By the same author

Sharks & Custard
EuroManagers & Martians
Great Britain Little England
The NewComers: Austria, Finland and Sweden
Have You Heard This One? An Anthology of European Jokes
Us & Them

D0188164

**Visit us on the Web at
understanding-europe.com**

Published by Europublic SA/NV,
P.O. Box 504, B-1180 Brussels.
Tel: +32 2 343 77 26   Fax: +32 2 343 93 30

email: info@europublic.com

Illustrations: Bob Pater
Cover design: Marc Segond

5th edition, February 2002.

Printed in Belgium. Edition et Imprimerie, Brussels.
D/2002/6421/1   ISBN 90-74440-11-8

This book is dedicated to Karin, who made it happen. It also owes a lot to many people who provided inspiration, encouragement and practical assistance, including Paul Aass, Paul Adriaanse, Gordon Aitken, Betty Averill, Luisa Bandini, Diederik Bangert, Dr Viktor Bauer, Horst Baumann, Rudolf Beger, Róbert Bencze, Anissa and Karima Ben Salah, Monique Bruyndonckx, Alison Bye, Miguel Cordero del Campillo, Marie-Rose Delaunoy, Jean-Philippe Deschamps, Jean-Lou d'Haeye, Colette Diercks, Sven-Erik Edlund, Harry Elhardt, Elisabeth Esberger, Alexandra Ferreira De Sousa, David Fields, Geoff Gibas, Norman Gilbertson, Philippe Glade, David Grossman, Rolf Gustavsson, Rita Gyarmati, Jason Hadick, Anna-Maria Hagerfors, Mats Halvarsson, Lazaros Hatjinakos, David Haworth, Eva and Helmut Hildebrand, Wendy Hofmaier, Marjalien d'Hose, Harald Hotze, Manos Iatridis, Bo Manderup Jensen, the two Michael Johnsons, Kata Kollár, Otmar Lahodynsky, Ingrid Lehmann, Arild Lillebø, Klaus Lojka, Angus Macdonald, Frank Malkwitz, Philip Marchand, Bill Martin, Marcel De Meirleir, Roeland Moens, Richard Neff, Lilian Nielsen, Michel Odelga, Athanase Papandropoulos, Richard Plumridge, Gilbert Sauber, Ursel Schuback, Dr Hans Schultze-Berndt, Isabelle Segond, Lenke Simon, Krister Svensson, Paul Thorne, Tom Thorsteinsen, Alan Tillier, Ana Trascasas, Nigel Tutt, Dominique Vancraeynest, May Vassilikou, Maurits Verschueren, Ilios Yannakakis, Mike Wade, Peter Willis, Nick Winkfield and Tim Wood. My apologies to those I have omitted.

Introduction

*"Toutes les généralisations sont dangereuses, même celle-ci"
(attributed to Alexandre Dumas but modified, for the purpose of
this book, to: "Toutes les généralisations sont dangereuses,
même celles-ci")*

*"A definition is the enclosing of the wilderness of an idea within a
wall of words"* Samuel Butler

*"Men of sense allow that each nation has a peculiar set of manners,
and that some particular qualities are more frequently to be met
with among one people than among their neighbours"*
David Hume

*"In all the circle of knowledge, there is not perhaps a more pleas-
ing employment than that of comparing countries with each other"*
Oliver Goldsmith

*"Culture is a system for creating, sending, storing and processing
information. We analyse the culture to determine how it operates
and what its messages mean"* Dr Edward Hall

*"Generalising about nations is a tricky and not entirely respectable
business, even though whole careers are built on it"*
Patricia Morison, *Financial Times*

The idea of putting my observations and thoughts to paper first came to me in 1988, on a beautiful autumn night in Nice. Standing on a balcony and sipping a gin-and-tonic, I watched the cars descending the hillside opposite. All the headlights were yellow.

For the benefit of non-Europeans, as well as ignorant Europeans, I should explain that cars registered in France were obliged to sport yellow filters on their headlights (all other European headlights used uncoloured glass). There were two reasons for this: (1) the determination of the French to protect their car industry and (2) the desire of the French to be different*. Their fun has since been spoilt by the Commission of the European Union...

So the embryo of this book had been gestating more than a year when, very abruptly in November 1989, the Germans started to tear down the Berlin Wall.

A week later I was standing at Checkpoint Charlie, on the one hand admiring the symbolism of a Czech pushing a broken-down Skoda across the frontier into West Berlin, and on the other hand wondering what the end of the Cold War meant for Europe - in the sense that people of my post-war generation understand the term. We had got used to thinking of an Old World bereft of the countries of Eastern Europe. Yet the latter had been an integral part of the European ideal and have contributed enormously to the thinking and culture of the Europe of today.

With or without the eastern European countries, Europe has rarely been perceived as a historical entity even by its own peoples (the entity has been the nation state). This is a pity because Europe is something to be proud of. Within a relatively limited area of the globe, it encompasses the widest range of cultural influences and the greatest variety of natural features of any continent, North America included.

Europe does not have rain forests or tropical jungles. But it is, geologically, the most complex of all the continents of the world. It has glaciers, tundra, fjords, archipelagos, islands, mountains, fells, semi-tropical seas, even a real desert (the area around Almería in southeastern Spain). From the lakes of Sweden to the hilltowns

---

* The official reason is that they were introduced in 1936 as a military measure "to distinguish our vehicles from the Germans" (Ministry of Transport, Paris).

of southern Italy, from the human warmth of the western islands to the sparkling folklore and music of the Slavs, this Europe, often unsuspected and unseen, is unique. It offers a richness of cultures and languages unparalleled anywhere else in the world.

This is something most non-Europeans don't appreciate, and something even Europeans still have to get to grips with. After all, we have at least four centuries of history to roll back if we want to get at the truth. Rolling back the past is not the easiest thing to do, particularly when you are likely to find some surprises under the carpet...

Let's roll back the carpet a fair way - to New Year's Eve of the year 406 AD. That night the great river Rhine froze over and, for the first time since the Romans built the *limes*, the frontiers of supposedly civilised Europe collapsed. The sequal - like other debacles that followed - actually enriched Europe enormously. According to eyewitnesses, a lot of people skidded across the ice on that and succeeding days.

Amongst them were the Vandals (who emigrated southwards through Andalusia, hence the name, and ended up in North Africa), the Alans and the Suevi (both comfortably resettled in Spain until the Visigoths came along) and the Burgundians, whom the French today consider to be the *crème de la crème*, seemingly failing to understand that they are not Latin, but Germanic.

In fact we, as Europeans, are most probably Germanic in some way or another, unless we are Basque, Celtic or Finno-Ugrian (and there's not all that much chance of that!) - or Slav or Ugro-Finnic if we come from the other side of what used to be called the 'Iron Curtain'.

What this book is not about

To cut a long story short, European history has been disgrace-fully distorted over the last few centuries and it can't do any harm to take a fresh look at things. Moreover, if we can agree on our common origins then, in looking at our national idiosyncrasies, we can agree to differ.

One thing this book is definitely *not* intended to be is a book about the Single Market or Maastricht - more than enough has been published on that subject already. Nor, I hope, will it read like the cross between a traveller's guide and a current affairs manual that so many other books of the 'understanding Ruritania' genre turn out to be. Least of all is it a statistical analysis of the European reality, whatever the latter may be. The fact that three per cent of Europe's males are now over 1.8 metres tall, or that 50 per cent of Europeans aged 60 and above snore (apparently the case in 1990), leaves me unmoved.

What this book *does* try to do is fill in some of the background to a reemergent Europe and, at the same time, show that the European ideal is more than an endless succession of conferences with the same old personalities on the platform and the inevitable boxes of interpreters.

My aim is to make a qualitative and, of course, objective assessment of the different temperaments present in the European House. This means there is relatively little room for statistics in this book: much of the data available hardly lends itself to intelligent interpretation, and that which does ages rapidly.

In any case, I am trying to deal with underlying characteristics rather than their external effects. To use an analogy from psychology, I am looking at the cultural 'ids'. That certainly means going deeper than the values of the moment like environmentalism or separatism, the 'superegos' which seem to be increasingly a mirror of international fashion. It also means going deeper than the habits of the moment, the 'egos' or the aspects within reach of the statisticians. I doubt if we can learn much from either of these, whereas there is something to be learned from the cultural 'ids' if we can identify them.

Please note *cultural* 'ids'. It is not my intention to plumb the ultimate depths of the European mind - the instincts of survival, sex and related manifestations of the human subconscious. The subject here is not the collective aspects of human behaviour, but the tribal variances.

As for the character sketches which form the core of this book, they show a desire to combat the ethnic folklore that has clouded Europeans' perceptions of one another for far too long: the rude frivolous Frenchman, the idle pretentious Spaniard, the dull humourless German (not forgetting his archetype, the bull-headed sabre-scarred Prussian), and so on. Curiously, it can be the victims themselves who hold most steadfastly to these stereotypes, sometimes reinforcing them in a spirit of defiance or self-mutilation.

12

Stereotypes of the 'one-liner' kind are best avoided at all costs. Apart from the fact that they treat the truth with the finesse of a blunt instrument, they are not calculated to improve mutual understanding. Based on a mix of historical resentments and folklore, they sometimes distort reality shamelessly. There are some people I know who will tell you for example that they have never met a rude Frenchman.

In his book, *The French*[1], Theodore Zeldin offers the following words of caution: "To describe a nation of 54 million, still less one of 220 million, in a single phrase, to attribute to all its inhabitants identical moral qualities, that in any case are hard enough to be certain about when dealing with one individual or family, is a natural reaction in the face of the complexity of the world, but it is a habit born of despair, which persists because there seems no obvious way of avoiding it".

Unexceptional in their ordinariness

Even so I feel the attempt to correct some of the most pernicious deformations of national character, in more than a single phrase, can serve some purpose. The fact that the French seem rude to many foreigners may in fact, as I try to demonstrate in Chapter 4, conceal a much more subtle complex of characteristics: self-absorption (my favourite), directness, eagerness to spark a response, and *désinvolture* - something that is not easily translatable. The Harraps New Standard Dictionary gives three interpretations of this very French word: (a) unconstraint', which sounds far too contrived, (b) 'free and easy manner', which defines the effect but not the cause, and (c) 'lack of deference', which is an Anglo-Saxon rendering of a very Gallic syndrome...

Elsewhere in his book, Zeldin makes the point that most people of most cultures are unexceptional in their ordinariness. Fill a room with a mixed bag of European nationalities, and even the most cunning ethnologist will have difficulty in deciding who's what. The problem is further complicated by the fact that people are divided more by region, class and, increasingly, generation than they are by race.

If the generalisations in this book do something to correct the folkloric stereotypes of the past, they will have served their purpose. In any case I offer no excuse. It seems to me that there is no better combination than British inventiveness, French wit, Slav music,

Italian cuisine, German perfection, Spanish reality, Dutch decency, Scandinavian fairness... in short, the best combination in the world.

In addition to the 'common factors' listed in Chapter 10 and at the end of this book, we Europeans have something else in common: the fact that with some exceptions we are, even if subconsciously, aware of our roots (often at as modest a level as the local community or township), yet we sense the fact that we belong to something bigger - an awareness that is most keenly felt in the younger generations.

This emotional response, because that is what it is, has nothing whatever to do with conformity in the American or the Japanese sense, it is something atavistic that comes from the fact that we are all brothers and sisters under the skin. Most of us don't want to recognise the fact, yet we show it in moments of real emotion (look how generously the English footballers responded after the Germans won the 1990 World Cup semi-finals!).

My favourite example of this phenomenon is the case of a pet accessories salesman I met on a train between Strasbourg and Wiesbaden, traversing the Latin-Germanic border and, simultaneously, the Rhine. This putative Frenchman explained how, after WWII, he had joined an *association des anciens combattants* in Strasbourg. After some years of happy camaraderie, one of his French colleagues asked him what he had done in the war. He told the truth: he had been dragooned into the Todt Organisation, a civil engineering adjunct to Hitler's army which conscripted manpower wherever it could.

This admission produced a stunned silence that lasted about six months. But, in the final analysis, sense prevailed and the management committee of the association decided that, since the parties concerned had enjoyed five years of friendship this, after all, was worth more than old enmities.

And that is what Europe is, or should be, about...

European Aberrations

Why do...

the Austrians... offer a glass of water with every cup of coffee (like the Greeks and the Hungarians)?

the Belgians... persist in the dangerous principle of according driving priority from the right *(à la belge/op z'n belgisch)*?

the British... think black cats are lucky when everyone else thinks the opposite?

the Bulgarians... shake their heads as if saying 'no' when they're saying 'yes'?

the French... insist on saying *soixante-dix* and *quatre-vingt* when the Swiss manage with *septante* and *huitante* (or *octante*)?

the French call a ship a building *(bâtiment)* and the Germans an airplane a machine *(Maschine)*?

the Germans... put the past participle at the end of sentences, the cause of breathlessness in the speaker and confusion in the listener?

the Greeks... nod as if saying 'yes' when they're saying 'no'?

the Hungarians... insist on putting the family name before the first name?

the Italians... eat their *pasta* with nothing but a fork?

the Portuguese... put their money sign in the middle, e.g. 32$40?

the Spanish... list words beginning with 'ch' in the dictionary after 'czar'?

the Swedes... finish their alphabet with 'X, Y, Z, Ä, Ö, Å?

the Swiss... stick a diminutive suffix on so many things, including even their surnames?

The Folklore Factor

"Some people... may be Rooshans, and others may be Prooshans; they are born so, and will please themselves. Them which is of other nature thinks different"   Charles Dickens

"That's the French. Great art, lousy organization"
                    Mary Moran, US coach at 1992 Albertville Winter Olympics

"A German child, twelve years old, has never spoken a word in his life. Over dinner one evening he turns to his parents and says "Salz, bitte" ('salt, please'). His astonished parents ask him why, if he could speak, he had never said anything till now. His reply: "bis heute war alles in Ordnung" ('up to now everything was OK')"   Joke reputedly told originally by the Poles about the Prussians

"But Lord! to see the absurd nature of Englishmen, that cannot forbear laughing and jeering at everything that looks strange"
                    Samuel Pepys, Diary, 27/11/1662

"A Belgian found a monkey and asked a gendarme what he should do with it. The gendarme told him to take the animal to the zoo. The next day the gendarme saw the man walking along holding hands with the monkey. 'Look', said the gendarme, "I thought I told you to take the monkey to the zoo". "Yes", said the Belgian, "We went to the zoo yesterday. Today we're going to the cinema".
                    French joke

"The trouble with Europeans is that they don't play cricket"
                    Clement Attlee, British Prime Minister, 1945-1951

Anyone who dares to talk about a 'typical' Italian, etc, only needs to spend a day in that country to realise the error of his or her ways. But, outside Italy, the stereotype reasserts itself.

There are strong variations within most European races, in terms of different morphological types as well as the physical and psychological differences between generations (compare the young Spaniard or Sicilian with his or her grandparents...). In fact you can often see a similarity between foreigners of the same morphological or psychological type that far outweighs their national characteristics.

Yet these national characteristics, the stuff of stereotypes, are real and palpable enough to encourage an attempt to put them on paper - an act comparable to walking wittingly into a minefield with the prospect of emerging an arm or a leg the less. Most people would say one has to be deranged to take on the invidious task of trying to pigeonhole one's fellow Europeans.

National characteristics exist not just because of history - and certainly not because someone-or-other won the battle of something-or-other, as the history books imply. They are there as a result of exposure to a particular set of influences: geography, culture, diet, family and legal systems, even language (in a curiously round-about way) and fashion.

They surface as stereotypes. These stereotypes are often wild and wide of the mark, yet they say something about the race in question. My intention - in Chapter 4 of this book - is to try to identify the catalysts of cultural chemistry that lead to the amalgams of national character. It has at least proved to me, if to no one else yet, that these stereotypes are explainable, even if not excusable.

One thing for sure is that, once established, these stereotypes are devilishly difficult to extirpate. The square-headed *kraut*, the bowler-hatted *limey,* the bereted *frog,* the mustachioed *dago* will be around for a long time after the European Union has done its job. Likewise, Continentals and Americans still think fondly of London's *peasoupers* even though there haven't been any for thirty years or more.

Such cultural mindsets, reflecting seminal attitudes and prejudices, have roots that go deep into a country's collective subconscious. I had a striking example of this when publishing an article by George Mikes in the Spanish edition of an international magazine.

In his English-language original, talking about a row with a friend at a football match, he used the rather convoluted phrase "he called your mother-tongue barbaric". The translator, having a mindset about traditional forms of Spanish abuse, rendered this as *"llama-ba a su madre un bárbaro del tribu tonga"*. Translated back, this means "he called your mother a barbarian of the Tongue tribe", wherever or whatever the "Tongue tribe" may be.

Now, if you know the traditional Spanish propensity for attri-buting all sorts of dubious behaviour and antecedents to the other party's mother in times of stress, you will understand everything. If you don't, never mind. Just take it that it demonstrates the ease with which one can slip into the habit of thinking a particular way about a culture, even one's own.

Folklore is fun...

The world at large is aware of these broad national character traits without necessarily understanding them very well or the underlying reasons. They are generally given expression in one of two ways: first the traditional outlet of ethnic jokes, or what I call 'foreigners folklore', and secondly journalistic confirmation in the form of what more often than not amounts to an apologia.

Let's deal with the 'foreigners folklore' first, not just because it came first (journalistic comment is largely derivative) but also because it's more fun.

The most venerable joke about Europeans deals with our con-cept of heaven and hell: "Heaven is where the police are British, the chefs French, the mechanics German, the lovers Italian and it is all organised by the Swiss. Hell is where the chefs are British, the mechanics French, the lovers Swiss, the police German and it is all organised by the Italians".

That gives us the following functional matrix to start from:

Nationality	+	−
British	policemen	chefs
French	chefs	car mechanics
German	car mechanics	policemen
Italian	lovers	organisers
Swiss	organisers	lovers

So we're off to a good start, even if we think the French are miscast in the 'hell' scenario. Since that joke took shape, they have learned a lot about cars. The Swiss might say it's unfair on them, too, though I know of at least one Swedish girl who endorses the judgment wholeheartedly. In fact there's a specifically Swiss variation of the 'hell' joke where the Germans provide the humour, the Italians the organisation and - wait for it! - the Swiss the romance.

A not-so-funny joke I heard in Germany also gets fairly close to the mark. It tells of the captain of a cruise liner who has difficulty in persuading his passengers to abandon ship (the lifeboats are stuck in the davits so he has to get them to jump in the water). He does this by appealing to the dominant instincts in each of the nationalities present: "I told the English it would be unsporting of them not to jump, the French that it would be the smart thing to do, the Germans that it was an order... and the Italians that jumping overboard was prohibited".

Another piece of folklore going around the European business community says that the ideal employee should have the following qualities: "The internationalism of an Englishman, the humility of a Frenchman, the charm of a German, the linguistic ability of a Spaniard, the precision of an Italian, the road manners of a Belgian, the generosity of a Dutchman, the gaiety of a Swiss, the ready wit of a Scandinavian and the sensitivity of a Greek".

A variant quoted in *The Economist* has a twist in the tail: "Jumble up a few national stereotypes and you have the old joke about a nightmare European. He has French moral courage, Italian fighting spirit, the British work ethic and a German sense of humour. In short, he is a Belgian".

Since we are dealing with acts of rank irony, I will not attempt to repeat the matrix. In fact the Spanish are now learning English, and the Belgians - who certainly deserve better than the cavalier treatment meted out above - have learned to drive, though not everyone agrees with me about this (see 'The Belgians', Chapter 4). That a very severe driving test has been in force in Belgium since 1977 seems to escape the attention of many foreigners, who prefer fiction to fact.

Another variant of the ethnic joke concerns the smallest books in the world. It includes a Compendium of German Jokes, a History of Italian War Heroes and the Norwegian 'Who's Who'.

The concept of culture has been around for a very long time. Aristotle thought that people from warm climes were intelligent but not very heroic, while people from cold climates were brave but stupid. The Greeks, being in the middle, got the best of both worlds...

European national stereotypes have also been around for some time - witness the pieces of this 'jigsaw puzzle' produced in the 1780s, the reproduction of which I owe to Geert Hofstede.

DUTCHMAN.
Industrious and hardy, cleanly in their persons, ships and houses.

ENGLISHMAN.
Generous and affable, desirous of liberty in the greatest extent.

FRENCHMAN.
Of a changeable disposition, and fond of amusement to excess.

In 1868 another Englishman, John Guy, was reflecting much the same attitudes in his book Geography. Here is what he wrote:

"The French are a gay, active and lively people, graceful in deportment and very polite, possessing however no inconsiderable share of vanity.

"The Italians are a discreet and polite people, but extremely effeminate.

"The Spaniards are considered a grave and haughty people, possessing elevated notions of honour: but they are indolent and revengeful.

"England, as a nation, stands without a rival; the intelligence, the industry, and the enterprise of her people have raised her to a greatness enjoyed by no other power."

Ethnocentricity, the curse of the European nations, is self-evident here. England, inevitably, comes out on top. But it is nice to see that the French for once, like the Italians, are found to be polite.

Ethnic jokes make neighbours easier to live with. They also make people laugh, though not necessarily the people that are being joked about.

Stories about Belgian drivers demonstrate that folklore can even go beyond the ethnic joke. I have had an earnest Swede tell me (and most Swedes are earnest) that Belgian courts used to enforce lower sentences if drivers could prove that they were under the influence of alcohol at the time. This, the Swede claimed, led to many Belgian cars being equipped with a half-empty bottle of booze by way of evidence...

Culture, as I hinted earlier, shapes language and language shapes culture. In this symbiotic relationship, the way people speak can tell you volumes about their environment. The clipped Prussians compare starkly with the singsong Rhinelanders. The Spanish extrapolate their environment simply when they open their mouths, as do the Dutch and the Greeks. One of the oldest recorded European aphorisms relates to language. It was Charles V, the Holy Roman Emperor, who is supposed to have said: "I speak Spanish to God, Italian to women, French to men, and German to my horse."

Most racist jokes (intercultural comparisons in polite language) tend to involve just two nationalities, like the Belgian jokes about the Dutch and *vice versa*, and the French jokes about the Belgians and *vice versa*: just change the label. But sometimes you will find the same joke being told about people a long way away, as can happen with jokes about the Irish and the Poles, States-side and Europe-side.

Speaking of the jokes told about the Galicians of northwest Spain, Flora Lewis comments[2]: "They are often almost word for word the same jokes that are told about Galitzianers, the people from the area of southeastern Poland once occupied by Austria that is also called Galicia, and about Scots and Bretons." But, she adds: "They probably had common Celtic ancestors a long time ago". English jokes about the Celtic Fringe tend to drag in everyone - Scots, Irish and Welsh - but these are probably exceptions that prove the rule.

Neighbours are inevitably fair game, with the emphasis on low IQ levels. A particularly neat 'couplet' hails from Scandinavia, where the Swedes describe the typical Norwegian response to an opinion poll as two per cent 'yes', two percent 'no' and ninety-six per cent 'don't know'. To which the Norwegians retort that, in

So we don't change, then...?

It would be wrong to get the idea that we Europeans are immutable in behaviour and attitudes. Cultures, particularly national ones, are as much the product of political will and passing fashion as they are of less synthetic things like geography, climate and family structures.

That some manifestations of culture can be passing too is borne out by history. Gesturing was considered vulgar at the French court until Caterina dei Medici came along with her Italian retinue (she also brought good cooking and perfumes with her).

In the 17th century, Englishmen kissed one another on the lips - at a time when both the English and the French, as it happens, thought washing was harmful to your health. The English simply didn't wash whereas the French, encouraged by Caterina, developed a perfume industry.

At the time both the English and the French were convinced, until events proved them wrong, that the Germans were unnaturally easygoing and lacked any military spirit.

And, just to show you how things can change, in the 19th century it was the French who used to queue - until they passed the habit on to the British.

There have also been great and sometimes repetitive sea-changes in cultures through history. England, for example, has lurched every 50-80 years from puritanism to permissiveness, France from hubris to despondency, Spain from hyperactivity to inertia.

The stereotypes help to remind us who we are!

Sweden, the reponse to the same question is two per cent 'yes', two per cent 'no', two per cent 'don't know' and ninety-four per cent 'don't understand the question'.

Some ethnic jokes (they really should be called 'cultural jokes') set out to be more than abusive and actually tell you something about the cultures in question. A good example is the one about the three Allied pilots - a Frenchman, an Englishman and an Italian - shot down during the Gulf War. Captured, they are subjected to 'ways of making them talk'. The Frenchman, quite logically not interested in suffering unnecessary pain and disfigurement, talks on the first day. The Englishman, true to his 'stiff-upper-lip' tradition, holds out for a week. The Italian is tortured by his capturers for a month and never talks. Released from captivity, he is debriefed by Allied intelligence who can't understand how he held out so long. "But 'ow could I talk", he says, "with my 'ands tied behind my back?".

A lot of jokes concern the frugality of folk. One of them, which has been used with the Dutch and, of all people, the Pontic Greeks, but apparently not the Scots, goes like this: "So-and-so (Dutch, Pontic Greek, etc) survives a plane crash on a desolate mountain. He or she, hungry and exhausted, finds shelter in a cave. A Red Cross search party scales the mountainside, spots the cave entrance and calls: 'Anyone in there?' 'No', comes the reply, 'I've already donated'."

Caves (as well as shipwrecks, icebergs and mountain tops) seem to crop up a lot in ethnic jokes - see 'The Norwegians', Chapter 4! A lot of European mythology revolves around holes in the ground. Not many people realise that, after the Pied Piper had led the children of Hameln underground, they reemerged in the Siebenburgen area of what is now Romania. And, of course, in *Journey to the Centre of the Earth* Jules Verne had his explorers go underground in Iceland and surface off the coast of Sicily...

Some ethnic jokes end up formalised in proverbs and the like. One example is a Russian maxim which says: "Greeks all tell the truth, but only once a year". The punchline seems familiar to me - all Russian jokes about Radio Yerevan end the same way. Example: "Caller to Radio Yerevan: 'Is it true that the Moskvitch car will corner at 120 kph?'. Radio Yerevan: 'Yes, but only once'." It seems the Russians think the same way about the Armenians as they do about the Greeks.

Another variant is the question-and-answer joke, of which a fine example is told by Italians, and others, at the expense of the Sicilians (who don't seem to mind too much):

"Q: Why are Sicilians so small?

A: Because, when they were little, their mothers told them they would have to work when they grew up."

Of such idle amusements are national stereotypes made. This one reflects at least three *idées reçues* about Sicilians:

1. they are all small

2. they are all mother-fixated

3. they all hate work.

Which of course is not entirely true. Also, like most ethnic jokes, it also tells you something about the joker. Like the Belgian *bon mot*: "The quickest way to make a profit? Buy a Frenchman for what he's worth and sell him for what he thinks he's worth."

Sometimes stereotypes go beyond thought and end up in the language. The British and French have made up their minds about one another to the extent that, where the British talk about "taking French leave", the French reciprocate with *"filer à l'anglaise"*, and the French call a French letter *"un capot anglais"*. Thwarted in getting the better of the French, the British talk about "Dutch auctions" (which ultimately implies driving a very hard bargain) and "going Dutch" (which is almost the same thing). These, and similar phrases involving the Dutch, are in fact the echoes of an English propaganda campaign conducted against their maritime rivals in the 17th century.

When folkloric sources run dry, you come up with your own. My favourite relates to the standard European anatomy which, from personal observation, doesn't exist. The French reach for their livers, the British for their bowels, the Belgians for their blood pressure, the Germans for that and their libidos, and the Spanish and Italians for just about everything...

So much for the folklore. As for the individual expression of such prejudices, journalistic or otherwise, this can be equally revealing - despite the fact that, compared with the ethnic joke which has many parents, media comment may bear the marks of the commentator despite the derivative nature of the ideas expressed.

Here, on the following pages, are some examples of the verbal violence, epithets and others, perpetrated on different nationalities. It should be understood that, regardless of what I just said, these are not perforce the opinions of the parties concerned (thank god), but should be taken as their assessment of public attitudes. They illustrate the sort of verbal violence that can be done to different nationalities in order to cope with the complexities of European life.

They also provide a common starting point for an exploration of the national psyches that make up the Old World. My intention is to get under the skin of these stereotypes - after all they are living, if redundant, organisms - and attempt to throw light on the varying value systems that gave rise to them.

Serious work, some of it described in Chapter 5 onwards, has been done in getting under the skin of these stereotypes. While some of the most helpful contributions have come from the other side of the Atlantic, this can hardly be said of one American business academic who has developed a 'metaphor' approach to cultural mindsets, viz "the German Symphony", "the French Vineyard", "the Spanish Bullfight" and "the Italian Opera".

Even if the analogies of German symphonic order and Italian operatic display have some merit (see Chapter 4), a metaphor is not much better than a stereotype. One could in any case be a bit more imaginative about it. I would prefer to talk of "the German Gemeinschaft" (a cultural club), "the French Flea Circus" (jumping up and down, showing off and irritating the onlookers), 'the Tortilla Espanola" (a simple, solid and nourishing dish) and 'the Italian Fireworks Display" (lots of show and noise). But, on second thoughts, I won't.

Dualistic by nature

Of course, stereotypes generally dwell on the most outrageous of the characteristics of a people. They ignore the fact that national temperaments, like individual human personalities, are dualistic by nature [see the *functional matrix* above]. They reflect the Hegelian cycle of thesis, antitheses, synthesis - except that the synthesis often eludes us. The same race, viewed over the centuries, may look very different to different observers. We do, after all, change with time.

Most national characters, indeed, have an obverse and a reverse side (thesis + antithesis = synthesis). I liken this to a clock with two faces, and a mechanism in the middle, and am reminded of the joke about the Englishman who, waiting for a train in Ireland, remarks loudly and indignantly that the station's clocks are showing different times. "But", retorts the Irish stationmaster who overhears the comment, "what would be the point of having two clocks if they told the same time?". In addition to illustrating the point that every culture contains logical inconsistencies, this joke says something about the power of Irish logic on its own.

History bears the thesis-antithesis-synthesis theory out in the case of the Germans (maybe Hegel really does have something to answer for). David Marsh[3] elaborates on the dichotomy of the German mind in thoughts quoted later in this book: "Only a thin line separates idealism from escapism, pride from arrogance, discipline from servility." John Ardagh, another British journalist[4], says much the same: "The contrast between the Germans' passion for orderliness and their tendency towards romanticism, irrationality and extremism has long puzzled observers of this nation, and the two elements would seem to be inter-related."

Over the generations, the English have not always been eccentric (and by implication creative), they are also at times, even now, inhibited by a natural tendency to puritanism. The Spanish, depending on the age, have been both actively exhuberant and passively morbid. The French can be both intellectually active and morally apathetic, the Italians creative and despondent, and the Greeks just about everything all at the same time (which may help explain why many people find them ambiguous).

To understand national psyches you have to identify the psychological checks and balances that make people behave the way they do. I tend to call these phenomena 'psycho-poles'.

Having said there are at least two sides to every national character, I have to concede that there are others relating to class and regional differences. Their incidence varies widely by country. Some nations (if that's the word) like Belgium or Switzerland show little class divergence, others being less money-oriented and more status-conscious show a lot. But, when it comes to regional divergences, it's difficult to name a single nation that escapes the rule.

Class influence, where it applies, attenuates national temperament the higher you go. Europe tends to converge at the level of the

ENGLISH

Sociable, flexible and under-prepared *EuroBusiness*

FRENCH

Rude, chauvinistic, even greedy *The Economist*
Friendly, humorous and sardonic
International Management

SPANISH

Dramatic, jealous, lazy *International Management*

PORTUGUESE

Quiet, law-abiding, introverted *New York Times*
Easy-going, smiling, patient, good-natured
Insight Guide to Portugal

ITALIANS

Operatic, subtle, romantic, hard-headed
International Management

La dolce vita minus all that Angst *The Economist*

GERMANS

Warlike, folkloric, relentlessly efficient, humourless
International Management

SWISS

'Mauschwyzerdütsch' unidentified

AUSTRIANS

Devious, snobby, xenophobic unidentified

BELGIANS

Formal, petit bourgeois, materialistic
International Management

Each book's [romantic] hero will be from a different EC
country. Yes, even Belgium *The Economist*

DUTCH

Stingy, philistine [!] *International Management*

SCOTS
Drunken, feckless depressives *The Economist*

IRISH
Amiable, ignorant *International Management*

WELSH
The Welsh, as all the English know, are a clannish sort, notoriously hot-blooded, voluble, good at singing, and as fond of leeks as they are unfond of the truth *Financial Times*

SWEDES
Naive, cautious, weakwilled *Communication World*

NORWEGIANS
Smug, pompous and hostile to foreigners *Riviera Reporter*

GREEKS
Mercurial, poetic, devious, hospitable
International Management
Slow, loquacious, impulsive, irrational, chaotic
La Vie en Grèce

GENERAL
Not all Americans are loud, lazy, overbearing and overweight, nor are we all preachy, pompous, naive bullies. The Germans are not all obnoxious, arrogant lager louts. The French are not all baguette-munching xenophobes. The Japanese are not all myopic, camera-wielding lemmings. And the English, thank God, are not all gray, humorless, supercilious, patronizing twits.

The Germans are aggressive, bullying, egotistical and sentimental, have an inferiority complex and are prone to angst. The British, as we all know, are smug, lazy, ill-schooled, snobbish and insular and suffer from excessive negative class consciousness. The French, of course, are chauvinistic, self-aggrandizing, too individualistic by half and always right. The Finns suffer from both inferiority and superiority complexes. As for the Italians, well! But, as they say themselves, "Nessuno è perfetto". So what's all the fuss about?
(Letters to *International Herald Tribune*)

upper middle class, thanks to the influence of *haute couture*, *cuisine nouvelle* and one or two things the French didn't invent like l'après-ski and holidays in the south of France.

By contrast what is left of European nobility, and there's quite a lot of it still around, has retained some of the values distilled by the culture surrounding it. Personalities are often wholesome yet distinctive, certainly when compared with the pretentiousness-cum-blandness of the international jet set. Hereditary nobility still represents, despite some awful exceptions, the better side of Europe.

But most countries take their colour, and earn their stereotypes, from the ordinary folk. The one notable exception is England. Everyone on the Continent knows, loves or despises the image of the English 'gentleman'. Awareness of the character of the English *hoi polloi*, other than contemporary clashes with the lager louts, is virtually non-existent.

As for regional variations, they reinforce the national stereotypes in many cases (look at the peasant communities of Austria!) and challenge them in others.

Region, county, township, club

One thing the European countries have in common, in addition to making jokes about their immediate neighbours, is handpicking a region of their own for the same honour.

As the butt of foreigners' jokes, the Belgians reciprocate generously between the two linguistic communities. The Flemish say that when they're in trouble they talk, whereas with the Walloons it's the other way round ("when they talk, they're in trouble"). The Walloons get their own back in various ways, including the story about the Flemish peasant who drives south into France en route for Calais. Just over the frontier he sees a roadsign saying 'Pas de Calais', so he turns back...

In most European countries, the qualification for treatment as a national scapegoat is perceived slowness of response (which may have nothing to do with quickness of mind). In Germany, the honour goes to the people of Ostfriesland, in France to the Savoyards, in Belgium to the Namurois, in Switzerland to the Bernese - and, according to Peter Collett[5], in Denmark to the people of Jutland and in Ireland to the Kerrymen.

One Swiss joke recounts the case of the Bernese paratrooper who is told to count to three before pulling the ripcord (contrary to what many people think, the German Swiss have a lively sense of humour). Halfway down, our Bernese friend says "one". Just before hitting the ground, he says "two". Rushed to hospital, he manages to open his mouth in the ambulance and say "three"... The Swiss also say you should never tell a Bernese a joke over dinner on Saturday night for fear he will burst out laughing in church on Sunday.

In fact, the Swiss regard any community more than 20 kilometers away as foreigners, thereby feeling fully justified in telling jokes at their expense. The same goes with greater geographical justification for Norway. As a foreign observer comments: "Norwegians are very nationalistic. They are proud to be Norwegian. But they are not only Norwegian - they are from the West Coast, from Oslo, from the North, and they are all different. When someone from the North is in Oslo, people can identify him, joke about him, because he is different"[6]. Perhaps not surprisingly, since a good 3,000 kilometers separates the two. Northern Norwegians are also reputed to be unNordically garrulous.

Some regions within the European nation states have always demonstrated seemingly irradicable idiosyncrasies. Nobody, British or otherwise, will argue about the differences within England itself. A survey published in late-1992 showed, amongst other things, that "couples in the south of England are far more likely to quarrel than those in the north or the Midlands".

Spain is one of the best examples of regional differences. A century-and-a-half ago the English traveller, George Borrow, said at different points in his epic book *The Bible in Spain*[7]: (a) "he is an *Aragonese*, and when one of that nation gets an idea into his head, it is the most difficult thing in the world to dislodge it", (b) "*Catalans* think only of their own affairs", (c) "*Valencians*, people infamous for their ferocity and bloodthirstiness", and (d), in this case reported speech on the subject of the *Galicians*, "the men in general seem clownish and simple, yet they are capable of deceiving the most clever *filou* of Paris" (they sound like a fair match for the Auvergnats...). I think the Valencians have since cooled off a bit but, for the rest, amen. Add to this the fact that the Galicians, largely thanks to Generalissimo Francisco Franco, earned the reputation of being the only Spaniards who could do at least three things at the same time. Maybe this matches up with their reputation for being dispassionate.

The curious thing is that, of all the European nations, the Spanish temperament (see 'The Spanish', Chapter 4) is in my view the most distinctive. The dominant feature is the tough, elemental streak bred in the central uplands of this very large country. But the people of the surrounding littoral, 'Spanish' or not, vary every bit as much as the climate. Salvador de Madariaga tried to systematise such observations in his book *Spain*[8]. I paraphrase for brevity:

Galicians:	shrewd, intelligent, hardworking, thrifty
Asturians:	less reserved, vivacious but cautious
Basques:	stern, loyal, uncompromising, narrow
Aragonese:	spontaneous, frank, stubborn, intuitive
Valencians:	expressive, spontaneous, passionate
Andalusians:	graceful, aesthetic, innately wise

I omit his references to the Catalans since the issue was already politicised when he wrote this book in 1942!

In some particularly idiosyncratic areas of Europe, one can detect strong differences between separate parts of the same region. The county of Yorkshire is a case in point. It is said that it took 20 years to amalgamate the Prince of Wales's Own Regiment because "the east Yorkshiremen were a serious bunch, while the westerners were a happy-go-lucky mob". For a long time the regiment had a split personality.

Yet another phenomenon is antipathy toward the centre, particularly toward the denizens of capital cities. It is the conviction of almost all French provincials that the Parisians are unremittingly loathsome. The same is generally true of Italian feelings about the inhabitants of Rome, as expressed in a letter to the *International Herald Tribune*: "Most Romans are obnoxious, they don't know how to drive, they have to be first in everything or they get hysterical and they've never learned how to wait in line": the last comment suggests to me that the writer is less than a fullblooded Italian, but the sentiments are certainly shared by most non-Romans. Big city living does seem to have an alienating effect on people but different perspectives and - who knows? - simple jealousy may also contribute to such attitudes.

Within even narrower geographic confines, one can detect loyalties and a sense of identification that qualify, in a term used by George Borrow, as *localism*. It is certainly true of the old wool towns of Yorkshire. It equally applies to the Flemish towns of Belgium (a citizen of Lier will want nothing to do with Antwerp,

Culture is a matter of nurture, not nature. Yet blood and genes still have a habit of getting in the way, more often than not without reason. Southeastern Europe is particularly strong on this score. The people of what used to be called Yugoslavia invoke their genetic differences all the time, yet the Serbs, the Croats and even a large proportion of the Bosnian Muslims are blood-brothers, whether they like it or not. The Greeks make a great deal of their Hellenism, yet their links with the people of Ancient Greece are as much surmise as scientific fact.

While directing the European Human Genome Diversity Project, Sir Walter Bodmer, a genial British scientist, set out to investigate the incidence of an inherited blood disorder, thalassaemia, on the island of Cyprus where 'Greek Cypriots' and 'Turkish Cypriots' cohabit uneasily. His carefully controlled study showed that the disorder was shared equally by both 'races', a conclusion that has disturbing socio-political implications for the people concerned. He announced the results to some Cypriot Greek Orthodox monks in a conversation which, in synthesis, went something like this:

Sir Walter: *"There's one type of thalassaemia common to Cyprus."*
First Cypriot: *"It's different from other types in the world?"*
Sir Walter: *"Yes, it's commoner than in Greece or Turkey."*
Second Cypriot: *"Couldn't you prove we descended from ancient Greeks?"*
Sir Walter: *"You're a little different, an older population..."*
Second Cypriot (confused): *"So you think we just feel Greek culturally?"*
Sir Walter: *"You're all Cypriots, Greek or Turkish, one people."*
First Cypriot (even more confused): *"It's very surprising to hear it."*
Sir Walter: *"It is."*

In fact, they should have known. The 'Turkish Cypriots' were simply converts to Islam when the Turks occupied the island.

33

only 15 kilometers away) and even to Wallonia if you know where that is. The spirit of localism also applies to the towns of Galicia in northwest Spain, as to many other parts of the peninsula, and to the historic cities of Italy.

The lowest common denominator - in descending order, Europe, nation state, region, local community - is the family. In the European context, this can take many forms, often starting with the letter 'c': the *clan*, the *club*, the *camorra*, the *camarilla*, the *cabala*, the *clientele* (*clientelismo*), not forgetting of course a word beginning with 'm'.

Whatever the word used, we are talking about the principle of grouping together to protect or foster mutual self-interest. In the days of the mediaeval guilds, even in the case of the *quartiers* of the Italian city states, the motive was honorable. Today, now that clubbing together has become a European way of life (egged on by the Americans who call it 'networking' and think they have discovered something new), its credentials are a little more suspect.

Yet the fact that countries, regions, even individual communities and groups have acquired their own distinctive identity is little short of a miracle when you consider the confused history of Europe - not the history that is still taught in the curricula of the nation states, but the common history of an open continent awash with ethnic movements a thousand years ago and more.

A lesson in European alternative history may not be out of place (if you think it is, then leapfrog to Chapter 4).

In the meantime, one historical fact is, I think, in order. A recent display of satirical cartoons, published in various countries between 1770 and 1830, depicted the British as fat, drunken, ill-mannered and unkempt, the French as foppish, vain and untrustworthy, the Russians as boorish, the Spanish dirty and the Dutch complacent. So not much has changed, in prejudices at least...

How Europeans see themselves...

Some clues as to how stereotypes survive may be offered by a study undertaken by International Research Associates (INRA), a worldwide network of leading market research agencies with its central coordination office in Brussels.

Known as the INRA Country Image III Study, the research took the form of personal interviews with statistically representative samples of 1,000 respondents in all western European countries (the research also extended to eastern European and other countries, but it is the western European perceptions that interest us here). The research was undertaken in the Spring of 1994.

Because of the number of 'country images' to be measured, each country sample of 1,000 was divided into two groups to make the subject manageable for respondents. Half the ballot gave their judgments on ten countries, the other half on the remaining ten.

Various 'country image' aspects were investigated. The responses to the two propositions that interest us most - the two pertaining to behavioural traits - are set out below.

The overall responses to Proposition A - 'the inhabitants are friendly and cheerful' - leave one in no doubt. The friendliest and most cheerful of Europeans are the Italians and the Spanish. No one can argue with that, least of all the Italians and the Spanish, both of whom voted for themselves *en masse*.

The least friendly and cheerful are, it seems, the Germans and the British, with the Irish and the Finns keeping them fairly close company. Evidently the Irish have a genuine image problem, the Finns too, come to that. Few foreigners seem to know the Irish for what they really are - despite the fact that, according to a Eurostat survey in 1993, they spend more of their household budget on recreation than anyone else, topping the European Union's so-called 'Fun Index'!

The comparison between how other people see them and how people see themselves is interesting. The Irish, for a start, are in total disagreement with their European neighbours: they put themselves at the top of the 'friendly and cheerful' chart, level-pegging with the Greeks.

It is no surprise to find that the Greeks, the Spanish and the Italians think themselves so friendly and cheerful: this is the established image, perpetuated in the travel ads. But it is mildly surprising to see that the French and the Belgians also feel the same way about themselves, though to a lesser degree. The most self-critical are the Germans and the Finns - unjustly so, especially the Finns who are the friendliest of people once they get over their inhibitions.

Another lesson drawn from this major study is that, whereas neighbours are habitually abusive about one another (consider the 'cave jokes'!), they can be mutually supportive when a researcher comes along. In their responses to Proposition A the Irish give their vote to the British, and vice versa. And the Dutch are very generous to the Belgians - a rare experience in ordinary life! - but the compliment is not returned. Equally, the Austrians, quite rightly, rate the Italians highly for friendliness and cheerfulness, and the Italians consider the Austrians hostile and morose - which they certainly are not.

Evidence of good-neighbourliness also reaches us from the frozen North, which is great 'cave joke' country. The Norwegians, of all the Europeans, turn out to be the biggest fans of the Swedes - an opinion not shared by the Danes and even less by the Finns! The Swedes and the Danes, and to a lesser extent the Finns, go out of their way to judge the Norwegians as 'friendly and cheerful', giving them ratings way above the norm (could this be a 'gesture of solidarity? The Norwegians are certainly friendly folk, but not the most cheerful in the world). But all the Nordics, including of course the Finns themselves, seem to have it in for the Finns!

Responses to Proposition A also demonstrate the North/South divide. While northerners evidently appreciate the friendliness of Mediterranean folk, the latter regard the natives of northern climes as hostile. I suspect that misplaced ideas about love in a cold climate plus lack of first-hand experience (after all, how many Greeks go to Ireland or Norway on holiday?) have something to do with this. In those cases where the North/South factor does not apply, I suspect that mutual incompatibility gets in the way, as between the British and the French.

Proposition B of the INRA study deals with the more intimate matter of trust: 'People are trustworthy, keep their promises'. The most trustworthy, in the opinion of this international sample, are the Swiss and the Germans. The least trustworthy are the Italians, with the Greeks not far behind. In fairness it has to be said that the Italians find themselves almost as untrustworthy as the others do. Inter-country prejudices tend to follow the pattern established with Proposition A.

The INRA study also asked people which countries they liked and had favourable feelings towards, summing up the emotions aroused in the two Propositions. The sometimes surprising responses - country measured (top vote/bottom vote) - went as follows: Belgium (Spain/Sweden), France (Belgium/UK), Spain (Italy/Netherlands), Germany (Austria/Italy), Ireland (France/Spain), Greece (Switzerland/UK), Netherlands (Belgium/Portugal), Italy (Switzerland/Denmark), UK (Portugal/Spain), Finland (Germany/Spain), Austria (Sweden/Italy), Sweden (Austria/Finland), Norway (Denmark/Italy), Denmark (Norway/Italy) and Switzerland (Spain/Ireland). There seems to be a love affair going on between the Swedes and the Austrians, while the Italians can't stand the Nordics!

How does this match the results of the Eurovision Song Contest?

An Alternative History of Europe

"The great events of history are often due to secular changes in the growth of population and other fundamental economic causes, which, escaping by their gradual character the notice of contemporary observers, are attributed to the follies of statesmen or the fanaticism of atheists"   John Maynard Keynes

"If without languages we are colour blind, without history we are groping in total darkness"   Sir Michael Howard

"...from humanity, via nationality to bestiality"
     Franz Grillparzer

"There's nothing new in the world except the history you don't know"   Harry S Truman

"All civilisations ... are omelettes made with broken eggs"
     The Economist

"History never repeats itself, it stutters" [L'histoire ne se répète jamais, elle bégaye"]   Unidentified

"Those who cannot remember the past are condemned to repeat it"
     George Santayana

"History would be an excellent thing if only it were true"
     Tolstoy

"History is more or less bunk"   Henry Ford

"One damn thing after another"   A cynic's view of history

Once upon a time... there was a cosy little continent crammed with alien cultures, each of them strange, even sinister, to its neighbours, most of them recently emerged from a series of devastating wars.

That was how Europe looked to observers only fifty years ago. Yet the greatness of Europe is precisely the variety of its cultures and the interaction between them - a process that, set against the cultures of other continents, leaves an impression of homogeneity.

This vexatious state of affairs, the fact that we are both alike and different, is examined in the chapters that follow. Even if it is easy to demonstrate that there are still real differences between one country and another - enhanced as they have been by that great but hopefully temporary phenomenon, the nation state - the things we Europeans have in common are just as important.

What's more, faced with momentous events in our immediate surroundings, we now have the perfect opportunity to settle with our past.

It's not just the countries of eastern Europe that need to take a fresh and unpoliticised look at their histories: everybody knows that truth was falsified to suit the doctrines of the time. Unfortunately, while people there can still remember how things were under communism (western Europeans have to go further back into their history to set the record straight), they seem to be more interested in creating new myths and pseudo-identities to replace the plain old lies.

Yet, viewed in a historical perspective, we in western Europe have a worse record of misrepresentation. The falsifications of the fascist regimes of Germany, Italy and Spain - where the history books have since been put to right, with occasional gaps - reflect a tradition of ideological and often brutal totalitarianism that started with the Crusades and became institutionalised in the Inquisition, the obscurantism of the Catholic Monarchs of Spain and the pogroms, both civil and religious, that ensued across the Continent over the centuries.

The countries of western Europe can benefit from a fresh and more objective look at their individual and shared histories. The culprit today is no longer totalitarianism, but general party political obfuscation allied with the need to justify past colonial and other adventures.

These motives have prompted the superimposition of a patina of pregnant silences and furtive half-truths on the reality of our national pasts. In some cases the nation states have deliberately and deviously instilled hatred towards 'the foreigner' in the hearts of their citizens. The consequences - maybe also the causes - are evident. Of the past 2,000 years, one in five has been a year of war.

National history books have also tended to link little of their own country's events with those of neighbour nations, except when at war. Occasionally there is even a kind of Machiavellian conspiracy: the combined geniuses of Yugoslavia, Serbia and Greece managed to invent, for a range of strictly irredentist reasons peculiar to each of them, a modern 'Macedonian' race which now looks more and more like a historical if not a hysterical nonsense.

When the author went to school in post-WWII England, nobody talked about a particularly important event in the British and European history of the last 100 years: the Boer War was passed over in silence. Yet Italian schoolchildren were at the same time being told all about it - and nothing about the bloody goings-on in Abyssinia (as Ethiopia was known at the time), for which their own parents were responsible.

British history used to have a curious habit of stopping short about the time of the battle of Borodino - perhaps appropriately so, since it was Tolstoy who made the essential point that history is not about kings and dates but about people.

French history used to have a habit of *starting* on 14 July 1789, though there were occasional lapses in favour of the Sun King and, even further back, Jeanne d'Arc. German history still understandably skirts the first half of the present century.

Often what surprises is what remains unsaid. There are remarkable lacunae in what the nation states have chosen to tell their citizens, whether out of self-interest or myopia. It was only recently that the British public became aware that, in the closing years of WWII, three million people died of famine in what is now called Bangladesh in order to keep the Burma Army on its feet - a conscious act of British defence policy at the time.

Little is also said in the perpetrators' history books of the effects of the Scottish clearances of the 1850s (except in Scotland), of the Turkish massacre of over one million Armenians in 1915, of the Ukrainian famine of 1932-33, of the Austrian role in the 'Final

Solution', of Czechoslovak bullying of the Sudetendeutsch in 1945, of exact events in the history of *l'Algérie française*, and so on.

Nation state policies, reinforced by economic constraints, have also managed to dispose of generations without killing them. Walloon ironsmiths went to Sweden; Scottish crofters emigrated to Scandinavia, the Baltic States and even Ireland in search of a better living; some of the Scots in Ulster thought better of it and went on to the southern United States; many German, Norwegian, British and Irish labourers and farmers travelled westwards in the same direction; Ukranians and Croats flocked to Canada; and Italians, and even Cornish and Yorkshire miners, emigrated en masse to South America.

Untypically, in the context of European history, there were even some major movements eastwards: the Pontic Greeks to the south-eastern shores of the Black Sea and the Volga Germans to the northern shores of the Caspian and - much later, with the help of Stalin - even further east to Kazakhstan.

The truth is that, today, many of us know little about such events. They are hiccups of history, part of the process of cultural digestion. While the original motive may have been political and within the narrow criteria of the era justifiable, time has since buried the reality in an accretion of contemporaneous and irrelevant data. Thanks to the intrusion of the nation state, much of Europe has lost contact with its past.

As individuals - English, French, German or whatever - we all have our own perspective of a common European history and each of these perspectives is different. National histories plough parallel furrows. Even the history of Europe as taught in the schools of Europe is still partly a travesty, partly a cover-up.

So I find it encouraging that comparative European, even world, history books are now starting to emerge, and that the most serious effort of clarification relates to the period after AD 1000, with the advent of the nation state. Rather surprisingly, some of the best initiatives are the work of French historians.

The nation states, with their practices and prejudices, are like massive boulders blocking the path to our common past. Right now, the French government is still doing its best to stonewall attempts by Alsatians to learn the language of their Swabian relatives. And it's not that long ago that the United Kingdom government announced its intention to *increase* the emphasis on British history in the country's schools: evidently some of us are going backwards!

The self-serving versions of history concocted in the interests of the nation states ultimately do a disservice to the European 'ideal' of a community of races that have cohabited, traded, created a common culture - and of course fought with one another - over many centuries.

Our roots are in the East

The collapse of the Berlin Wall (nobody ever talks about the Iron Curtain!) challenged a western European *Weltanschauung* that had hardened over fifty years. We had to step back in time and remind ourselves that our history and culture find their roots largely in the East. If we go back to prehistory, we find evidence that the earliest settlers came southwestwards out of the depths of the Eurasian landmass. Many of them then moved on westwards along the shores of the Mediterranean, both north and south, from the area known as the Fertile Crescent.

Without going into the credentials of people known to some as the Atlanto-Mediterraneans (the people who hewed, dragged and raised the monoliths of Carnac and Stonehenge around 3000 BC), we can see that, like so many to follow, they felt the impetus of a *Drang nach Westen* that has characterised European history from that day to this.

The Celts, a people speaking a tongue derived from a proto-European language base known as Indo-European, provided the first major recorded settlement in what we now call western Europe, advancing in waves at various intervals up to 1200 BC. Historians are uncertain who was here when they arrived - certainly the Basques and the Iberians (who appear to have arrived earlier from North Africa), likewise the Ligurians and the Etruscans. A Mongolian people, the Finns, were also well established in the far north.

But the Celts were to be overtaken by other Germanic tribes coming from the same direction and ended up in what can be called the *Celtic Fringe*, with their backs to the Atlantic Ocean.

Agriculturalists of undetermined origin also moved westwards from Asia Minor, bringing their genes with them - or rather, according to a study undertaken by a team of American sociobiologists, six distinctive proteins still evident in the inhabitants of the earliest European regions to be cultivated.

It was the Celts who laid the initial foundations for a pan-European trading network. From their early civilisation in the Hallstatt region of what is now Austria (*Hall* from the Greek hals = salt), they developed a salt and iron trade that acted as a catalyst for commerce in many other commodities: amber from the Baltic, skins from the far north, spices from the south.

The Celtic salt roads, generally following the uplands for fear of raiding by unfriendly folk on the way, were primitive by comparison with the Roman roads but helped open up Europe to civilisation. As so often since, trade preceded politics: left to its own, it could have put a very different stamp on the history of Europe.

It would be wrong, however, to think of the Celts as a united people. They quarrelled frequently, a fact that encouraged the Romans to undertake the conquest of Gaul, today France, and thereby create the first European Union (the second being the empire of Charlemagne and the third, and the most perfect in my opinion, being the 'Open Europe' of the 12th and early-13th centuries).

John Casey of Durham University's department of archaeology makes the point that for the first four centuries of this era the present members of the European Union, with the exception of Ireland, Denmark, Sweden and Finland, were in part or whole provinces of the Roman Empire. That means Austria, Italy, Spain, Portugal, Greece, France, Germany (in part), the British Isles, Belgium, Luxembourg and the Netherlands.

As Casey explains: "The disunity of the Celtic societies which made up the population of the Iberian peninsula, Gaul comprising France and Belgium, Germany west of the Rhine, Britain and the lands bordering the Danube, made possible piecemeal Roman conquest of this vast territory by a combination of force and diplomacy." The rivers were as important to the Romans as their new and impressive road network. Like the Rhine, the Danube comes up frequently in early European history, as much for its importance as a transportation route as for its significance as a barrier.

The Roman road system, unlike the Celtic salt roads, was created to serve the army and the administration. "For civilians land transport, except over very short distances, or for very high-value goods of low bulk, was uneconomical... Archaeology allows us to build up a picture of this trade which supplements the historical sources. Corporations of shippers are found at key ports, both coastal and inland, as at Ostia (Italy), Arles (France), Cologne (Germany) and Lyons (France). London was a major port...".

Life at the other end of the Roman Empire was more confused. Barbarians kept on dropping in from the East. Diocletian, beset with these and other problems, decided they were too big to manage alone. So he split what has more recently been known as Yugoslavia between his own empire and the Greek-speaking Byzantine empire of the East. This was the first of many arbitrary decisions that were ultimately to have serious consequences for late-20th century politics: administrative division led to a schism of the churches (Roman and Orthodox) and to the introduction of separate alphabets. Diocletian, incidentally, then retired to his palace in a city appropriately called Split and spent what was left of his life cultivating cabbages.

As history has shown, the Romans of course got it wrong, but they did succeed in driving the Celts into the westernmost corners of Europe - although the ones in Britain made it back to Brittany, one of the few examples of a folk movement from west to east.

The frontiers of the Roman Empire crumbled partly through the fortuitous aid of nature when the Rhine froze over on 31 December of the year 406 AD (an easy date to remember). The Roman Empire then disintegrated progressively despite the assimilation of colonised peoples.

The first across the Rhine, helped on their way by the Huns, were evidently so glad to get out they could hardly stop. They were also obligingly accommodated by what was left of the Roman Empire, which really couldn't do much else.

The Marcomanni and Quadi tribes of the Suevi group of peoples (Suevi = Swabian) settled in the northwest corner of the Iberian peninsula, present-day Galicia and northern Portugal; a clan of Alans of Iranian stock went a bit further south for a while; and the Vandals conducted an elegant 'reverse', ie west-east, pincer movement taking them through Andalusia (hence the name) and Tunisia to Rome, whence they disappeared off the map.

The rest of the Swabians, the Alemanni (who became synonymous in the French language with the Germans), stayed relatively close to home, contenting themselves with land offered to them on the left bank of the Rhine - an early case of poacher turned game-keeper.

In one of the more coherent examples of European colonisation, they created a stable and longlasting community of peoples that took in - and still takes in today - an area extending from Alsace in France to the Austrian Vorarlberg, spanning southwest Germany and Switzerland. The Bavarians, a much more mixed bunch of people, settled alongside and later colonised the Ostmark of the Frankish Empire, today's Austria.

Other westward or southward bound folk included the Burgundians (a Germanic race who did a great job getting themselves assimilated into French culture!), the Lombards (the 'longbeards' from the far north who settled in Northern Italy), the Goths, both western (Visigoth) and eastern (Ostrogoth) branches, and of course the Franks who gave their name to France. The Goths in fact dithered for a while, heading southeastwards from Poland to the Black Sea and Asia Minor before they turned west and headed for Greece, the Balkans, Italy and Spain.

They had all originally come from further east as did, in chronological order, the Huns (a Mongol folk from Central Asia who were eventually defeated by a combined Roman, Frankish and Visigothic army in 451 AD and disappeared), the Slavs (some of them also known as Wends or Sorbs) who moved into the vacuum left by the Germanic peoples in what is today Mecklenburg, Pomerania and areas to the southeast, the Avars (another Hunnish lot) and the Turko-Finnish Magyars who, after a round trip (see below), ended up in Hungary.

A Germanic by any other name...

Western Europe then slid slowly into what historians choose to call, for want of a better phrase, the Dark Ages. Whether they were that dark is debatable. The western Roman emperor was deposed in 476 AD, but immigrant barbarian leaders still tried to legitimise themselves by seeking recognition from Constantinople. Meanwhile Irish missionaries, coming back from the outer edge of the Celtic Fringe, proselytised across wide swathes of the European Continent.

The so-called Dark Ages were also considerably enlightened, technically and culturally, by the arrival of the Arabs in southern Spain in 711 AD. In any case these Dark Ages didn't last that long because by the year 768 Charlemagne, the illegitimate son of an upstart king with the unlikely name of Pip the Short *(Pepin le Bref)* and a lady graciously referred to as Bertha of the Big Foot *(Berthe au Grand Pied)*, had popped up on the European scene and Europe was being recreated.

Charlemagne was crowned Emperor in Rome on Christmas Day 800 AD (another easy date) and by his death in 814 AD he had created an empire covering - to use the analogy suggested by John Casey - most of France and Italy, western Germany, Belgium, Luxembourg and the Netherlands, as well as Switzerland, Austria and lands further east. He had even embarked on a plan to link the Rhine with the Danube, rather precociously anticipating the opening of the Rhine-Main-Danube canal in 1992.

The Celtic Fringe, including the Brittany peninsula, was notably absent from Charlemagne's empire, along with Britain and most of Spain - which he had ventured into in the year 778, only to be rebuffed by the Arab Emir of Saragossa. On the way back through the Basque country, his army sacked Pamplona and deservedly got ambuscaded by a Basque force in the Pyrenees. This event entered European history books as one of the first but certainly not the last distortions of reality. Charlemagne's rearguard got chewed up by a bunch of Basque guerillas, not by an army of 300,000 Saracens as legend would have it, and Roland certainly didn't burst a blood vessel blowing his horn...

The close of Charlemagne's reign is an appropriate point at which to draw the first balance. The findings to date, we suggest, are threefold. First, that the majority of the invaders were of Germanic stock (one used to say 'Aryan', which also included the Celts, but Hitler turned this into a dirty word). Moreover, they got just about everywhere, Franks and Burgundians to France (Luigi Barzini maintains in his book *The Europeans*[9] that almost half the inhabitants of present-day France are the descendents of Germanic tribes), Visigoths to Spain, Lombards and Ostrogoths to Italy, Vandals to North Africa, and so on.

Secondly, by the year 800 AD, there had already been two relatively successful attempts to create a European Union - which is hardly surprising in view of this *brassage* or stew of different peoples.

Third, one should treat racial descriptions with utmost care: the Franks, the Burgundians and the Lombards are Germanic or Nordic, not Latin. As often as not, the name used by one European nation to describe another is a misnomer. The English call the inhabitants of the Netherlands the Dutch (from *duitsch/deutsch*), the others, with equal disregard for racial origins, Hollanders. The right label, according to the Dutch, would be Batavians, pace the Frisians.

The French, unless they're being rude, know the Germans as *les Allemands*, yet the Alemanni (German: *alle Mann*) were just one small confederation of Germanic tribes which happened to be geographically the closest to French civilisation at the time. The Italian know them as *tedeschi* from the Old English theod, itself derived from the Old High German *diot*, the word for a people or nation. Surprisingly only the British seem to have got it absolutely right: Germans, a word of Celtic origin.

Some changes in direction

So Charlemagne came and went and his empire, like the Roman Empire, slowly fell apart. The Vikings, who had been little more than a thorn in his side, now got down to serious business, establishing the 'Dane-law' in Britain and - after a series of forays up the Seine to Paris - negotiating, in 911 AD, the conditions necessary for the creation of a fine new culture in Normandy. At about the same time, their fellow-Vikings established a highly successful trading station at Novgorod in Russia, which shows that the Vikings were capable of a lot more than rowing hard, wearing silly hats with horns in them (a myth, as it happens) and plundering.

The same period saw two other important developments. The first was prompted by the Magyars, today's Hungarians and the first non-Germanic settlers in western Europe of our era, who embarked on one of the few examples of a racial 'round trip'. This took them through Germany and France, over the Alps into northern Italy and back home to Hungary (nb 'the land of the Huns'). They then settled down, adopted Christianity and a written constitution, but, along with the Finns, stuck loyally to their Finno-Ugrian languages.

The second development, following on the taming of the Magyars, was a genuine counter-movement eastwards across the northern half of Europe. The Wends, who had settled along the Baltic coastline, encouraged Germanic peoples to come back with their agricultural techniques, their crafts and their laws. This movement later extended even further eastwards with the Germanic settlements in Poland and the colonies of the Teutonic Knights. Further south, Bavarians and other frontier settlers drove a wedge between the Slav communities, effectively isolating those that later became known as the South Slavs from their fellows.

It was at the end of the first millenium that the prime example of the modern nation state, in the European sense, reared its head. Its beginnings, in 987 AD in what is now called France, were not that auspicious - a minor noble, Hugues Capet *(Hugh the Cape)*, was crowned in a small place called Noyon - but, thanks to a clever strategy of local alliances directed against both German competitors and Rome, the Capetian dynesty laid the foundations for the modern French state. About the same time, Otto the Great founded the Welf dynasty from Hanover and sowed the seeds of a Holy Roman Empire that slowly matured into a modern Germany.

However some good things were going on at the same time. The emergence of an artisanal class, a minor intelligentsia, along with the first city states, even the creation of new towns (*Villeneuve* and *Villefranche*, the town of the Franks, are common placenames in France) prompted what some historians call the 'Open Europe' of the early Middle Ages. These developments were accompanied by rapid population growth: it is estimated that, between the year 1000 (when the world was rumoured to be coming to an end in any case) and the year 1300, the western European headcount more than doubled.

It was a time of enquiry, of relative give-and-take, of an awareness of the riches to be rediscovered in both the Classical and in contemporary civilisations, particularly the Arab and Jewish cultures. One fine aspect of this cultural flowering, anticipating the Italian *Rinascimento*, was Romanesque art and architecture ('Norman' to the British) which, through the extension of monastic life, permeated Europe, both West and East.

Commerce also opened up again on a European scale, picking up where the Celts and the Romans had left off. At first this trade was essentially land-based. Thanks to its central position,

Champagne became almost a 'Single Market' in its own right, with traders from all over Europe converging on the four annual fairs at Troyes, Provins, Lagny-sur-Marne and Bar-sur-Aube. At the end of the thirteenth century, commerce shifted back to the sea-routes, with Bruges, Genoa and Venice as the principal poles for this traffic. To the north the Hanseatic League reigned supreme.

The 'openness' of this Europe is well demonstrated by the life of Frederick II of Hohenstaufen. In 1198 AD, at the age of four, he inherited the Kingdom of Sicily from the Normans of all people - who, not content with staying Vikings, had established a second and equally fine empire in the Mediterranean. Frederick was a very eclectically educated lad who developed equal sympathy for the Arab and European cultures, both of which were well represented in Sicily at the time. He was elected Holy Roman Emperor in 1212 AD and then spent most of his life quarrelling with the Popes - one of whom, Gregory IX, sent a crusade against him and excommunicated him, after which he rather reluctantly headed his own crusade to the Holy Land.

Frederick has been called variously 'the first modern man', *stupor mundi* ('amazement of the world') and even, to Italian peasants today, *il Gran Frederigo*. When he failed to quell an unruly Arab community on the island, he had the intelligence to create a new township for them on the Italian mainland, Lucera (cited rather unkindly on mediaeval Italian maps as Lucera *delli Pagani*). And as King of Jerusalem he officially made his new possession a city of the three 'non-pagan' religions, Christian, Jewish and Muslim.

The Hohenstaufen dynasty hailed from Waiblingen, a burg close to today's Stuttgart. The best the Italians could make of this impossible Germanic placename was 'Ghibbeline', a name they gave to the Hohenstaufen faction (the people who built those pretty castles with the swallowtail battlements). The opposing faction were the Ottonian Welfs from Saxony, whom Frederick finally silenced through the intervention of Philip II of France at the battle of Bouvines (a nondescript yet significant corner of France close to the Belgian frontier). Hence Max Beerbohm's immortal phrase "enter Guelphs and Ghibbelines, fighting". So much European history has been distorted phonetically: the French even managed to transmogrify the calvinist *Eidgenossen* ('confederates') into *Huguenots*.

But the real message here is that, as dear old Frederick II so ably demonstrated, Europe was a mishmash of cultural interests spilling over from one so-called state to another. Yet in addition to the good things, this 'Open Europe' bore the seeds of the mistrustful Middle Ages that followed. The Church of Rome was in such a parlous state by now that it created a breeding ground for heresy. The most famous of the heretical sects was the Cathars, followers of a manicheistic faith that had found its way to western Europe from Bulgaria. The epithet 'Bulgar' became synonymous with heresy and suitably associated habits, hence its survival today in the word 'bugger'. Another example of how history distorts things.

Anyway Rome, in the form of Pope Innocent III, eventually put paid to the heretics. Taking advantage of the growing estrangement between the south and the north of France - the people of the *langue d'oc*, the *hoc*-speakers, and those of the *langue d'oïl*, the *hoc ille* or *oui*-speakers - his Holiness summoned the northerners to a Crusade against their fellow-Europeans under the leadership of a well-meaning but, as time passed, increasingly nasty character called Simon de Montfort. The ensuing bloody sieges of the cities of Languedoc between 1209 and 1229 AD contributed to the destruction of this first 'Open Europe'.

Simon's dirty work was aided and abetted by a monastic order created specially for the purpose, the Dominicans. Its founder, a certain Dominic de Guzman, was another apparently well-meaning individual who happened to be passing through the Languedoc on his way back from the Holy See to Burgo de Osma, a place that once boasted a bishopric but today claims 5,000 inhabitants and a large cathedral. Dominic (on no account to be confused with Guzman el Bueno) set a standard for later Spaniards by enforcing conversion through, to use a nice word, coercion - an initiative that ultimately metastased into the Spanish Inquisition.

It is perhaps worth noting parenthetically that Fernand Niel, a distinguished French historian who roundly condemned this intra-European Crusade, tempered his strictures with the comment that, by bringing a number of provinces to heel, it did after all contribute to the unification of the French nation state. So?

Similar dastardly deeds were being done at the same time by Conrad of Marburg who, as chief Inquisitor of the area we now call Germany, roamed up and down the country on a mule, terrorising the population, conjuring up the demons of mass psychosis (as

Adolf Hitler did more recently) and applying summary justice on a grand scale in the name of religion.

Ironically, conditions in Spain - destined to become the *haut-lieu* of the Inquisition - were relatively serene at the time, probably due to the presence of the Arabs and fellow-Muslims from North Africa (variously called Saracens or Moors). The Arabs showed the rest of the world, in varying degrees during 600 years of occupation, the virtues of religious tolerance, allowing Christians and Jews to practise their religions in the occupied territories, sponsoring the arts and the sciences, tending the land with superb irrigation systems, and passing on the accumulated knowledge of the Classical civilisations.

A concept of Europe...

Few Europeans acknowledge their debt to the Arabs (or, parenthetically, recognise the poor deal the latter got in return, something that is now catching up with us). Most of us are totally unaware of the fact that it was the real or perceived threat they posed to the existing order, religious and social, that helped give our continent the identity it has today.

Peter Millar made this point in an editorial in *The European* newspaper: "It took a long time and a lot of bloodshed, the sacking of Rome and the sacking of Constantinople to create the concept of any sort of European continental identity based on habitation of a contiguous land mass. The catalyst was Islam - the threat from without. It is dubious whether a concept of Europe as any sort of coherent body would ever have emerged had the followers of Mohammed not first ripped the southern bank of the Mediterranean from the influence of Rome and challenged the northern bank in a giant pincer movement that reached from the Pyrenees to the gates of Vienna."

The Arab invasion of Spain had one particular consequence which also contributed to the realisation of an 'Open Europe' even if it was, again, a defensive reaction to an alien system. This was the creation of the pilgrimage route to the supposed tomb of Saint James in Compostela. Millions of ordinary folk in search of an indulgence, prisoners walking out their punishment, and simple adventurers travelled down the old Roman roads to Galicia in the early middle ages and later.

Religious orders and lay benefactors built hospices, hospitals, causeways and bridges to help them on their way. They leave behind traces that comment on the continental scale of this venture. On the one hand, sites and names on the pilgrimage road that testify to a cosmopolitan past, for example a village in the mountains of northwestern Spain called Ruitelán, a rough transcription from the native Rutland of a man who opened an inn there. On the other, traces of the pilgrimage in faraway places, like the fresco of a *Jacquet* in a tiny village lost among the lakes of Mecklenburg in distant northeastern Germany.

Spain, in the form of a nation state created by the Catholic Monarchs Ferdinand and Isabelle, put a stop to such sentimental nonsense in 1492, after the fall of the Moorish Kingdom of Granada. The 'Catholic Kings' reneged on their promise of freedom of religion, they expelled the Jews of Toledo and, later, the *moriscos*, the Muslim converts to the Christian faith. Ironically but happily, thanks to an enlightened individual by the name of Sultan Bayezid II, the Sephardic Jews found a new haven in the Ottoman Empire.

So we come back, irrevocably, to the ultimate supremacy of the nation state. Not much more needs to be said in this alternative history of Europe - except perhaps that Napoleon, much later on, managed to bully and maneouvre much of Europe into living together again, in crude imitation of the Romans and Charlemagne. But he was motivated by the spirit of *La Patrie*, the nation state extended, and didn't give a damn about the European ideal.

The concept of the nation state found its origins in France at the end of the first millenium and was later sealed, for both the French and the English, by a new sense of identity born of the awful experiences of the Hundred Years War (1337-1453). Yet, in most other parts of Europe, it is a relatively recent creation. The Netherlands and Spain took shape in the last five centuries, Italy, Belgium, Greece and modern-day Germany in the last two.

With its gift for self-justification and colonial adventures, this modern emanation of the nation state is a striking but hopefully shortlived feature on the historic landscape of Europe. It is certainly not contributing to the creation of a New World Order. As an American anthropologist Virginia Hine pointed out, the League of Nations and the United Nations "failed because they were built upon the very form of social organization they were designed to supersede - the nation state". We see the same phenomenon here within Europe...

These nation states were artificial political creations, rather than coherent ethnic entities, as hopefully the preceding pages have shown. And the concept of the strictly ethnic state, now back in vogue in eastern Europe, is an even greater abberation which only took shape in the last two hundred years.

Yet it is uncanny how ethnic, as opposed to nation-state, frontiers so often coincide with marked changes in terrain. One of the rare exceptions to this rule is the Flemish-Walloon borderline in present-day Belgium - where, fifteen hundred years ago, the Great Referee blew his whistle for 'time' on the playing fields of history.

There are even localised examples of changes in terrain acting as barriers to the movement of both peoples and ideas - and I am not just thinking of the English Channel. One is the 'drumlins' of County Down in northern Ireland, a range of glacier-formed hills which separates the people of Ulster from the rest of the Irish. Another is the Landsker line of hills in southern Pembrokeshire which divides a mixed community of English, Norman and, yes!, Flemish stock from the native Welsh to the north. Yet another is the hills and forests on the northern fringes of Sweden's southern province of Skåne, which delineated an area that was more akin to Denmark - and was occupied for centuries by the Danes - than to the Sweden to the north.

It is also worth remembering that 'our natural heritage' is not as natural as we Europeans pretend it to be. For a start the hand of man - the Englishman, the Dutchman, the Frenchman, etc - is evident enough if you fly from London to Frankfurt, irregular hedge-lined fields giving way to landscapes cultivated in squares, then strips, then squares getting larger and larger (no doubt the EU's Common Agricultural Policy will eliminate these differences and turn our land yellow and blue with its sunflower, oilseed rape and linseed production subsidies!).

Cultivation of the olive tree changed the face of Mediterranean Europe even before the present era. Many of our fruit trees and herbs came to us by courtesy of the Arabs at the end of the first millenium. The famous oak forests of Europe are a result of the uninhibited land clearance movements of the early Middle Ages. The Scots moors and the Irish bogs - now treasured by travel connoisseurs for their distinctive landscapes - were rich forest country until the Celts cut all the trees down. Even the woodlands of Denmark disappeared several centuries ago. The planetrees that line the *routes nationales* of France only arrived from the East in the 1700s. And the tulip, a symbol of the Netherlands, arrived from Turkey in the mid-16th century. And so on...

So anyone who talks about 'our natural heritage', as if time had stood still all these centuries, is talking rubbish. Even in the so-called 'Dark Ages' - a misnomer if ever there was one - Europe was surprisingly open. It was only with the emergence of that upstart phenomenon, the nation state, that the idea of sovereignty and independence took hold.

As history has shown time and again, we are interdependent. In the words of the French historian Jean-Baptiste Duroselle, "no region in Europe can be fully understood in isolation from the rest". And our interdependence goes much further than the confines of Europe. One of the most traumatic events in pan-European history - for no region was spared - came with the arrival from central Asia in 1348 of the Black Death, ferried to us on a galley from the Genoese trading station of Caffa in the Crimea. The subsequent decimation of urban populations encouraged a ghetto mentality, but then led to the economic revival that spurred the development of the nation state...

Historical whodunits

We tend to talk of races as if they acquire immutable characteristics. Yet, every now and then, we see startling evidence of change.

Obviously, some of us wonder what happened to the Ancient Greeks - those fine, athletic, blonde creatures of the Classical legends. There's not much evidence of them today.

We also wonder where the Basques came from. An original-minded people with a particularly high rhesus negative factor, did they really come from the Caucasus or thereabouts, like most of the rest of us. And we wonder what happened to the Etruscans. Did they end up in Raetian Switzerland as some people suggest?

But probably the most dramatic and indisputable example is provided by the Vikings, who transmogrified from a relatively wild and migrant warrior folk ("warmongering, ale-swilling rapists", in the words on one historian) to the Normans, the highly cultured settled civilisation of the early Middle Ages.

More recently, we have the case of the Prussians, reputedly the most work-oriented and best organised of all Europeans. Attributes claimed for them (forgetting their militarism for a moment) included modesty, honesty, tolerance, pragmatism and thrift. What happened to all of this?

Well, for a start, the original Prussians or Prusi, a Baltic tribe related to the Lithuanians and Latvians, were butchered by the Teutonic Knights and disappeared in the Middle Ages. The people that then usurped the name earned their reputation - with the help of *der alter Fritz*, Frederick II - partly on the battlefield, partly through industry. Today, in the eastern lands of Germany, there is not that much evidence that the Prussian tradition survived. Foreign investors complain relentlessly about a lack of a work ethic.

Yet I suspect that some of the qualities associated with the Prussian tradition have survived: orderliness, discipline and a sense of social responsibility. What we are witnessing is a shift in values.

Fifty years of life in a collectivist environment, however badly managed, have accustomed people to the benefits of a cocooned society, unexciting yet satisfying. But the Prussian virtues of intelligence and industry, particularly in the newly emerging entrepreneurial and administrative classes, will find their proper place - and reassert themselves - given time!

The British (or English)

A sentimental society

"The British are notable for their sentimentality, which they mistake for a virtue: hence their ability to deceive themselves, which others mistake for hypocrisy." Lord Hailsham

"It is my Royal and Imperial Command... that you exterminate first the treacherous English..." Wilhelm II of Prussia

"There is nothing so bad or so good that you will not find Englishmen doing it; but you will never find an Englishman in the wrong. He does everything on principle" George Bernard Shaw

*"The French want no-one to be their **superior**. The English want **inferiors**...* Alexis de Tocqueville

"You never find an Englishman among the underdogs - except in England of course" Evelyn Waugh

"An Englishman's mind works best when it is almost too late"
Lord d'Abernon

"Heavy Fog Over Channel, Continent Cut Off" Times headline

"The accursed itch of class difference" George Orwell

"The British are brave people. They can face anything, except reality" George Mikes, How To Be Decadent

"In the last analysis, the government's defence of the status quo boils down to little more than 'this is the way we have always done it.' As with so many things in Britain, that is precisely the problem. Reginald Dale, International Herald Tribune, 4/6/1993

Putting the British first may be interpreted as an act of favouritism. Not so. It is a declaration of interest. I am British and, however hard I try, I cannot avoid some degree of subjectivity, positive or negative.

This declaration will put other European nationalities on their guard, and rightly so. Any observations on the personalities and quirks of the French, the Germans, etc, will be better received and understood, precisely because the reader (German, French, etc) will know where we are all starting from. But any ethnocentric (or, rather, culturocentric) bias should be put down to innocence rather than intention.

So what are the trademarks of the British? Lord Hailsham, if his comment can be taken at its face value, feels that they are misunderstood. Indeed we are, but no more than anyone else.

Certainly the British are a complex lot, like all Europeans and possibly even more so, due to their hybrid origins. In fact these origins are so hybrid that the only way of approaching the subject is by rephrasing the question: what are the trademarks of the *English*? For the benefit of foreigners, who frequently misuse the word 'English' (whether they understand the realities underlying it or not), we have disposed of the Scots, the Welsh and the Irish and what's left of the Cornish. They have been consigned to 'The Celtic Fringe', the subject of a later chapter.

Not that this simplifies things all that much. The English are a heterogeneous lot, divided both by class and geography. The only way of approaching them is by trying to understand, in the first place, their class structure - what Sue Townsend, the British author, calls "our terrible class system which strangles people".

As far back as 1937, George Orwell said "whatever way you turn, this curse of class difference confronts you like a wall of stone." That wall is still there, stony in its subtleties, often impenetrable even if you think you can can see through it. In the words of Flora Lewis[2], a keen observer of the British scene: "Acceptance, indeed assertion, of the right to class consciousness is too deep, almost as though class were an inalienable aspect of identity".

Let's start at the top of English society. There is still a real nobility and loads of landed gentry, of varying degrees of authenticity. There are also a lot of aspiring 'squires', who use their money to acquire estates in the Home Counties and elsewhere in order to gain respectability (a manoeuvre which will not fool anyone in the class he or she is trying to enter).

Then come the middle classes - and this is where the problems really start. While the dividing lines have blurred since Victorian times, it is still possible to typecast people as 'upper middle', 'middle middle' or 'lower middle' class. It is particularly easy to spot the 'lowers' or 'middle middles' trying to break into the 'upper middle class'. Again, money on its own is not enough - contrary to the reality in other modestly egalitarian societies like Belgium, Switzerland or Scandinavia, where money can buy you into most things. And, in England, the further people progress up the social ladder, the firmer they turn their backs on their past.

As for the English working class, some people would say it doesn't exist any more. Yet it is remarkably resilient, but more as a declaration than a reality. Ordinary English people - the ones who talk with an accent, balance processed peas on the blades of their knives and wipe their noses with their hands - are particularly anxious to declare themselves members of the working class in order to avoid being confused with any of the other classes they consider, paradoxically, 'beneath them'. Even people who do *not* talk with an accent, balance peas or wipe their noses with their hands now prefer to identify themselves with the so-called working class.

The result is that, in a MORI poll conducted in 1991, while only 52% of the respondents said they identified themselves as working class (the official standard survey classification put the working class at 61% of the population at the time), no less than 66% of respondents said they preferred to be called 'working class'. Moreover this 66% represented a 50% increase on the national survey figures of 40 years earlier!

Northerners will even claim that there are subtle class distinctions, five in all, within the working class itself: the upper working class, the working class proper, the lower working class, the "scruffs" and the "scroungers".

This situation bemuses foreigners. Japanese businesspeople living in Britain are shocked both by the lack of consideration shown by the rich towards the poor, and the lack of deference shown by the poor towards the rich. Evidently they still perceive some class distinctions that the rest of us have lost sight of.

Certainly the assertiveness of ordinary English people is of growing social significance, perhaps as a result of years of Thatcherism and union-bashing, perhaps more as a reaction against the snobbery implicit in social symbols and perceptions: accent, dress, eating habits and simply origins (some regions, such as Lancashire or the London East End, are more suspect socially than others).

British class-related perceptual mechanisms can be subtle in the extreme. The aforementioned criteria of accent, dress, eating habits and origins have now been complemented by the size and shininess of one's car - increasingly, thanks to the tax system, a company 'perk' and a managerial status symbol. The ultimate symbol, the personalised number plate, is regarded by Continentals (with the exception, it seems, of the Austrians) as positively daft.

It was a pleasure for me, since writing the above, to come across the following words from the novelist David Lodge: "English social life is controlled by an intricate system of signals recognised by the natives." It was also intriguing to hear the views of a British sociologist who believes that the class system developed to compensate for the fact that the country lacks a written constitution[10]. 'Social order' begets social order, it seems.

But it is the signals that decide things, not the substance. Interviewed on French TV, Jeffrey Archer - a man who has demonstrated that British political life can, even if temporarily, attract people with above-average intelligence - offered his elevation to the House of Lords as evidence of the absence of a class system. But it is precisely the willingness of even intelligent individuals to be absorbed into the system that demonstrates its potency.

Class attitudes influence the manner in which English children are brought up. While the working class is inclined to say "shut up and don't ask questions" to its kids, the 'upper-to-middle-middle' classes tend to adopt a bossy and no-nonsense approach, jollying the youngsters along without necessarily giving them the answers either. You sometimes need to be a mindreader to guess there's any parental love involved. This matter-of-fact, nanny-knows-best attitude is particularly highly developed in English women doctors and British Airways stewardesses.

The English also attach symbolic significance, raised to the level of a religion, to certain words. The most potent combination at the moment is 'Brussels bureaucracy'. Not even the French can muster such Pavlovian responses as the English do, negatively, to words like 'federalism' (the 'f-word') and, positively, to the word 'sovereignty'.

But on the matter of sovereignty, as Samuel Brittan points out, "the latter has already been eroded ... by Britain's own elective dictatorship". To which I would add that the squeals about losing sovereignty to an independent central bank, when the Bank of England is still essentially a tool of government policy far removed from the interests of the electorate, smack of total humbug.

Next to class, the most noteworthy structural aspect of English society is its politics. Here the system is sufficiently rigid to shield the public from any really interesting surprises other than the sexual indiscretions of cabinet ministers, which are cheerfully amplified by the media. When the indiscretion is a purely political one - for example, choosing to differ from the Prime Minister on a matter of substance - then, try as the media may, the real truth never comes out. The offending minister goes to his political grave, lips sealed (or at least he used to as long as Mrs Thatcher was around).

One wonders whether this is an effect of the 'clubbishness' of the UK establishment or a reflection of what is still essentially a two-party system or something resembling it. On the other hand, when things go seriously wrong, even the ruling party takes matters into its own hands. As Arthur Balfour noted in 1922, long before Margaret Thatcher was even thought of: "It is not a principle of the Conservative Party to stab its leaders in the back but I must confess that it often appears to be a practice."

Cyril Northcote Parkinson, the creator of Parkinson's Law, said this of Westminster: "The British [his choice of words, and in this case he's right], being brought up on team games, enter their House of Commons in the spirit of those who would rather be doing something else. If they cannot be playing golf or tennis, they can at least pretend that politics is a game with very similar rules."

The exposure of the Lower House (appropriately named?) to television has demonstrated conclusively to the British electorate that politics is, indeed, a game and that the majority of those involved behave like kids. Even allowing for the possibility that the two-party system encourages a 'yaroo' mentality, these goings-on are totally unparalleled in any other European legislature. In Italy, they fight.

Events at the time of the Maastricht summit led me to conclude that even Ministers of the Crown were more concerned with party political point-scoring within their own little Westminster world than with what was going on outside. In fact the whole dismal experience demonstrated, once again, a fundamental lack of vision. As a German negotiator said at the time of the Single European Act, "we knew it was another step towards an ever closer union, but the British never look ahead".

The power of the media also has a lot to do with British life, with newspaper circulations double or more those of most other European dailies. What used to be known as 'Fleet Street' journalism has an oversize scoop mentality which has done the country's image abroad untold harm through spreading stories about truculent workers, rowdies and other unsavoury aspects of English society.

Even BBC TV and radio journalists resort to levels of investigative journalism - where the interviewer does everything imaginable to trip up the interviewee - which make the hairs of their peers on the Continent stand on end. But the BBC generally has a record of objective reporting which deserves to be, and in the minds of many people is, the envy of Europe. Maybe that's why the government doesn't like it.

It is certain that English sensibilities regarding class are far more subtle than those of the other European nations. In many cases social judgments on the Continent are made either in terms of region or apparent wealth and very little else. As a result, many Continentals have difficulty in perceiving the innuendos of English life. Of course, everyone knows the stock concepts of the English 'gentleman', Major Thompson or the eccentric and mustachioed elderly boor. But these are as much a part of international folklore as the musical comedy Italian or the naughty, naughty Frenchman.

Even so, the English still have more than their fair share of sententious, pompous people who are expert at producing the well-rounded and often self-serving phrase. Presumably there were even more of them around in Walter Bagehot's time, prompting him to declare that "dullness is our line, as cleverness is that of the French". The Belgians must be positively dazzled by the French: even today, to judge from a survey made in 1990, they find the English boring by comparison.

Which is a slur on the English. They have even managed to produce a type of seemingly frustrated intellectual - almost as culturally rootless as the English middle class, but in another sense - that engages in such arcane pursuits as poetry readings in Druidic shrines and musical tours on French canal boats. Some of these people even refuse to use the first person singular, 'one' being infinitely preferable to 'I'. They also tend to be incurably romantic, a quality that is not so evident in the other strata of English society.

Along with eccentricity, whatever the Belgians may say, another feature attributed to the English is their sense of fairness. Amongst competitive Continentals, being gratuitously fair is a delightful but dotty example of the eccentricity of the English (the term 'fair' has even found its way into the French and German languages, for want of an equivalent). They admire it, they emulate it in their better moments, but a blind tradition of being fair strikes them as sheer madness. In fact, the English like to pretend they are fair, but there's no guarantee that they will ultimately be more compassionate than anyone else.

This brings us back to Lord Hailsham's aphorism which, in fact, only tells half the truth. The British (read *English*) can be sentimental - but mainly towards animals and, occasionally, towards children. They certainly do deceive themselves, as does everyone, but they can also knowingly deceive others (the Belgians say the English "camouflage their emotions"). In fact, the 'others', i.e. foreigners, are absolutely right. As often as not, what they mistake for hypocrisy is indeed... hypocrisy. So, as George Mikes said, "if you want to be really and truly British, you must become a hypocrite".

Confusion about the average Englishman's intentions is not helped by British diplomatic tradition. Luigi Barzini[9] talks about the ability of British statesmen to "resort with equal ease and elegance to what seemed to foreigners Levantine duplicity, Greek ambiguities, Florentine intrigues and, but more rarely, outright treachery. This unexpected flexibility", he adds, "offended the French in particular, perhaps because they alone felt entitled to resort to such dubious techniques."

The Marqués de Ximenez had reason to talk of "perfidious Albion", a phrase that was picked up by the French and then used afresh by the Spanish over the Gibraltar issue - *"la pérfida Albion"*.

Yet, as one of my Spanish friends pointed out recently, hypocrisy has a bad face and a good face: the good face is the readiness not to say things that are better left unsaid.

Why do we English manage to dissimulate to the extent that many foreigners think we are hypocrites? I am not talking here about 'keeping cool' which, curiously enough, is normally identified with the Gallic term of *sangfroid*. Peter Collett, in his book *Foreign Bodies*[5], offers an explanation: "This reticence may be connected to the shyness of the British, but it probably has more to do with that cardinal rule, which says that one must not make a scene in public. This desire not to cause any trouble is a very powerful motivating force in British life - one which sometimes threatens to be more important than life itself."

From self-observation, I would say that the problem is that many of us have indeed been brought up to spare other people's feelings - an extension of this misplaced idea of fair play. So we bottle up our own feelings (the Stiff Upper Lip?) until, later, a provocation triggers the truth. And, then, the unwitting foreigner assumes we have been pretending all along. Hypocrisy, no?

Maybe Churchill had this in mind when he said that the typical Briton says little, and what he says is always obscure. He even keeps his hands in his pockets more than the average European (could this be body language to let the other party know he's giving nothing away?). Examples of verbal obscurity abound: the insidious preamble, in debate, of "*if I may* say so..." or the opening remark of a traffic policeman to a speeding motorist: "*I'm afraid*, sir, you have committed an offence". As a Canadian woman novelist remarked in public not long ago: "I know the British are famed for their plots, not saying what they really mean".

In drama, TV and other, the trait comes across in the best cases as creative understatement, in the worst cases as innuendo. By comparison with the TV outpourings of other European networks, it can be terribly effective. In real life, it can confuse and hurt...

But this is the better, more mechanistic, form of hypocrisy. There is another kind that can be much more brutal. Being really double-faced is something some English excel at - surprisingly since they are basically very decent people. Humbug is evident in both public and private life and, uncharacteristically, it extends to all classes.

Perhaps as an extension of the wish to spare other people's feelings, the English can be extremely and genuinely polite. Unfortunately, this does not necessarily extend to their relations with foreign visitors, where the response to an appeal for help in finding the way is as likely to be a lesson in the correct use of the English language as the help itself.

But if the English can be sensitive at the personal level, few nationalities can beat them for insensitivity culturally, with attitudes ranging from naive insouciance to sheer hubris. Dutch prime minister Ruud Lubbers must have been thinking of the latter when he said: "I am worried that there is a tradition that it feels good to say 'No'." Making a point of one's uniqueness is a particularly English trait, like a spoilt child refusing to eat its dinner. In international affairs, as demonstrated in the late-1991 negotiations over European Monetary Union, British delegations used a combination of deception and stonewalling to frustrate the intentions of the majority.

It is when parodying foreigners that the English demonstrate that they do, in fact, have acute powers of observation. Witness the television series 'Allo, Allo'. Here their creativity and sense of fun compensate for everything else. But in day-to-day situations, the tendency to behave in a foreign environment in exactly the same way as at home is highly developed, as much out of a total lack of awareness as anything else.

Sadly, in the 1980s, this insensitivity or the desire to appear different (the eccentricity trait again?) started deteriorating into a form of xenophobia. Even more recently, traditional suspicion of the Germans has had a new lease of life, prompting the Germans to dub the British generally as the 'Sicilians of the North' (implying perhaps a little more than the fact that both live on islands).

Europeans' perception of English insularity is sufficiently developed to be categorised either as an accepted fact or as a stereotype, depending on your point of view. I feel it partly arises out of misinterpretation of a unique combination of two characteristics: 'fellow feeling'-induced dissimulation and the desire to appear different, something that the English display as much among themselves as towards foreigners.

Alien understanding of the English is ultimately and utterly confused by what I call 'the puritan/peacock syndrome'. Values shuttle back and forth between two poles - from the exuberance of Elizabethan England to Cromwell's Puritans, from the Regency

Rakes to the Victorian *paterfamilias* (a case of true hypocrisy?), from the austerity of post-WWII England to the permissiveness of the 1960s. English values are too easily influenced by fashion: not just in mores and in the Rag Trade itself, but even in the destruction of the urban tramway system and the post-WWII erection of eggboxes in place of architecture. This yo-yo environment may contribute to the apparent hypocrisy and the lack of *cultural* sensitivity. It also contributes to the creativity.

The influence of that strip of water appropriately called the English, and not the British, Channel is undeniable. It was a revelation to hear, as late as 1991, a British transport minister defend the principle of driving on the left with the following words: "I see no reason why the people of this country should have to change the habits of a lifetime, and of generations, just because we are members of the European Community."

He could simply have said that the conversion costs would almost bankrupt the nation. Even better, he could have announced that the government was funding a study to assess the costs of coming into line with the rest of Europe, except Ireland, and most of the world. But, instead, he chose to indulge in an empty appeal to the hoary old principle of sovereignty, rounding off with a petulant harrumph at that neo-Napoleonic and almost satanic institution, the EU.

'Little Englandism' is a deep-rooted, almost atavistic instinct that crops up in many forms and at various levels of society: earnest middle-class ladies and gents demonstrate it in their railings (an appropriate word) against the high-speed London-Chunnel rail link, which now looks like going almost nowhere (Stratford) in a very long time (the year 2005 AD).

Politicians, with a pragmatic eye on the environmentalists, echo the sentiment and screw up Britain's transport logistics in the process. It's ironical that the Stratford option should have been challenged by the environmental watchdogs in the European Commission! It's all a far cry from events a few miles away - nb miles, not kilometers - in northern France where people have been falling over themselves to get a slice of the 21st-century action (see next chapter).

A curious feature of British life is the ability to come up with creative ideas, reject them as unsuitable for domestic consumption and force them on unsuspecting foreigners. In the aftermath of

WWII - the time when German history came back into the books - the British civil service, the Control Commission and others worked on ideas which might have done as much for Britain as they did for Germany: consolidated trades unions, the 'additional member system' (comparable to proportional representation), two-tier management structures with worker participation, *Der Spiegel*, the revitalisation of VW, the *Grüne Welle* traffic control system, even a federal constitution. Many of these ideas were too radical, even too professional, to stand a chance of being accepted at home. As Sir Nikolaus Pevsner, an anglicised German, was able to say in a different context: "The British character is too much against revolution, or even logical consistency, drastic steps, and uncompromising action".

The mirror-image of English eccentricity is the cult of the amateur. Even a prime minister, the Earl of Rosebery, felt prompted to say in 1900 that "it is beginning to be hinted that we are a nation of amateurs". Despite such hints and the fact that amateurism has caused untold harm to the country over the years, it is still a favoured phenomenon of the 'middle-to-upper' classes who tend to regard business, just like Parliament, as a form of sport. "Never take yourself too seriously, old man, it's not good form" - an attitude described by *The Economist* as "the contempt of the squirearchy for useful knowledge". Sadly it has to be acknowledged that Britain has fewer business schools and a smaller stock of trained professional managers than any other member state of the European Union.

This *laissez-faire* attitude extends to a visceral fear of anything that suggests a doctrinaire approach to social or economic issues to the extent that, not long ago, a junior minister felt entitled to characterise the principle of a minimum wage as a threat to the economy - ignoring the fact that (1) the economy was already in an enormous mess and (2) other European economies which feature both a minimum wage and indexation have done much better. Pragmatism at any price.

A leading international management consultant says that "the English... are perceived as sociable, flexible and under-prepared...". Another consultant who works extensively on trilateral British-Dutch-German projects comments that the English contingent excel themselves as mediators, presenters and after-dinner speakers - having none of the inhibitions of the Continentals - but are poor on preparation and often disappointing on follow-up.

The dilettante approach of the English extends beyond the self, through business or professional life, to ultimate values: quality of life in preference to wealth. This happens to be a particularly insidious form of snobbery. Engineers, technicians, salesmen are regarded by the upper classes as inferior forms of life. Even the lower orders tend to be work-shy. An American author, Richard Critchfield[11], talks about the pervasive lack of ambition among British youth, especially the working-class young. As for the idea that England might be a nation of shopkeepers (whether attributed to Napoleon, a Corsican, or Samuel Adams, an American), this is so far from the reality that it really doesn't matter.

Shopkeepers no, entrepreneurs yes. The spirit that galvanised an apparently otherwise staid generation, the Victorians, into action is very much back in evidence today, albeit in a less spectacular form. Unfortunately recent government policy has tended to kill off the most praiseworthy initiatives.

But back to the cult of the amateur, which is still as strong as the entrepreneurial instinct. The obverse of the dilettante attitude is a mistrust, particularly among the Establishment, of anyone guilty of precocity or cleverness. Such attributes, which would be the envy of all in France, are likely to qualify the British perpetrator as a 'bounder' or upstart. It is precisely such a Pavlovian response that cost Michael Heseltine his bid for the premiership in 1991. He also happens to have been one of the most successful entrepreneurs of recent times.

The American journalist Katherine Stephen sums up much of the aforegoing when she says: "I have come to believe that the key to an excessive snobbery about Americans is the key to much of what divides Britain internally: a morbid consciousness of class and a related fear of the combination of newness and success."

But this disapproval of the parvenu reflects, on the credit side, the underlying civism of the English. They perfected the queue, having only recently inherited both the habit (and the word) from the French[5] and, when motorised, they are about the only Europeans apart from the Portuguese to give way at pedestrian crossings. Speaking of roads, they also have some of the dirtiest streets in Europe. This is even evident in London, a remarkable amalgam of superficial grace and fundamental grubbiness.

Allied to civism is the genuine hospitability of British people at all levels of society, with the possible exception of the suburban lower middle class.

But the most admirable trait, in my humble if subjective opinion, is the openness or receptiveness of the educated and quite often uneducated English mind. Sometimes this is more apparent than real, but the fact that it does exist is demonstrated by the creativity and the lateral thinking qualities of the English, indeed the British generally, in some of the more freewheeling pursuits of society, in particular the arts, both fine and applied - including TV, witness 'Allo, Allo' and 'Blackadder', and pop music. Even quite ordinary English people have few inhibitions about making positive fools of themselves on the sillier types of TV game shows - it's democratic and it shows you have a sense of fun.

As a TV addict with access in Belgium to at least 30 channels, I recognise in the BBC (ITV not yet being available) a readiness to experiment, a sensitivity to social issues at the *personal* rather than the purely philosophical level, and a real sense of commitment to creating a better world.

It is still a truism that the best advertising is produced in London. The English certainly believe this and so do many Continentals, even if other centres, French and Spanish in particular, are catching up fast. Unfortunately, because of the cultural liberation all classes of English society have enjoyed in the last 25 years, this so-called creativity sometimes deteriorates into little more than meretriciousness, simply a striving after effect. Some observers speak of "a lot of style with not much substance".

Commenting on this trend Norman Stone, a British academic, goes further: "The change downward of England's intellectual life in the last 30 or 40 years has been pretty dramatic. We are much more parochial than we used to be and, so far as I can judge, much less well-read."

This superficiality is also evident in everyday life. The English picked up the habit, in the 1960s, of kissing everyone in sight. Further evidence is provided by the fact that, in terms of pep talks to passengers, they have the chattiest pilots in the world - an institutionalised and up-market version of the informality or rank familiarity practised by the man-in-the-street.

Openness is of course a close cousin of informality - a quality not always associated by foreigners with the English (Major Thompson again), but one that has blossomed in all classes since the end of WWII. Occasionally this directness can lead to major misinterpretation by more formal-minded Continentals. Even an

American, Richard Critchfield, felt sufficiently provoked recently to talk about "lack of civility and sheer meanness".

But this English quality of openness, an innocent prerequisite of familiarity, is precious. I only needed a few weeks out of the country, on coming to Belgium, to realise that something profound had happened to my life: out in public, walking along the street, there was a total absence of casual eye-contact from passers-by (the only thing the elder generation of Belgians seem to look at are your shoes, apparently to assess your wealth and status). In Britain generally, people actually look at one another in an interested way. By comparison the average Belgian face is closed, often wary.

Another quality evident in those English people with, one suspects, a sense of their rightful place in the world (the materially and socially comfortable upper middle classes?) is a gentleness about the eyes, a healthy geniality which one sees too rarely in any other race. It is very seductive.

To come back to Lancashire and the London East End (to which one can add the West Country, East Anglia and all points north), the truth is that there is a real England out there: people who are hardly aware of class, people who, like the provincials of many other countries, are friendly, warm and relatively uncomplicated.

Which inevitably brings us back to the matter of the 'middle class' and the process of gentrification. It tends to be a problem everywhere, as it takes people away from their roots, but it is a particular problem in England - precisely because of the power of class symbology in the English culture.

So there is both good and bad in the English. Which only shows how subjective one can be.

Being a 'Weak Uncertainty Avoidance' people (see Chapter 5 for illumination), the English - even in this case the British - have a different approach to many of the fundamental aspects of living. The differences even show up in the trivia, although whether these have a deeper significance or are just further evidence of British bloodymindedness (they never liked Napoleon), I wouldn't know. Here are some examples, with possible explanations opposite.

Black cats   *British Isles:*   Lucky
                    Continent: Unlucky

There is a British story about a black cat running between the front lines at the Battle of Waterloo (Napoleon, you see?). With the benefit of hindsight, it seems, this came to mean good luck for the British and their Allies, bad luck for the French and theirs. Unfortunately, everybody except the British thinks it means bad luck. I suspect it has something to do with the Catholic Church, another British bogey.

Salt cellars   *British Isles:*   One hole
                    Continent: Lots of holes

No idea, but the Continental solution seems to make more sense. Salt being hygroscopic, it should pour better through more than one hole.

Children at meals *British Isles:* Hands under table
                    Continent: Hands on table

The British worry about kids' hands on the table, Continentals worry about what they get up to when they're under the table.

Washing options *British Isles:*   Baths
                    Continent: Showers

Various studies prove it, the British are bath-oriented, Continentals shower-oriented.

Health   *British Isles:*   Stomach/bowels
                    Continent: Heart/liver/etc

Pure culture-related stuff. When something goes wrong, the French think it's their liver, the Germans their heart and the British their digestive system (see Chapter 6).

Driving   *British Isles :*   Left
              Continent :   Right

Napoleon again. French logic convinced him that, in a time of horse-drawn carriages and mainly right-handed coachmen, it made sense to change sides to avoid whips of passing carriages getting intertwined. The worst that could happen, on the right, was that they ended up in the trees. Too logical for the British.

Carousels   *British Isles :*   Clockwise
                Continent :   Anticlockwise

No idea - ask 'Lovejoy'.

Titles on   *British Isles :*   View from left on shelf
book spines   *Continent :*   View from right

The British being empiricists favour the arrangement that ensures that, when a book is on a table, they can still read the title. According to the French, Continentals prefer the title the other way for extremely Cartesian reasons which have something to do with neck muscles.

<u>The French</u>

The inquisitive individualists

"France is the most brilliant and the most dangerous nation in Europe and the best qualified in turn to become an object of admiration, hatred, pity or terror, but never of indifference" [*"La France est la plus brillante et la plus dangereuse des nations de l'Europe, et la mieux faite pour devenir tour à tour un objet d'admiration, de haine, de pitié, de terreur, mais jamais d'indifférence"*   Alexis de Tocqueville

"They are doomed to be abstract. Talking to them is like trying to have a relationship with the letter x in algebra."   DH Lawrence

"Let's drink to the King of France and **** to the King of England who declared war on us" [*"Buvons un coup au Roi de France et merde au Roi d'Angleterre, qui nous a déclaré la guerre"*]
French corsairs' song

"How can you be expected to govern a country that has two hundred and forty-six kinds of cheese?"   Charles de Gaulle

"In France we don't have energy, we have ideas" [*"En France on n'a pas d'énergie, on a des idées"*]   Speaker on Radio France

"In France, if we think, we don't do anything" [*"En France, si on pense, on n'agit pas"*]   Michel Würtz, Deputy Mayor, St Louis

"In the heart of every Frenchman there is a piece of Jean Monnet, but also a piece of de Gaulle and of Richelieu"
German Government spokesman

"The English rely on their intuition and the French on their grey matter"   Anthony Burgess

"Parking tolerated" [*"stationnement toléré"*]   Paris street sign

De Tocqueville's words are those of a Frenchman, blunt and with none of the hesitancy or circumlocution of the English. The contrast is apposite since, picking up the thread from the last chapter, there is a love-hate relationship between the English and the French.

Bluntness or, better put, assertiveness is indeed one of the characteristics of the French. It is no doubt born of the belief that, because they are endowed with such acute powers of reasoning, they must be right. After all, it was a Frenchman who invented value-added tax (TVA), the elegant concept of *taxe en cascade*, and sold the idea to the other members of the European Union.

Certainly the French have agile minds, particularly the Parisians who are almost a race apart and dominate French life, even today when the country is at last moving away from terminal centralisation. Perhaps they owe this to the crisp, stardust-spangled climate of their capital city. There is a radiant quality to the light which you will have difficulty in finding anywhere else in Europe.

The French pride themselves on being cartesian, at times wrongly so, since their idea of cartesianism can get so abstract that it is self-defeating. Look at the way many French business documents are laid out: the paragraph numbering and presentation get in the way of the contents. The *Encyclopédiste* tradition of exactitude and rationality seems at times to be an end in itself. One observer quoted by Theodore Zeldin[1] even goes so far as to speak of French people, rather perfunctorily, as "brilliant intellectually, but weak in common sense".

As a Frenchman puts it, "we give too much weight to ideas and neglect their applicability". Another sums up his fellow-countryfolk as follows: "The French are logical, rational and Cartesian, but not to *do* logical things. It is only to be able to explain in an apparently logical way the illogical things they do."

Or, as yet another Frenchman says, "we always ask ourselves, 'OK, it works in practice, but will it work in theory?'". The French love to analyse - and some of them are sublime self-analysts, as these comments show. No wonder Woody Allen's films are so popular in Paris!

Woody Allen would, I think, appreciate the observation made a long time ago by a business compatriot of his, E Russell Eggers. He suggested that Hamlet would have added a line to his soliloquy if

Shakespeare had been French: *"Etre ou ne pas être. C'est là la question. Mais la question est mal posée"*.

In her perceptive book French or Foe?[12], another American, Polly Platt, takes the thought a step further and confirms something that many foreigners suspect: "The French like circles. Thinking and talking in circles comes naturally here. It's a kind of French-preferred protection from showing one's hand too soon, from taking risks and making mistakes. And circles are more aesthetic than grids."

A German businessman, who has lived over 25 years in France, has this to say: "Often the French seem to concentrate on phenomena rather than causes and solutions. Perhaps this is due to their education. They learn to analyse and to express themselves verbally very brilliantly and *have a need to do so*" [my italics].

This touches on an important characteristic: an almost childlike need to show off, generally in a very likeable and entertaining way. In groups, the French positively sparkle and spark off responses among themselves. One is reminded of a flock of squabbling sparrows (their Belgian neighbours would say "little cocks").

'Squabbling' is the operative word. Not because the French are more quarrelsome than other European nationalities (though they can be), but because they enjoy nothing more than a verbal spar. As two American sociologists[13], explaining the French to their fellow-countryfolk, point out: "Americans need to be liked. French people do not. Americans tend to like people who agree with them. French people are more likely to be interested in a person who disagrees with them... A conversation where disagreements are exchanged can be considered stimulating by a Frenchman, while an American will likely be embarrassed."

Unfortunately spirituality, to use a big word, can get the better of the French. Apart from their natural desire to show off or provoke a reaction, the French have a taste for complicated things just for the sake of them, a form of perfectionism (for example French design is often idiosyncratic and clever, but not always practical). Commenting on the foreign affairs scene, *The Economist* speaks of "a neurotic urge to be different" and of the average Frenchman's "refusal to admit that he could be wrong".

This desire to show off or be different permeates most aspects of life. French television, apart from its dubious technical quality which it largely owes to a determination not to accept other people's standards, is remarkable for the sophistication of its childrens' programmes: the real-life characters of *Dorothée* are light years removed from the sensible cosiness of BBC TV, while some of the cartoons make intellectual demands on the viewers that would leave British children openmouthed. I am tempted to think that the French are as much child-adults as they are adult-children.

There is certainly something of the spoilt child about the way the French, individually often the most sensible of Europeans, behave in public life. The moment they get into official groupings, they tend to go daft (more of this below). David Granick[14] suggests the inevitable emphasis on *La Patrie* may be compensation for the lack of homogeneity of French society as a whole. French journalist Anne-Elisabeth Moutet, describing the 1992 Winter Olympics in Albertville, described the occasion as "pure, unadulterated gut chauvinism in motion". Other words she used to describe her fellow-countryfolk in the same article included, significantly, "division", "self-absorption" and "an inability to accept the truth". She is one of many who feel that such immature behaviour does more harm than good.

But at the personal level - despite English suspicions (in the words of an American observer, "on Albion's side of the Channel, the Hundred Years War goes on") - the tendency to show off is harmless enough. If capable of summoning the will and more importantly the wit, Anglo-Saxons and others are well advised to join in. The French will not think the less of them for it - unlike the Germans, who have a highly developed sense of ridicule where foreigners are concerned.

The real problem is the fact that the two races, French and English, are so different in certain essentials, such as the way they speak. The French mock the Anglo-Saxons (some of them) for their contorted accents and, to judge from the advice offered by Dave Barry, an American journalist, on how to speak French, the Anglo-Saxons reciprocate: "You say it with your tongue way back in gargle position and your lips pouted way out like you're sucking grits through a hose...".

Anglo-Saxon observers in particular have falsely concluded that the French are frivolous and lightweight - rather the sort of image the French put out about the Spanish 100 years ago. Nothing could be further from the truth. They can be exceedingly formal, sometimes almost mandarin-like, to the bewilderment of offshore visitors in particular. If they are well-bred, Parisian and/or organisationally involved, don't expect smiles let alone sympathetic laughter - one high-up official had to hire a 'professional laugher' to encourage his guests to react to his terrible jokes.

The French can also be very hardworking when it suits them and extremely consequential. Whilst some of them - particularly the politicians - tend to be too clever by half, often tripping themselves up in the process, they are as capable of fairness as the British. This may be due to their need to be appreciated (as opposed to loved) by the rest of the world. It also has to be said that the two nations, French and British, share a tendency at the level of the individual to want to be both themselves and different: again this propensity to show off. The Germans just want to be themselves.

Like most Europeans, the French are also prey to sudden and profound moments of self-doubt. A contributor to the *International Herald Tribune* talks about "a certain perversity in the national temperament, impelling the French intermittently to destroy their success". They are easily 'psyched', positively or negatively. It is remarkable to see how a French professional tennis player responds, up or down, to the mood of the crowd - particularly his or her fellow-countryfolk.

In parenthesis, this volatility is evidently too much for some people. A Japanese psychiatrist based in Paris speaks of the "Paris syndrome, which includes hallucinations, depression, paranoia and shocks to the nervous system" (he means to the nervous system of the Japanese, not the French). "French people tend to be moody", he says, "They can be very kind one moment and very mean the next". Ah, so.

French perversity can, of course, be directed towards others as well as their own kind (in that sense they are great egalitarians). There is a certain naughtiness of spirit which can get the upper hand and lead to temporary consternation in those at whom it is aimed, while rarely being fatal. This is evident at all levels of human activity: in private relationships, in the manifestations of an at times batty local bureaucracy, and in public affairs. A GATT official remarks that it is customary for French delegations to "stonewall" before making a last-minute deal: "It's the French way of doing things."

With this open invitation not to be taken seriously, it is hardly surprising that the French - while still crying *cocorico* - often give voice to the most articulate and penetrating pessimism about their country's world status: the country long agonised over the loss of its perceived role as an independent force between the US and the USSR. At moments the French demonstrate, in the words of Frederick Painton of *Time* magazine, "that endemic French affliction called *malaise*... a volatile mixture of ennui, anxiety and irritation with the potential for triggering sudden acts of collective furor".

But, as if that were not enough, at other moments they suddenly and inexplicably hear the sound of trumpets and transmogrify into highly emotional personifications of *la gloire* and *la défense de La Patrie* (*La Patrie* being a useful rallying cry in a country which, in a very different way from Britain, also has profound class and regional differences). We wretched foreigners are left wondering which are the real French. Today, they all are. I say 'today' because as a Dutchman, A H Heineken, points out (see Chapter 11): "At the time of the French Revolution, when the French got their 'Marseillaise', the majority of the population did not even speak French and were not able to sing the national anthem."

Yet the trumpets, when they sound today, herald great acts. Partly due to their ability to summon energies at the national level that no other nation can command, thanks to the synergism of a corporatist state, the French can show great vision. Witness the 19th-century reconstruction of Paris and, more recently, the TGV, the Minitel revolution and the digitalisation of the French telecommunications network.

The French can also use their sense of vision in a sinisterly dirigist way, plus what *The Economist* calls a "passion for grand gestures". The gestures can also be significantly absent, suggesting a remarkable if occasional meanness of mind.

President Mitterand conducted a 15-minute televised interview marking the end of the Gulf War without once referring to the United States (he also never acknowledged the help he received from Britain in WWII). Later, equally cynically - and maybe naively for someone who claimed to epitomise French vision and statesmanship - he took care not to call Gorbachev during the Putsch. The main aim of French foreign policy, says Luigi Barzini[15], "is to flatter the people's high opinion of their country and prod them to accept the necessary disciplines and sacrifices".

At a more mundane level, the government aided and abetted a counter-attack by the Chronopost organisation against foreign express air courier services - an interventionist move that won back 40 per cent of the French market over three years by mobilising the services of local post offices and demanding special advertising rates from French radio and TV. What was that about being fair?

Yet such dirigist tactics can go sadly wrong when applied outside the framework of French society. They rely for effect on the establishment conspiracy that underpins the Gallic way of life. Renault lost the Skoda automobile deal because they went to the top instead of working at the base. As Marian Caffe, the Czech prime minister at the time undiplomatically pointed out: "First, the French came late. Second, the French began by visiting the ministries; the Germans (began) with the company. Third, the French came here; the Germans invited our people to go to Germany." Evidently the Czechs like to travel.

Devious foreigners may even point to the fact that some French nuclear power stations are located close to the country's frontiers, as on the Meuse and the Moselle. In matters pertaining to state and national survival, the sense of fairness still lingering in the average Frenchman's breast metamorphoses into the sort of bare-faced cynicism that puts the amateurish hypocrisy of the English to shame.

I had personal experience of this - even if it hardly classed as a case of corporatist life and death - when helping a foreign company to obtain French type approval for its franking machines. All approaches, including diplomatic intervention, failed. The head of the technical department in the French PTT then invited the chief executive of the foreign company out to lunch, when he told him, firmly but with great charm: "We have no intention of according you type approval until our national suppliers have perfected their machine. But, if you repeat this admission to anyone else, we will deny it categorically."

Ah, the French! I am reminded of the senior businessman interviewed years ago by David Granick[14]. After expounding at length on a series of points, the respondent said: "Whatever you may think of my answers to your other questions, this answer is really true". *Touché!*

Ultimately, we are talking about a strange troika of traits: intellectual arrogance and cynicism harnessed to lingering notions of *grandeur* and to a peculiarly Gallic form of the Not-Invented-Here (NIH) complex, namely "anything you can do, we can do better". The French always think they have a better solution to everything in matters both intellectual and technological. Where others referred to '1992' as the start of the Single European Market, the French talked about 1993. Logically they're right of course, but I wouldn't mind betting that they were seduced by the thought of, once again, being different from the herd.

Often they are, thanks to their inventiveness and tenacity (the British would probably say 'bloody-mindedness'), as witness the successes listed earlier. But this burning desire to be different can produce abberations like the Secam television system, attempts to create a French computer industry, French pop music much as I like it and, dare I say it, *cuisine nouvelle*. After all, what's the point of having a plate in front of you that looks like the cover of a seed packet and sometimes tastes like the contents?

Intellectual arrogance is paralleled by intellectual curiosity: the French are easily seduced by ideas or by a well mustered argument. My first encounter with a group of French business people was instructive. When an issue arose over the contract, the French started discussing tactics amongst themselves. They were naively astonished to discover that I spoke their language well enough to grasp what they were planning to do. Far from creating ill-will, this enhanced their respect. To me this is sufficient proof of their ultimate magnanimity...

In fact the French, both ordinary people and professionals, often convey an impression of great rectitude in the best sense of the word. A sense of decency, of simple humanity, is the overriding impression derived from the character sketches that make up Theodore Zeldin's book. It is also evident in the reaction of many people, eminent or ordinary, to recent outbreaks of xenophobia. Possibly the confidence the educated French have in their own powers of analysis allows them to be very fair with the rest of the world, even if they may mock the British for their apparent commitment to fairness.

Egalitarianism - a concept the French nailed to their mast a long time ago - is still conspicuously absent from the attitudes of many French males towards the opposite sex. As Edith Cresson had reason to lament when she became prime minister: "Every time a woman gets nominated or elected somewhere, it is customary to hear that she made it by her physique or by providing favours to some man. Not one woman has ever been selected without the explanation that she slept with so-and-so. Unfortunately, we're still at that stage."

Their sense of fairness, a general but often volatile quality in the French, can also desert them when dealing with people of less secure background as, for example, the immigrant workers of the Maghreb. Evidently, they felt the same away about Europeans a century or two ago: apart from the strange ideas they put around about the folk south of the Pyrenees (see 'The Spanish'), the French did a great job of ridiculising the people south of the Alps, as Luigi Barzini[15] points out.

The French also have some funny ideas about the people up *north*. Here the problem seems to stem more from a poor understanding of European geography than from any preconceptions. I was stunned to have a French university undergraduate ask me where Holland was, but that was a long time ago. Imagine my surprise, then, when I recently read an otherwise excellent French book on Europe which suggested the Netherlands has a common frontier with Denmark!

Maybe there's a 'Belgian block' in the French mentality that prevents them thinking any further (all those bad jokes about so-called 'French fries'!). In fact the most recent study undertaken in France reveals, among other things, that an indecently high number of respondents think Amsterdam is located somewhere between Copenhagen and Moscow...

To judge from their reactions, the Belgians - both Flemish and Walloons - seem to feel they have been dumped in the same boat as the Dutch and the Italians. According to a recent study, Belgian businessfolk of both communities find the French arrogant, flowery of tongue, rich in false promises, often poorly prepared and, frankly and surprisingly, not that good at figures. They also love holding meetings on the slightest pretext - generally arriving late.

A Flemish Belgian who ran a car rental company in France describes the French temperament, appropriately, as *"laisser-aller.* Because they think they are smart and *débrouillard*, they leave things like car bookings till the last minute and then wonder why there are no cars available!"

Happily, our Belgian sample also sees the good side of the French: their openness, their flexibility, their charm and, a great quality, their humour. French humour is dry and can often be a bit cruel. But it also tends to be self-deprecating, regardless of the joker's ego. Curiously, the British have only one word, 'humour', to describe both wittiness and one's state of mind, whereas the French have two, *humour* and *humeur* (though Theodore Zeldin tells us that the *Académie Française* only admitted *humour* to the French vocabulary in 1932).

For sure the French have egos, as any foreigner will tell you. This is an inevitable by-product of their individualism. Every French national is a little law unto him or herself. They have an autonomy born as much of self-absorption as of *amour-propre*. This means among other things that 'putting themselves in the other chap's shoes', as the English would do, does *not* come to them naturally, making them poor marketers instinctively if not creatively. They also tend to institutionalise their communications: an international market researcher I know confirms their fondness for memos (business letters are generally out!) and notes that it is difficult to get a response to a research study without making a formal approach.

In day-to-day life French self-absorption can emerge as what looks like downright rudeness: how many foreigners have been elbowed helplessly out of the way on a French sidewalk? Yet, when their attention is drawn to their misdemeanour - or to another person's plight - the French can be the most genuinely considerate and kindly people in the world. Some people rationalise these con-tradictions by saying that the French are rude in public, polite in pri-vate - but I think self-absorption is the real culprit.

Getting a group of French people to work together virtually defies the laws of dynamics: each of them runs his or her own lit-tle fiefdom and the operating principle - from the top down, which is the only way French business works - appears to be 'management by information retention'. This independent spirit can be a source of great creativity in fashion, pop music, advertising and TV com-mercials (to the astonishment of Anglo-Saxon agency people), but it also implies a lack of discipline.

The French establishment gets over the discipline problem by organising the upper echelons of society in such a way that they at least more or less conform within their own ranks. This even extends to a conspiracy of silence on matters likely to prove disruptive. Socialist politician Michel Rocard challenged taboos by openly volunteering the fact that his marriage had broken up. But, as an American journalist observed, "the notion that an extramarital affair could terminate a politician's ambitions strikes many Frenchmen as absurd."

What goes for politicians goes for the corporate establishment too, since the fates of the two are interwoven - in some instances for the worse, to judge from the newly found verve of the judiciary for exposing cases of collusion and corruption. But the private lives of public figures in France, both in and out of government, are scrupulously protected by law and tradition. This is in startling contrast to Britain, where the indiscretions of eminent persons are pretty well fair game all round. In fact, the private life of any French national, however lowly, is strictly nobody else's business. As *The Economist* puts it, "asking a Frenchman how he votes is like asking him how much money he earns".

The *Grandes Ecoles* - in particular the ENA and the 'X', as the Polytechnique is known - are institutions which far surpass any social infrastructure invented by other European nations including the British 'public school' system. They create and perpetuate an administrative elite which effectively holds the reins in its hands, staffing the ministries with like-minded bureaucrats and, whenever appropriate, 'parachuting' them into the upper ranks of business and industry. Many of them make the establishment grade as *Inspecteur de Finance* of all things, something that would be cause for perpetual banishment in the UK and some other countries.

In this way, French society has achieved a symbiosis between government and the private sector that is the envy of every other European nation. This appropriately *dirigiste* solution has produced one of the most hermetic and successful 'clubs' of all Europe. In fact, if the other nations could achieve it too, Europe would probably be at war again.

While you don't necessarily have to explain the way the French behave in terms of the social structure of their country, unlike the English, the class system is well defined and well entrenched, particularly at the upper levels. But status depends more on educational level and origins, occupation and political views than on money. Quite the opposite of the English, the engineer is held in high esteem, thanks to the *Grandes Ecoles*. On matters of class, if it comes to the crunch, the French can rise above it or below it - depending on where they start from.

The biggest social gulf in France is, of course, between the Parisians and the rest, although Lille, Lyons, Montpellier, Nantes and other centres - thanks to a well-meaning but to some extent symbolic change in emphasis early in the Mitterand administration - are emerging to challenge the intellectual and business supremacy of the capital. This trend can only cause rejoicing in the provinces, where the Parisians, many of whom are recent arrivals from the provinces themselves (hence the word *arriviste*?), are regarded as the lowest form of Gallic life.

The fact is that Paris has systematically drained the French provinces - an ensemble of geographic, cultural and gastronomic variety and richness unmatched by any other European nation, Spain and Italy included. France is still a supremely centralist and dirigist country, unlike consensus-run Germany, and is likely to remain so for a long time to come. It still even boasts a five-year plan that might have been inspired by one of the erstwhile central command economies.

Unfortunately this *dirigisme* (a distinctively French concept) can lead, both at the regional level and in certain areas of public life, to a sustained distortion and, in some cases, an outright abuse of power. Inspired by the example of Colbert's work for *le Roi Soleil* (and how many French presidents have aped the latter?), successive governments have determinedly and often cynically maintained a policy of defending national interests at all costs.

This has now got to the point that Paris milks its nationalised cash cows, banks *and* industrial groups, to keep the others out of the bankruptcy court - again, all for *la gloire* and to hell with the logic, the European Commission and the consequences. To ward off the Japanese threat, the government resorted to old-style dirigism, organising a shotgun marriage between the state's semiconductor, consumer electronics and nuclear businesses. A strange match! Even the AFP news agency is subsidised by the state - one suspects to foster French influence internationally - and is challenging Reuters.

French universities, too, are hampered in realising their mission fully: the country concentrates its research and development potential in state-controlled technology centres which, again, are an instrument of government policy.

Through their elitism and dirigism - and as the corporatist state par excellence - the French have succeeded in betraying many of the traditions of *liberté, égalité* and *fraternité* they are supposed to have inherited or, as some French people would say, invented.

Dominique Frischer[16] speaks of a different set of values: *liberté* (to do what one wants), *inégalité* and *egocentricité*. Theodore Zeldin quotes a German journalist who has worked out that three-quarters of the managers of the 200 largest firms in France are the sons of rich families (the figure for Germany is one-quarter).

These leitmotifs of the French way of life, cartesianism and corporatism, are curiously juxtaposed in the fortunes of the French computer industry. On the one hand, chauvinistically inspired state intervention in hardware manufacture has produced such dubious results as the Bull saga. On the other hand, we have the full flowering of French cartesianism and the Gallic entrepreneurial spirit in the software side of the industry, making the French the European leaders in software services.

Indeed, when they get their act together, the French are virtually unbeatable in both the high-technology and service industry sectors. Some of the old French provincial towns have been impeccably brought into the 20th century, historic buildings rubbing shoulders comfortably with new shopping malls, pedestrian concourses and well conceived and run hotels. They beat the Germans at their own game. But when they don't (as in the extraordinarily tacky residential and commercial suburbs of these towns, not to mention the Parisian *périphérique*), the result is horrific and idiosyncratically French.

Certainly, when they identify with a cause or opportunity and succeed in firing themselves up, the French draw on deep wells of energy and creativity that foreigners can only admire. The difference between the British and French responses to the Channel Tunnel challenge is an object lesson.

Where the British pontificated and procrastinated, effectively putting the concept out of joint, the French went into action. Their realism, helped along by the usual dose of government dirigism, ensured the rapid establishment of high-speed links from the Chunnel to both Paris and the Belgian frontier. Local councils fell over one another to make sure that the track ran through their constituency and not the one next door (the spirit of Clochemerle?) - in complete contrast to Little England, where the gentlefolk did everything possible to ensure that the track went through somebody *else's* backgarden.

In fairness to the French (and to Clochemerle), some of them do still put quality of life before progress. One *commune* on the proposed high-speed rail link was determined to frustrate the planners' intentions by any means possible. With typical Gallic ingenuity, they bought a plot of land bang on the proposed route and sold it in one-square-meter lots to people in places like Hawaii and Hong Kong, creating a legal web that not even the French government would have been able to unravel. Not content with this, the mayor gave instructions, in the event of his untimely death, to have his remains buried on site. With all the excitement, he then had a heart attack and died. But French dirigism had the last word: the planners expropriated land alongside the plot and repositioned the line.

Many of us Europeans - the ones who don't necessarily happen to think that European culture started and ends in Paris - deplore French centralism but greatly admire the spirit of Clochemerle. If anything could rally sentimental Europeans to a common cause, it would be the simplicity and self-awareness of generations of French people. People who spirited up a variety of glorious concepts teetering on the brink of zaniness. My favourites include the following:

– *Association des Anciens Combattants et Mutilés du Métro,*
– *Grand Bal des Anciens Combattants et des Mutilés de Guerre,*
– *Ministère de l'Education Nationale, Centre National de la Recherche Scientifique Appliquée, Section d'Art Gastronomique*
and
– *Grand Critérium Cycliste International Féminin des Producteurs d'Asperges de la Vallée du Dropt.*

All of these, I assure you, are genuine.

At the epicentre of life, elitist Paris harbours its own elitist cultures, both legitimate and dubious (in the words of the ex-*Die Zeit* correspondent Roger de Weck: "Paris is a city where everyone writes books which nobody reads and everyone talks about"). How else can one explain the gulf between the high fashion or the architectural flair of the capital and the total absence of good taste evident in the check shirts, screaming colour combinations and bijoux residences of the French provincial? Half an hour's drive out of Paris is sufficient to convince you that you have entered another world, the world of *steack & frites* and tacky highrise developments poised self-consciously on wooded hilltops.

Bad taste is forgivable, cartesianism is another thing. Anthony Burgess, referring to Roger Peyrefitte's book *Le Mal français*, says: "The French disease (echoing the title)... is neither syphilis nor arrogance but excessive logicality, which is called Cartesianism. He (Peyrefitte) thinks the French ought to be more like the English - empirical, pragmatic, self-disciplined, patriotic, adaptable to change. The French will never be like the English. The Channel remains the Great Divide. Concord and Concorde fly parallel and will never meet". Maybe, but the French won that particular battle. The supersonic plane was officially christened 'Concorde', i.e. with an 'e' at the end. Which the English ruefully came to call 'the French letter'...

This is only one of the cross-Channel battles the English have lost. They also felt outmanoeuvred when they cheered Concorde on its maiden flight: they shouted "Fly, Concorde!" where the French cried "Allez la France!". But the British did win Waterloo, whatever the French may say.

That battle may have been prompted in English minds, more than anything else, by the realisation that Napoleon was getting far too big for his boots: he had already launched the Napoleonic Code, the metric system and the sugarbeet industry, and institutionalised driving on the right. So it was high time to get rid of him.

As Napoleon showed, the French have enormous potential for both good and, occasionally, evil. Too often they have been demoralised by history, by politics or by sheer bad luck.

For the English, the French are both infuriating and fascinating. Which is exactly what the French feel about the English.

The Germans

The methodical mystics

"It was at that time [in the 1400s] that the German personality developed traits that have survived to today... This literal-minded, narrow world of small townships, lacking the authority of a nation, produced the little man who seeks self-glorification in trivial things, who has himself buried under the shrouds of his skittle club... the title-seeker who seethes when he's not addressed as 'Herr Doktor'... and the infamous 'silent protestor' who swallows everything simply because, right back to the 1400s, he's never had the authority of a nation behind him" Joachim Fernau

"How appallingly thorough these Germans always managed to be, how emphatic! In sex no less than in war - in scholarship, in science" Aldous Huxley

"Foreigners stand astonished and attracted by the riddles revealed in the contradictions of the German soul" Nietzsche

"The Germans are the most honest people in the world" George Borrow

"It's the Germans who love order" Vladimir Bukovsky, Russian dissident

"The Germans make everything difficult, both for themselves and for everyone else" Goethe

"The Germans always buy platform tickets before they storm a railway station" Attributed to Lenin

"Our firm has been functionally organised for the past 95 years" Answer to industrial survey

"What gives me Angst is worrying about whether or not I ought to feel Angst" German student quoted by John Ardagh

Joachim Fernau, speaking as a German, has a privileged insight into the mindset of his fellow countrymen. Most foreigners fail to look that far into the depths of the German psyche, preferring to indulge in the kind of superficial stereotypes made famous by the late Sir Nicholas Ridley.

Sir Nicholas lost his job for this, maybe unjustifiably. After all, he was saying what a lot of other people thought. But he wasn't clever enough to go beyond bombast and get at the real grounds for these prejudices. His comments put paid to his career in British politics for the simple reason that he committed the unspeakable and totally un-British sin of telling the plain truth as he saw it.

But while Ridley could be laughed away by his fellow-Brits as a 'comedian' (and was indeed called that by a member of Her Majesty's Opposition), the committee of so-called experts, assembled at Chequers earlier the same year to advise on 'the German problem', had absolutely no excuse at all. As university dons, they should have known that trying to explain the German psyche in terms of words like 'insensitivity', 'self-pity', 'excess' and similar *Supermensch* cliches is, frankly, less than half the story - and certainly the less revealing half. However they *did* evoke the concept of *Angst* (after all it's a German word) and, there, they were much closer to the truth.

The existence of such words helps explain the German mentality. It is extraordinary how much the language has contributed to the English, French and other vocabularies of philosophy and perception, through the lack of suitable alternatives: *Angst, Doppelgänger, Fingerspitzengefühl, Gestalt, Heimweh, Lebensraum, Leitmotiv, Realpolitik, Schadenfreude, Wanderlust, Weltanschauung, Weltschmerz, Zeitgeist* and, more recently, things like *Nachholbedarf* and *Endeffekt*. The 'philosophical' French have come up with *existentialisme* and *maladie du siècle*, but not much else.

This should tell us something about the Germans, namely that they are a philosophically inclined people. Since the cream of Europe's philosophers are German - Hegel, Kant, Leibniz, Nietzsche, Schopenhauer, Jaspers, Heidegger and others - there may be something in this idea. The German language is intimately intertwined with the German psyche - as all languages are, but only more so.

One can even go further: the German language has helped *shape* the German psyche. An eminent professor active at Cambridge

University post-1945 (and who happened to be one of my early inspirations) maintained that Hitler excited his audiences precisely because he was out of breath before he got to the 'active' verb at the end of his very long sentences. But this, along with the conclusions of the so-called Chequers experts, may tell you more about the intellectual powers of British dons than it does about the oratorial powers of Hitler.

The English, while we're on the subject (and I mean the *English*, not the British), are the Abominable Clubmen *par excellence*. But their concept of a club is a device to cut one class of Englishmen and women off from the other classes. In the case of the Germans, the concept of a club is much more supportive than divisive: it serves to create a sense of German *togetherness* in an otherwise hostile world. To quote an oft-used phrase: *"Wir sind ja unter uns!"*.

Which brings me back to Joachim Fernau[17]. The keyword in the remarks quoted at the beginning of this chapter is this term 'club'. Not a club in the English sense, not even a skittle club, but quite simply a CLUB. Every European nation has its club (see Chapter 10), but the German type of club is far more effective than any other.

The German club is nationwide - even if recent applicants from what was the German Democratic Republic are not considered, by many of those already in the club, as deserving of full membership. Apropos the people of the eastern *Länder*, they differ markedly from their fellow-countryfolk in their value judgments: the jury is still debating how much of this is due to the transient influence of communism and how much is innate (see page 56). But the differences are important enough to justify the caveat that what follows is written more with 'Wessies' than 'Ossies' in mind.

This idea of a German club is a challenging thought because, despite its mark on history, Germany has never really been a nation. Rather, it has been a concept: *Deutschland über Alles*. And the disruptions caused by upstarts like Kaiser Bill and Adolf Hitler have overshadowed the real contribution of German culture to European history, with a bit of help from the Austrians (who, incidentally, also helped Hitler a bit). People like Goethe, Schiller, Bach, Händel, Beethoven (the offspring of a Flemish peasant family from Heist-op-den-Berg), Schumann, Kleist, Kant, Heine, even Nietsche and Wagner, created the core of European humanism and gave the Continent a spiritual flywheel which is still turning. It is therefore totally unfair to diminish or ridiculise the Germans, and not the easiest thing to do in view of their evident success.

Even so, this sense of clubbishness is prevalent in all areas of German society. And the reason for this clubbishness is conservatism. The Germans are the most conservative and cautious people in Europe. Their great claim to fame is the fact that it was really *they* who invented the NIH (Not-Invented-Here) complex. The obverse side of the coin is that they often wrongly assume that the rest of the world is uninformed on matters German.

The underlying motive is insecurity, which is exactly what Joachim Fernau is talking about, albeit somewhat brutally. Yet, as Flora Lewis points out in her book *Europe - a Tapestry of Nations*[2], the result is not an exaggerated sense of class, as with the English, but an exaggerated sense of status.

In this German conservatism is indeed a measure of arrogance. Günther Grass, talking of international fears of a newly united Germany, has spoken of megalomania fuelled by a sense of insecurity. The Germans genuinely believe that their system is superior to any other, certainly the British, possibly the French. They admire the French for their chic and their wit - and that's about it. They admire the British for their *sangfroid* and their supposed sense of fair play, but that's about all.

On the other hand (being British, I *try* to be fair, even if I don't succeed), it has to be said that these days the Germans observe the rules of good citizenship with their neighbours as much as with themselves. It was instructive to compare the television coverage of the Nobel Prize award to Mikhail Gorbachev: German TV showed Soviet citizens who endorsed the choice, whereas the BBC showed the sceptics and the dissenters. Essentially, the German mind is supportive, whereas the British mind is disruptive.

The point about insecurity (read *Angst* if you wish) is certainly well-founded. Take an international and unheralded initiative at the level of the European Union - as I have done on occasions - and you can be sure that, while the others will respond enthusiastically, the Germans will show suspicion.

Insecurity has played a decisive role in German history: it also helps explain the importance many Germans attach to *Kultur* as a way of validating uncertain personal status. Even German youngsters seem to favour highly cluttered pinboards in their homes -

maybe to challenge the principle of discipline but more often, I think, to tell themselves that they are busy and successful.

There are so many stories about the cautiousness and conservatism of the Germans that there is no point in repeating them here. They are clearly happily entrenched in their bogs, mists and forests, living much the same life as they lived in the time of the Roman Empire, when even Caesar had to admit defeat. The same, of course, can be said about my countrymen: *The Times* once ran a memorable headline "Fog over Channel. Continent cut off". Yet the German attitude, I suggest, is even more pervasive: "Mists over Germany. Europe cut off". This is not meant to suggest that the Germans are *not* good Europeans or are not, these days, friendly to foreigners. Quite the contrary.

The fact is simply that, like Varus, we other Europeans have enormous difficulty in penetrating German society and the German world of business. The Germans prefer to deal with their own kind (even if the buyer comes from Munich and the seller from Soest which, in their terms, is a world away). It's almost as if they had never emerged from their primeval forests, despite all the evidence of history.

Trees must have played an important role in the shaping of the German psyche. Even recently - despite the combined effects of autobahn construction, logging, *Waldsterben* and the like - a geographic survey undertaken by the German Bundeswehr concluded that the view across 80 per cent of the pre-1990 BRD was only 1000 metres (is the integration of the *Neue Länder* changing attitudes...?). A sojourn in as pastoral and parochial a town as Bamberg or Freiburg is enough to give anyone, German or foreigner, the feeling of being hemmed in by nature and, as a matter of extension, by oppressive neighbours.

This is linked to what Edward T Hall, the eminent American sociologist (see Chapter 6), describes as the Germans' well developed territoriality. "For the German", he says, "space is sacred. Their sense of being geographically crowded is a contributor to this territorial behavior. Homes are protected from outsiders by a variety of barriers: fences, walls, hedges, solid doors, blinds, shutters and screening to prevent visual or auditory intrusion." It also extends to using your towel to stake a claim to the best spot by the swimming-pool and defending your rights to a table in the restaurant. Just nudging his car is an outrage to a German motorist. With a Frenchman, it won't merit more than a Gallic shrug.

The same compartmentalisation applies at the macro level. While a highly cohesive society, Germany as a nation still hardly exists. John Kennedy declaimed, in an act of association: *"Ich bin ein Berliner"* (which means "I am a bun", rather like saying "I am a hamburger"). Equally, a man from Munich will say *"Ich bin ein Bayer"* before he will admit to being German. In that respect, he is not much different from the Belgians, the Spanish or the Italians. But it goes further than that. John Ardagh[4] quotes a *Münchner* who said "I feel Bavarian first, European second and German third". This attitude is far from uncommon.

Even so, and understandably in the light of history, the Germans have some difficulty in accepting the word of other nations at their face value (the other nations have exactly the same problem). So they keep their cards close to their chest. The average German businessman will hesitate to deal with a foreign company unless it has a German subsidiary and deals with the right banks. In many business situations of my experience, the German attitude towards ideas or opinions coming from outside can only be described as one of 'stubborn hermeticity'.

This hermeticity of German society was brought home to me with a bang when I heard that a friend of ours had been selected for a major assignment on the German business scene. When we called to congratulate him, his wife answered the phone with the words "Of course, living in Brussels, you wouldn't know about this, but...". It is they who are parochial.

It is my conviction that many of the attitudes I have been talking about stem from insecurity catalysed into a highly developed sense of social conformity, a particularly German version of 'what will the neighbours think?' or something I call the Social Consensus Effect (SCE). After all, if you think you're all on the right track, why quarrel with your own kind (which does not exclude a tendency to moralise)? Put more positively, it may explain the excessive use of the word *Partner*, not just in advertising, but in politics too.

A couple of examples of SCE should suffice. An Anglo-Saxon couple I know moved into a suburb of Stuttgart with two young children: it only took a few days for the neighbours to complain that the kids were leaving their pushcarts on the front lawn and diminishing the social status of the area.

Then there was the apparently far-fetched case of a celibate American acquaintance of mine who invited the wife of a close friend to spend the night at his apartment while her husband was attending an exhibition in another German city. Nothing improper occurred but, at eight o'clock the following morning, when our friend left his apartment, the woman from next door came up and said, very definitively: "Our neighbourhood does not condone such behaviour."

In fact, many aspects of social behaviour are subject to state legislation or local community rules, varying according to the area one inhabits, and the threat of prosecution by local administrators or even the neighbours. Examples include not mowing your lawn on Sundays or between the hours of 1 and 3 pm (the Belgians also have rules governing the siesta hours), not putting glass in your dustbin after 8 pm and even not taking a shower in your own flat after 10 pm. Things have now got to the point that, in the good city of Hamm in late-1992, the local magistrates ordained that dogs should be restrained from barking between 7 pm and 8 am.

With all these restrictions, it is little wonder that the Germans let themselves go behind the wheel of a car although, here again, they can be prosecuted for making rude signs at other drivers.

Unfortunately, there seems to be another side-effect of this urge to orderliness: *Kinderfeindlichkeit*. At the time of writing, federal legislators are trying to outlaw parental violence, "constant nagging or threatening children with the bogeyman". This is an aspect of German life that I find puzzling. John Ardagh thinks that, in addition to the fact that children tend to be unsocially noisy, it may have something to do with "failure to understand a child's imaginative world". Ingrid Hoffmann of the Deutsche Kinderhilfsdienst, quoted in the *International Herald Tribune*, suggested that "the lost war and total destruction stripped away our certainty about basic values. The relations between generations were poisoned for a time". *Angst* again.

For Germans, cleanliness and a quiet comportment are cardinal virtues (John Ardagh talks about the "profound Teutonic need for silence"). Cleaning chores in the public areas of multi-family housing developments are shared on a rota basis: if someone defaults, the others may end up taking him or her to court. Rules are there to be obeyed.

In discussing the German temperament, one seems to keep on coming back to what I call the 'con' words: conservatism, conformity, consensus, continuity, condoning. Their prevalence must surely reflect the traditionally authoritarian nature of German family life.

As I have noticed with regularity over the years, this sense of social conformity is particularly highly developed in Germans of the older generations: *gutbürgerlich* folk who generally look disapproving, particularly at only mildly eccentric Englishmen whom they clearly confuse with men from Mars. These elderly middle-class Germans dress in muted pastel colours, powder blues and dove greys, a form of social camouflage (unfortunately when the great German public does let itself go colourwise, it generally gets it terribly wrong: the less inhibited currently favour mauve). Many of them also wear matching shoes with thick crepe soles - what the Americans call rubber-soled deck shoes and what British nationals of my generation used to grace with the name of 'brothel-creepers' - maybe hoping that, in addition to not being noticed, they won't be heard either.

This talent for conformity, for merging with the background (what Peter Millar of *The European* calls "the habit of self-effacement") may help explain a lot of things including Hitlerism: the author Jonathan Steinberg speaks of an addiction to civic virtues, such as efficiency and dedication, as a potent factor in the history of those troubled times. Others talk of a "typical German over-respect for authority". One foreigner, who justifiably remains anonymous even if his nationality is self-evident, put it more crudely in saying that "the trouble with the Germans is that they're either at your throat or at your feet". I say, old chap...

A particular eye-opener for me was to read in Wolfgang Ebert's book, *Das Porzellan war so nervös*[18], that Goebbels hit on the brilliant idea of inviting all good German citizens in possession of a flagpole (which happened to be a regular feature of German suburban households in those days) to hoist the Swastika. It could be argued that, thanks to the latent sense of social conformity in the average German, this single move was largely responsible for the success of Nazism. Of course, the Treaty of Versailles may have contributed, too, as well as the Great Depression and, in the view of my Cambridge professor, the fact that the verb comes at the end of the sentence.

Bringing these thoughts into the present in his book *The Germans*[19], David Marsh leaves the reader in no doubt: "The Germans fear society without order and organisation; and so defer to older systems of guidance. This is the reason for an extraordinary slavishness to deep-seated principles of hierarchy, and to rules and regulations in general". The Social Democrat party, in the post-WWI period, ran a campaign under the banner *"Rot ist richtig, aber Ordnung muss sein!"*. And when a descendent of Catherine the Great's *Volgadeutsch* immigrant community was asked recently, on German TV, what he had liked about life in the USSR's erstwhile Volga Republic, he replied simply and conclusively: *"Es war Ordnung"*.

Maybe the orderliness of Germans in daily life explains their behaviour on the *Autobahn*. One class, the motorists, tends to drive either too fast - or not fast enough, but in the left hand lane. Another class, the *Alternativen*, which does not approve of cars, seems to spend all its time systematically painting often very high-quality graffiti on the soundbreaks. Certainly, the violently anti-establishment attitudes of the younger generations are an understandable response to the implicit authoritarianism of German society.

In the right environment, the "addiction to civic virtues" Steinberg speaks of is an admirable trait: where else would you have direct access, at a motorway service station, to public telephones on the apparently reasonable presumption that you declare and pay for your call?

Addiction to civic virtues does not, however, extend *per se* to individual initiative in a good cause. In an interview with the *Washington Post* Werner Hoyer of the Free Democrat party said a mouthful: "Our society's greatest weakness is an engagement gap. You don't get involved unless it immediately helps your business or family. We have no tradition of volunteerism as you do". Again, the pressure of social conformity - though it has to be said that the Germans have recently shown themselves to be as emphatic in demonstrating personal opposition to racism as any other European nation, perhaps even more so.

Moreover a sense of social conformity can have its advantages. My personal experience is that the Germans, with certain exceptions, are extremely polite in a rather matter-of-fact way. Even when they are being difficult, something that happens frequently in their relations with non-Germans, they still manage to be polite. It's a very successful form of hermeticity.

Some people - including the French who, as past masters in such matters, should be the first to recognise the trait - may class this as bloodymindedness. My personal belief is that polite behaviour is natural to educated Germans. Amongst themselves, they show a respect for their fellows together with a slight admixture of servility which, in a nation bred to clear standards of social conformity, is not altogether surprising. Like the Japanese, they tend to be even overpolite individually but very rude in groups, particularly when abroad.

Spurred on by Goethe *("Kennst du das Land wo die Zitronen blühen?")* and by Baedeker, the Germans have become inveterate globetrotters. Upmarket Germans, of whom there are many, now migrate in flocks to such places as North Africa, India and the South Pacific. This hankering after exotic distractions reflects an innate romanticism, maybe also a dissatisfaction with, and the desire to escape from, the emptiness of their own materially very successful society. Even the run-of-the-mill restaurant menu reads like a travel brochure.

Speaking of food, it seems that almost every Italian immigrant to Germany opens a restaurant or an icecream parlour - whether he or she can cook or make icecream or not. Germans will spurn their own *gutbürgerlich* cooking - which, in very simple places, can be extremely good - for the sake of something with an even mildly exotic atmosphere, gastronomic or other.

This fondness for the apparently exotic can lead to pretentiousness in the home, extending to the use of goldplated chinaware and other items which demonstrate the owners' wealth rather than their good taste. Essentially simple people, trapped as they are in their high-tension social environment, the Germans can be breathtakingly pretentious - a trait that the advertising profession has exploited shamelessly.

But, whatever the rights and wrongs of the situation, we have to take the Germans very seriously. With their *Gründlichkeit* (apropos of which how often one hears the phrase *'im Grunde genommen'*!), their social discipline, their industriousness and their accumulated wealth, they represent Europe's 'economic centre of gravity', even if they have lost a little of their fabled work ethic.

It may seem a backhanded compliment to suggest that the Germans are 'the Japanese of Europe', yet they demonstrate many of the same symptoms of industrial and social consensus: a symbiotic business/banking relationship, a sense of common purpose at industry level (even extending to the exchange of proprietary information) and a gift for hidden protectionism, making the German market seem sometimes as impenetrable to foreign exporters as Japan. And with the recent changes in Eastern Europe, they have the advantage of linguistic and cultural links eastwards that are superior to those of any other Western European nation except Austria.

Many companies - British, French and others - have tried to outmanoeuvre the German system to their cost. The Frankfurt correspondent of the *Financial Times* reported that, every time he tried to speak to a German bank other than the Deutsche Bank, the Dresdner Bank or the Commerzbank, he was referred back to... the Deutsche Bank, the Dresdner Bank or the Commerzbank. The same thing applies to the trade associations, the wholesaler organisations, in fact just about everyone. Don't try to beat the system. The Germans, out of a historically inexplicable sense of identity - after all, they are still a federation of highly independently minded *Länder* or states - simply don't break ranks. There's discipline for you!

Like the Japanese, the Germans have both the patience to find the right answer - *Nemawashi*, the time it takes to grow a tree - and a very matter-of-fact approach to problems (like the Japanese, some of them also still give a little bow when shaking hands). Yet, as David Marsh says in his book, "they have perfected a system of economic and political consensus which - partly because of worries about the consequences if society ever became less organised (here comes that *Angst* again) - has become notoriously inflexible".

A not necessarily apocryphal story is told about the different responses of a British board of directors and a German management board to the same situation: the news of the launch of a major product by a competitive company. The British directors, so the story goes, pondered awhile until somebody said "let's buy the company", to which proposal everybody said "hear hear". The German board went into a state of deep depression until, three weeks later, the engineering director came back with the first production model of an even better product. The British got round the problem, the Germans went straight to the heart of the problem.

Of course, we British would say this shows the power of lateral thinking. Yet the truth is that the Germans have a very systematic, even modular, approach to just about everything. One example is the relentless use of the word *System* to promote almost anything from skin care products to furniture. Another is the use of the *Baukasten* (building block) principle in the construction and other industries. The German environment is essentially rectangular and rectilinear: small-town apartment blocks tend to look like multi-storey barracks. Some towns even manage to look like scaled-up versions of Märklin model railway sets (one wonders which came first).

To some extent the modular approach reflects the technological past - another example of innate German conservatism. There is a strong attachment, in many areas of industry and science, to things electro-mechanical, a technology in which the Germans have excelled. Under the communists even the East German computer industry made good *printers*, if nothing else. And German scientists and doctors still prefer things with buttons and knobs on them (they like to have some measure of control, otherwise they get *ängstlich!*) than things that go buzz and whirr all on their own...

The miracle ingredient of German industry - so evident when you look at some of the country's neighbours - is the *Mittelstand,* that rump of well-run, often highly specialised, medium-sized firms that gives the economy so much of its relentless momentum. It is the companies from the *Mittelstand*, not the big combines, that have baled out the failing industries of the *neue Länder*.

For better or worse, many German companies are still the fiefdoms of their owner-managers, who work on the 'management by concession' principle. The concept of the professional manager only began to win respectability in the 1970s and it has been a hard fight for some of them to get into the club. Yet the idea of making a career in industry is respectable enough. In the words of David Marsh: "... the Germans have a much closer affinity to industry than the British or the French. This helps to explain why the most talented people go into manufacturing, not politics".

Depending on your prejudices, German matter-of-factness can be interpreted as literalness: they have difficulty in resisting the temptation to label even things that are self-evident. By nature the Germans tend to be serious to the point of severity. Businessfolk draw extensively on weasel words of two classes: relationally charged terms like *Mitarbeiter, Partner* and *Team*, and authority-pregnant ones like *Profi, Expert, Fach*-this-and-that and inevitably *Technik*. And no self-respecting German business would be without a generally rather ponderous slogan and, in the case of those manufacturing anything consumable short of the fastest of foods, never without a foundation date!

The Germans are systematic, often mechanistic, in their approach to many things in life. Even their pop music has a relentless quality, so much so that the performers, like the sorcerer's apprentice, sometimes don't seem to know how to make things stop: they generally get the engineer to fade out the sound. And we all know the stories and pastiches about German double-takes when jokes are being told.

It is also true that, when they get jokey, the Germans can be unnervingly hearty. It is at moments like this - for example at a letting-one's-hair-down evening at a local skittle club, as has happened to me - that a rather unsettling (for foreigners) mood of hubris can emerge. David Marsh makes the point: "The Germans have plenty of humour, but go in for organised burlesque rather than spontaneous levity. Leaning to *Schadenfreude*, the Germans like to home in on a target; they seldom have enough self-confidence to laugh at themselves, something which comes naturally - perhaps, too naturally - to the English".

Related to this is the highly developed sense of irony you see in some Germans, including essentially serious individuals like Karl Otto Pöhl, the combative ex-president of the Bundesbank. Irony is, of course, a particularly effective way of keeping some other Germans off-balance.

Yet German humour, as demonstrated by some of the TV shows masterminded by the younger generation, can be scintillating in its satire and its powers of observation. German current affairs programmes also sparkle by their powers of in-depth observation. But their big band, game and talk shows are as bad as everywhere else, maybe worse.

German TV is a clumsily conceived and engineered programming machine, remarkable for its gongs and sudden silences - and a preference, in the case of news programmes, for professorial *Kommentare* rather than the lively debates favoured by the French. It reflects, in addition to the rigidity and self-absorption of German society, the byzantine world of German politics.

By this I do not mean the political coverage offered by German TV, which can be excellent, but the political affiliations of the anchormen. Some of the TV commentators are geriatric political appointees and timeservers, members of the *ich begrüsse Sie, ich bedanke mich* brigade, while most of the entertainment (?) is provided by aging stars with wigs. They all seem to try to excuse their presence by being, not surprisingly for their age, excessively polite when addressing their audience.

Indeed, things are starting to change for the better. But the depth of resistance to change is evident from the fact that, even in 1994, ZDF journalists transferred to the 'n-tv' programme insisted on employing secretaries, since they were not accustomed to working with wordprocessors - much to the astonishment of their CNN sponsors!

The phrase *verehrte Zuschauer* (honoured viewers) is occasionally discarded in favour of *meine Damen und Herren* (my ladies and gentlemen). Only Spencer on Sesamstrasse, the children's programme, is allowed to say *Hallo Leute* (hi folks!). But that's all part of the formality of much of German society. In fact German children's TV, very largely due to Czech programme producers, is probably the best in Europe.

In other areas of the arts too (maybe because this is not real life?), the Germans are as capable of startling originality as they are of conformity. Maintaining the Berlin tradition from the inter-war years, their satirical cabarets are superb. They also excel in street entertainment, a tradition revived from mediaeval times. Watch open-air 'happenings', as I have done in the historic hearts of cities like Worms and Nuremberg, and you really feel you are sharing a cultural heritage with the jugglers, the jokers and the mimes. Even their pop music started to come to life in the mid-80s, after decades of slavish imitation.

With so many boyish-looking *Gruftis* looking for eternal youth as their role models on TV, it is not surprising that age is a great preoccupation for the Germans. Apart from omnipresent ads for miracle drugs and nature cures, a study conducted by one of Europe's business schools discovered that "the Germans were most preoccupied about aging and the pressure of time, probably because of their desire for accuracy and their extreme sense of responsibility". Fair enough! And, while on the subject, it is only recently that German doctors started prescribing anything but German drugs.

The Germans are certainly very thorough - but, in the view of the Dutch, by no means as systematic as the Dutch (something the rest of us Europeans regard as an act of hyperbole). This may be due to the fact that, in stark contrast to the Dutch, the Germans are a philosophical and ultimately sentimental folk who easily drift off into abstracts, foggy idealism and vague and verbose forms of expression. David Marsh quotes the author Horst Krüger: "The Germans are an unpolitical, romantic people who lean towards extremes - they confuse reality and dreams". Heinrich Heine, a century earlier, was blunter, saying quite simply that the Germans "are the unchallenged rulers of the kingdom of dreams". Maybe this explained the size and naivety of the German anti-war movement.

Elsewhere in his book, David Marsh sums up the dichotomy of the German mind: "Only a thin line separates idealism from escapism, pride from arrogance, discipline from servility." To which I would add 'perfectionism from inflexibility'. The drive to perfectionism is so firmly instilled in the German psyche that it tends to inhibit the development of the persona, both socially and professionally: one of the issues confronting German business schools is the need to foster a sense of creativity which, by definition, means departing from established procedures.

Yet, despite this dichotomy and despite their philosophico-romantic leanings, the Germans - and particularly the young people - demonstrate an articulateness which leaves me, as an Englishman, a bit ashamed of my own kind. They are an impressively educated people. A reflection on British shortcomings?

In deliberation, despite a tendency to philosophise, the Germans are articulate and make statements full of content. At the same time, in debate, they can pass hasty judgment on an adversary, perhaps just to demonstrate that they have minds of their own.

This ability to express themselves reflects a nervous or emotional intensity which is almost absent from the average Englishman. Even the prosaic business of walking around a public garden generates a level of observation and comment that would do justice to a *putsch*, or at least a general election, in any other country.

Intensity is certainly, to use an appropriate word, a leitmotiv of the German temperament: I have never known anything like the family sagas indulged in by my German friends and relations. They eclipse the emotive potential of Dallas and Dynasty combined. When really outraged, the Germans can display an incandescent self-righteousness that takes my breath away. So I guess we're back to *Angst*.

The Spanish
The egocentric egalitarians

"The Englishman, German or Frenchman who thinks about public affairs contents himself with entering the local branch of a party, working in favour of a hospital, giving his time to town administration... or to another of the numerous private or public collective institutions which come to hand. The Spaniard sees his country in its entirety and local issues seem small to him next to the immenseness and importance of himself" Salvador de Madariaga

"The truth is that the Spaniards are a simple race in comparison to the English and the French" Gerald Brenan

"Their incorruptible sense of humour and their dignity"
Laurie Lee

"... I will say for the Spaniards, that in their social intercourse no people in the world exhibit a juster feeling of what is due to the dignity of human nature, or better understand the behaviour which it behoves a man to adopt towards his fellow-beings"
George Borrow

"When I speak of Spain, I speak of Man" Antonio Machado

"If your wife tells you to throw yourself off the balcony, pray to God it be a low one" [*"Si tu mujer quiere que te eches de un balcón, pide a Dios que sea bajo"*] Spanish proverb

"The Spaniard... shuns abstractions as much as any Englishman and is as free from inhibitions as any Frenchman can be"
Salvador de Madariaga

"You have neither beauty nor money, but you love my mother and for that I love you" [*"Ni hermosura, ni dinero, ya lo se que tu no tienes, pero quieres a mi madre y por eso yo te quiero"*]
Spanish folksong

"God gives nuts to the toothless" [*"Da Dios nueces a los que no tienen muelas"*] Spanish proverb

"Long live Death" [*"Viva la muerte"*]
Battlecry of the Spanish Foreign Legion

"Thank God for the Spaniards... If there were no Spaniards, the Italians would be the last people in Europe" Gioacchino Rossini

Jumping from the Germans to the Spanish might look like a feat of intellectual acrobatics. But, contrary to popular misconceptions, the two races have a great deal in common: seriousness sometimes bordering on perfectionism, a rather rudimentary style of cooking (which, in both cases, has its moments of glory), even a banking mafia running much of the economy.

Added to these are a deep-set fascination with death and a reputation for political fanaticism, both of which are hopefully now exhausted - though it has to be said that the Spanish have the disarming gift of owning up collectively to their past mistakes where the Germans, pre- and post-Stasi, have been heard to say "we didn't know" or "it wasn't our fault".

There may also be other historical reasons for the inherent likemindedness of these two races. There is the element of German blood in many Spaniards from the Visigothic connection. Apart from traces still evident in words with Germanic roots like *ganso* (*Gans* = goose) and *queso* (*Käse* = cheese), could this explain the fact that the women of both races have uncharacteristically low-pitched and melodious voices?

Then there is the Habsburg link, originally a German dynasty, and the refuge offered to German immigrants over the centuries, ranging from the Andalusian colonies of the 18th century (places with romantic names like La Luisiana, La Carlota and La Carolina) to German political refugees after WWII.

Add to this the fact that the Germans go all *schwärmerisch* over the Spanish climate and folklore, contributing in the process to the false image of the people (see more below), while the Spanish adore the Germans for their discipline, their organisational skills and their approach to federalism - something they are now imitating fervently.

I admit that this affinity between the Germans and the Spanish intrigues me, because it seems to run counter to all the received wisdom about the two races. But the English writer Jan Morris throws some helpful light on the issue[20] when she says: "The shape of Spain is symmetrical, and the Spaniard likes everything else to conform [one of those 'con' words - see previous chapter]. He distrusts loose ends and anomalies. *Limpieza*, purity, is one of the great Spanish abstractions." Maybe it is not surprising that the country's capital, Madrid, is at the geometric centre of Spain, a country which (*pace* the Portuguese) nature ordained should be the most symmetrical of all Europe's parts.

Later on in her book Jan Morris comments that "the cities of Spain are often wonderfully tidy and closely knit, and the ports of Spain often look like model harbours in a museum." That, again, makes me think of the 'miniaturism' of German towns I referred to earlier.

I owe a particular insight to the author when she says in her con-clusions: "Watch the Spaniards at a bull-fight [I don't go to bull-fights], and you will see that when a matador succeeds, a frightening tide of hero-worship sweeps instantly around the crowd, and that when one fails, then the catcalls and whistles echo across the city, the insults are chanted like incantations, and not a single dissent-ing tremor of sympathy breaks the unison...". That sounds familiar.

Not only do the Germans feel this affinity with the Spanish, the Spanish don't have to envy the Germans for their sense of industry. Contrary to yet another brand of folklore for which the French are to blame, the Spanish work as hard as the Germans and are apparently now working harder. A market researcher friend of mine maintains, from extensive dealings with the Spanish busi-ness community, that they combine the rigidity of the Germans with the self-assurance of the British. More of this anon.

One thing is for sure. The Spanish can be both dynamic and inventive, and are currently showing the rest of Europe a thing or two. Some engineering companies - particularly Basque ones, the Basques producing brilliant engineers - are as good as anything Europe can offer. In fact engineering enjoys as exalted a status as in France, possibly more so.

This challenge to the traditional image of the Spaniards is hard for many people to swallow, precisely because of the nonsense put around by mainly well-meaning Frenchmen like Merimée, Gautier, Bizet, Barrès, Daumier, Lalo, Debussy and Ravel since the last century. The image was composed of more or less equal parts of Carmen, Don Quixote, Don Juan and wild fantasies of Mexican-like types in *sombreros*.

Admittedly the Spanish were also to blame, certainly for Don Quixote - a masterly creation who, with Sancho Panza, represents the light and shade of the Spanish character, idealism and common sense. They also spent a lot of time mooning over the loss of the last remnants of their empire in 1898, got dragged into no less than 43 *coups d'état* between 1814 and 1923, and finally perpetrated a heroic but thoroughly nasty civil war which only ended in 1939 - when the rest of Europe went off on a rampage of its own.

Partly because it was cut off from the rest of Europe for such a long time (Spain only really turned around and came to terms with the rest of the Continent in the 1960s), also because it is such a huge, beautiful and in many ways genuinely mysterious country, Spain is still an enigma to most Europeans.

Understanding has not been helped by the fact that, despite the undeniably steady and stalwart temperament of the countryfolk, some sea changes in the apparent character of the Spanish have been evident over the centuries. The swashbuckling 16th-century adventurer gave way to the 19th-century romantic, and the early 20th-century revolutionary succumbed to the late 20th-century materialist, someone in search of "The Three C's": *coche* (a car), *compañera* (a girlfriend) and *casa* (a house).

But then it seems that the relatively recent arrival of prosperity has made materialists of both the Spaniards and the Italians. Fur coats are as popular here as there and the Spanish can boast the philosophy of *amigismo* as their answer to the M-word and the C-words of the Italians (see next chapter). Recent events have highlighted how far *pelotazo*, the cult of the fast buck, has gone. Corruption in high places is up to the standard of other Mediterranean countries.

There is also a permanent dichotomy in the Spanish psyche, to be found in one and the same person (in that respect the Spaniard is no different from other Europeans). But, in this case, it is human warmth cohabiting with the occasional brutality. It may be indicative that that most talented of Spanish painters, Francisco Goya, moved from rococo to the most violent realism in a lifetime.

In talking of Spain, I am not referring to that devastated seaboard known to tourists which, excepting the northwest coastline, has nothing to offer in my book. For most Europeans, experience of Spain is the waiters and the bad cooking in package-tour hotels.

Nor am I talking about some very special communities within this remarkable subcontinent: the Catalans, in my opinion the most cosmopolitan of all the European peoples, endowed with an almost indecent degree of inventiveness and taste, counterbalanced by a strange fondness for scatology; the Galicians, part of the 'Celtic Fringe'; the Andalusians, a sparkling, lyrical folk; and the Basques, the enigma of Western Europe, with a rhesus negative factor that is mind-blowing and a language that appears to find its inspiration in the Caucasus...

I am talking about the heart of Spain, that remote tableland stretching southwards from the provinces of Aragon, Castile and León to La Mancha and the Sierra Morena, in short at least 70 per cent of the land area of the country.

Writing in *The European*, Tom Burns-Marañon stressed the difference between this Spanish heartland and the deep south: "Castile-León, with its extreme continental climate, is a dour, no-nonsense land with conservative ethics of traditional family values, hard work and thrift... Andalusía, the southern swathe of Spain, with its flamenco and fighting bulls, is where most of the national stereotypes flourish. As the cliches have it, Andalusía is the home of quick wit and imaginative flights of fancy; a land of poets where sustained periods of indolence follow sudden bouts of energy."

This difference, both physical and cultural, is even more marked than the substantial differences between Castile-León and the other cultures of Spain, in particular Catalonia, Valencia, the Basque country, Asturias and Galicia.

I share the opinion of Jan Morris when she says "for some the other provinces may be Spain plus; for me they are always Spain minus. It is in Castile that the proper magic of Spain resides, casting its spell from Finisterre to Almeria, and projecting its familiar image to the four corners of the world."

But we are supposed to be talking about the people, not the country. Yes, but to understand the people of this Spanish heartland, you have to know the country, see how the people in these remote parts live. It is a land of harsh but majestic outlines, stones, scrub, pinewoods, olive groves, moulded in a climate of extremes, oven-like in summer, icy in winter. Everything expresses itself in tactile, elemental terms, even the placenames. And, throughout, the dominant colours are browns, yellows, mauves and purples.

If toponymy appeals to you - in this case the way places owe their names to their situation or their role in history - then this is the country for you. But the landscape has not left its mark on the language alone, it also flavours the cooking, simple but sustaining, and shapes the personality of the people, even their voices. The Spanish, both men and women, talk as if they had pebbles in their mouths - an extension of their environment, just as the Dutch talk through their teeth as if they were whistling into the wind on a North Sea dyke. Both nations are people who have a close relationship with the elements. And the more southern the Spanish, the more they swallow their words, whatever this may signify.

Spanish society has something of the earthiness one associates with the Russian culture, elemental and close to its roots, yet stiffer and less sentimental than the Russian version. "In Spain", says Lorenzo Silva Rodriguez, "there's a tradition of women being powerful and physical. This is a power that comes from within." Both countries claim novelists and playwrights with an exceptional talent for revealing the intricacies of human nature.

Many recent observers, the British more than the French, have understood this Spain and its people (in my view, the French parody Spain, the Germans worship it, the British understand it).

This is how Jan Morris describes the central tableland of Spain: "The light is brilliant, the atmosphere is preservative, the colours are vivid - so vivid, for all the vast monotony of the *meseta*, that sometimes this seems like a painted country, as the mauve and purple shadows shift across the hills, as the sun picks out a village here, a crag there, as the clouds idly scud across the candlewick landscape of olives or cork oaks, and the red soil at your feet seems to smoulder in the heat. It is no accident that the Spaniards are masters of floodlighting."

Another British writer, VS Pritchett, adds graphic detail in his description of the central plateau [21]: "Dust and yellow earth have begun; the grass, if there are patches of it, is wire, the trees only mark the roads, there are no others, and the roads, too, are rare. It is steppe, not desert, a steppe variegated only by wilderness. And there appear those strange flat-topped hills of the country. A half-mile long, perhaps, and anything from 400 to 450 feet high, they have been planed off at the summit and are water-hollowed in their flanks...".

Of course, progress is now blurring the ancient reality: people are leaving the land, pouring into the cities and living in apartment blocks, but it will be a long time before the impact of this unique environment is effaced for ever. The authorities, in their wisdom, have even tried to install gypsies in multi-storey buildings, but the donkeys get jammed in the stairwells. Football has long since supplanted bullfighting as the national sport (though the Spanish are still harassed on the issue of animal rights by the British, who are harassed on the issue of *human* rights by the rest of the European Union). And women are no longer expected to wear hats in church - much to the consternation of the English contingent at a recent 'mixed marriage' who looked as if they were dressed for Ascot.

The Spanish indeed have a sentimental affinity with the Germans and share the same curious blend of superficial romanticism allied with deeper-set irrational impulses. Their affinity with the Italians is close to zero (a typical syndrome in neighbours) even if, despite themselves, they tend to like them. For Spaniards the Italians are lightweight, for Italians the Spanish are sombre and severe.

Those from the European North who confuse the two races have absolutely no excuse. Despite the stories put about by the 19th century French, the Spanish are essentially sober people, secure in their Spanishness, while the Italians are as viscerally uncertain as only Italians can be (see next chapter). The Spanish reflect the colour of their surroundings - browns, yellows, sombre hues - while the Italians are, well, colourful.

This was already evident nearly half a millenium ago. Talking about the arrival of the Spanish Emperor Charles V in Italy, the Italian writer Luigi Barzini[15] comments: "While Italians were dressed in the bright and gay colours fashionable at the time, in silks, brocades, velvets, laces, and woollen cloth, of red, green, yellow, pink, blue, the Spanish wore black suits with black silk stockings, black boots or shoes, black velvet caps adorned with black plumes." While black may not be so fashionable with them today, the Spanish still have more sober tastes than their Italian neighbours. This reflects their gravitas, a far cry from the frivolity and folkloric nature of the traditional stereotype.

A much-travelled Englishman, George Borrow[7], sensed this over 150 years ago when he spoke of "the silent, reserved men of Spain, with whom a foreigner might mingle for half a century without having half-a-dozen words addressed to him, unless he himself made the first advances to intimacy, which, after all, might be rejected with a shrug and a *no intendo* (sic)." Borrow, a keen and close observer of the Spanish scene of the time, mingled with the people rather than with the bourgeoisie, who were already picking up frenchified habits.

This elemental simplicity of the Spanish - which Gerald Brenan, another Briton who understands Spain, alludes to in the quotation at the head of this chapter[22], should not be interpreted as artlessness. The Spanish, and not just the emancipated ones of whom there are more and more these days, have a very highly developed and innate sense of style. This in no way diminishes the importance they attach to substance - in the best of all worlds, everyone is a *hidalgo*, a *hijo de algo* ('the son of a somebody'), but it does distinguish them from their Portuguese neighbours, who tend to put substance before style.

Curiously, and this is a very personal opinion, in many respects the Spanish most resemble, of all people, the English - in their relaxed manner (in civilised situations, that is, rather than civil wars), in their dress, in their fondness for roasts and, more recently, in their fondness for monarchy (even their coins look like English currency!). In fact, in their dress, they are even more conservative than the old-style Englishman: far from taking the easy option of espousing a 'uniform' like the pinstripe suit, they demonstrate natural good taste. They also occasionally, like the English, show a gift for eccentricity - like the company secretary I knew who ran an advertising agency on the side, never ate anything but *serrano* ham and always drove with one hand, the right one, with the left hand trailing out of the window and slapping the side of the car...

Respect for a leader - a king, a duke, a Caudillo, a union leader, even a *cacique* - has been a feature of Spanish history. Here there are echoes of German social conformity, but the Spanish version is more personal and has little to do with what the neighbours say. There is a fondness for ceremonial and occasion, as a group of wealthy women demonstrated in huddling around a TV set in an Aragonese mountain hotel to watch a British royal wedding. A leading falangist must have been thinking of such things when he said "the Spaniards love a uniform, provided it is multiform...".

Spanish life has always been complicated by the fact that different Spaniards have had different leaders - at the local level, at the level of the community or of any one of the little nations which eventually became Spain. Hardly surprising, then, that the modern Spanish state comprises 17 autonomous regions and may eventually end up with more.

Jan Morris elaborates on this point: "Spain is not merely a regional country, but a passionately local one as well. To many Spaniards, patriotism goes no farther than the village, and Spain in the abstract is only a tax-collector or a sergeant-major. The Spanish language varies not only from province to province, but actually from village to village, and so self-contained is the village entity that in the Napoleonic Wars the Mayor of Mosteles, a hamlet near Madrid, personally declared war on France". In the typical small town, people will be hailed as *El Segoviano*, *La Toledana* and so on, a reference to their origins even when they have lived there for years.

Only Spain, certainly not Russia, could have produced a phenomenon as bizarre as the anarchist movement of the Spanish Republic: towns and villages which declared unilateral independence from the state, burned the national banknotes and printed their own with the skull and crossbones on them and, when they went to war, refused to nominate commanding officers. In its most absolute form, government was reduced (or raised?) to the level of the individual - an eloquent expression of the status accorded the human being in Spanish thinking.

Totally misguided, the movement was visionary in a uniquely Spanish way. In fact the chain of events known blandly as the Spanish Civil War could have become one of the purest and most natural expressions of the revolutionary spirit in the history of the western world, working as it did from the grassroots upward. As it happens it just deteriorated, with the help of outside intervention, into a very bloody mess.

As with so many things Spanish, such quixotic behaviour stands in stark contrast to the commanding feature of the Spanish personality: the sense of the importance of the individual, both oneself (cf the words of Salvador de Madariaga at the head of this chapter) and one's fellow humans, or at least those worthy of respect - a definition which excludes one's enemies. It seems that just about everybody qualified as an enemy of someone else in the Civil War: individuals counted for nothing when they were at the receiving end of a knife or a gun barrel.

Spaniards traditionally judge people by what they are, not what they possess. As George Borrow noted in the mid-19th century, Spain "is one of the few countries in Europe where poverty is not treated with contempt, and I may add, where the wealthy are not blindly idolised". And, elsewhere in his book, he comments that the Spanish demonstrate "a spirit of proud independence, which it is impossible but to admire".

Unfortunately, the Spaniard's sense of his (or to a lesser degree her) own worth can get in the way of everything else. The Spanish can be extremely curt, even dismissive, in their relations - sometimes downright rude like the French, but in a more impersonal way. They have a tendency, like the Greeks, to shut off mentally at what are vital moments for the other party.

On the other hand, they are known to pull out all the stops if someone criticises or just disagrees with them: their *dignidad* is at risk. As Jan Morris says, "Spaniards prefer not to be laughed at, and do not much like losing". They also do have a rather casual attitude towards time - not a *mañana* mentality, but an erratic appreciation where something that has been hanging fire for years becomes the burning issue of the moment.

Though I have had plenty of experiences to the contrary, an acquaintance of mine insists that the Spaniards increasingly demonstrate an inability to cope with the demands of a service-industry age, seemingly confusing service with servility: their dignity inhibits them in being helpful to others. In the words of Salvador de Madariaga[8]: "The instinct for preserving his own liberty makes him [the Spaniard] eschew all forms of social co-operation, since all collective work tends to enslave the individual and to reduce him to the status of a piece of machinery."

This view was even being voiced as long ago as 1836, when George Borrow encountered an innkeeper in Valladolid who was "far too high a cavalier to attend to the wants of his guests". At least it can be added, put the other way round, that the average customer treats the person serving him as an equal - which is more than can be said of some countries. Having made the connection earlier with Russian tradition, it gratifies me to evoke Jan Morris' words: "In normal times Spaniards of all classes treat each other with a casual courtesy, almost a familiarity, that suggests to me the oddly easy relationship between master and serf in Tsarist Russia."

Gerald Brenan examines Spanish social attitudes in his book *The Face of Spain*[22]: "The whole of Spanish life, one may say, is organized in a sort of clan system. Within the clan - which consists of relatives, friends, political allies, and so forth - all is warmth and friendliness: outside it all is distrust and suspicion."

There is a nuance here which differentiates Spanish from Italian attitudes (see next chapter): Italians are driven to hunt in packs because of their basic distrust of the system, whereas the Spanish make a conscious choice of the people they like to be associated with and the ones they don't...

But back to Brenan: "For this reason [the Spanish dilemma of the identification of friends and enemies] new acquaintances must be provisionally brought into the clan by the offer of bread and salt - in modern terms, of a cigarette. Hence too all those pats on the back, those touches on the arm: they serve to give reassurance. It may be that this way of conducting social relations is the mark of a primitive or imperfectly organized society, but at least it avoids the English vice of indifference."

Further on, reinforcing his first point, he adds: "they live by a tribal or client system, which makes it a moral duty for them to favour their friends at the expense of the State and to penalize their adversaries". VS Pritchett echoes Brenan's words: "The Spanish live in castes, but not in classes, and their equality - the only real equality I have met anywhere in the world - is in their sense of nobility or, rather, in the sense of the absolute quality of the person."

Gerald Brenan recalls the words he used in a conversation with a Spanish schoolmaster he met on a train: "...you have a certain aristocratic quality, a sort of pride in yourselves which is fortified by Oriental stoicism; and it is this that makes you liked and esteemed wherever you go. It's a quality for which we English no longer have any word, but which you call *nobleza*." Another virtually untranslatable word is *castizo* (of good breed?), a quality which can be applied to a lot of otherwise very ordinary people in the upland provinces.

Perhaps because they rate the individual so highly, the Spanish accept the principle that all human experience, with all its contrasts, can reside inside a single person. So contradictions are part of life, as Cervantes demonstrated with Don Quixote and Sancho Panza. Despite the relative tameness of life today, you will still find Spaniards who demonstrate a sincerely held devotion to eccentric individuality, striking poses and saying things that the observer, for want of a better word, can only class as quixotic.

No doubt Gerald Brenan was also thinking of Cervantes' odd couple when he wrote: "The Spaniards are great realists - that is what we are always told. Certainly they see things minutely and objectively. But this reality hurts and wounds their pride: too often they look on life as if it were the enemy. And it is precisely the cruelty and precision of their vision (consider Goya) that throws them back into themselves with the desire to transcend what they see. Hence their nobility, their generosity, their extravagance."

VS Pritchett says much the same thing: "The fact is that they are people of excess: excessive in silence and reserve, excessive in speech when they suddenly fly into it...". He describes a group of Spaniards he meets on a train: "There was no conceit or vanity in these travellers. The nervous pushing bustle of the European was not in them. The quick vanity and sharp-mindedness of the French, their speed in isolating and abstracting a problem, were not there. Nor were there the naïve vivacity and affectibility which electrify the agreeable Italians. These races care to attract or please continuously; the Spaniard cares very little and leaves to us to discover him." Even the old-style stereotype of the Spanish male, the little cock (who is probably a gypsy), has this hard core of reserve, natural dignity, inside him.

I had an elegant example of this natural dignity, which is often worn so unassumingly, in a small provincial town in the Spanish uplands nearly forty years ago (things have not changed that much since - though, where they have, as in the treatment of animals, it has generally been for the better). A labourer on a building site saw me giving a tip to a beggar - one of many at that time but one who, evidently, didn't have the right credentials. Prompted by a sense of decency as a Spaniard at this exploitation of a naive foreigner, he made amends by offering me a cigarette (see Brenan's comment, earlier), no mean gesture at that time. It was important to him, through this simple and disarming act, both to apologise for the dishonorable conduct of his fellow countryman and identify with me as a fellow being irrespective of origin, race or class.

This sense of identity, allied with a pride in their heritage, continues to surprise me. I saw it years ago in the little Castilian town of Arévalo, when an old lady insisted on showing me the fountain in her private courtyard where, as she explained most persuasively, Saint Teresa of Avila had washed her feet. Likewise an old lady in Villaverde de Sandoval who showed us around a ruined Carthusian monastery. Neither of them was looking for a tourist's tip (tourists don't go to these places in any case): they were simply proud of their place and happy to share it with us. I am reminded of yet another old lady in Mansilla de las Mulas (what wonderful names these towns have!) who came up to us and asked us if we were *Asturianos*: she thought we were lost (it seems that Asturians get lost in Castile).

I have had the privilege of knowing two distinguished gentlemen from the equally distinguished city of León on the Spanish *meseta*. They are both in their mid-sixties and retired from active life. They are both courteous, generous, well informed and interested in the world around them. They both know all the landmarks, the local rivers, the traditions. They both have a close contact with, and awareness of, the physical world around them. They tend their gardens lovingly, watch the seasons go by with wonder, speak proudly of their country. The only difference between them is that, before retirement, one of them was a university professor, the other a truckdriver.

Indeed the Spanish have a consequentiality, for want of a better word, a sense of involvement only matched by the *Gründlichkeit* of the Germans - maybe another reason for the affinity felt by these two races. You see it in the intensity of Spanish children in situations where they sense the need and the opportunity to be involved, like looking after children smaller than themselves. And Spanish respect for old people is praiseworthy and practical, in the context of a falling birthrate and an aging population.

Unfortunately consequentiality stops short of respect for the environment. Maybe the sheer size and majestic desolation of the country explains why people so scrupulous about personal hygiene are so indifferent to public pollution, as evident in the huge rubbish tips sited strategically around the peninsula. They feel there's room for everything.

The quality of commitment, which is responsible for both the good news and the bad news in Spanish history, is exemplified in certain characters, both real and fictional, that have acquired world renown. Don Quixote, Ignacio de Loyola, the founder of the Jesuit order (a typically Spanish institution, like the Opus Dei), St Teresa of Avila, even a man who is now building a cathedral with his own hands on the meseta east of Madrid.

Dignity, commitment and fatalism are closely related. The serious or even sad-faced Spaniard, with his strong admixture of Moorish blood, is indeed Europe's great fatalist. *Ojalá, inchallah*, Spanish and Arabic words respectively, are only dialectically different. In his seminal book on the Civil War, *The Spanish Cockpit*[23], Franz Borkenau sums it up, quaintly but accurately as always: "The Spaniards, amid their terrible ordeal, keep quiet and poised as individuals, because they are basically healthy". So much for the folklore which would have it that the Spanish are excitable and panicky.

In this connection, no one should underestimate the contribution of the Moors, better known these days as the Arabs, to Iberian and ultimately European culture. They gave it and us much of our understanding of the world around us - the plants, the trees, irrigation, the stars, passing on to us all the wisdom of Classical Greece with added value. Despite the violence they exhibited during their invasion of the Iberian peninsula, they taught the equally brutal mediaeval world of Europe a thing or two, particularly the nuances of chivalry and the art of religious tolerance (something that, sadly, the Spanish subsequently forgot). And they helped give the Spanish their respect for the individual, their fatalism and their fierceness.

The Italians

The artless aesthetes

"Even if untrue, it is well found" ["E se non è vero è ben trovato"]
Italian aphorism

"The charm of Italy is akin to that of being in love"　　Stendhal

"The delightfully natural human beings one could always be sure of in this land of human nature unabashed"　William Dean Howell

"...Italians have always excelled in all activities in which the appearance is predominant: architecture, decoration, landscape gardening, the figurative arts, pageantry, fireworks, ceremonies, opera, and now industrial design, stage jewellery, fashions, and the cinema"　　Luigi Barzini

"The Italian quest for simplicity and harmony within the welter of human complexity"　　The Reverend John Navone

"To trust is good, not to trust is better" ["Fidarsi è bene, non fidarsi è meglio"]　　Italian proverb

"Italians are the only disturbing element in a magical land"
19th-century English traveller

"Italy is like a bumblebee. It shouldn't fly, but it does"
British TV director Richard Denton

"We need to think more like Italians"　　Washington Post

"Let me sing. I'm Italian" ["Lasciatemi cantare. Sono italiano"]
Italian lyric

The Italians are, for me, the most difficult of all Europeans to explain, yet they seem to be the least complicated. Maybe that's the reason. We spend a lot of time trying to fathom them out when, in fact, there nothing particularly to fathom. They are content as they are, they have no intention of going to war, and they love the good life: bread, love and dreams. But...

I find myself moving almost subliminally from the Spanish to the Italians because of a sideline of history at the time of the Spanish Civil War. Confronted with Italian armoured divisions, an emanation of Mussolini's braggadocio *Mare Nostrum* escapade, the Spanish had little more than rifles and donkeys. A courageous people to the point of foolhardiness, they took on the Italians who, as long as they were in their whippet tanks and fighter bombers, felt dashing and not particularly vulnerable. Unfortunately for them the weather turned nasty, heavy rain fell, the Italian tanks got stuck in the mud, the Italian planes couldn't get off the ground - and the Spanish moved in with their rifles and their donkeys and created mayhem.

That made me think, out of ignorance, that the Spanish were vastly superior to the Italians. In war, maybe, though there are plenty of Italian examples of personal bravery contrasting with their marked and admirable reluctance to get annihilated in droves. But happily war - even a struggle over issues of principle, as the Spanish Civil War was for many - is not the be-all and end-all of life. Moreover the Spanish approach to war has been, historically, rather nasty.

It was only later, having abandoned the history books and resorted to personal observation, that I discovered that the Italians (who?) are just as fine a people as the Spanish but, quite understandably, with different qualities.

I say 'who?' because there are, once again, all sorts of Italians: the Italians of the plains of the Po, who are descended from German stock even if they don't like to be reminded of the fact; the Italians of the South who could be part-Greek, part-Arab for all we and they know; and the Italians in between who may be Italians.

Not that it matters very much, since the nation only took shape 120 years ago. As Flora Lewis says[2], "Italy has a weakly organised state and an intensely clannish society whose people do not easily identify national interest with their own". Which does not mean to say that they are not proud of being Italian, quite the contrary.

And being still a fragmented country, Italy is also a flexible one: the Italians make a virtue of their weaknesses. Maybe that's what they're proud of!

Another reason for saying 'who?' is that the average Italian changes personality as fast as a chameleon changes colour, even faster. One moment everything is fine, the next moment life Italian-style gets too much for him or her, and he or she turns moody, even truculent or dismissive. The Italians are like water - they take their colour from the sky.

But that is only half the truth. Far from the simple people we for-eigners believe them to be at first sight, the Italians are in fact very complex. The purest insight comes from a fellow-country-man, Luigi Barzini [15], who argues that they lead a double life - out of a visceral sense of insecurity in an albeit beautiful but essential-ly ungovernable country.

"An Italian", he says, "will often utter grave and sincere words (dictated by wrath, jealousy, the defence of his interests and dignity, or passionate love) and, at the same time, look out of the corner of his eye to check the impression he is making on his public". This almost childlike self-awareness is one of the traits many of us for-eigners appreciate. And, further on, "In other parts of the world sub-stance always takes precedence and its external aspect is considered useful but secondary. Here, on the other hand, the show is as impor-tant as, many times more important than, reality". Anyone who has seen Vittorio De Sica posturing as the *Maresciallo* in the *Bread, Love and Dreams* film series will understand.

Despite this complexity, perhaps because of it, the Italians are delightful people - as they should be, living in god's own country. Luigi Barzini speaks of "a tense, dramatic quality, a shameless directness, about the Italians which is refreshing to foreigners accustomed to nordic self-control, to feigned or real frigidity". He also talks of the fatal charm of Italy which gives "middle-aged and resigned people the sensation of being, if not young again, at least daring and pleasing to others, and the illusion that they could still bite the fruits of life with their false teeth".

Speaking of teeth, false or real, the Italians (those that can cook, by no means all Italians) also have, in my book, the finest cooking in the world *pace* the French: "Things frankly smell, look and taste as they should, every component sharply differentiated and true to its nature", says Barzini. Forget the singing waiter syndrome, the plastic grapes and the studied gaiety: this is all part of the insecurity syndrome you have just heard about (the Italian answer to German *Angst*).

Despite their association in foreigners' eyes with *dolce far' niente*, the Italians are by no means as superficial and frivolous as other Europeans expect them to be. Many of them are extremely hard workers and, if they give the appearance of being better lovers than the rest of us, so what? Moreover they produced the most creative and democratic of all Western European cultures. Look at their mediaeval city states, where whoever happened to have the highest tower could use the force of gravity to intimidate the rest...

In that respect, their vibrant city societies and the Renaissance that followed, the Italians have a natural advantage over the Spanish. How many Europeans, for example, know who Lope de Vega, Calderon, Juan de Herrera or Granados were? There's a bigger chance they've heard of Boccaccio, Michelangelo, or Verdi - although I came across one British journalist who thought Fra Angelico was Frau Angelika, a genetic and sexual *tour de force*. The only luck the Spanish have in winning real recognition is with their painters: Velazquez, Goya and, of course, Picasso and Dali.

But we're talking about the Italians. These delightful people clearly demonstrated their creativity and flair in the Renaissance and they are still demonstrating these qualities today: in their design, in their films, even in their pop singers with their chainsaw voices. As *The Economist* put it in an editorial: "Italy beats France for style, and in culture is second to none. Yet [said with feeling] politics lets it down".

Italian excellence in art and design reflects the fact, as Barzini points out, that his fellow-countrymen have such natural acting talent: he suggests that many of them even impersonate *themselves* (the 'singing waiter syndrome'?).

Unfortunately, both Italian expatriates and foreign writers now note that this flair is deteriorating into a facile striving after effect in people who have no need for such pretensions. Stuart Miller quotes a Roman physician [24]: "The biggest change in the last twenty years has been in the way people feel and behave everyday... in the streets courtesy is forgotten, people are rushing, tired and unhappy... They have cars, fancy clothes, and now it's even boats they are after! It is a paradox, this increase in general wealth and decrease in courtesy and good humour". Is it?

Affluence is, it seems, eroding the warmheartedness and graciousness of Italian life. The traditional taste for eccentricity verges these days on the vulgar. Many Italians, including a notorious ex-Foreign Minister, look like characters from a Fellini film. Normally paragons of extreme good taste, Italian women have taken to wearing fur coats (and Swatches!) everywhere, even when skiing. As the country that imports more furs (also diamonds and whisky) than any other, they have to do something with them.

Comparing his people with the Norwegians (an unlikely match!), an Italian business executive said: "The average Italian is more disposed to exhibitionism, to show off his status symbols"[6]. "In wealth, we are like the last of the newly rich", adds Paul Bocca, a columnist with *La Repubblica* newspaper. "We don't know how to use the wealth and we have all the neuroses of the newly rich." Aided and abetted, of course, by the eternal striving after *la bella figura*...

Another old Italy hand, who has an Italian mother and spent his formative years in the country, acknowledges the parvenu element in Italian society and blames the political and business establishments for this state of affairs. He feels that materialism has 'uprooted' his people and is turning them rapidly into an exclusively 'get-rich-quick' society. He offers the awful quiz games and Z-rated films on Italian TV as evidence, and wishes his mother had been born in Spain.

But, even if it is going out of date, there is still some dignity around, maybe thanks to the Spanish who also introduced a taste for titles. I am reminded of a Felliniesque encounter with an aging *commendatore* or 'knight commander' who, bereft of financial means but well endowed with dignity and a venerable motorcar, had me tip, on his behalf, an equally aging and toothless parking attendant whose main attribute seemed to be the ability to raise his cap and repeat *commendatore* at five-second intervals. No self-esteem was lost in the process by any of the parties.

Perhaps surprisingly for such an apparently easy-going people - who also have a disarming ability to laugh at themselves when they can afford to - the Italians have a highly developed sense of perfectionism. Take the case of an Italian machinery importer who found the wide tolerances practised by his American suppliers so offensive that he had their machines recalibrated at his own cost.

Conveniently, this perfectionism is complemented by an adaptability which frequently comes to the rescue of individual Italians and of the nation as a whole. The Italians have a highly developed sense of survival. How many times has the rest of Europe and the world written them off? But, in the words of Franco Ferrarotti, one of the country's leading sociologists, "we always manage to do well whenever we are on the verge of disaster".

Economically, the Italians pulled a miraculous rabbit out of a hat in the 1960s and, despite all the twists and turns of political life, go on repeating the act. "This miracle may be more illusory and paradoxical, but it is quintessentially Italian", says Luigi D'Amato, a politician and economist. Yet the simple fact is that, in recent years, Italy has surreptitiously evolved into the world's fifth biggest industrial powerhouse.

"Se non è vero è ben trovato...": this is positive opportunism, a syndrome far removed from the Mr-Fix-It mentality of the Greeks. When Barzini speaks of "an enthusiastic feeling of improvisation", he is talking of the Italians' readiness to bend the rules - as any foreigner who thinks that Italian drivers obey city traffic lights after midnight will learn to his or her cost. Italian improvisation is an art in itself, extending to the *coloratura* principle in opera, the essentially Italian art form.

How does the balance sheet of the Italians look so far? Inventiveness, perfectionism, pragmatism. And beyond these lie the traditional clichés: wit, vivacity, verve, charm, love of life and so on, all of them true, yet all slightly dismissive. Unfairly so, since they are great qualities. The Italian 'new realism' cinema was one of the most moving, humorous and meaningful experiences of post-WWII Europe. Italian film makers demonstrated a sense of the picaresque, a Spanish term, far in excess of anything the Spanish ever imagined.

There are, of course, less certain features of the Italian mentality, even if they find their roots in the people's natural ingenuity. To use the words of a business journalist who has made a study of things foreign, "a formidable Italian strength is active inertia - the paradoxical science of seeming to run towards something while in fact retreating, a concept busily practised by local lawyers [sounds like those jokes about the Italian army]". This is almost reflexive, a form of passive resistance developed over two millenia of foreign

131

occupation by the Greeks, Normans, French, Germans, Austrians, Americans, and many others."

It may also explain the philosophical fatalism of the Italians - that expressive shrug of the shoulders *('che sarà sarà')* - and a remarkable passivity, even patience, in situations that would drive any other European absolutely mad. Yet they can be moody to the point of truculence.

The mercurial nature of the Italian character should not be confused with a lack of principles. The Italians do indeed have principles, and one in particular: the importance of enjoying life to the full and being grateful for life's blessings. This is an artless wisdom which we other Europeans could well afford to adopt. In well-groomed Italian women, it even extends to unselfconsciously stroking one another's hair in public.

The active inertia spoken of earlier can even be a career choice for an increasing number of younger Italians, it would seem. Writing in the 1980s, Stuart Miller reported that "70 percent of the generation of Italy's famous economic boom, the kids born between 1960 and 1965, albeit coming on the labour market during a time of national budgetary cutbacks, have the following aspiration: they want to find a *posto fisso*, a permanent government job, the kind that cannot by law ever be cut from any budget, even if society doesn't need it anymore".

Luigi Barzini speaks of *sistemazione*, the dream of most Italians: "It does not necessarily signify hard work, responsibility, good wages, and the possibility of getting ahead, but often nothing more than a mediocre but durable position, protected from unseen events, with a predictable career, some moral authority, and a pension at the end". Plus the opportunity to moonlight on the side.

One such excessively durable situation was brought to light in the late-1960s when an auditor uncovered a department for 'the regularisation of fascist affairs', some 15-people strong, which the government did not know existed. The present administration is well aware, it seems, of the continued existence of other outdated yet still state-bankrolled organisations. One of them is the National Association for the Distribution of Medicine to the Allies, another the Society for the Corrective Education of Miners of the Ancient Kingdom of Sardinia in Turin.

The 'jobs for the boys' phenomenon is as deepset in Italian society, particularly in the south, as it is anywhere else in Europe. As one Italian journalist disarmingly points out, "we have always asked the saints to intercede on our behalf".

These practices stem from the political tradition of party patronage: the trade in votes and favours known as *clientelismo* (what the *Financial Times* calls "a system of *cheques* and balances"!). A related phenomenon, *lottizzazione*, is the habit of filling top public-sector and banking posts with political acolytes. Sadly, the country doesn't seem to have enough of these jobs, elevated or lowly, to satisfy everyone.

"Italians", says Robert Graham, talking about the 'great *mamma* state' in the *Financial Times*, "are still greedily sucking this gigantic breast in thousands of legal ways: jobs for life, indexed wages, discounts, subsidies and generous pensions. The system is ever more abused: from illicit tapping into electricity supplies to the 16 civil servants found receiving overtime - on the basis that they were working 29 hours a day".

But the 'great *mamma* state' now offers less opportunity for breast-fed Italians than it used to. It is also the cause of very mixed emotions in the mind of the average citizen: dependence on the one hand, revulsion on the other. There is an instinctive fear of central (and therefore by definition corrupt) government, based on a series of nasty historical precedents. Respect is not encouraged by the fact that, at the time of writing, the country has had over 50 governments in as many years.

In the words of an editorial in the *International Herald Tribune,* historically "Italians more often than not experienced government as a hostile power controlled by foreign interests". And, now, even the Vatican has roundly charged the Italian state with being "without law, feudal... dominated by privilege and threatened by criminality" (couldn't the same be said of the Vatican?).

In other areas of endeavour than the administrations, similar systems apply: cliques, gangs, *camorras, camarillas, cabalas* (the C-words) - all specifically Italian versions of the 'club'. This herd instinct is so highly developed that it moves Barzini to exclaim that "Italians are not, as foreigners believe, individualists". Well, well!

But forgetting the boom generation, jobs for the boys, *Tangentopoli*, the bankers, the Mafia, etc, how do the Italians that are left harness their indisputable natural inventiveness - creativity, flair, whatever - to everyday life?

Well, for a start, they keep a lot of things, including profits, up their sleeves: the *economia sommersa* must have something to do with the country's ability to execute economic U-turns whenever it needs to. There is even the well-known case of a ceramics factory near Rome which was mounted on wheels in order to evade the tax collector.

All you see of the national economy is the tip of the iceberg. Or, as an Italian businessman put it, with a typically disarming turn of phrase: "Other Western economies are like battleships, beautifully constructed but easily torpedoed. The Italian economy is a raft - and how do you sink a raft?" He omitted to mention the bit underneath.

Tax evasion comes as naturally to the Italians as it does to other Europeans. An Italian MP puts it succinctly: "In exchange for enduring some of the worst public services in Western Europe, Italians count on the authorities turning a blind eye to fiddling on tax returns. This is our silent pact". Yes, but the reason for such poor service from the state railways and postal services is precisely that their employees resent having demands made on them when they are much more interested in their second or third jobs (80 per cent of all government employees in Rome are reckoned to indulge in this habit).

A *Reuters* report puts it bluntly: "Tax evasion is as much a part of the Italian way of life as *pasta*." So is moonlighting. Yet, while the Italians will go to inordinate lengths to avoid paying taxes, they cheerfully lend their savings to the mother-country. "In a way, Italians treat the state as the homemaker in a family", says Luciano De Crescenzo, a popular social philosopher. "They work and earn money and gladly give their earnings to the state to spend so it will make their lives comfortable and secure."

Italians' ability to act pragmatically and respond fast to necessity or opportunity is encouraged, in the business sphere, by the structure of their industry - essentially small-to-medium sized companies, many of them privately (read 'family') owned, like the machinery company mentioned earlier.

The concept of family ownership may also conjure up images of the Mafia, but the family has its own *raison d'être* outside gang warfare, both in business and in private life. As Luigi Barzini says, "the Italy of the families is definitely the real Italy, distilled from the experiences of centuries, while the Italy of the laws and institutions is partly make-believe, the country Italians would like to believe was or will be but know is not". These days, where the family offers and earns loyalty, the state earns cynicism or outright hostility.

Barzini's *The Italians* dates back to 1964. In her more recent book, Flora Lewis quotes a survey which showed that 86 per cent of adults still felt family unity "must be defended at all costs" and 57 per cent pronounced "family honour" as coming before the rights and interests of its individual members. Yet, surprisingly, 76 per cent considered children "too much of a responsibility". This jars with the *mamma*-oriented tradition best known to foreigners.

After all, the exclamation *mamma mia*! has no equivalent in any other European language. One foreigner I know, a Belgian businessman (probably the closest European equivalent to an Italian businessman), regrets he doesn't live in Italy because, as he puts it, "I could then be sure of getting a plane home the same day. Italian pilots, regardless of weather conditions, cry *mamma*! and simply take off...".

Affinity with their own kind, as well as insecurity, seems to encourage Italian businessfolk to hunt in packs - again challenging the stereotype of the Italian as an individualist. The disruptive effect they can have on other business cultures comes up again and again. A research consultant I know comments that, in international gatherings, the Italians are remarkable for keeping very much to themselves. The Spanish by comparison - in stark contrast to the stereotype of the proud, distant *hidalgo* - are much less exclusive in their relationships.

A significant feature of the Italian business scene is the very high percentage of organisations employing less than 200 people, partly because of the constraints put on larger companies by Italian law. So, as a company grows, it simply spawns another to supply it, for example, with components. To outsiders, the taxman included, the link is not evident.

This dynamic element in Italian business is, sadly, matched by the inertia of the country's state-owned businesses and a serious lack of large companies in the private sector. Many of the bigger organisations, both public and private-sector, are in any case controlled by a gerontocracy in step with the political elite.

Equally sadly, another major element in Italian business, mainly at the bottom end of the scale though not exclusively so, is the Mafia. In 1991 it was estimated that 60 per cent of all retail businesses - shops, bars and restaurants - were paying extortion money to organised crime. What started as a *Mezzogiorno* speciality is now spreading to the whole country.

A peculiarly Italian phenomenon is the concentration of small industries, competitive as well as complementary ones, within a limited geographical area. This generates a sense of solidarity which allows them to take on the rest of the world. Examples are the automotive and engineering component suppliers around Bologna, the specialised steel makers of Brescia, the textile firms of Prato and Biella, the tilemakers of Sassuolo and Reggio Emilia, the furniture manufacturers of Pesaro and the domestic appliance manufacturers of northern Italy who make 70 per cent of all European 'white goods'. Nothing quite like this exists anywhere else in Europe, so it must say something about the Italians...

Of course, their natural design flair helps. Barzini maintains the Italians are obsessed with symmetry, which he also attributes to insecurity. Obviously, though, this is a far cry from the more rigid, modular approach of the Germans - the *Baukasten* principle - which is, in the writer's view, more prompted by a love for functionality than by *Angst*. It has to be said, though, that Italian attachment to symmetry sometimes gets the better of their good taste. Venice's 'new town', Mestre, reminds me of nothing more (or less) than East Berlin on a bad day.

The search for balance in Italian design goes a long way back. Many of their mediaeval, pre-Renaissance, cities were planned in six more or less equal parts (a concept which was later modified to four by the French, hence their *quartiers*, viz Quartier Latin). Later, they were equally successful in breaking the basic rules of symmetry, with their exaggerated perspectives, their theatrical settings and other baroque effects. These could be architectural analogies of the Italian psyche: theatricality in a world where things are not quite what they seem to be.

Italian design skills were summed up for me in a food processing plant I visited in Poland. On one side of the building was a German canning line: functional, down-to-earth, efficient, technically advanced but with no particular imagination. On the other, an Italian tomato paste line: a symphony in stainless steel, sculptural, equally functional but with such flair and style. A tomato paste line! And, when I asked, I was told the Germans had also bid for this line, but the Italians had undercut them.

At the time of writing, Italy again looks like a basket case: the public services are collapsing, labour costs are soaring and the social security system is close to bankruptcy. But never underestimate the Italians: they're full of surprises. To quote an Italian phrase, *finire in bellezza*!

The Belgians

The openminded opportunists

"'Belgianisation' - the abandonment of national responsibility in favour of totally commercial values"   Leon Trotsky

"I'm not a tart because I'm the owner of a four-storey building, so think about that!" ["Je ne suis pas putain puisque je suis propriétaire d'un immeuble de quatre étages, figurez-vous!"]
                                        Overheard on a Brussels street

"Access to the maternity services is strictly forbidden to children under 14 years of age" ["L'accès des services de maternité est strictement interdit aux enfants de moins de 14 ans"]
                                        Notice in Brussels hospital

"I've paid for your seat, don't get up!" ["J'ai payé ta place, ne bouge pas!"]
                    Belgian mother to child offering his tram seat to an old lady

"Buy the Belgian grape. Foodful and healing"   Advertising panel

"Monsieur le Juge, je parle français sais-tu!... Nous sommes de braves gens, il n'y a pas d'architek dans la famille"
                    Untranslatable quote from Marollian legend of De Skieven Arkitek

"Do not throw foreign bodies in the toilet"   Sign on Belgian ferry

140

The best way to understand Belgium is to imagine a Belgian road junction. Four drivers coming from four different directions, none of them giving way. One of the cars contains the Flemish, the second the Walloons, the third the Brussels Community and the fourth the German speakers from the *Ostkantone*. They all meet in the middle, but they don't crash. They simply block one another's way, including their own.

That sums up Belgian politics today and also typifies the sadly blinkered mentality of many influential people who should know better. Belgian politics, described by *The Economist* as "straight from Ruritania, via Freedonia", are byzantine. It is no reflection on the driving skills of the Belgians. They drive as well, or as badly, as any other European nationality these days. The stories about bad driving simply demonstrate the lasting power of folklore.

But many Belgians do indeed suffer from lack of imagination, even tunnel vision. They take cover behind phrases like "that's impossible!" or, more frequently, "we've never done it like that!" in Flemish or French, or both, or even English (they're great linguists). This results in kafkaesque confrontations with communal administrations where you begin to wonder whether *you* really exist.

Yet lack of imagination can also be a great strength, since there's less danger of distraction. And it would also be wrong to suggest that the Belgians are not creative: they are extremely imaginative in well-defined areas such as strip cartoons (Hergé, etc), singers (Brel, Adamo, Johnny Halliday, not to mention Annie Cordy), humourists (Raymond Devos) and showbiz generally (even Christine Ockrent of French TV fame is Belgian).

The real problem lies elsewhere. Belgium, simply, is not a country, it is an accident of history, other people's history. It could even be seen as a *happy* accident since Belgium has the enormous distinction of bringing together the two great western European traditions, the Germanic and the Latin, but those Belgians who admit this are probably in a minority at the moment. Yet anyone who suggests that there is no individual awareness of being Belgian, no sentiment, no pride, has failed to talk to the people or is politically inspired.

Of course, no one would deny that Belgium as a nation state is a nonsense. Created in 1830 from the leftovers of Western Europe, it happens to take in both sides of the northern frontier of the

Roman Empire. The *diutisc*-speakers, with a stretch of the imagination today's Flemish, still look down on the descendents of the settlers to the south - with an even greater stretch of the imagination, today's Walloons. Yet among themselves, despite such accidents of history, the so-called Belgians have managed to make something worthwhile out of this little country.

The Belgians are the Italians of northern Europe. They have a pragmatism, both in politics and in everyday life, and a nose for opportunity that has seen the country through many crises. They can also work very hard but, like the Italians, much of the effort is conducted below the surface. In the words of a German woman journalist long established in Belgium and very happily married to an Antwerper, "the Belgians are essentially anarchists at heart."

The existence of a parallel economy, as in Italy, is matched by the influence of an establishment mafia clustered, in this case, around the Société Générale and a few other major holding companies. The 'old lady' as she is unaffectionately known (particularly unaffectionately by the Flemish, since the Société Générale represented all the best and worst in the Brussels francophile and francophone élite) has, after a flirt with Carlo de Benedetti, now revealed her true character by succumbing to the blandishments of the French.

In any case, despite the general belief that until recently, she controlled some 40 per cent of the Belgian economy, the Société Générale is *not* Belgium. The true Belgium is a politically elusive and geographically complicated entity which, more than any other region, offers a microcosm of Europe past and future. In this relatively small area, you have at least three races (apart from the substantial European community), Romance and Germanic languages, and a richness and variety of heritage and nature which other countries, even large ones, have difficulty in matching. Sadly much of this remains unknown to the Belgians.

Maybe being the prey of so many other nations - the Spanish, the French, the Austrians, the Dutch, the Germans - has something to do with it. After all, almost everybody has laid claim to Belgium at some time or another. So the Belgians, quite naturally, have stayed close to their roots. They have a bit of a 'bunker' mentality. Launch yourself at them as a complete stranger and the first reaction will be suspicion.

But if you show that you are friendly, you will eventually earn a friendly response. This lesson came the hard way to a group of foreigners who set out to chronicle the opportunities for English-language education at Belgian universities: rank suspicion of their initiative was followed by enthusiastic cooperation. Personal criticism is ill-received, self-criticism is at times excessive and often unjustified.

The deep-rooted Belgian instinct for survival obviously has its good side and its bad side. The good side is pragmatism, the bad side is muddle. Although the country is now starting to get its act together with untypical concepts like 'zonings' and industrial parks, you can still see plenty of physical evidence of this muddled approach to life: splendid old parish churches stuck in the middle of oil refineries, oases of opulent green stuck between regimented streets of terrace houses, radar dishes looming over 12th-century monuments. It has its charm as well as its horrors - an amiable disreputableness of the kind you can easily find in neighbouring France, but never in neighbouring Holland or Germany.

There is also an absence of humbug in Belgian public life - something that often surprises Anglo-Saxons and others. When acting for a foreign company that was closing down a subsidiary in a small town called, let's say, Molle, I received a letter from a government minister asking for reconsideration of the decision. The latter said exactly what one would expect in such circumstances except for a footnote which read: "PS, please note that I am the mayor of Molle". Maybe that's why serving as a mayor and a government minister at one and the same time is no longer tolerated in Belgium!

History has taught the Belgians to be defensive, maybe a bit complacent, even fatalistic. Foreigners are sometimes surprised how little people, even in high office, react to criticism. A pity because they have so many qualities including, paradoxically, an admirable open-mindedness towards the rest of the world, despite all the dirty tricks played on them by history.

This is in stark contrast to their frankly ridiculous narrow-mindedness on their own so-called community affairs. Imagine a Flemish commune that advertises the Burgomaster's Ball with the admonition "no admittance to beggars, hawkers or French-speakers". Yes, in that order!

If they do try to get their own back on the rest, the Belgians do so by changing the names on the road signs (so that it requires a very educated Frenchman to know that, as far as the Flemish are concerned, Lille is Rijsel, etc) or by restructuring the Brussels telephone directory in line with their internecine quarrels to the point that it is virtually unusable for anyone who doesn't have a very precise knowledge of the local geography.

There is even the case of a well-meaning Brussels resident who offered funds for the preservation of a venerable tree in the commune of Uccle/Ukkel. He chose to do this with the help of an ecological trust which, probably like the tree, happened to have *'francophone'* roots. When the initiative came to the attention of the Flemish minority on the (let's be careful here) Ukkel/Uccle council, they insisted that a second tree be designated and sponsored by a *'nederlands sprekend'* organisation. The result is that Uccle/ Ukkel - Ukkel/Uccle now has a French-speaking tree and a Dutch-speaking one, both of them protected.

In fact it is particularly nonsensical to talk about the 'Belgians' as I have been doing. You have the clean-limbed Flemings with their innate good taste, severe and stern-faced, firm and factual, the intellectual ones wearing the beards of mediaeval Germans, some of them as sallow as victims of Count Dracula, others as swarthy as gipsies (their Spanish blood is irrefutable). Yet the Flemish middle class also boasts some wildly non-intellectual members who behave like a cross between a mad professor and an unhorsed cowboy.

Then you have the ruddy-faced Walloons, hearty and short-winded, overemphatic in voice and gesture, often over life-size (there are Flemings like that, too, as Brueghel the Elder showed). They share, with the *classe moyenne* of Brussels - a phrase not to be confused with 'middle class' - a fondness for knees-up-mother-brown and related social activities.

Then you have the Brussels bourgeoisie, often pretentious, sometimes plain, the worst being the women who demonstrate their BCBG *(bon chic bon genre)* potential by being superficially over-formal or over-friendly and fundamentally poisonous. And then you have the ordinary folk, scruffy and amiable. And of course the German-speaking minority, who have belatedly qualified for a special mention at the end of this chapter.

All these, with the admixture of nationalities drawn to the European institutions, international organisations and the headquarters of major corporations, have created a unique multilingual and multicultural environment. But let's hope the Belgians don't spoil it, either through their silly internecine squabbles or through the opportunistic attitude of developers, landlords, traders and others towards the Eurocrats, collectively and individually. Otherwise, the day could come when Brussels will be better known as the *Ex*-Capital of Europe.

But, with such provisos, it still has to be said that the cosmopolitan environment of Belgium produces some fine and relatively unspoilt human beings from all levels of society - individuals whose only real fault is the fact that other people know they are Belgians and therefore tend to make jokes about them, partly because of their accents. The worst offenders are the French, yet what the French understand about *égalité* would fit on the little finger of a Belgian's left hand. Even the tax inspectors have a human quality and a sense of fairness that would put their peers in most other European countries to shame.

The French jokes about the Belgians (as well as the Dutch ones) tend to be more silly than revealing and bear the hallmarks of all jokes about immediate neighbours: they are based on ignorance as much as prejudice. Unfortunately, they encourage ingrained attitudes. I remember the words of a French businessman, who quite possibly didn't even realise there is a Flemish-speaking half of Belgium: *"oh, les Wallons sont superficiels - ce sont des grands 'hâbleurs'"*. In fact, even the Flemish authorities find their toughest task is persuading ignorant foreigners that there is a *second* language in Belgium - and it is actually the *first*.

The main French TV chain ran a talkshow on *Les Belges* which was notable for two indiscretions. The principal Belgian participant, the president of the Brussels Region, presented a copy of Manneken Pis in French colours. On his side, the French TV moderator thought the person offering him this dubious gift was the Belgian Prime Minister. (In this connection confusion over Belgian Prime Ministers is rife. There are three of them, one national, one Flemish and one Walloon: all three turned up in Japan at the same time, unbeknown to each another, and convinced the Japanese *qu'ils sont fous, ces Belges*).

Needless to say the Belgians have their own jokes about the French, also the Dutch, but very few about their other neighbours, the Germans. There could be at least two reasons for this: either the

145

fact that the Flemish majority have a certain sympathy for the German way of doing things, or because the Belgians find the Germans insufficiently eccentric to tell stories about them.

It is less easy for the Belgians to tell jokes about themselves because of their identity crisis and the problems of deciding which side everyone is on. This situation is not helped by the fact that the Belgian you meet with a Flemish-sounding name turns out to be French-speaking, and *vice versa*. Even a seminal piece of community law, the Scheurs-Couvreur proposal, was named after a French-speaking politician with a Flemish name (Scheurs) and a Flemish colleague with a French one (Couvreur).

Incidentally, the importance attached to making a proper distinction between the Flemish and the Walloon cultures throws Belgian advertising agency copywriters into a paroxysm of invention in order to avoid coming up with a direct translation from the 'other' language. The result looks decidedly silly when it turns up on the same advertisement hoarding or the same product pack: how can a deodorant be called *Senteur des Iles* and *Coralfris* at one and the same time?

Having waited so long for them historically, the Belgians *insist* on their individual rights - encouraged by a crazy hangover from a highway code which, at unmarked junctions, gives priority to the driver coming from the right. This leads to the crossroads hiatus described at the beginning of this chapter, where everyone glares at everyone else: history speaks from behind the wheel of a car. And the foreigner who conducts a saucy road manoeuvre of any kind is likely to be classed as mad or incompetent, whether the manoeuvre is dangerous or not.

Of course the truth is that the so-called Belgians, like virtually all European 'nations' other than the Basques, are a pretty bastard race and have gone on interbreeding happily regardless of separate linguistic communities and idiocies like that. But whether Flemish, Walloon or hybrid in origin, most of them apply the attitudes and value judgments of the 'community' in which they live. The people in the northern, Dutch-speaking half of the country have a much stronger civic instinct and sense of social responsibility (something some Flemish employers exploit shamelessly) than their counterparts in the French-speaking south where militancy, even bloodymindedness, is part of the game.

Attitudes to the use of money also differ between the communities. Where the Walloons can be fairly liberal with what money they have (and it may not be much these days), spending a fair proportion of the household budget on food and other fun things, the Flemish will use their money to impress the neighbours. In the view of a Jewish Brussels antique dealer - as neutral an observer as you can expect to find in this country - the Walloons spend where the Flemish are traditionally tightfisted. That sounds like guilt by association with the Dutch.

The overriding features of the Flemish culture, best demonstrated by the females of the species, are primness and a materialistic attitude to life. Surprisingly, even in their great art cities, they can be breathtakingly parochial busybodies. But the culture is very much there, often forcibly fed on both sides of the country: where the Walloons entertain with slot machines and sideshows, the Flemish offer folk music and farm animals.

One of the great qualities of Belgian society, the upside of the 'bunker' syndrome, is the importance attached to the family and the community. A person from Lier for example (where, you may well ask?) will be terribly upset if you take him for an Antwerper, even if only eight miles separate the two towns. In some cases neighbouring towns speak different dialects and have difficulty in understanding one another. If you happen to be a foreigner, you sense the intimacy of local life, a far cry from the anonymity of existence elsewhere.

But the real nucleus is the family itself, where the different generations are mutually supportive and share their existence, even to the extent of many wedded children staying in the parental home for the first years of their marriage. It may help explain why I have rarely, if ever, seen a young Belgian girl with a 'sugardaddy': they have the real thing. This admirable sense of family, even if overdone, also extends to the wholehearted and totally unselfconscious integration of Third World children, adopted or not, into the home.

Provision is often also made for the grandparents, either under the same roof or close by: this does not prevent them feeling treated like second-class citizens by their nearest and dearest, according to a recent Eurobarometer survey. Maybe the reason not more old folks end up in homes is because these rather dubious institutions - ironically dubbed *Ma Paix, Tranquillité du Bois, Avondstilte* and the like - are almost always located on the noisiest traffic intersections, close to railway lines, etc. At least some senior citizens have uninterrupted entertainment as the cars crash and the trains go by...

Inevitably there are some Belgians who find the family environment unduly stifling. They include a few who have been known to go out of their minds, or off the map, when they should have been chauffeuring the wife's mother on her ritual Sunday outing. There are others who take refuge in things like pigeon-fancying.

A popular car sticker, with drawings of pigeons and hearts, reads *mijn man houdt duiven en ik zie ze vliegen* ("my husband keeps pigeons and I watch them fly"). This is the Flemish equivalent of a *double entendre* (*"Ik zie ze vliegen"* means much the same as "I'm bats"). Yet, in addition to humour, the sticker demonstrates the importance of the pigeon culture and a certain machismo.

But generally the social system works, and works well. Belgians have the best-trained children and the worst-trained dogs. And the Belgian family survives as an example to all other European societies, the Spanish included.

A patriarchal, even autocratic, spirit also survives in Belgian industry outside the major holdings. I had good evidence of this in the response of a secretary when I asked to speak to her boss: "He's on holiday and no decisions are taken in his absence" (*"Il est en vacances et aucune décision n'est prise en son absence"*). Even more outrageous was the public avowal of another boss that "I need mediocre people" (*"J'ai besoin de médiocres"*).

You will note that, in both cases, the people were French speakers. As in normal life, the differences between the Flemish and the French-speaking communities show up in business. No Flemish entrepreneur, however self-serving, would ever make such an admission to the press. A headhunter reports that when he calls 'sources' for leads on potential candidates, the Flemish always cooperate openly whereas the French speakers, Brussels or Walloon, are typically reticent.

But secrecy is symptomatic of many sectors of Belgian business. Sometimes, companies really have something to hide. Mostly, they think it's nobody else's business. A general manager went on record not long ago with the following words: "Our company has no obligation to make things public. Our sector is very concentrated [like a lot of other sectors, as it happens]. Therefore we take extreme care to avoid information getting through to our competitors".

In such matters, as in many others, the Belgians are pretty shameless. An international journalist resident many years in Brussels says they have no "blush factor".

Like French industry, Belgian industry is still dominated by engineers, though the marketing people are slowly making their influence felt. A study by the PA Consulting Group found that Belgian manufacturers focus too little on what products they make and too much on the process by which they are made. Others comment that Belgians are stronger in day-to-day management than in long-term planning and, rather surprisingly, don't perform too well in an international marketing environment. One thing they *are* good at is straightforward exporting: the average Belgian salesman can sell refrigerators to eskimos. Unfortunately most of the products made in Belgium today come from factories owned by foreign groups. Belgium is becoming a satellite economy.

This sense of dependence, more exactly vulnerability to external events, was evident in the opening days of the Gulf War when many Belgians revealed a deep-set and atavistic siege mentality. Within 24 hours of the outbreak, stocks of many essential products - sugar, pasta, flour, coffee, cooking oil - had disappeared from retailers' shelves. Foreigners were amazed: one woman was seen leaving a supermarket with 70 kilos of washing powder in her trolley.

This kneejerk reaction throws light into the murkier depths of the Belgian mind. They seem to share the siege mentality (and some other things) with the Italians, who also had to be asked to resist the hoarding instinct at the outset of the Gulf War. Memories of past deprivation are certainly strong in the older age groups: most Belgians coped relatively well during WWII, thanks to a thriving black market, and some of them even have something to show for it today!

Maybe Leon Trotsky was right: the Belgians have abandoned national responsibility in favour of totally commercial values. In fact, when Napoleon talked about a "nation of shopkeepers" (or was it Samuel Adams?), he should have been thinking of the Belgians, not the English. Belgian tradesfolk, both Flemish and Walloon, are so adept at making a sale that they sometimes seem preprogrammed, responding to customers' demands in a weirdly mechanistic way.

The Belgians do have a 'shopkeeper' mentality, for all the reasons mentioned earlier. They are indeed materialistic people, but generally in the right sense, *pace* the Gulf War. They have a natural affinity with creature comforts, the sort of things that money will buy, like good food, a cosy home (every Belgian has 'a brick in his belly'), a smart car, and delicious beers with names like *Verboden Vrucht* and *Mort Subite*.

They also have a remarkable affinity with the world around them. Though there are glaring exceptions at the industrial level, individually they respect nature and care for it in a way that makes the countryside look well groomed without being over-organised. Both Flemish and Walloons tend to be born with green fingers, and nobody grows taller or more luxuriant trees.

The Belgians have learned the art of sharing the pleasures of the good life, both with their own kind and with foreigners (read Walloons in the case of the Flemish and *vice versa*, plus real foreigners). There's nothing much wrong with that. Of course some of them, mainly the metropolitan climbers, are exceptionally status-conscious in a money-related way and tend to make devastating judgments on the social relevance or irrelevance of others, particularly those in proximity.

Unfortunately this has recently taken a nasty turn with the emergence of right-wing racism - one can only hope that this reflects as much revulsion at the intrigues of mainstream politics as anything else. In fairness, it has to be said that xenophobia and anti-semitism are not part of the Belgians' daily diet: of the 60,000 Jews living in the country at the outset of WWII, more than half survived thanks to the compassion and decency of the ordinary people. There is still a tradition of providing foster homes for the less fortunate of this world, regardless of origin.

Due to the byzantine nature of Belgian politics, compounded by the latest crop of scandals, the country's legislators have largely succeeded in alienating the electorate. They do however illustrate well the strengths and weaknesses of the country. Individually, Belgians are brilliant opportunists but, collectively, they lack cohesion. So, sadly, the whole system falls into disrepute.

On the subject of mores, the contrast between Belgian attitudes and those of their neighbours to the north (see next chapter) is as marked as everything else. Witness the tongue-in-cheek reaction of a Belgian politician to a press report that two Dutch mayors had got into trouble when asking for directions to a local house of ill-fame: "In Belgium such a thing would be unimaginable: we *know* the way."

It would be nice to finish on this note, which says so much about the essentially no-nonsense attitude of many Belgians. But I have something to add, as a result of my shabby treatment of the German-speaking community in the *Ostkantone*, whom I referred to in the first edition of this book as "well, German"...

As I found out on a subsequent tour of the region's schools, this well-intentioned description is considered by the younger generation as little less than libellous: their Frankish forefathers settled in the region in the 6th century AD. But the real problem is that, annexed by the Kingdom of Belgium in 1918 and subjected, before and after, to the historical irrationalities that are typical of this crazy little part of the world, they have become more Belgian than the Belgians.

The key to this search for an identity - which runs completely counter to the attitudes of Belgians of longer standing, both Flemish and Walloons - is a nasty little episode at the end of WWII, when the government deprived those who had continued to work under the Nazi occupiers as administrators, schoolteachers, etc of all their civil rights.

This act of civic vindictiveness has produced a generation, now emerging from college, that is distancing itself as much as it possibly can from the German culture. In the circumstances, the only way out is to be 'Belgian'. When Edward Mortimer of the *Financial Times* asked one of them what he would do in the event of the breakup of Belgium, he replied: "We are the only real Belgians... If Belgium breaks up, we'll probably ask to join Luxembourg". A strange comment on our times!

Equally strange is some of the recent history of the *Ostkantone*. There is a town tucked into the corner bordering Germany and the Netherlands which used to luxuriate under the name of 'Neutral Moresnet'. It, and its neighbouring community of Kelmis/La Calamine, were once home to a zinc carbonate or smithsonite mine, now abandoned. But the site was of sufficient strategic importance in 1815 to make it the subject of a condominium between the Kingdom of the United Netherlands and the Kingdom of Prussia. The former was supplanted in 1830 by the Kingdom of Belgium and the latter, in 1870, by the *Deutsches Reich*. But throughout, until the abandonment of the mine early this century, Moresnet remained admirably 'Neutral'.

If only the rich and varied country that is Belgium today could have been declared neutral too...

The Luxembourgers
The introvert internationalists

"Of all the countries I have visited, the Grand Duchy of Luxembourg is the smallest, but it is the one that has charmed me most, and where hospitality has been most simple and cordial"
Winston Churchill

"Prosperous little oasis"   Financial Times

"Too small to be a country, too big to be a town"   Irving Berlin

"A patient, home-loving, stalwart little nation"
Arthur Cooper-Pritchard

"Here there is so much greatness married with grace, so much earnestness mingled with charm..." ["Hier findet sich so viel Größe mit Anmut, so viel Ernst mit Lieblichkeit verbunden..."]
Johann Wolfgang von Goethe

"They have all the pernicketiness of the French with the boorishness of the Germans and none of the dignity either"   Bill Gosling

"They are hard-working and thrifty, phlegmatic yet hospitable; and somewhat conservative in outlook. Less dour than the Germans and less animated than the French, their essential feature is perhaps their good-natured robust individualism"
US Naval Intelligence Division

"Luxembourg only differs from Munich's North Cemetery in that the North Cemetery is livelier" [Luxemburg unterscheidet sich vom Münchener Nordfriedhof eigentlich nur dadurch, dass es auf dem Nordfriedhof viel heiterer zugeht"]   Saphir

Egged on by Winston Churchill's words of encouragement, it is hardly surprising that the good people of Luxembourg hold fast to the motto expressed in their native Lëtzebuergesch, a distinctive patois deriving from Middle German, of *'Mir wëlle bleiwen wat mir sin'* ['We want to remain what we are'].

Churchill had, after all, discovered during his visit to the Grand Duchy in 1945 that the Luxembourg Minister of Foreign Affairs was also Minister of Viticulture. As he said at the time, "if all Ministers of Foreign Affairs were at the same time Minister of Viticulture, world affairs would be much better than they are!"

The words of the Luxembourg motto, *'Mir wëlle bleiwen wat mir sin'*, is taken from a poem written by a Luxembourg bard. In itself, it tells you something about the character of the people. The sentiment expressed, while full of good sense, conveys a mood of self-satisfaction, something that is not far removed from the mentality of this *burger* folk.

Jul Christophory speaks in his book *Luxembourgeois, qui êtes-vous?* [25] of a learned Luxembourger with the unlikely but appropriate name of Dr Antidotus who said that, if his fellow-countryfolk stuck to the motto, they would be *petit bourgeois* to the end of time. Dr Antidotus said that in 1866.

Everything about Luxembourg and the Luxembourgers (Christophory calls them 'Luxos' for simplicity) tends to make good sense. This is another way of saying that life *à la luxembourgeoise* can be dull. The Luxembourgers sound smug and provincial yet, by vocation, they are very international - and not just because of the international banks.

In the words of an eminent Luxo working with the Commission of the European Union (another important international presence), "the shrinking of our borders has not made us Luxembourgers abandon our deep feeling of belonging to a community defending the same values. We were here before the bankers and we'll be here after they've gone."

The official catalogue of the 1989 exhibition, marking the 150th anniversary of the sovereign state, commented that "the history of Luxembourg is a continual oscillation between two poles; opening up to the outside world and turning in on oneself. The first dominates most frequently, because the Luxembourger has a sense of reality, but the second is a temptation that is rarely absent."

Yet 'turning in on oneself' is, in Luxembourg terms, a cosmopolitan act in its own right. Of the 400,000 or so Luxembourgers, 125,000 come from immigrant families, mainly Portuguese, but also Italian, Spanish and other.

A Belgian journalist researching for a feature on the country remarked that, in the average Luxembourg restaurant (and where else would a Belgian journalist do his research?), he was able to order his spaghetti in German, have a Yugoslav waiter (those were the days!) serve him a glass of Bordeaux, pay the bill with Dutch florins and *'filer à l'anglaise'* ('take French leave') after a glass of vodka. It was in the personality of the country, he said, to be able to do all these things.

A Luxembourger, Josiane Kartheiser, said the same thing in a different way: "We speak Lëtzebuergesch, are sentenced in court in French and colonised by Springer [the publisher] in German. We have Italian wives, Portuguese names and Spanish neighbours. The Americans infiltrate our economy and the English fill our bars."[26]

Independence, under the treaty of 1839, came late in Luxembourg's identifiable history, which started as a County in the year 963 and continued as a Duchy in 1354. Before becoming the Grand Duchy of today, it passed through the hands of John the Blind, Philip the Good and Charles the Mad and, as if that weren't enough, reported to the French Ministry of Forests for a while, before becoming the private property of the King of the Netherlands. Fortunately for the Luxembourgers, things have settled down since.

To demonstrate its cosmopolitanism at the same time as its parochiality, Luxembourg communicates in four languages: French in matters of economy and law, and in all official functions; English in banking and finance as well as, with French, in business generally; German in the news media and for reading and writing; and Lëtzebuergesch as the normal language of conversation. Such versatility demands an acute sense of occasion! As Jul Christophory says, "our cultural identity can surely not be viewed outside our particular language situation. It shapes all our interests and attitudes."[27]

Arguments about the linguistic status of Lëtzebuergesch are known to raise blood pressures locally. Some assert it belongs to the family of West Middle German dialects called *Moselfränkisch*, others claim it is a language in its own right. Whatever the truth, it was elevated to the status of official language by an act of parliament in 1984.

Luxembourgers from the northeastern corner of the country - can you imagine that? - speak a dialect called 'Echternoocher' (after the chef-lieu of Echternach), southerners speak 'Minett'. According to Joelle Diderich, writing in *The European*, "there are seven variations in between". Lëtzebuergesch spelling, regardless of dialect, was established by government decree in 1976.

Physically, according to the *Geographical Handbook Series* published by US Naval Intelligence in 1944 (what on earth where they doing there?), the Luxos "are mainly broad-headed, are of medium stature and are dark rather than fair". Christophory's book also cites Henry Miller's comment that "the faces of the inhabitants were stamped with a sort of cow-like bliss".

The country is European history in microcosm - it couldn't be anything else since it is only some 2,500 km2 and has been invaded 22 times. In this last respect, it has had much the same experience as its neighbour, Belgium, and has acquired many of the same reflexes. These internationalists are, in their private lives, inward-turned. But, in their dealings with foreigners, they are almost invariably friendly and polite.

The cosy and cosseted nature of Luxembourg home life, if you are ever privileged enough to witness it, is immediately evident. Being quintessentially *Luxembourgeois*, with the accent on the last two syllables of the word, they cherish material things. One couple I visited had accumulated so much furniture that I had difficulty getting through the front door. They also avoid any hint of eccentricity in their dress or behaviour (Dr David Weeks of the Royal Edinburgh Hospital, please note).

Despite such technicalities, Luxembourg hospitality is as simple and cordial as Churchill says. It can even contrive to be sophisticated and cordial. At the time of writing, Luxembourg boasts more Michelin stars per square kilometer than any other country (that may not be a lot of Michelin stars, but it tells you something). To compensate, the country has local specialities like *kuddelfleck* and *quetsch*.

Yet Luxembourgers have some difficulty in cohabiting with culture with a big 'C' (or 'K', depending on the choice of language). This made living up to the challenge of nomination by the EU as 'European City of Culture 1995' more than taxing. Luxembourgers spend less on culture than any other country in the Union, and the government normally allocates little more than a 0.5% of its budget to cultural matters, most of this going on the preservation of buildings and the purchase of library books. The country has no museum of contemporary arts and no university - though, as Luxembourg journalist Gilbert Sauber points out, this has the incidental advantage that it obliges young people to go abroad to broaden their minds.

The cosy nature of Luxembourg is projected onto public life. According to informed sources, the country is run by eleven ministers and twelve families. It seems it is even impossible to run a trial by jury in the country because everyone knows everyone else. As the *International Herald Tribune* stated, "problems in Luxembourg are never the same, because of the long-established and cosy relations between politicians, business and government leaders."

In many respects, despite their apparently *petit bourgeois* mentality, the Luxembourgers are disarmingly simple and sensible in their social and public behaviour. The American *Fielding Travel Guide* reported that, if you called the Prime Minister's office switchboard, you would be greeted by an attractive female voice saying *"gouvernement, bonjour!"* ["government, good day!"]. It would be a miracle to get a similar welcome in most other countries I know.

Of course, there are some Luxembourgers who find this degree of cosiness overbearing. This may help explain the homicide rate which, at 9.7 murders per 100,000 inhabitants in 1988, was nearly twice as high as that of any other European nation. That works out at 35 murders for the whole of Luxembourg.

However John Dunning, an American resident and avid observer of the Luxembourg scene, considers the inhabitants' driving habits even more murderous. In his words, "Luxembourg must suffer from the greatest number of single-vehicle accidents in the world". Change 'murderous' to 'suicidal'. As a percipient British consultant queried, could this have anything to do with the Portuguese element in Luxembourg society?

But non-conformist attitudes are generally frowned on in this cosy little country. A 1987 Eurobarometer study found the Luxembourgers, of the twelve member states of the time, the least enthusiastic about liberating the little woman from the kitchen sink: *"Die Frau bleibt zu Hause"*.

Yet Luxembourgeresses do get out, at least in the afternoons. The visitor will still witness the scene described, back in 1974, by an English observer: "Particularly in the late afternoon, the cafes and tea rooms are packed with plump ladies of mature age, expensively dressed and all eating the most enormous cream cakes". The ladies have just got plumper and more mature since.

The presence of so many foreigners in the country owes much to Luxembourg's emergence as an industrialised nation with iron and steel production in the mid-19th century. Even as long ago as 1912, 15 per cent of the population were immigrants[28]. In recent years, though, heavy industry has given way to the service and administrative sectors, particularly banking, a number of European Union institutions and, of course, TV and radio.

CLT, the company that runs the RTL programmes, and a more recent arrival, the SES satellite TV organisation, are testimony to the international vocation of the country. Yet, here again, you see the tug-of-war between the competing sirens of cosmopolitanism and cosiness. Luxembourgers live in perpetual fear that their 'home-grown' creations will one day fall prey to foreign interests.

The stability of the Luxembourg culture is well expressed in the famous 'dancing procession' of Echternach: three steps forward followed by two steps backwards or sideways. Such is the Luxembourgers' vision of progress.

Whatever else, the Luxembourgers are intelligent people and hard workers. How else explain the fact that they lead the member states of the European Union in meeting the criteria set for monetary union: an infinitesimal budget deficit, a low national debt, low inflation and a stable currency? Maybe they owe some of this to their marginal investment in culture - and also to the fact that the Luxos rarely strike. Jul Christophory attributes the latter to the close links between rural and industrial life in this little country: the smallholder working in a factory, and the factory employee doing evening work on a farm.

In fact the only strike ever recorded between 1921 and 1980 (nearly 60 years!) was a protest action directed at the Germans. Few foreigners are aware that the Luxembourgers showed a stoic and anything-but-passive resistance to their Nazi occupiers during WWII. These modest people have many hidden qualities. Quite a number of them joined the French Foreign Legion.

According to *Euroscopie*[29], discretion is a natural virtue (this, which I can confirm, may explain why it is difficult to say more about the Luxos). Rather surprisingly for us foreigners, it seems they don't like talking about money - certainly not about their personal incomes. But they love taking it from the Belgians, who flock into the Grand Duchy on daytrips.

This must please the Luxos a lot, since they sometimes resent the activities of their neighbours. Before achieving its present truncated state, the Grand Duchy embraced the French-speaking Belgian Province of Luxembourg. In recent times, the two have developed a symbiotic relationship by virtue of the 40,000-odd Belgians who commute into the Grand Duchy every day to work. They have also developed a healthy rivalry.

This was evident when an American company decided to set up a manufacturing plant in the area. First the Americans looked at the Grand Duchy, then at Belgium's Luxembourg Province, an initiative that provoked a preemptive and rather ceremonial visit to the US company's headquarters by a close relative of the Grand Duke.

The Americans opted for Belgium, then decided to organise an international gala opening for their spanking new plant. They overlooked the fact that the only suitable arrival point for the charter aircraft, loaded with American VIPs, was Luxembourg (Grand Duchy). When they asked for the red carpet treatment, the word got back to the Grand Duke and, regally, he said *'nyet'*. It's a small world, particularly in the Grand Duchy...

Curious that the President of the Commission of the European Union should be a Luxo called Jacques Santer. Coming from so small a country, it makes sense that his name translates into English as 'John Lackland'. In Luxembourg, almost everything makes sense!

<u>The Dutch</u>

The democratic dogmatists

"To be Dutch still means coming to terms with the moral ambiguities of materialism in their own idiosyncratic but inescapable ways: through the daily living of it, in Sunday sermons on nuclear weapons and Monday rites of scrubbing the sidewalk"

Simon Schama

"The Dutch occupy one of the world's most densely populated countries, and they structure life in it by means of a seemingly irrevocable commitment to a meticulously detailed but at the same time flexible system of interlocking organization"

William Z Shetter

"We have no balconies, so we have no revolutions. Our balconies are at the back" Wim Kan, Dutch entertainer

"Just be yourself, you're silly enough!" ["Doe maar gewoon, dat is al gek genoeg" Dutch saying

You should plan to go by taxi, but you still take your bike" ["Je moet plannen om met een taxi te gaan, maar je gaat toch met de fiets"] Another Dutch saying

The moment you cross the border from Belgium into Holland you know you have entered another world: the motorways narrow from four lanes to three, then two, the overhead lighting disappears. You realise you have passed in seconds from an essentially expansive country into an essentially frugal one. If you happen to cross the frontier on a country road you have the same effect in microcosm: the road gets narrower (and prettier due to the charming Dutch habit of using red roadtiles in towns rather than asphalt) and the houses get smaller.

But if you start talking about these differences, the Dutch will probably anticipate you by telling a joke which, it goes without saying, dates from the Cold War: "If there's going to be a nuclear conflict, I want to be in Belgium when it comes. They're at least five years behind everyone else", a jibe that is followed by gales of hearty laughter.

This sense of difference, while justified ethnically, is surprising culturally since the two countries have shared much the same destiny for centuries, ever since they got a mutual pasting when the Spaniards arrived in the Low Countries.

The Dutch joke is also surprising because, if anything, Belgium has caught up on the Netherlands and even overtaken her in some respects in the last few years. Some Dutch people even envy the Belgians their softer phonetic approach to their shared language - something that astonishes most Belgians. They also remark on the defensive Belgian habit of closing the shutters at night - Dutch curtains are left wide open and their rooms well illuminated so everyone can see they have nothing to hide.

'The Netherlands' is once again a vague amalgam, although the little country has had a relatively homogeneous history over the last 500 years, thanks largely to its success as a mercantile and ultimately colonial power. The calvinist island people of Zeeland in the southwest are a far cry from the catholic folk of Noord-Brabant and the almost 'Romanesque' communities of Limburg in the southeast – all of whom are equally distant, both geographically and ethnically, from the Frisians in the north.

Physically what they share in common is water - none of the Dutch are far from the sea or a major river or canal system - and a flat environment relieved by some little hills close to the German frontier. These features have shaped a people whose attitudes reflect their historic fight with the elements: wind, water, open skies and, increasingly, other people's pollutants since they are downstream from all the other Europeans. They also prompted a tradition of 'grassroots' democracy which eventually matured into the principles of mutual help and responsibility that pervade Dutch society today.

It has to be added, in passing, that this flat and flooded landscape has contributed to a more intimate aspect of Dutch life, namely an obsession with cleanliness thanks to an abundance of water (not so evident in the younger generations).

This flush and lush landscape has also contributed to the volume of animal waste produced by cows, sheep and pigs - an environmental challenge of major proportions. The casual observer might be forgiven for thinking that much of this has ended up on the regulation bow tie and dinner jacket of the average Dutch waiter, a segment of society that also seems immune to this obsession with cleanliness.

The Dutch are a plucky, emphatic people who spend as much time fighting with their own inhibitions as with the problems that inevitably confront a small, resource-poor country. This has produced qualities defined by the Dutch historian Johan Huizinga[30] as "honesty, a scant receptiveness for rhetoric, an immunity to political extremes and an abhorrence of national self-glorification that goes hand in hand with a certain urge for national self-abnegation". They are also great lovers of individual liberty, something for which other Europeans have reason to be grateful.

Historically, the Dutch have been caught between the Old Testament imminence of natural disaster wreaked by a wrathful god and the inevitability of wellbeing resulting from their intelligence and industry. As Simon Schama says in the conclusion to his superb book, *The Embarrassment of Riches*[31], "We end, then, where we began: in the moral geography of the Dutch mind, adrift between the fear of the deluge and the hope of moral salvage, in the tidal ebb and flow between worldliness and homeliness, between the gratification of appetite and its denial, between the conditional consecration of wealth and perdition in its surfeit". This is, in his own words, "the classic Dutch counterpoint between materialism and morality".

This Dutch dilemma is something totally unknown to most Europeans other than, maybe, the Norwegians. It is forged by the elements, by history and by religion - calvinism or catholicism depending on where one happens to be, but predominantly calvinism. In fact this is a historical hangover: 70 per cent of today's Dutch no longer go to church and the two institutions, catholic and calvinist, have now developed a ecumenical empathy, largely due to the innovative spirit of the Dutch catholic church.

The traditional toughness of the Dutch environment, socially as well as climatically, may also explain a tendency to dogmatism, even didacticism. As one of them puts it, "we have a tendency to lecture, preach and teach on any subject that is not our business" (some people say that, with foreigners, they just say what the latter want to hear). The writer J van Laarhoven describes the Netherlands as "a country... of practical tolerance and impractical pedantry". No wonder the English say that 'he talked like a Dutch uncle': the moralising streak is highly developed. As an eminent sociologist put it to me, "we Dutch think helping is important, as long as we're not on the receiving end."

But Rentes de Carvalho, a Portuguese who has spent many years in the Netherlands, puts it more trenchantly: "The Dutch definition of averageness is not the wise middle course of the golden mean but more the obsession to crush everything that falls outside acceptable standards, the rejection of any form of adventure, including of the spirit."

In the circumstances it is not surprising that when in 1987-88 Dr Rajendra Pradhan, a Nepalese anthropologist, set out to study the good people of the Dutch village of Schoonrewoerd, he found their religious beliefs puzzling. As recounted by Geert Hofstede, a Dutchman and in my view the world's most eminent expert on cultures, the bemused Dr Pradhan said: "Everybody over here talks about believing, believing, believing. Where I come from, what counts is the ritual, in which only the priest and the head of the family participate. The others watch and make their offerings. Over here so much is *mandatory*. Hindus will never ask 'Do you believe in God?' Of course one should believe, but the important thing is what one *does*." [32]

The Dutch do strike many foreigners as being opinionated, bureaucratic and inflexible (the Flemish think they are just plain mean). Those who have spent time living in the country speak of the average Dutch office worker as institutionalised and lacking in initiative.

Related to this institutionalisation is, understandably, a highly developed sense of togetherness which, at the family level, goes under the name of *gezelligheid*. An American William Shetter, in his book *The Netherlands in Perspective* [33] cites an example that is worth quoting: "In 1975 one of the TV broadcasting associations started a series of programs called *Kerkepad* ('Church Route') consisting of short documentaries on three or four historically interesting churches and inviting viewers to visit them, not just any time but on two prearranged successive Saturdays. The careful viewer could 'subscribe' to the whole series of that year by mail, which brought a brochure with maps and timetables, pictures and explanatory notes. Or the more venturesome could simply go (the churches selected were always close together in the same region or city)."

"The visitor to any one of the churches on the day's 'route' would find an identifying flag waving on the tower, throngs of people milling about in a festival atmosphere, coffee and tea readily available - sometimes in the church itself - and meals for sale close by. Just inside the door of each church would be a long table in front of which visitors could line up to get an official stamp on their card certifying that they had made that point on the 'route'. As this is being written, *Kerkepad* is now in its eleventh year and shows no signs of diminishing in popularity."

Hugo van der Poel of Tilburg University also insists on his people's attachment to *gezelligheid*, but in another way: "The Dutch seem to be a kind of home-loving people". Well said! Just look at the interiors portrayed by the Old Masters. No wonder they take their homes with them when they go on holiday: caravan holidays cost less (in 1992 there were 400,000 caravans in the Netherlands for a population of 14.8 million). They also take their fellow-countrymen and women with them, creating Dutch camping ghettos in significantly unflat places like the Belgian Ardennes and the French Ardèche. There is even a Dutch subculture at the Alpe d'Huez every time the Tour de France comes round, just to make their cyclists feel at home.

But back to Dutch discipline. Foreigners, particularly their neighbours, can easily misinterpret this tradition of rectitude. To me, it comes across at times as superciliousness in the older generation, arrogance in the young. They tend to hunt in packs, shunning all but their own kind, and can be very dismissive with those with whom they do not directly identify (Dutch children, a boisterous bunch, demonstrate these qualities at an early age).

This partly derives from the traditionally structured, even clannish, nature of Dutch society along philosophical lines, a phenomenon examined by William Shetter in his book: "In Dutch society as it was from about the 1930s on to about the mid-60s, we find a society that was fragmented into blocs [*zuilen* = pillars] based on ideology - religious or otherwise - and strongly isolated from each other." There were essentially five such blocs or 'pillars' - Roman Catholic, Orthodox Reformed (Calvinist), Reformed (Calvinist) and other Protestant, Socialist, and General and Non-church - which extend through all levels of society.

Traces of these blocs have survived today in the affiliations of the political parties, and particularly in the educational system and the broadcast media. Shetter concludes that what makes the Dutch system unique in Europe is "the development and elaboration of a pluralistic pattern to the point where it became the shape of the society itself." But he maintains that "there is a gradually decreasing identification with organizations exclusively on the basis of ideological position, and in general association with others across the old invisible lines is much freer."

But the dogmatic tradition is still around. Anyone who has had dealings with Dutch people will testify to the existence of both individual and collective egos. Of course it is precisely this that has earned them such a glorious past. Unfortunately it can also lead to a charismatic state of mind which excludes the possibility of error or wrongdoing by the party concerned and can lead to acts of great impetuousity, if not opportunism.

Assertiveness, often but not always tempered with tolerance, is a dominant feature of the Dutch: it springs partly from their confident relationship with their society whichever it happens to be (the *zuilen* phenomenon), partly from the fact that with exceptions they are a relatively well educated, if not over-educated, bunch of people. They have reason to feel superior, even if they shouldn't.

They even feel superior about their coffee culture, much to the astonishment of foreigners, myself included. The Dutch process much of the coffee that ends up in other Europeans' cups, and you see the 'fresh coffee' sign *(de koffie is klaar)* wherever you go. My formative Dutch led me to conclude early on that this meant that Dutch coffee was clear rather than cloudy (like some other people's coffee) and raised my expectations beyond hope of fulfilment. I now think the Dutch would do better to keep off the subject. Instead, they are running posters putting the question that evidently exercises them more than any other: "Is there coffee after death?" *(Is er koffie na de dood?)*. Speaking for myself I hope not, unless it's Spanish or Italian.

Despite such acts of apparent self-assurance, Dutch society now seems to be passing through moments of doubt - something that Prime Minister Lubbers evoked when he said that "Holland is a sick country". Reviewing this most un-Dutchlike turn of events, Peter Brusse of *Elseviers* magazine commented: "The Dutch are troubled. They seem to have lost a sense of direction and they do not know where to go". And, significantly, echoing Simon Schama's thesis: "We want moral persuasion, at home and abroad, because our history has taught us that our weakness is our strength. We are a small country surrounded by big powers. Due to our lack of political and physical strength, we want to reason". Aldous Huxley called Holland "a haven to the rationalist" (similarly placed, their Belgian neighbours eschew reason for resourcefulness).

To Johan Huizinga's reference to the Dutchman's "scant receptiveness for rhetoric", as opposed to didacticism, I would add any form of extravagance. This may help explain the experience of a British consultant who uses role-playing as a way of improving management performance: it doesn't work with the Dutch, because "you can't get them to compete with one another publicly...". In fact, despite foreigners' claimed experience to the contrary, the Dutch tend to be much less assertive with other races than among themselves.

William Shetter elaborates on this aspect: "Today Dutch people still tend to be distrustful of too-conspicuous individual achievement or even 'show', to dislike anything perceived as excessive display of affluence, to maintain a discreet public reserve that meticulously respects the privacy of others, to accept outsiders readily and unquestioningly, and above all to cherish the forms of social organization that help assure all this."

The point about achievement is well made: a number of observers, myself included, have been surprised at the reluctance of young Dutch people - and Flemish youngsters too - to draw attention to themselves as academic achievers. As an American says, "you're simply not allowed to 'win'."

As for the world of show business, well the Dutch are, it seems, at least less reticent than the Germans. Witness the number of top spots occupied by Dutch nationals on the German entertainment scene: Rudi Carel and Linda de Mol on TV, and the brilliant Herman van Veen on the boards.

Even in everyday life a bit of showing off by Dutch adults is permissible. A Dutch businessman, interviewed for his impressions of the Norwegians[6], admitted the following: "The Dutchman is a member of a club, not only for the joy of the sport but for showing this off to the immediate surroundings. Families will seldom mention that their little girls are attending dancing school without adding the particular name of the school to create a sense of status." Maybe this is not surprising in so close-knit a society.

A Belgian brought in to run the Dutch subsidiary of an American multinational (a challenge if there ever was one) first noted the tendency to close office doors, rather like the Germans, but later came to acknowledge the relative readiness - compared with their neighbours, the Belgians and Germans, or even the French - to accept the advice and experience of outsiders. He describes the Dutch, seen from a Flemish Belgian standpoint, as "traditionally introverted and cautious, but extremely well educated, intelligent and ready to learn...".

Most Belgians, both Flemish and Walloons, seem to think they know everything there is to know and don't need help from anyone, thank you - particularly when it costs real money. The Dutch, by comparison, are not too dogmatic to seek a third-party opinion and not too mean to pay for it. So much for the stereotypes!

Yet what no one will argue with is the frugality of the Dutch, fully understandable in the light of their centuries-long battle winning land from the waves. But one frequently wonders if their natural caution about money, often reflected in tight budgets, doesn't ultimately do as much harm as good.

Frugality can, of course, be as much of a virtue as a vice and, in the case of the Dutch, can be accompanied by great generosity in the right circumstances. In fact prosperity is teaching them to be less tight-fisted. It has even got to the point that Belgians charge the Dutch with ostentatiousness for driving around in large smart cars (to compensate for their almost universally small houses, which they can do nothing about?). This has also produced the domestic backlash of a back-to-basics movement which extols frugality and publishes a monthly called the *Vrekkenkrant* (Misers Magazine).

In any case the reputation for meanness probably owes as much to the perception the Dutch have of themselves as to reality: a number of major consumer marketing fiascos can be traced back to underestimation by Dutch managers of the ability of their fellow-countryfolk to accept a higher price for the sake of quality. But they are learning fast!

Meanness, the first cousin of frugality, can sometimes lead to trickiness. Under pressure the Dutch, who are generally a very correct people, look for solutions which do credit to their ingenuity but not necessarily to their sense of honour. As a battle-scarred independent American businessman says, "whenever I had a real problem, there was always a Dutchman at the heart of it!"

To their closest neighbours, the Belgians, the Dutch businessman is determined, ambitious, "a real fox". In supplier/customer situations it is often a question of "all or nothing" - the relationship is either a roaring success or it goes straight off the rails. Curiously, the Dutch are also great natural gamblers - a neat way of sidestepping the materialism/morality issue?

Belgian businesspeople find the Dutch can be less than wholehearted in their respect for the letter, let alone the spirit, of the agreements they sign. The problem, they claim, can be either deviousness or plain bad faith. At the same time, they give them the highest marks of all the European business communities for creativity. There may not be a contradiction here.

As an example of this creativity - apart from all the silly jokes, some of which you will find elsewhere in this book - it is worth recounting the case of the Dutch director of a manufacturing company who was dissatisfied with the performance of the director of his French marketing subsidiary. Without warning the latter, he decided to advertise for a replacement in the French newspress. He then decided that the incumbent was OK after all, so he allocated the advertisement costs to the wretched Frenchman's operating budget...

This class of ingenuity can serve the Dutch well. It may help to explain the fact that, when Young & Rubicam and *The Economist* investigated the working lives of Europe's business élite, 90% of the Dutch respondents said they drove themselves to and from work while, in answer to another question, 34% of them said they read a paper on the way home. It is not clear whether the 4% of Dutch chief executives who commute by bicycle indulge in the same ingenious but dangerous practice.

Another characteristic, aggressiveness under pressure, is well demonstrated by a humbler but equally important constituency in the Dutch international trading community: the truck drivers who handle 37 per cent of Europe's long-distance road transport traffic (not bad for a small country!) So, when a juggernaut pulls out right in front as you come up in the fast lane, the odds are it's a Dutchman.

This aggressiveness can, in some circumstances, emerge as vindictiveness - an old testament fire-and-brimstone view of life where the normal sense of fair play of the Dutch deserts them. And the ordinary person can be particularly beastly to the Germans. There is some justification for this - history plus German disdain for the Dutch language and culture - and, for the Dutch, such justification is enough.

But the world of international affairs is well removed from the reality of everyday life, cosy little towns with their narrow, winding streets, gabled brick houses and *gezelligheid*. On the reasonable assumption that Dutch classical art comes closer than any other school to portraying life as it really was at the time (another measure of the matter-of-factness of the Dutch), not much has changed.

Admittedly the cosy little towns are now adorned with red-tiled pedestrian concourses, unexpected *art nouveau* hotels, bearded environmentalists and cyclists in swarms. But the social ethic, catholic or calvinist, continues to reign supreme. Little old Dutch ladies peep out from between their *petit point* curtains and potted plants, draw conclusions and whisper their judgments to their neighbours. The young, out of desperation, do everything they can to enrage the old. Depending on age-group and to some extent sex, they either adopt a slightly hysterical kick-my-heels-over-the-windmill attitude or retire into drugged silence. The unending Dutch battle between propriety and permissiveness goes on.

But, an essentially sensible people, the Dutch are learning to accommodate themselves to a changing world and, in the process, are producing a genuinely pluralistic and democratic society - although one which, in the opinion of many of its people, has become overorganised to the level of a kafkaesque nightmare. In this they have been aided by their churches, which have vied with one another to meet the challenge of the times even on the airwaves. Dutch television airtime is still largely a carve-up between the different ideological blocs or *zuilen* - religious, ideological, cultural or other - plus new and somewhat destabilising commercial stations. The pressures created by the advent of the latter may however mean that this bastion of Dutch 'pluriformality' will also change beyond recognition.

Moreover there are two caveats about Dutch democracy. A meritocracy once known as 'the Mertens 200', largely peopled these days with graduates of Leiden University, still masterminds many of the real issues. And the Dutch elite is as susceptible to foreign fashions - like using French words where Dutch ones will do - as anyone else. Along with the Münchners and Düsseldorfers of West Germany, they can be as snobbish a people as you will find. Fortunately they are in a minority in an otherwise egalitarian Holland.

As one of the smaller countries, the Netherlands also finds itself in a minority situation vis-a-vis the rest of the world, but does not allow this to blunt the innate bullishness of its citizens. I once met a Frenchman who didn't know where Holland was. Another, the author of a book on Europe, attributed the Netherlands with 'a common frontier with Denmark'. And a survey conducted in the United States by the Dutch tourist authority in 1990 revealed that 56 per cent of those polled thought the Netherlands was "a group of countries somewhere in northwestern Europe" (they got warmer than the Frenchman). Twenty per cent thought the national language was *German*. The tourist board thinks that identifying the country with the geographically inexact label of 'Holland' rather than 'the Netherlands' would help.

The latter obviously runs the risk of association, oh horrors, with Belgium, the northern part of which is as low as the Lowlands themselves. A rather silly joke, presumably American in origin, neatly sums up foreigner attitudes (European and other) to both the Dutch and the Belgians. It recounts the story of a rookie airline pilot briefed at JFK for his first flight to Brussels. His navigator explains: "You fly due east until you reach a major landmass. That's Europe. The first thing you'll see is rows of freshly washed toilet paper out to dry. That's Holland. Turn 90 degrees to starboard and descend. That's Belgium."

This makes a couple of points. Belgium lacks an identity and a lot of people are not even sure where it is. And the Dutch, to come back to our subject, are seen to be both clean and frugal. Which no one will deny...

The Swiss

The practical pacifists

"A curst, selfish, swinish country, placed in the most romantic region in the world"   Lord Byron

"The Swiss are not a people so much as a neat clean quite solvent business"   William Faulkner

"When a Swiss banker jumps out of the window, jump after him, there must be money to be made"   Voltaire

"The Swiss are both prisoners and their own warders at one and the same time" *["Die Schweizer sind gleichzeitig Gefangene und ihre eigenen Wärter"]*   Friedrich Dürrenmatt

"The Swiss rise early but take a long time to wake up"   Anonymous

"The whole world loves the Swiss franc; but only the Swiss adore the Swiss centime"   George Mikes

"I look upon Switzerland as an inferior sort of Scotland"   Reverend Sydney Smith

"Scarsdale with mountains"   American commentator

"Question: what goes... boom (long silence)... boom (long silence)... boom. Answer: a Bernese machine-gun"   Zürich joke

"Ne pas introduire les chiens"
                    Sign outside Swiss post office, immediately below the mailbox

"The Swiss make a success of not minding"   Italian EC official

"Switzerland washes whiter" *["La Suisse lave plus blanc"]*
                                          Title of book by Jean Ziegier

The Swiss must have regretted Lord Byron's interest in the Château de Chillon, even if it helped their tourist trade. He manages to make the word 'romantic' sound like an insult.

Poetic licence or not, the outburst does seem a little unfair. The *Eidgenossen* have run their country so pacifically and profitably over recent years of its seven-century existence that they only occasionally feature in the history books of the other European nations. So the Swiss have to content themselves with what *The Economist* calls "a chocolate-box image" - a folksy composition of sing-song *Schwyzerdütsch*, alphorns, yodling, *Hudigäggeler*, cuckoo clocks and hairy old stories about boys with apples on their heads.

In reality, the centre of the cuckoo clock industry is the German Black Forest, the Swiss having graduated to Swatches. And, far from being implacably bourgeois and conformist, they are now breeding a younger generation which is one of the most militant in Western Europe.

In defence of the Swiss, it also has to be said that, surrounded by larger neighbours with whom they share the same languages, they look outwards culturally as well as inwards. And, in addition to bringing together four language communities - German, French, Italian and Romansch - they have delicious sun-dried meat, cheeses and wines, and strange pursuits like wrestling in short pants, curling and a high-powered game called *Hornisse*.

A practically minded people, the Swiss are firm believers in comfort and security, virtues which they are prepared to share with foreigners - at a price. They claim to have invented both the zip fastener (Simon Frey) and the Velcro cling fastener (Georges de Mestral). Tut, tut, Harry Lime - nothing more remarkable than the cuckoo clock? And it was a Swiss who devised Pascal, the most widely used academic programming language in the world.

So the Swiss have tidy minds as a nation. Traditionally everything, including the viewpoint of the *petit bourgeois*, is firmly buttoned up. I should explain that I am talking about the German Swiss: the French and Italian Swiss, on the other side of what some people call the *Rösti-Graben* ('the roast potato ditch'), tend to be rather more relaxed about things, but not always.

However, even the concept of 'the German Swiss' is difficult to sustain, since the inhabitants of a town 20 kilometers away are likely to be classed as 'foreigners', with all that implies: dirty habits, unreliability (turning up 30 seconds late), and so on. Even direct neighbours are suspect. No wonder the German Swiss try to be as unlike the Germans as possible - an impulse that has been encouraged by historical fears of being caught up in a German-run superstate.

Security-mindedness has a half-sister, suspicion - which often finds expression in revenge. The *Neue Zürcher Zeitung* reports that 75 per cent of all tax evasion cases brought in the canton of Zürich are based on denunciation by fellow-citizens. But, unlike the Austrians who love doing their dirty washing in public, the Swiss tend to close ranks when the country's reputation is at stake: solidarity with the system, at least for the older generations, is synonymous with patriotism.

Collectively, the Swiss subscribe to the principle, best expressed in their second language, of *vivons caché, vivons heureux.* Individually, they are not *that* reluctant to show off their wealth: Flora Lewis makes the point[2] that "apartment windows are not curtained; if they were, neighbors would whisper suspiciously about what must there be to hide."

A German colleague, who has worked for a number of international organisations, has no illusions. Having spent two unforgettable years living and working in Zürich, he likens Switzerland to a police state. "The whole country is full of mistrust - you would think everyone regarded everyone else as criminals - everyone else being not just foreigners, but upright Swiss *Bürgers* too!".

He speaks of "envy compounded with a paranoic search for law and, particularly, *order*". Note the weasel word...

George Mikes puts it even more bluntly[34]: "If 'Love thy neighbour as thyself' is the first Christian duty of any true-born Swiss, 'Hate they neighbour more than thyself' is the second" (the only exception being mother, who as often as not still lives opposite and washes her son's underwear). Such hatred should not, however, be demonstrated openly: the Swiss prefer to be polite, they are rarely rude, never abusive - which of course is why foreigners find them so irritating.

Personally, I find them perplexing, particularly the German Swiss. On the one hand they are very *sachlich*, matter-of-fact: they sometimes demonstrate a schoolmasterish, sardonic manner that intimidates even the Germans.

On the other hand they are, well, full of surprises ranging from stupifying naivety to breathtaking *insouciance*. My moment of truth came during tense negotiations with a Swiss SME, when I became uncomfortably aware of the fact that the financial director was a Porsche-driver with a fondness for the same sex and his Number Two was a raving alcoholic. Nothing wrong with this *per se*, but it didn't really add up - even in terms of conventional Swiss double standards.

Coming back to the subject of security, my German informant insists that every negotiation invokes the principle of security or guarantees. He should know. Setting up flat in Zürich and needing a tape measure, he persuaded a local shopkeeper to loan him one - for a deposit of ten Swiss francs. He made sure he gave it back!

Some two weeks after arriving in Zürich his phone rang at five o'clock in the morning. "Please stop playing the alphorn" said a voice (in Switzerland, almost all such phonecalls are anonymous). My friendly informant is not in the habit of playing the alphorn, least of all at five o'clock in the morning: the idea is preposterous. But for the anonymous Swiss caller, he - as the most recent foreigner to arrive on the scene - was the most suspect.

He recounts the case of a fellow executive from Germany who flew into Zürich twice in the same week and had the misfortune to get the same taxi. The second time, the immigration police were in his office within half-an-hour. The taxi-driver had reported him on the basis that his regular presence indicated he was working illegally in the country.

On the issue of Swiss law and *order* - that word again! - numerous anecdotes spring to mind. Not long ago the news media were buzzing with the case of a farmer who was instructed to remove the cowbells from the fair necks of his herd (Swiss cows *are* beautiful) between the hours of 8 pm and 7 am. Of such stuff is Swiss life made.

Another equally important case concerns the chestnut sellers in Zürich's Bahnhofstrasse. Individual entrepreneurs had concocted stalls of various sizes, shapes and colours. This offended the Swiss urge for tidiness so, at considerable expense for those involved, new standardised stalls were introduced. People then complained that patrons were leaving the empty chestnut shells on the pavements, so the local administration spent 250,000 Swiss francs worth of public money producing a double-compartmented pack, one for the chestnuts, the other for the shells.

The Swiss mania for tidiness is, of course, epitomised in the *Putz-Geist*, the 'cleaning spirit' of the average Swiss housewife (and what could be more Swiss than the average Swiss housewife?). These good ladies put their German sisters to shame. Orderliness reaches the point of hysteria when household matters are exposed to public view: a Scots daughter-in-law discovered that, when putting her washing out on the clothes line, she was expected to group all her socks together with colours matching...

Despite the sternness of their attitudes, the Swiss are not always as competent as legend would have them be (it's not uncommon to get the wrong shirts back from a Swiss laundry). This shows they're human after all. They can also be very slow. The average Swiss calculates everything down to the last centime and this, of course, takes time.

It has to be conceded though that, despite a rather narrow-minded approach to the enormous business of living (male *Eidgenossen* complain that the female of the species marries for security, not for love), the Swiss can also be creative. The very existence of things like zip fasteners, Velcro fasteners, *Hornisse*, cheeses with holes in them, Pascal, *Bündnerfleisch*, Swatches, maybe even Swiss army knives, shows that they can be very innovative about anything not threatening the social order of their little country.

The Swiss have the oldest constitution of any European state, a time-honoured (yes, the Swiss honour time!) and questionable status of neutrality, and the best railway system in Europe.

They also have a rugged, if rather primitive, form of democracy. When drafted into annual military service for the first time, enlisted men get their Swiss army knives free of charge whereas the officers have to pay for them. Which means there is a distinction between enlisted men and officers. Democracy still has some way to go.

Yet the Swiss have, as George Mikes points out, "two special and attractive institutions: the referendum and the right of initiative. Private citizens (under conditions laid down in the Constitution) are entitled to initiate legislation; and the Federal Government can quite easily be forced to submit certain measures to referendum and, in fact, in many cases does so without any coercion at all."

This may not be so surprising when you consider that, at the time of writing, the 'Federal Government' is just seven people strong (a reflection of the fact that the revenue - and the power - stays in the cantons?). Indeed the institutions George Mikes speaks of find their origin in the admirable spirit of rural democracy that developed in the cantons of Uri, Schwyz and Unterwalden all those centuries ago - a tradition of enlightened self-interest which is also evident in Dutch society. Unfortunately the Swiss public seems to be losing touch: the turnout at recent polls has been less than half what it was 20 years ago.

For Swiss youth to get serious and use these instruments of democracy as effectively as their forefathers did seven centuries ago would be a definite change for the better. Of course there are constitutional obstacles to match the constitutional opportunities. One of the more evident consequences of the Kopp affair, when a minister was caught confusing public with personal interest, was a crackdown on younger delegates in the national parliament who came to sessions wearing open-necked shirts.

But the ice is starting to crack. Four university students took on the might of parliament early in 1992, when they demanded a referendum after the deputies had awarded themselves a 100 per cent pay rise. Appropriately, members of the Swiss *Nationalrat* vote with their feet. To show their support for a motion like a pay rise for Swiss deputies, they stand up. I lie not.

What the Swiss *don't* have is a very distinct identity compared with their German, French and Italian neighbours. But Switzerland, as everyone knows from reading newspaper reports about money laundering and so on, is a very international community, so that's hardly surprising. Which is not the same thing as saying that the average Swiss is particularly open towards foreigners: a mood of resentful acceptance would be closer to the mark. Yet, when all is said and done, 20 per cent of Swiss nationals end up marrying a foreigner. *Gruezi miteinand*!

Apparently this doesn't stop them being happy folk, largely thanks to the benefits that accommodating foreigners bring them: a recent survey made European history when 95 per cent of respondents declared themselves 'highly satisfied with their lives' (out of respect for the security/suspicion syndrome, the research organisation guaranteed absolute anonymity).

Like the Netherlands, Switzerland is a traditionally cosy and conformist society and, like the Netherlands, the dropout rate amongst Swiss youth is high. The incidence of drug-taking and AIDS is also high, in fact the highest of any European country at the time of writing. But more than the Netherlands, it is a place where people tend to violence when tempers get out of hand.

This is evident in two things: the student riots of recent years in the cities of German Switzerland, and the high level of road accidents. Swiss standards of courtship can also be rough. Techniques for making an advance on the opposite sex range from knocking the person over to spilling beer on his or her head. Even Swedes, erstwhile Vikings, find their approach lacking in finesse.

But the maintenance of Swiss cosiness and conformity at almost any price encourages an almost manic defence of the *status quo*. Early in 1990 evidence emerged that the police was keeping personal files on 900,000 people, again prompting violent public demonstrations. As it happens, only 260,000 of the 900,000 were Swiss nationals. All the rest were immigrants.

This is not altogether surprising since, despite their natural aversion to 'the enemy in their midst', the 6.7 million Swiss tolerate the presence of 1.1 million foreigners on their hallowed soil. The reason for this is that they need someone to do the work they don't want to do themselves, to wit dishwashing in Swiss catering establishments, cleaning Swiss office buildings, and the dirty jobs in Swiss hospitals, old peoples' homes and laundries (sic). In fairness to the Swiss, though, the rest of us are just as happy to have foreigners do our dirty washing.

One of the few exceptions to the principle that foreigners do the dirty work was a nightly check by the local administration of refuse bags in the streets of Berne. This was aimed, with the help of the bags' contents, at identifying those householders who infringed the rule that waste bags be put out in the morning and not overnight! It was felt that it would be demeaning to have foreigners spying on the Swiss, so this particularly dirty job, in more senses than one, was reserved for Swiss nationals. The project foundered, of course, because non-immigrant labour is too expensive.

In case you get the idea that the Swiss accept foreigners, even on tolerance, please note that asylum-seekers are herded into nuclear shelters (the ones that are not used as wine cellars) and then escorted out of the country. The country's insistence on pursuing its bunker construction programme in a rapidly denuclearising universe suggested a combination of pigheadedness and a natural instinct for taking cover. Swiss holes-in-the-ground, proliferating like the holes in Swiss cheese, can always come in useful one way or another.

Religious holidays also provide a god-sent opportunity. When the Italian immigrant workforce went home for Christmas some years ago, the Swiss slammed the frontier gates behind them. This neatly solved the immigration problem for a while but caused a furore inside Switzerland - which shows that the Swiss do have a sense of fair play. More recently, they have demonstrated this in their generous acceptance of refugees from Yugoslavia, a policy that puts some other countries with a claimed tradition of asylum to shame.

It is also curious that a nation which is neutralist to the point of indifference towards the problems of the rest of the world should be home to the International Red Cross, the WHO, the ILO and others. Though it is not a member of the United Nations (not out of principle but because, it is rumoured, the Swiss balked at the idea of having to pay for the rest of suffering humanity), the country at least supported the UN boycott of Iraq. Maybe this was a case of what the German magazine *Stern*, talking about the Swiss phenomenon, called "an occasional attack of bad conscience".

No review of Switzerland would be complete without reference to that splendid institution, the Swiss army.

This august institution is renowned for its knives - or what enterprising businessmen, Swiss and others, pass off as Swiss army knives - best known for the bit that helps boy scouts take stones out of horses' hooves. So it may come as a surprise to learn that, before passing themselves off as pacifists, the Swiss were regularly at war with others (their foreign escapades ended with the battle of Marignano in Lombardy in 1515) and with themselves. They then settled down to being good mercenaries, a trade for which they are well suited.

But the Swiss army of today is something else. It is the idiosyncratically Swiss version of what every European dreams of: a *club*. Rather than rushing around warding off putative enemies the Swiss, during their annual terms of duty, go into huddles with one another, planning commercial alliances, forays into foreign markets, and so on.

One Swiss, a career general, went a bit too far. Just to prove that corruption can overtake the *Eidgenossen* too, he arranged to take kickbacks on a network of frontier fortresses. The resultant concrete constructions faded away like, and with, the sands of time.

Maybe the Swiss army will, too. Grassroots democracy of the Swiss kind has now produced a lobby called 'The Group for Switzerland Without an Army': 27 per cent of citizens, mainly young people, voted for its demise in a recent referendum. It has also produced the 'Auto Party' - something that sounds sinisterly like an *autonome* militant faction but actually started life as a lobby for Swiss motorists, an equally aggressive bunch of people. This is demanding the deployment of army units along the frontier in a bid to halt illegal immigration. What it has in mind for the Swiss Navy, a handful of frigates on the Rhine, is not so clear.

Overall, Switzerland's record in the art of war is not a very flattering one. A recent addition was the claim by the country's Socialist Party that 48 Swiss companies supplied advanced weapons technology to Iraq just before the Gulf War.

Despite its seven centuries of history, the country does now show signs of change - and not just at the level of the youngest generations. Swiss women, who first won the right to vote in the 1970s, now hold 17.5% of seats in the 200-member lower house. They also go on strike.

It also comes as a considerable surprise to learn that, as far back as the early-1980s, the Swiss had the highest mobility rate of any European country, with Ireland claiming the lowest. The explanation lies in the fact that the figures for home ownership are in inverse ratio: almost 80 percent of the Irish own their property against only 29 per cent of the Swiss (70 per cent of whom live in apartments in any case).

In business, the Swiss are generally if not always efficient and punctilious. Various observers speak of them as being exasperating negotiators, rigid in outlook and with a great talent for 'nitpicking'.

Some people say that, socially, they cast off their inhibitions when climbing mountains - but there's not much opportunity for that in a business environment...

Robert J Brown, a consultant psychologist, tells the story of a joint venture between a Swiss systems company and an Italian manufacturer of computerised materials handling equipment, a story that says as much about the Italians as the Swiss. After three months of working together "the Swiss engineers complained that their Italian colleagues were always changing their minds, that they never met the deadlines and did not seem to think time was important. They complained that the Italians invariably came back within a few days of provisional specifications being agreed, seeking modifications that would optimise performance of the mechanical equipment but would delay further programming. The Italians, meanwhile, complained that their Swiss colleagues were inflexible...".

Brown concludes that the central element in this problem was a conflict over the *sense of time*. "The Swiss team were heavily steeped in their cultural understanding of time as a commodity of precise and specific measurement... The Italians, separated geographically by a solid wall of snow-covered peaks, have endured and enjoyed a more casual attitude towards time. Like their moods, their sense of time is more fluid and is imbued with a temporary and transitional flavour". This endorses what was said earlier about the Italians.

For all Swiss from the businessman down, via the railway official who keeps the trains running on time, to the ordinary man or woman in the well-ordered Swiss street, punctuality is probably the greatest virtue of all. No wonder they make good watches! My German friend learned this early on when he invited mixed company - Swiss and foreigners - to a party at 8 pm. The Swiss guests turned up at *one minute to eight*, to be sure that they weren't late: he even suspects they rendezvoused outside his front door. The foreigners of course failed to appear for another half-hour or so.

'Sense of time' of course now applies to the Swiss in another, newer way. They sense that the time has come to review their values and their place in the world. As Rainer Gut, chairman of Crédit Suisse, said not so long ago: "After years of almost unbelievable prosperity, it may be time to scratch our heads and ask where we are going."

Some commitment to their neighbours in more than just meeting the demand for numbered bank accounts (though even the Swiss are now trying to inhibit money laundering) may be timely - things like backing down slightly from their tenet of neutrality and joining the European Union.

Even how the Swiss rally individually to the idea of membership of the European Economic Area as an interim step is questionable (they have reason to jib, since it's a bit of a pig in a poke). And, then, there's the problem of the imposition of new operating methods on the cantonal structure. Currently most revenue stays in the area where it is generated: the introduction of a standard Union-wide fiscal system like the present value-added tax, would shift funds to the centre and challenge the viability of a political formula the Swiss cherish so dearly.

The smugness *(Selbstgefälligkeit)* and the self-interest still get in the way. It is not that long ago that Zürich's leading daily, the *Tagesanzeiger*, asserted that "Switzerland is a model for Europe, not Europe a model for Switzerland". Cynics suggest that pro-EU mumblings from the gnomes of Zürich are prompted by the realisation that life outside the European Union would hurt Swiss pockets too much. If you listened to my German friend, any change would be a change for the better. Asked to sum up Switzerland in three words he said: "a fascist Disneyland" (maybe *Mauschwitz* or *Mauschweiz* would do it in one). But, he added, fascism is supposed to have vision: Switzerland's *petit bourgeois* fascism spies on its people, inhibits expression, ignores the real problems of society.

To judge from the massive if temporary migrations to Florida and California, and the more recent events northeast of Paris, there are many Europeans who would be happy to be part of the Disneyland thing, fascist or not. But for the Swiss it poses an awesome prospect. Faced with fundamental changes in their European perspective, in the words of *The Economist*, "the German-speaking majority are the most worried, fearing absorption into a new German empire. The French-speakers and Italian-speakers have few complexes about closer ties to France and Italy. The idea of a 'Europe of regions' is fashionable in Geneva and Lugano." Unfortunately the end-1992 referendum showed that even the Italian Swiss have their doubts.

The trouble with talking about the Swiss is that we Europeans tend to suspect there's always an element of self-interest in everything they do. Even George Mikes fell for that one. Yet, on examining my conscience, I have to admit I have met a lot of nice Swiss people and they have made me feel very much at home - and not just because they wanted to make money out of me. So there's good and bad in the Swiss, just as there is in the English.

The Austrians
The sentimental schizos

"Austria is Switzerland speaking pure German and with history added"   JE Morpurgo

"I think the good Austrian mentality is particularly hard to understand, it is in a particular sense subtler than any other, and its reality is never on the side of probability!"   Ludwig Wittgenstein

"The Austrian soul is a soft-centred truffle, the Swiss identity is bank secrecy" ["Die österreichische Seele ist die Mozartkugel, die schweizerische Identität ist das Bankgeheimnis"]   Dr Franz Schuh

"The situation in Germany is serious but not hopeless: the situation in Austria is hopeless but not serious"   Viennese proverb

"We're clever people. We turned Hitler into a German and Beethoven into an Austrian"   Austrian joke

"With your hat in your hand you make your way across the land" ["Mit dem Hut in der Hand kommt man durch das ganze Land"]
                                                                    Austrian saying

"Happy is he who forgets what cannot be changed" Johann Strauss

JE Morpurgo makes the Swiss sound pretty dull, which they're not. Yet, compared with them, the Austrians are a constant source of surprises. Not only because their German is anything but pure, though it sounds better, but because they have so much history to offer - history of a peculiarly dynastic, convoluted and schizophrenic kind. No wonder Freud had a ball!

'Dynastic' is the key word. Today's Austrians, and the Viennese in particular, have inherited the psychological and emotional trappings of the Habsburg Empire. To it they owe their understandably confused sense of identity. They are the heirs to an identity crisis which has not been helped by events since the turn of the century: World War I (when they nearly got beaten in the final phase by the Italians), the Anschluss of 1938, World War II, the Neutrality Treaty of 1955 (which now looks rather like injury time) and, most recently, accession to the European Union.

Once again we need to pause to decide who or what classes as 'Austrian'. A sojourn of 18 months in a Tyrolean peasant community in the late-1940s taught me that the Austrian west and east are worlds apart. With justification. The people in the mountainous west are of Swabian stock, while the Tyroleans have Bavarian, Celtic, even Nordic blood. Strike out eastwards beyond Linz and you move into Slav country.

So you have the peasantfolk at one end of the country and the scale of sophistication, and the Viennese at the other. The men of the Western provinces, a cross between Arnold Schwarzenegger (suntanned sallowness and all) and Maximilian Schell, are characterised by an amiable and folkloric good nature which occasionally turns very nasty. These characteristics are perfected, at the other end of the country, in the fine art of the Viennese.

Vorarlberg and Tyrol tend to look west to Switzerland, Salzburg and Oberösterreich north to Germany (while resenting the latter's wealth), Carinthia and Styria south to Italy and what used to be Yugoslavia, and Vienna and Burgenland east. Theoretically the country could disintegrate from centrifugal force. Yet history has created an unlikely but very real cohesion.

Maybe we have a lot to thank the Habsburgers for. Only centuries of dynastic history could have produced such an unlikely concoction of peoples. But, if this looks complicated, take the case of Vienna itself - amputated from its other half, Budapest - a microcosm of the old Austro-Hungarian Empire with bells and whistles attached.

Vienna was built by Czech workers on the orders of its Habsburg rulers. The Czechs were told to suppress their Slavonic instincts and help create an arch-Teutonic community. They were also encouraged to 'naturalise', in every sense of the word, in exchange for Viennese citizenship.

The first bit worked: Vienna has the Germanic grandiosity of Munich and Berlin, with the appropriately added touch of kitschiness. The second bit didn't: the Czech workers not only couldn't change character (they are Slavs after all), they proliferated. So ironically, with the help of both earlier and later migrations, we are now confronted with a German-looking city full of Slav-looking people! Statistically, Vienna has the largest ethnic Czech community after Prague.

Austria has lost, but not forgotten, half of its historical *raison d'être* - the Hungarian half which anchored the nation firmly in a common *Kaffeehauskultur* plus a tradition of committed bureaucracy. Although now a member of the European Union - having finally, though not entirely convincingly, turned its back on a role within a 'Greater German Space' - the country is still responsive to the siren song of *Mitteleuropa*.

The German link is not just a matter of shared language. Long before the Anschluss and the emergence of Austria's active Nazi element in WWII, a national assembly had voted in 1918 to have the country merge with the German Republic of the time, a decision that was vetoed by the Allies. All this prompts the question of whether or not Austria really exists - a question that contributes heftily to the country's psychoses.

If a clear political identity has been lacking until recently, the cultural identity has not. The Viennese take in culture in the same way other Europeans go to football matches - regularly, enthusiastically and with almost as much extrovert involvement as the average football fan. Their participation in musical events has always ensured 'critical mass', even if the critical bit has been largely destructive, as it was for poor old Schoenberg. And the number of bookshops per square kilometer in Vienna's First District must be the highest in Europe.

In these and other respects, the Austrians have pretensions plus a historical tendency to anti-semitism (maybe they do have something to reproach Freud for). But as a relatively exotic branch of European culture with their Slav overtones, their memories of historic grandeur and their formidable artistic record, they probably think they are entitled to their airs and graces.

This cultural stew emits a sophisticated sweetness that charms some and curdles the blood of others. At their best, the Austrians are charming and courteous people with a gift for making the stranger feel wanted. At their worst, they demonstrate a 'bellboy' mentality: *Habe die Ehre, Herr Generaldirektor* or *Herr Universitätsprofessor*, and *Küss die Hand, gnädige Frau*.

But the interest, when it's there, is genuine. Contrary to what many foreigners might expect, even the Viennese are likely to put human values before social judgments. An expatriate comments that the Catholic tradition has taught the Austrians the art of being considerate towards their fellow beings, despite occasional and flagrant lapses.

Some foreigners also note that, if you scratch the surface charm, there's a latent aggressiveness underneath which has its roots in uncertainty. *GEO* magazine insists the Austrians have an inferiority complex, the Vorarlbergers, Salzburgers and Tyroleans excepted. These lastnamed, to be different, suffer from pigheadedness tempered with wiliness.

But, as an Austrian observes, "Vienna remains Vienna, and that's the worst one can say of this city". The Viennese sense of irony is a saving grace. No doubt this is also a defence mechanism: their reticence about accepting a shared responsibility for the less happy moments in recent history is still remarkable.

Polly Platt, a consultant in cross-cultural affairs who knows Austria well, must have the Viennese particularly in mind when she says that "Austria is ... a nation with a Germanic passion for rules and Latin ingenuity for getting around them... German efficiency, Latin love of fun and macho Slav individualism all sheltered in the same breast." That's quite a tall order, though one wonders whether the "Germanic passion for rules" is as highly developed as she suggests.

Other writers offer equally fascinating formulae for the Austrian psyche. Ernest Marboe, in *The Book of Austria*, describes the country's *genius loci* as "Gothic imagination, Hellenic spirit, Celtic love of form, and Slav melancholy." Hans-Georg Behr, in *Die österreichische Provokation*, speaks of "Bavarian [Bajuvar] love of life, Slavic melancholy, Balkan business sense, Levantine cunning and Hungarian temperament." Take your pick.

On this evidence, it should surprise no one that, dubbed a *Skandalrepublik* by some of its citizens, Austria is renowned for corruption in high places. As memories fade, people find ingenious ways of rekindling the image. There has been a particularly persistent outbreak of cases in recent years, ranging from payola on public contracts like the AKH hospital project to collective fraud like the wine scandal. But the fact that these things become such public knowledge says something for the Austrians...

As in Italy, the principle of patronage extends down from the political establishment into other sectors of the community: here, *lottizzazione* is known as *Proporz* (the philosophy is similar). There is also a repressed violence not far below the surface, which may explain why one in ten Austrian males owns a firearm.

In his book *Die österreichische Seele*, the late and lamented Erwin Ringel[35] said that his fellow-countrymen "oscillate between sentimental self-deprecation and boundless feelings of grandiosity". I have seen this confirmed in a pathological tendency to switch from wild enthusiasm to apathy, and back, in perfectly ordinary conversations. Resentment over German wealth - and over what some Austrians perceive as a German plot to hijack their culture - is certainly rife. The not-invented-here (NIH) complex is highly developed.

Professor Ringel, who says Freud would have had to be deaf and blind not to stumble across the Austrians' neuroses, offers a theory on the root causes. He maintains that complexes are incubated in childhood through the authoritarian attitudes of parents who impose standards of obedience, politeness and thrift which engender a love-hate relationship between the generations. Children are treated as 'property' until they leave the family - although, for whatever reasons, Austrian parents spend more money on toys for their children than other European parents do.

Such things, says the Professor, create a dichotomy in the Austrian mind, a seesaw mentality with superficial courtesy and conformity at one extreme, hidden resentment and jealousy at the other. He quotes the words of a Dutch observer, Bernard van

Beurden: "The Austrian has a two-roomed house. One room is bright and friendly, a well-furnished room where he receives his guests. The other room is dark, with the blinds down, locked, inaccessible, completely out-of-bounds to strangers."

Foreign friends living in Vienna argue that attitudes to children have now evolved to the point where Austrian parents are as permissive as European parents anywhere else. But they concede that the Austrian adult leads a very private existence (the influence of the 'dark room'?). Professor Ringel cites research which claims to show that, even within the family, much is left unsaid - hardly surprising since the research finds that "1.4 million Austrians have practically no contact with their friends, outside their place of work, in an average month". Moreover "married couples speak to one another an average of seven minutes per day (!)". Maybe the recent proposal to oblige Austrian husbands legally to participate in housework is designed to encourage improved communications within the home...

Professor Ringel suggests difficulty in communicating and in eliciting a response from one's fellow-beings may also help explain the country's high suicide rate. To that could be added the high level of illegitimate births.

On the business front, the image of little men with plastic attache cases is fading fast, though the *Doktor Doktor* syndrome is still very much alive. Sometimes, there seems to be a great deal of activity with little delivered at the end of the line. But once they get their act together, Austrian companies can outperform their foreign rivals: industry leaders include businesses like Plansee in cutting tools, Engel in plastics machinery and Plasser & Theurer who make those smart little railway maintenance machines that most of us think are Swiss. Much of the most recent growth has, in fact, been in the Alpine provinces at the western end of the country.

Many small-to-medium family firms, particularly in the engineering sector, are competent international marketers. Despite the fact that they have only a small vehicle manufacturing industry, the Austrians manage to return a favourable net balance of trade on automobile-related products. And they're now teaching the Czechs and others the art of management.

In fact there can be no doubt that the country is basically well run. Try to relate today's Austria to the quaint and chaotic country I remember 40 years ago and the overall improvement is striking.

For a start there is surprisingly little environmental spoliation: the country has more stringent environmental standards than those reflected in the norms of the European Union. Almost all one sees impresses: roads, railway systems, agriculture, city development, even the architecture manages to combine contemporary imagination with traditional charm (light-years ahead of the aseptic approach of much German architecture).

Maybe the identity crisis will resolve itself with time in any case. Comparing the younger generation of Austrians with their elders, Friedrich Torberg remarked: "When you say Austria, they know what you mean and when they identify themselves with this Austria, they know why."

But, in the meantime, the Austrians can still offer us their wistfulness combined with a wry sense of humour. The Viennese tell a charming story about Otto von Habsburg asking his valet to turn on the television set. A football match is in progress. "What's the match?", asks Otto. "Austria-Hungary", replies the valet. "Ah", says Otto, "but who are they playing against?"

The Celtic Fringe
The wonder in the west

"The Irish are a fair people - they never speak well of one another"
Samuel Johnson

"Other people have a nationality. The Irish and the Jews have a psychosis"
Brendan Behan

"The world of the imagination, the unseen world, has carried for many Irishmen as much conviction as the visible universe"
E Estyn Evans

"All races have produced notable economists, with the exception of the Irish who doubtless can protest their devotion to higher arts"
JK Galbraith

"The noblest prospect which a Scotchman (sic) ever sees, is the high road that leads him to England!"
Samuel Johnson

"A young Scotsman of your ability let loose upon the world with £300, what could he not do? It's almost appalling to think of; especially if he went among the English"
Sir James Barrie

"Severitas, which means being stern with oneself"
Paul Scott, Essays on Scotland

"...the character of Welshmen in general, who are proverbially obstinate when opposition is offered to them...
George Borrow

"'The Welsh,' said the Doctor, 'are the only nation in the world that has produced no graphic or plastic art, no architecture, no drama. They just sing', he said with disgust, 'sing and blow down wind instruments of plated silver'"
Evelyn Waugh

L ook at a map of the British Isles in the late Roman Empire and, beyond the westernmost frontiers you see two words: 'Picts' where Scotland is today and 'Scots' where Ireland is. This sets the tone for anything to do with the Celts: they have their own way of doing things and should not be confused with apparently rational people like the English.

The Celtic communities are a colourful lot, full of surprises and remarkable in their variety. Collectively dubbed the Celtic Fringe or more respectfully the Atlantic Arc, they are strung along the shores of the western ocean like pearls on a fine necklace. They include the Scots, the Irish, the people of the Isle of Man, the Welsh, the Cornish, the Bretons of France (forced back eastwards out of the British Isles by the Anglo-Saxons in the Fifth Century, it seems) and the people in the northwest corner of the Iberian peninsula.

Without going too far back into prehistory (there is a theory that they originated in the Himalayan foothills), the Celts were established throughout Europe when the others - Greeks, Germanics, Romans - came along. How much they were a distinct ethnic group is a matter for continued and typically enthusiastic debate. Anyway it seems the Greeks gave them a gentle push westwards, the Germanics helped them on their way, and the Romans set the seal. Apart from recolonising Brittany, they then stayed put.

There are two main branches of the Celtic language, Goidelic (Gaelic) and Brythonic, and a rich variety of customs and traditions. One of the things they have in common - and that unites the rest of Europe against them - is their love of the pipes, whether the bag-pipe in Scotland, the *Uilleann* pipes in Ireland, the *cornemuse* in Brittany or the *gaita* in Galicia, to which should be added Ireland's addiction to the flute and the tin whistle. Another is their affinity with the world of the spirits (non-alcoholic in this case) - the water kelpie of the Scots, the leprechauns of the Irish, the *estadinhas* of the Galicians - and of giants and the like.

Sadly this affinity does not extend to the spirits of the trees. Little remains of the post-glacial forests of Scotland and Ireland and, in the view of E Estyn Evans[36], Irish countryfolk still demonstrate "a continuing hostility to trees". According to the same authority, they also still demonstrate "a predilection for incendiarism"! There may be a connection.

Within their similarities, the peoples of the Celtic Fringe display some dramatic differences of temperament which add up to one of the most remarkable funds of human resourcefulness Europe can offer today. In varying degrees, its people have retained a feeling for life that much of the Old World has lost, together with a refreshing sense of creativity and a remarkable gift for both words and song. They are also a very egalitarian lot, having little of the class-consciousness of the English.

Although it takes a lot to match up to a Scotsman like Rabbie Burns or a Welshman like Dylan Thomas, it's probably the Irish that make the greatest impression on foreigners. Yet Ireland has one of the lowest population densities of any European country, though you wouldn't think so when you go into an Irish pub. A lot of folk seem to spend much of their time drinking and telling stories, except when they're eating, sleeping or going to church. But, while informal, the Irish have none of the meretriciousness of the English: historically, the Celts are a people with strong moral precepts. And there are a lot of very able Irish folk in business, where they combine charm with unexpected efficiency.

In the words of *The Economist*, "the British have often identified a riotous sense of fun in Irish people". The Irish have not earned their image of amiable inconsequentiality without reason. They even contrive to have the only capital city where, in some cases, the house numbers start in the middle of the street.

Nora Chadwick[37] must have had the Irish particularly in mind when she wrote that "the most widespread entertainment of the Celts probably was that derived from story-telling and talking, accompanied by feasting and drinking. These pleasures appear to have been enjoyed by all grades of society, whether the drink was the expensive imported wine of the nobility or the native beer and mead of the less wealthy."

In his enlightening book *The Personality of Ireland* E Estyn Evans (curious that a Welshman should be one of the great authorities on Ireland!) offers us an insight when he says that "it may be said that constantly changing weather brings a sense of uncertainty and perhaps encourages an indifference to time and a predilection for gambling and for alcohol."

Climate has certainly had a formative influence on the cultures of the Celtic Fringe. Elsewhere in his book, Evans remarks that "there has been much speculation on the possible relationship between the warm humid conditions of south-western Ireland and the soft accents and supposed laziness of the Kerryman". And, looking at the opposite end of the island in a surprising allusion to present-day problems in Ulster, he says that "the climate is cooler here the whole year round and the growing season shorter. The landscape in places approaches the austere. Tree-fruits such as chestnuts and walnuts rarely ripen and one will see no sweet-scented cowslips in the fields. As a habitat it is more familiar and attractive to Scotsmen than to lowland Englishmen."

Another formative influence was history and the proximity of the English. In the appalling potato famine of the mid-19th century the English were both perpetrators and, as the descendants of 14th century settlers, the victims. It is even said that the supremely Gaelic sport of hurling was brought to Ireland by these English invaders. But what many foreigners are even less aware of is that there was an English Irish elite known to the locals as the 'West Brit' Irish which, until recently, tended to monopolise the best jobs in business and the professions.

The image of the Irish has been institutionalised over the centuries, largely by the Irish themselves. An editorial in the *Irish Independent*, written on the brink of industrialisation in the 1960s, said that "there can be no doubt that much of the responsibility for the distortion lies... on certain Irish-born writers and artists who for the sake of currying favours in some quarters may seek to perpetuate the tradition of the stage Irishman and to present our people as wastrels, drunkards, ne'er-do-wells and irresponsibles."

Ireland and the Irish are indeed great fun, even if the image of "a land of pubs and peat", to quote *The European*, has given way to science parks and smokestacks. It is astonishing that respondents to the INRA Country Image III study referred to in Chapter 2, asked to sample the statement "the inhabitants are friendly and cheerful", gave the Irish such a low rating: -13.1 compared with 49.2 for the Italians, 46.5 for the Spanish, and even 24.6 for the French who can be as churlish as anyone.

The fact is that the Irish are such a long way away that they are a totally unknown factor for many Europeans. Ask the Irish themselves and they will vote more enthusiastically than any other European country for the fact that their fellow countryfolk "have a positive attitude towards life".

Rather surprisingly for an otherwise easygoing people, the Irish are inclined to be sexist, to the extent that a mixed pair on a golf course almost ranks as an indecent act (parliamentary committee guidelines now state that clubs must provide 'full and equal treatment for men and women members'). Yet they have one of the healthiest birth rates in Europe. The explanation, on both counts, is that they are still staunchly Catholic - although there are signs that the younger generations are now questioning the convictions of their elders.

One of the great contributions of the Irish to society is their habit of spreading their humanity around the globe by dint of emigration - encouraged of course by religious fervour (Irish missionaries christianised much of northern Europe) and by potato famines, the English, job opportunities in the Chicago police, and the like. Even in the 1980s they were still leaving the Emerald Isle at an average rate of 40,000 per year, mainly heading for Britain, Canada or the United States. The stick-in-the-muds, by comparison, seem well embedded: the Irish have the highest rate of home ownership in Europe.

The Scots (note the spelling) also have a habit of spreading themselves around, encouraged by the virtual absence of all natural resources except coal, timber and more recently oil - which the English have claimed for themselves in the name of the British.

Examples of sizeable Scots communities on the Continent can be traced back to the early Middle Ages, particularly in France, Sweden, the Netherlands, Germany and Denmark. Magnus Linklater, editor of *The Scotsman*, makes the point that the Scots feel more at home in continental Europe than in England: "Scotland has had strong links with the countries of Europe. Whether it was supplying officers for the king's guard in France, mercenaries for Flanders, engineers for Poland, shipbuilders for Russia or whalers for Norway, the Scots have been confidently exporting manpower and expertise across the North Sea for more than 500 years."

Gustavus Adolphus of Sweden boasted a bodyguard and an army corps composed entirely of Scots, hence the number of Swedes with Scots names you find in the Stockholm telephone book (try it sometime).

Later came ill-fated attempts to establish Scots colonies in Nova Scotia and on the Darien isthmus, of all places, followed by the emigrations prompted by the Highland clearances of the nineteenth century (sheep being more profitable than the traditional activities of the Scots crofters). About the same time a middle-class movement developed which has taken generations of Scots to London and, from there, out to the British Empire.

If the English provided the administrators, the Scots provided the accountants. They also produced the scientists - the list of Scottish inventors is a long one. They owe this to a canny belief in the importance of education for its own sake, a strong university tradition, and a distinctive combination of native inventiveness and a talent for hard work. By comparison with the Irish, the Scots are a very level-headed people, determined and dour to the point of self-deprecation. But if they tell you, as they are likely to do, that they are humourless, don't believe them.

In fact their humour is as idiosyncratic as the people themselves, which may explain why foreigners sometimes have difficulty in detecting it. Douglas Muecke[38] offers enlightenment: "Scottish humour is particularly rich in understatement and especially dry off-hand expressions of mock-commiseration that are grossly inadequate to the cruel and grim situations that call them forth." Uh huh.

Though they have little of the whimsy of the Irish, the Scots share with them a strong sense of nationhood. While this seems to come naturally with the Irish, in the case of the Scots it is helped along by education, both within the family and at school. Ambitious by nature and condemned as they are to cohabit with the English in a tight little island, the Scots offer a unique example of potential nation-statehood that has so far not been realised. As a well-educated Scot of my generation explains (and almost all Scots are well-educated): "The primary school pupil is fed a history diet of the Wars of Independence - Stirling Bridge and Bannockburn, Wallace and Bruce and the treachery of the English stooge Balliol." Again, you see what history books can do.

While the Irish had only a passing relationship with the French Revolution, the Scots have had a love affair going with the French for a very long time and this has helped cement Scotland's close links with the Continent. But, as a Scot puts it wryly: "The French connection is something the Scots remember much more than the French".

The Welsh, like anyone within the orbit of English history (their name comes from the Old English word 'wealh', meaning 'slave'), also have a tendency to emigrate. In their case, it was to even more unlikely places like Patagonia (the Scots, after all, only got as far as the Darien Peninsula in Central America).

Whilst sharing the Celtic lyricism of the Irish, the Welsh can be just plain verbose: 'The Welsh Windbag' is a character that pops up regularly in both fiction and public life. They also sing a lot, again like the Irish and to a lesser degree the Scots - though less in the bathroom (according to the Graham report cited in Chapter 6, where they only register 32% against an all-time high for southeast England, of all places, of 44%).

The Welsh also have a reputation with the English of being devious, something at which the English themselves excel. They are certainly obstinate, as George Borrow knew full well, a quality that is often perceived as a kind of dogged truculence.

It is particularly difficult to say anything coherent about the Bretons as, apart from superficial things like funny clothes and a fear of death, they have very little in common. Theodore Zeldin[1] goes so far as to say that "their delight in the Breton language comes from the fact that almost every village speaks that language differently, so that it becomes the expression of their very local particularism. The differences are enough to make them use French when they meet Bretons from a different district: if Breton were standardized, 'it would no longer be their own private possession'". But, thanks to the efforts of a determined minority they still hold, collectively, the world record for alcoholism, it seems.

As for the Galicians of northwest Spain, some of the things said about them suggest an amalgam of the Scots and the Welsh. Flora Lewis makes the point[2]: "Gallegos, as the people are called, have their own character, speak a dialect near to Portuguese and are the butt of many jokes about *dourness, slyness, shrewdness, stinginess, conservatism*" (my italics). But, though they shared Celtic ancestors a long time ago, this may have more to do with the Swabian strain in their blood!

Ultimately, the decisive factor common to all components of the Celtic Fringe is their passion for being what they are, a passion that expresses itself through their music (brass bands for the Welsh, fiddles, flutes and bagpipes for the rest), their folk-dancing and their story-telling.

The Norwegians
The obstinate outsiders

"A permanent sense of diversity is at the base of Scandinavian cohesion" Flora Lewis

"November always seemed to me the Norway of the year" Emily Dickinson

"In a situation where one has the choice of being straight and honest or tactical, there is no doubt where you will find the Norwegians. The Swedes are honest to a less degree, the Danes not at all" Finnish business executive

"Although Norwegians believe they belong to the best country on earth in terms of quality of life, they need constant confirmation of this opinion" French visitor

"If Walt Disney had been Norwegian, there would have been a dwarf called Gloomy" Roland White, *Sunday Times*

"It is commonly known that one of the worst things for a Norwegian is to be taken in by a Dane" Unidentified Danish businessman

"A race formed by climate and history into a somewhat dour, Puritanical and hard-working mould" Robert Ball, *Fortune*

"From a French point of view, a Norwegian businessman appears often more open-minded than, for instance, a Swede" French business executive

"Norwegian ladies are of natural beauty without make-up. Ladies wearing knapsacks are typically seen in Norway. This custom, which seems strange to the foreigner, is very functional, since walking people get both hands free" Japanese visitor

Having committed the unpardonable sin in the first edition of this book of lumping the Norwegians, Swedes, Danes and Finns together under the title of 'The Nordics' - I did so because I didn't feel confident enough to make a clear distinction at the time - I now plan to make amends. This is a risky business.

It's risky because, even now, I sometimes have difficulty in telling the difference (it's easier for a Norwegian, a Swede, a Dane, a Finn, etc, etc). It's also risky because I have to make a judgment of Solomon in deciding where to start.

So I will start with the Norwegians, simply because they are as Nordic as anyone can get - namely opinionated and, seen from a relatively centralised western European standpoint, insular.

We Europeans, with haunting memories of Viking raids and rapes in our collective subconscious, tend to think of all these good people, even the Finns, as Scandinavians. But strictly speaking in the geographical sense, Scandinavia is just Sweden and Norway (*pace* SAS). If we talk about the languages, then we are justified in adding Danish. But we tend to talk of them all as 'Scandinavians' - at this point adding the Icelanders, who are of Norwegian stock.

Since we've brought up this business of the Vikings, let's get them out of the way before we go any further. They came in three varieties: Swedish, Norwegian and Danish (definitely no Finns). They were all Vikings in their formative years, as different tribes descended from the same race. The Norwegians, of course, claim that they were the *real* Vikings, looking westwards and taking the Celtic Fringe, Iceland, Greenland and even North America's Vinland into their marauding stride (giving the name 'Greenland' to a barren expanse of snow and ice, in order to attract settlers, rates as one of the great public relations stunts of all time).

The Nordic region certainly has its fair share of folklore, mainly in the minds of non-Nordics. All Norwegians are obstinate, all Danes are frivolous, all Swedes are sullen, all Finns are taciturn. Lumped together by Europeans from further south they appear, quite wrongly, to be uninspiring.

But their apparent dullness doesn't prevent them from sharing a series of ethnic jokes where you just fill in the spaces according to your nationality (the Finns don't fit as easily into this form of verbal folklore, although if the evening is long enough and the drink good enough, anything is possible).

An example is the story of the Norwegian, the Swede and the Dane who find themselves caught in a snowstorm on the side of a mountain. They stumble across a cave and decide to take shelter. On entering they are greeted by an awful stench which, on inspection, turns out to come from a half-dead goat which has already taken refuge in the cave. The three of them debate what to do and (depending on your nationality) the Norwegian goes back in first: five minutes later he staggers out sick with nausea and collapses. Then the Dane goes in and, ten minutes later, crawls out and expires. Finally the Swede goes in and, fifteen minutes later... the goat comes out.

The Swedes colonised the Finns for four centuries, the Danes colonised the Norwegians for what the latter prefer to term 'the 400-year night', the Swedes regularly besieged the Danes in Copenhagen and the Danes regularly gave them a bit of Norway in order to get rid of them. The Swedes and Norwegians even participated in a century-long and thoroughly uncomfortable union which ended in 1905. All of which helps explain the story about the half-dead goat.

While there is inevitable resentment about 'big brother' next door, stories of Norwegian-Swedish antipathies are greatly exaggerated. Swedes will tell you they have a better relationship with the Norwegians than with the other Nordic peoples. Mutual comprehension is helped by the fact that they can understand one another's languages, a capacity neither of them shares with the Danes, where the Danish accent gets in the way, and even less with the Finns.

In reality all the Nordic cultures have great qualities which, of course, are rarely acknowledged by the others. The Norwegians, for a start, have a very comfortable relationship with nature, something they wrongly think the Swedes are forfeiting through industrialisation and material progress - and which, they fondly believe, explains the Swedish crime and suicide rate.

The Norwegians, again like the other Nordics, demonstrate a total absence of pomp and circumstance in public - and in public life. An Italian visitor makes the point[6]: "Even if the Norwegian has the same material goods as the average Italian, he does not have the same need to show it. An aspect of this is the ease with which you can get in contact with top-level people. At first, I was surprised to be invited to have breakfast with a minister in Parliament at 8:00 or 8:30. And then I would see all these different ministers, including the Prime Minister, serving themselves at the self-service counter. In Italy, it is completely different." Most elsewhere, too.

Lack of pretention is accompanied by natural politeness. It is quite something to have a German, a representative of one of the politer European races, say this: "The phenomenon of being able to tolerate anything is widespread and found in many situations. I have not yet discovered whether this is because Norwegians are polite, or if they simply do not dare say anything when there is something that bothers them." Since the Norwegians are anything but cowards, I put it down to tolerance *per se*.

They are also, sometimes too transparently, honest. A Finnish businessman says he has never met a Norwegian who has tried to cheat him. Yet he adds, on second thoughts, "except for an exporter who sent me a lobster with two left claws and told me that they were both on the same living lobster when it left Norway!"

What they can also be is obstinate. In the words of another Finn (not themselves one of the most pliable of peoples), "Norwegians are exceedingly stubborn. Their approach is matter-of-fact. 'These are the merits, that's it!' They make a proposal and stick to it, come hell or high water."

Despite fits of gloom about both themselves and their neighbours, the Norwegians and their fellow-Nordics have a relatively upbeat view of life: "not cheerful, but optimistic, an intellectual attitude in which the future is expected to be good", says the American writer Stuart Miller[24].

Maybe for 'future' one should read 'afterlife'. In the case of the Norwegians Lutheranism, the Nordic brand of Protestantism, seems to have imprinted a rather cheerless view of life on earth. This view is reinforced by the sparse and rugged nature of the country - something that, in addition to the inevitable gulf between capital-city attitudes and provincial ones, may help explain the fact that the southern and western areas are far more fundamentalist (and anti-EU) than the Oslo region.

Almost all the respondents to the INRA Country Image III Study quoted in Chapter 2 gave the Norwegians a poor rating on the 'friendly and cheerful' scale - the only major dissenters, other than their fellow-Nordics, being the British. 'Cheerful'? Well, no. But 'friendly', surely. Maybe I just say that because I'm British.

Old Testament images of fire and brimstone have helped keep Norwegians on the straight and narrow. Maybe this helps explain the country's road safety record: a French research centre rated the Norwegians the most careful drivers in Europe in 1991.

Norway's Sunday press was stigmatised a century ago by the church because it was supposed to have a 'trivialising' influence on people's minds. And only 40 years ago, which is but an instant in the passage of Nordic time, Norwegian public opinion was engulfed in a nationwide debate on the nature, scope and location of Hell with a capital 'H' (not to be confused with a rather grim railway junction of the same name). As a Norwegian puts it, "we face this constant moral dilemma: can one find joy in life and, at the same time, be a good person? If you have fun, you're a sinner". Norway is still an island of prudery in a Nordic sea of permissiveness.

On the brink of the 21st century, Norwegians do seem at times to be a gloomy and introspective lot (maybe they think the world *is* going to end on the dot of midnight December 31 1999). An opinion study conducted among 1,000 Norwegians in 1991 found that 80 per cent agree with the proposition that Norwegians are sceptical about new ideas, and 70 per cent believe that the fear of looking foolish is a national problem. No wonder they resent the Swedish joking that, if there's a flash of lightning, a Norwegian will come out to have his photo taken. Recently the government has been mulling over a campaign to get the people to be more positive about themselves.

Such stories prove that the Nordic peoples have reservations about one another. While the Swedes think the Norwegians bucolic, the Norwegians find the Swedes both opportunistic and condescending (not surprisingly in view of the joke about the lightning flash), and both of them find the Danes rather lightweight.

The Lutheran tradition of doctrine and discipline finds its 20th century extension in rules and regulations. The Nordic populations are by nature socially obedient people - to the extent that, in structured situations, their normal powers of creativity and imagination desert them.

From time to time, of course, they kick over the traces. But where the Swedes embark on tax dodges and one-day alcoholic

210

blinds on the Kattegat ferries, the Norwegians tend to work out their frustrations by going on long and dangerous treks through the mountains.

Despite the equality that comes with it, the Lutheran ethic has encouraged a tradition of conformity which has its darker side, namely a disapproval of socially deviationist tendencies that almost amounts to a denial of any form of pluralism. In the Nordic region generally this can also lead to curious value judgments, for example the subtle distinction between the socially acceptable habit of going on the periodic blind (socially acceptable to males at any rate) and the unacceptable principle of being an alcoholic.

It also produces strange behavioural quirks, such as the dinner-time habit of banging cutlery on wineglasses to announce the inevitable boring speech, with heavy drinking and coarse humour as the equally inevitable sequel.

In their book *Made in Norway - Norwegians as others see them*[6], Kjell Habert and Arild Lillebø cite the words of a Japanese business executive: "Norwegian people are rather straightforward... They are kind of stubborn." Strong words for a Japanese, but the "straightforward" helps explain the rest. Norwegian people have a directness and, without any intention on my part of sounding condescending, a simplicity which makes them stand apart from many other Europeans. They also have a sense of their own worth, and often other people's worth too, which is not far removed from that of the average Spaniard. Both nations happen to live close to nature.

This affinity with nature makes Norwegians disregard little conceits which some other Europeans would regard as normal. This is even evident to as matter-of-fact a people as the Finns, one of whom comments that "Norwegians are outspoken to the degree of being naive... In a situation where Norwegians are confronted with being straight and honest, or 'tactical', there is no doubt where you will find the Norwegians." Trust, for them, is the rule rather than the exception.

Nature indeed marks the Norwegians. 'Nature in the raw' for, where it is a hint in neighbouring Sweden, it is a hammer-blow in Norway. Thirty minutes by tram from central Oslo and you are in deep forest. Norwegians immerse themselves in nature, they commune with it, they breathe it. With due respect for private rights, the land is theirs (as is Sweden for the Swedes). The word 'trespassing' is unknown in Norwegian language and law.

Much is explained by the sheer size of the country and the relative insignificance of the individual: next to Iceland, Norway has the lowest population density of any European country. As a Norwegian puts it: "If you pinpoint the southern tip of Norway and swivel the country around 180°, the northernmost tip will be on a level with Bologna or Bordeaux. Bergen in the west is on the same line of longitude as Amsterdam, and Kirkenes in the north is as far east as Istanbul." A curious lesson in geography but an informative one.

Remoteness from the rest of the world, and even within their own environment, makes the Norwegians 'uncertain in their certainty'. A British businessman quoted in Kjell Habert's and Arild Lillebø's book puts it in simple but, I suspect, unintentionally inflammatory terms: "Norwegians often appear to be 'village folk' as opposed to 'city folk'. In the main, they have not the self-confidence of, say, the Danes." And I thought the Danes lacked self-confidence.

A Frenchman elaborates on this more elegantly: "Although Norwegians believe they belong to the best country on earth in terms of quality of life, they need constant confirmation of this opinion." Inferiority complexes, many of them born of history rather than reality, die hard.

Outdoor exercise looms large in the minds of average Norwegians. They can prove their worth and enjoy nature at one and the same time. They call it their 'Nansen complex' and invoke it to justify queueing to cross Greenland on skis. They can even produce people like Erling Kagge and Boerge Ousland, each of whom trekked alone and unassisted to one of the Poles, Kagge the South, Ousland the North, just for the sake of it. By his own admission, Kagge thought about beautiful women and good food to keep going.

If you're older and less energetic, but still Norwegian, then you can always fall back on your country cottage and enjoy the good air. The Norwegian way of life was summed up unintentionally but succinctly by ex-premier Jan Peder Syse who, interviewed about his stormy life in parliament, replied: "I consciously turn my thoughts to my holiday cabin and reflect on bricklaying, composting and planting flowers there. After seven minutes, I'm fast asleep."

Such simple truths deserve to be better known. Yet much that happens in Norway fails to reach the ears of the outside world - and that's part of the problem. It even applied to Erling Kagge when he was at the other end of the world. You would have had to look an even longer way to find mention of his exploit, yet the papers were full at the time of the travails of two Britons who, despite egging one another on, nearly didn't make it. But they went *across* the South Pole and not just to it.

In the circumstances it's no wonder that, though they are really no different from their fellow-Europeans in most respects, the Norwegians make up for modest human resources by having their own way of interpreting reality. Witness the newspaper headlines about great sporting achievements quoted at the head of Chapter 8. With only 4.3 million people, they are even in a minority in Nordic terms.

The Norwegians deserve greater encouragement from the rest of us. No wonder they suffer from an inferiority complex. If they were in the middle of Europe, it would be different. But, then, they wouldn't have that country of theirs - and what's a little complex when you have a country like Norway?

And, after all, the Norwegians do have other claims to fame. They boast the largest community of Sami, better known to us in the south as Lapps ('community' is a questionable description, since the Sami are largely nomadic and no one can really verify the Norwegians' claim). No one is absolutely certain either about the Samis' origin, but they appear to be caucasian with an admixture of mongol and speak a variation of Finno-Ugrian. Contrary to popular belief, they did *not* cross the North Atlantic island-hopping or on icefloes.

A second pretext for Norwegian pride is that they can claim common lineage with the Icelanders, descendants of Norwegian settlers who colonised this mid-Atlantic island before the year 1000. The Icelanders, all 262,000 of them, live in splendid isolation, wanting nothing to do with the European Union. They speak Old Norse, the language of the Vikings, address each other by their first names only (which is the way you'll find them listed in the telephone directory!), and eat sheep's testicles washed down with a fiery potion called 'Black Death'.

I reckon that, if the Norwegians want to claim responsibility for something like this, nobody for once is going to argue with them.

The Danes

The entrepreneurial extroverts

"One day all Nordic lands were in your power
And England too - no longer your domains
A tiny land, but in the world you tower -
There ring the song and chisel of the Danes"

Hans Christian Andersen

"Denmark is a clean, well-regulated country populated by prosperous, literate people who all vote in elections, live in handsome and modest surroundings and have no hang-ups about sex. An American can find plenty to learn from here"   Garrison Keillor

"The Danes are regarded as informal, unpretentious, ironic and anti-authoritarian"   Per Himmelstrup

"In Denmark, breaking rules and laws is one of our most popular pastimes"   Danish business executive

"Whimsy - and a bloody-minded contrariness - play no small role in Danish politics"   Peter Millar, *The European*

"The Danish labour force is highly educated. Individual workers display a lot of independence, creativity and initiative. As an American, I especially notice the Danes' high expectations of their own results - they demand quality"   Connie Lindgren, IBM

"Danes go to their summer cottages for privacy. But Swedes invite real friends into their homes"   Swedish journalist

Even if they demonstrate less of the qualities traditionally associated with that warrior race, the Danes were also Vikings - the ones that raped, plundered and pillaged in a southwesterly direction much of the time. Tradition is actually wrong on a lot of points, one of them being that the Vikings had no decent instincts, the other that they wore silly hats.

One thing the Danish Vikings did do was turn up in the majority at the conquest of Normandy. There were Swedish and Norwegian Vikings there too but no one, least of all the French, could tell the difference since the frontiers between the Nordic countries were still arbitrary, and certainly different from today's, with 'Danes' living in the Skåne province of present-day Sweden.

On that occasion the Danes also demonstrated the sense of equality typical of Nordic society. The story goes that, at the siege of Paris, the Frankish commander had great difficulty negotiating with them because he couldn't fathom their hierarchy. They were all free men, so they had no leader in the French hierarchical or elitist sense. Things haven't changed all that much since on either side!

Historically, where the Norwegians have tended to look westwards and the Swedes eastwards, the Danes have looked southwestwards and south, both to England and to the European mainland - a corrupting influence which, according to the people from further north, has contributed to their acquiring unNordic tastes and other bad habits.

The language the Danes speak today, while looking like Norwegian with spelling errors, is incomprehensible to the other Nordics because of the curious way the Danes articulate or don't articulate it. The Swedes call it a 'throat disease', to the rest of us it sounds like a tape played backwards.

Even if it doesn't mean much by other European standards generally, Denmark can boast by far the highest population density of all the Nordic countries, with 119 people per km2 - compared with 19 per km2 in Sweden, 15 in Finland and 13 in Norway. Denmark was, as it happens, one of the first European countries to take a census, in 1769. The results were, at the time, a closely guarded military secret.

More important is the fact that Denmark is the oldest kingdom in the world. King Knud (Canute to the British!) ruled over an empire that extended to much of Scandinavia as well as to England, as Hans Christian Andersen's poem indicates. One of Knud's legacies was the Absolute Nuclear Family referred to in Chapter 5.

Today, Denmark comprises the peninsula of Jutland and 527 islands, 86 of them inhabited. Its highest hill is just 173 metres above sea level. The country is seductive in an undemonstrative way: wheatfields, water, beechtrees, ancient oak-lined alleyways, soft marine breezes, rarely anything spectacular. It is a country that inspires affection, that the Danish people love. They particularly love it during the magical two months of summer, *de lyse naetter* [the bright nights], when the sky glows softly throughout the late hours.

A pragmatic and independently minded folk, the Danes have earned the soubriquet from fellow-Nordics of 'the Italians of the North' (further south, they are rated as the Jews of the North). One wonders what Kierkegaard would make of all this? Even the Finns have their reservations about their neighbours. "The Swedes are honest to a less degree [than the Norwegians], the Danes not at all", says a Finnish businessman[6].

Danes are essentially light-hearted people. They manage to accommodate Lutheran-inspired frustration, such as there is in their country, by outbursts of hearty humour of the thigh-slapping type. They are also known not to pay their taxes.

In the eyes of the relatively straightlaced Norwegians, the Danes are a rather frivolous folk "addicted to ballroom dancing, good food and dirty jokes". A Swedish woman journalist adds the weight of her opinion: "Danish women smoke cigars", she says, severely, and then adds, "and Danish environmentalists smoke like chimneys." Obviously not very serious people.

I suspect that references to ballroom dancing and 'the Italians of the North' are made essentially with the people of Copenhagen in mind. By comparison, the Jutlanders strike one as much more sombre, seriousminded and thrifty (remember the villagers in the film 'Babette's Feast'?). In a study of Europeans by a Third World researcher - an experience not dissimilar to the Nepalese Dr Pradhan's work in the Dutch village of Schoonrewoerd (see page 165) - an Indian anthropologist, Professor Prakash Reddy, explored the attitudes of the people of the village of Hvilsager, in Jutland, in 1989. The personality traits most evident to him among these 104 Jutlanders were excessive i dependence (and not necessarily in the positive sense), loneline s and a lack of spirituality.

If the Danes, Jutlanders excluded, share the lighter side of the Italian character - they are fun-loving and know how to laugh at themselves - they also share their inventiveness and intrinsic sense of good design. They also demonstrate an addiction to planning, which extends to things like schedules and route maps (something the Italians do not share with them...).

In addition they have some distinctive traits their neighbours choose to overlook including the ability, first, to reconcile frankness with understatement and, second, to combine informality with apparent coolness socially. The Swedish journalist comments that "Danes seem more friendly, but this is 'social machinery'. Once you get over the threshold...".

The Danes themselves suspect this coolness may reflect a lack of self-confidence as a small country with a distinguished but distant past. They also demonstrate a marked degree of whimsy and of contrariness - they hate being pushed about by others and can be extremely obstinate.

In fact, the traditional Danish inferiority complex so many people talk about is difficult to understand, though it purports to derive from the defeat they suffered at the hands of the Prussians on April 18, 1864. This evidently traumatic event also engendered the will to "win inwardly that which outwardly is lost", words used by a Dane with the unlikely name of Enrico Dalgas who set out to convert the heather-strewn Jutland peninsula to agriculture. Centuries of glory as a major European power terminated overnight with the realisation that Denmark was a small country after all [39].

No chapter on Denmark would be complete without reference to a tradition of Lutheran pastors who have played an important role in history. The most famous internationally, though largely ignored in his own country, was the philosopher Søren Kierkegaard. The most famous in Denmark's own history was NFS Grundtvig, whose exhortations helped put the country back on its feet after the defeat of 1864.

Others from the same pastoral tradition, even if their roles in history were less significant, include Christen Kold, who pioneered the unique Danish 'free high school' system of adult education based on Grundtvig's thinking, and Pastor Eilif Krogager, who founded

Sterling Airways, one of Europe's most successful charter airlines in the 1970s. They all have something to be proud of.

Yet, to paraphrase the words of Axel Sandemose in his *Jantelov* or 'Law of Jante': "Don't think you are anything". Modesty is a national trait - a characteristic, though, that foreigners should not take at its face value. No less eminent a person than Queen Margrethe commented that: "We are very proud of our modesty. It is our inverted megalomania. It is highly sophisticated."

Åke Daun, the Swedish sociologist (see next chapter), elaborates: "According to the 'Law of Jante' [Jante was a fictional community featured in one of Sandemose's books] the highest acceptable degree of pretentiousness is 'sameness' - being like most other people. However, being worse than other people is commonly allowed."

The Swedes incidentally regard Sandemose as one of their spiritual fathers as well - whereas the Norwegians, being Norwegian, like to claim him for themselves, pointing out that he spent most of his life in Norway.

Maybe because they got to know them better during the Danish 400-year domination of Norway, the Danes seem to have more time for the Norwegians than for the Swedes. Mutual attitudes are well summed up by the comment of a Danish businessman: "If a Norwegian is badly treated in Denmark, it is because the Dane thinks he is a Swede..."[6].

Something else deeply ingrained in the Danish psyche is the *hygge* habit of hunkering down with fellow-Danes and sharing their pleasures and your sorrows. As described by Esther Edelsten, *hygge* is a Danish cultural phenomenon which cannot be exported or copied: "It requires a specifically luxuriant [NB not luxurious!] atmosphere, as well as the ability to view life on a Danish scale; to prioritise small pleasures, to appreciate a get-together with soft lighting and candles, the smell of freshly baked pastries and a beautifully laid table with lots of superb food, or just herring, beer and aquavit."

Maybe *hygge* also helps explains the fact that, while the Danes detest authority (look how the Danish voter took on Brussels!), they are better queuers than the Swedes and certainly better than the Norwegians. They even have a word for it: *køkultur!*

The Danes deserve to be more assertive these days: after years between an economic rock and a hard place, they have developed the Nordic region's most vibrant economy and, from a slender industrial base, are achieving excellence in many spheres of high technology.

Rather than the Swedish model, people now refer to "the Danish model" and cite entrepreneurial examples like Lego, a brilliant expression of Danish frivolity put to good account. *The Wall Street Journal Europe*, referring to Denmark's ability to survive in an international environment, called the country the 'Tomorrowland of the European Union'.

Entrepreneurial zeal (some people call it 'the shopkeeper spirit') is highly developed in the Danes: many executives voluntarily terminate a successful corporate career to go into business on their own account. Some foreigners suggest Danish entrepreneurialism goes too far, that some Danes lack a sense of fair play in business, that they even cheat. A matter of interpretation?

No section on Denmark should close without passing reference to the Atlantic dependencies of Greenland and the Faroes. Both have their own home-rule parliaments, with Copenhagen responsible for defence, foreign policy and the common currency. The 55,000 Greenlanders joined the European Union in 1973 and then pulled our six years later, while the 40,000-odd Faroe Islanders never joined. Excessive independence again!

The Swedes

The rational realists

"The beginning of freedom in Europe, and all freedom to be found among men, is to be found in Scandinavia"   Montesquieu

"Swedes are not philosophers, abstract thinking is not for them"   Professor Åke Daun

"Only a Swede, perhaps, can appreciate the political power that arises from the feeling of consensus"   Thomas Anton, American urban planner

"Only barbarism was once domestic"   Esaias Tegnér

"If Sweden had a revolution today, the defeated opposition would be sitting down to dinner with the revolutionary government tomorrow"   Lenin

"When conceit bursts, there is a bad smell"   Swedish proverb

"Outwardly in Sweden a behavioural pattern has developed which is characterised by calm, lack of aggression and emotions, calculated behaviour, compromise, rationalism, 'lagom' (not too much, not to little - just right) and by not standing out more than anyone else"   Jens Allwood

"The Swedes are more dynamic, pushy, aggressive than the Norwegians. Both are abrupt but in a different way"   Australian business executive

"Norwegians drink beer and wood alcohol, Danes drink beer and schnapps, Swedes just drink"
Willy Breinholst, a Dane, quoted by Jean Phillips-Martinsson [40]

"The most slovenly people Allah ever created"
Ahmad Ibn Fadhlan speaking of Swedish merchants in 921 AD

The Swedes can certainly claim their share of the Viking legend, having given their name *rus* (= red), which they borrowed from the Finns, to today's Russians.

Invited by the Slavs to help bring law and order to the Russian steppes - ironically you might think - they created a fine civilisation based on Novgorod and Kiev, and then went on to besiege Constantinople, forcing this great city to pay tribute. Some of these roving northerners then continued their excursions, warlike and commercial, into the Middle East.

It is the 'downside' of the Viking legend that seems to have stuck more relentlessly to the Swedes, even if it has evolved over time. As witness, I offer these lines written by British journalist Auberon Waugh: "Sweden works, of course, in the sense that Swedes are born (in ever decreasing numbers), eat, copulate and eventually (thank God) die, without the extremes of violence or starvation which one sees in such countries as the United States of America or Ethiopia. They put up repulsive buildings and live in them, washing their almost hairless bodies with great thoroughness under the shower whenever necessary. Their conversation is so boring it makes one gasp and stretch one's eyes, and they have not had an original thought between them in the last 150 years."

Now we can all quarrel with that, even if we think Mr Waugh didn't really mean it ("not an original thought between them in the last 150 years" - what about August Strindberg, Folke Bernadotte, Ingmar Bergman?). But it shows the image. One wonders how far in the minds of foreigners a rather sanitised lifestyle and the reality of the welfare state, a natural expression of the Nordic psyche, have come to overshadow the personality of the people.

In truth, the Swedes are as human and personable as anyone else. They even have weaknesses like the rest of us, but manage to keep them within bounds. Perhaps the most baffling thing about them is that they seem to do nothing to excess - not even washing! - and are at times almost irritatingly well-balanced. Their attitude is summed up in the word *lagom*, which implies "not too much, not too little, but just right!".

In the words of a Swedish film producer who has lived in both Sweden and France: "Where two Frenchmen will do anything to disagree, two Swedes will do anything to agree". Consensus is no idle concept. Yet in achieving it, their greatest asset is an ability, it seems, to sublimate their feelings: they rarely get really upset. They even queue better than the Norwegians.

This drive for consensus has a side-effect - something that is perceived by foreigners as indecisiveness. There is an inbuilt tendency to forgo judgment, to give the other party the benefit of the doubt. The Swedish sense of democracy is expressed in this willingness to respect the other person's point of view.

Sweden is a country where a free glass of water is served with every meal, bread has sugar in it, parents are punishable by law for smacking their children, and cars drive around in broad daylight with their headlights blazing (a habit recently picked up by the Hungarians).

The Swedes share with their neighbours such things as the climate, Lutheranism, and a preference for foldaway beds and doors that open outwards - peasant traditions that still linger on in many hotels, sometimes with disastrous consequences. They also share closely interlinked histories and, as someone has said, a quasi-mystical affinity with nature.

But the Swedes are not easy people to get to know intimately. They are great at living (they have a fine lifestyle) and at letting live. Yet at heart they remain great individualists in the sense that, as Bengt Anderson says, they have "a strong desire to be their own masters, but not to be different."[41]

Both nature and history have taught Swedes to value their personal independence, despite the environment of a consensus-oriented society. People are cautious about establishing relationships and, as they see it, committing themselves. This pops up in telling little habits, like buying a cigarette off a colleague at work, or taking your own sheets when you are staying with friends.

It is often said that creating empathy with a Swede is like trying to empty a ketchup bottle. At first nothing happens, then, all of a sudden, the contents splurt out all over the place (in the case of the Finns you first have to work out how to remove the cap).

As a Swede said, with typical Swedish understatement, "Swedes don't chat very much in bars with strangers." Also Swedes don't say "hello" to one another in hotel elevators, but may be shamed into doing so when they know there are foreigners in the hotel.

Perhaps it's not surprising that we so often get the Swedes wrong. Most of us are even wrong when we imagine that the average Swede is tall, gangling and flaxen-haired. There are as many dark-haired people, medium-height or small, as there are blond giants in the country.

Generally they are a gentle people, though some smaller versions of the race are, from personal experience, very dogged and assertive to the point of pugnaciousness. But the country, like most others, suffers from various versions of rowdyism, notably from the big-city yobbos, the Hell's Angels in the south and, some people would say, the *kask*-fuelled *bandy* supporters in the north (*kask* being a *brandy*-reinforced coffee and bandy a primitive form of ice hockey). Even life in Sweden can be complicated at times!

The Swedes have a very special type of humour, bitter-sweet and based on social observation, as exemplified by the films of Ingmar Bergman. Their culture, despite its obvious claims to social progressiveness, contains a very striking retro element - a throwback, I suppose, to the gracious life of the landed gentry in a country which was both large and generous enough to permit such things.

Sweden still breeds a scaled-up version of Clark Gable - slicked down black hair, pencil moustache and natty suiting, but with longer legs and smaller ears. And, then, there is an older generation of *grandes dames* wearing stylish clothes and startling hats. Until a few years ago, Swedish radio used to regale you with old-style ballads sung by mournful baritones. And they still insist on using wet snuff, as do the Finns.

Touches of formalism, in what is essentially a well laid-back society, still surprise the foreigner from time to time. You see it in the little speech of 'thankyou' *(tack-talet)* offered to the hostess by the guest of honour at a dinner and, even more, in the habit of saying *'tack för senaste'* ('thanks for the last time') when being invited for the second (or third) time round. Maybe this reflects surprise at being invited for the second (or third) time round.

Sweden is a beautiful country with its continual interplay of rock, wood, water and wild flowers, perhaps the most beautiful in Europe - an opinion that is most definitely not shared by the Norwegians, who think *their* country is the most beautiful by far. Moreover the Swedes enhance this natural beauty with their burgundy and mustard-tinted clapboard houses. The wild juniper trees are a particular delight.

So much of nature to commune with - with the added stimulus of *allemänsrätt*, the right of common access to the countryside - helps ensure that the Swedes are a healthy race (something, I suspect, Mr Waugh resents as well). The only 'downside', shared with the country's Nordic neighbours, is the short days of winter, particularly those between the late-autumn and the first snows, which seem to come later and later. If Sweden has a health problem, it is what is called Seasonal Affective Disorder (SAD).

Perhaps as an antidote to SAD, the Swedes are great artists in the use of artificial light, both practically and symbolically. In addition to using light therapy in growing numbers, they are the largest consumers of candles in Europe.

Little flames play a symbolic role on many occasions: the candles of the Santa Lucia festival, the cemetery lanterns on All Saints' Day, the Advent Sunday candles, the *ljusstake* candelabra visible in almost every window during the Christmas season. Candles are a sign of welcome outside cafés and private houses when a party's on. In some of the more desolate parts of the country a light is left burning in the front window of every house simply as a signal to the traveller.

For a relatively sophisticated country, Sweden has managed to retain the gift of simplicity. One feels that childhood memories of summer friendships are never far away - a cult that is helped along by the tradition of storytelling reflected in characters like Nils Holgersson, Kalle Blomkvist and, most famous of all, Pippi Longstocking - whose creator, Astrid Lindgren, maintained that a happy childhood was a prerequisite for creating a better world.

Besides being beautiful, Sweden is a well organised country, which may go some way to explaining Mr Waugh's bile. It has been so for quite a time. As Bengt Anderson points out: "The National Registration can account for every individual who lived in Sweden since 1749, not just in statistical terms but with personal details."

Having created a very remarkable society for themselves, something that was regarded as the 'Third Way' in the days of capitalism v. communism (the 'Middle Way' in Norwegian parlance), they now seem to find it either too boring or too expensive. High taxation has engendered a work-to-rule mentality which, encouraged by long holidays and a wealth of leisure pursuits, is now too deep-rooted to eradicate. Among the pursuits are the beautiful girls, which may explain the number of Italian and Greek car mechanics, restaurant owners and waiters in the country.

Students of Swedish public affairs assert that Swedish society comprises two essential streams of thought: those that are committed to the creation of wealth, primarily the business and industrial community, and those that are committed to redistributing it, which can mean almost anybody, business people and industrialists included.

Geert Hofstede classes all the Nordic cultures as relatively 'feminine' (see page 289) in the sense that they genuinely believe in social equality, put personal relationships before money and have a high regard for the quality of life.

While the welfare state is still much in evidence in Swedish society despite recent economies, industry runs on strictly free market lines and, in the major groups, represents the finest flowering of capitalism. Of all the Nordic countries, Sweden has the most prominent and powerful industrial base and, per capita, the highest concentration of large corporations in all Europe.

The country is no exception to the rule that the Nordic countries have the youngest managers in Europe and run their businesses democratically, as young managers should. As an example, at the time of writing the CEO of Electrolux is in his late-30s and the company's chief comptroller is only 32.

Swedish management practices quite understandably tend to reflect the egalitarian culture and social organisation of the country. Foreigners, however, harbour suspicions that much of what goes on is time-consuming window-dressing and that, in the words of a Finnish observer, Swedish management is ultimately "manipulative"[42].

Other studies carried out on the impact of the Swedish corporate culture on international business partners, particularly foreign subsidiaries, also show that the egalitarian or 'evolving consensus' approach can be easily misconstrued - particularly if it is accompanied by the curiously old-fashioned, almost colonial, habit of sending Swedish middle-rank executives on two-year tours of duty to their overseas dependencies.

Nordic business aptitudes in fact vary dramatically. If one is to believe the old Norwegian saw (it somehow seems right that 'old saws' should be Norwegian), it should be the Finns who design the products, the Swedes who make them, the Danes who sell them and the Norwegians - because, for once, they think anything foreign is better than the home-grown equivalent - who buy them.

The Finns

The passionate pragmatists

"... a sense of national identity intricately bound up with ideals of social equality and a deep psychic respect for the primeval"
Paul Binding, *The European*

"In Finland, as in other peripheral places like Britain and Portugal, people refer to Europe as if it were somewhere else"
The Economist

"The weak self-esteem of us Finns is, in fact, a pattern of behaviour originating from our culture... and we can learn to have strong self-esteem without being arrogant or pompous"   Pertti Widén

"Finns are rotten writers; we prefer the telephone to the letter, a telex is normally the nearest thing to a written confirmation"
Finnish businessman

"They are the most rigorously honest people in the world. They always pay you back. They are almost incapable of lying: if they ever try to lie to you, they get nervous. Good people to do business with"   American CEO

"We do not like to make a fuss in public; it's a question of style"
Heidi Hautala, MEP

There's no place for Vikings in this section on the Finns. In this and some other important respects, the Finns don't fit the Nordic mould - even if they share many of the characteristics of the others. Geographically they are the furthest removed from the Nordic epicentre and, being distant relatives of the Mongols, they boast ethnic origins and a language entirely their own.

Of all the Nordics, the Finns are the odd ones out. Locked into their environment, they share with the Swedes the legacy of a German-inspired educational system which tends to programme social attitudes and factor out personal eccentricity. They are even more pragmatic than the Danes: history and geopolitics have taught them that this is the only way to survive.

To foreigners the Finns seem an almost inscrutable people, taciturn to the point of silence. Both their nature and their education encourage them to keep their counsel until they feel they have something suitable to say. When they say it, it is likely to be direct, sometimes devastatingly so, but with the best intentions.

"The main motive of the Finn is not to ensure that he is liked, but that he is not disliked", says Peter Collett[5]. "It is a social strategy that is designed to reduce one's losses, rather than to increase one's gains, and is largely responsible for the Finnish attitude to silence."

Pertti Widén of Turku University puts his people's cautious behaviour in a more positive light: "Finnish politeness is not disturbing a person. That is why Finns do not look at the person, they do not address him directly, they avoid calling him by name". A young Finnish woman adds another factor: "When we are asked for an opinion, we go quiet, and foreigners think we are arrogant or embarrassed. Small talk is not one of our favourite pastimes." There, they are typically Nordic.

Finnish inhibitions about communicating extend to a reluctance to put things into writing. This reflects the recent emergence of the Finns from a rural environment, where relationships relied on word of mouth, plus a natural tendency to be cautious in dealings with authority of any shape or nationality. Now, of course, the Finns have the perfect excuse that they are the pioneers of mobile phone technology.

Not only does their language isolate the Finns from everyone else (Max Jakobson speaks of "the language curtain"), they even have problems in communicating among themselves: the dropout rate in Finnish language studies is astronomic. This may help explain the story of two old friends who meet up for a drink after a long-time-no-see. There is a protracted but comfortable silence until one of them says: "Well, how are you Matti?" To which Matti replies: "Look, did we come here to talk or to drink?".

None of this is meant to imply that the Finns are not bright, but that educational standards are very severe. An intelligent and essentially very outward-looking people despite their hermeticity, they often seem to lack self-esteem but are not inclined to indulge in self-examination. Perhaps they are wise not to try.

The Finns demonstrate a unique complex of complexes, both inferiority and superiority, at one and the same time. They are often impulsive and erratic yet, equally often, they can be obstinate. They have a fine sense of humour until it gets too boisterous and, despite the 'Matti' story, take great trouble to develop relationships with both fellow-Finns and foreigners.

Like their neighbours, the Finns have the excuse that they have to cope with a couple of grim realities. Mid-country, the winter sun hardly comes over the horizon for a number of weeks. In sympathy with the Swedes, the locals say there are three reasons for not visiting Finland: October, November and December. And, even more than their neighbours, their country is remote. Helsinki is on the same line of longitude as Athens. It also, as it happens, lies on the shortest and quickest air route linking western Europe with Tokyo.

The Finns have, even more than the Swedes, a mystic relationship to nature or, as Paul Binding puts it, "a deep psychic respect for the primeval". There are 400,000 second home-owners out of a population of five million: many of these holiday homes are farmsteads inherited from parents or grandparents. Pertti Laine, a forest industry representative, says that "owning a second home in the country and a little bit of forest to put it in is the ideal of every Finn."

An expert on Finland points to the "inner tensions" evident in the average Finn, created by the conflict between the Lutheran ethic and a natural inclination to have fun in order to lighten the load of living. It is not uncommon, he says, to have a well lubricated but professional lunchtime *tête-à-tête* terminate with soulbaring revelations of marital infidelity, deaths in the family and so on. Yet it has to be added that, with recessionary times and reduced expense accounts, long and well lubricated lunches are now a fond memory. My informant also says it used to be social suicide to wear anything but black shoes after 6 pm: the fact that you weren't able to stand up in them didn't matter.

Compared with their neighbours, the Swedes, the Finns are a relatively temperamental lot (no sublimation for them!). Questioned in a joint Finno-Swedish research study whether they easily lost their tempers if they didn't get what they wanted, 31% of Finns answered in the affirmative, compared with 19% of Swedes. A Finnish criminologist, Jussi Pajuoja, notes that his people are more inclined to violence than any other nationality in western Europe, but adds the fact that about 80% of assaults are alcohol-related.

The Finnish fondness for alcohol has to be put into perspective. Like camels and water, they are capable of going without refreshment for weeks at a time but, when the occasion presents itself, they can get riotously drunk in their saunas and elsewhere. 'Elsewhere' includes on the country's myriad lakes, since a recent check at the height of the admittedly very short Finnish summer showed eight out of ten boatsmen to be drunk in charge.

The Finns are 'bout drinkers'. In the words of David Haworth, a British-born Finland fanatic, "lengthy periods of abstinence culminate in binges where no bottle is left empty - a throwback to the farmer's weekly visit to market to sell his produce, the only time he had cash in hand."[43] In fact alcoholic excursions to St Petersburg have earned the Finns the label with their Russian neighbours of "our four-legged friends".

Asked by *The European* newspaper whether he had noticed any curious Finnish tendencies, Jeff Bickert, a Canadian journalist living and working in Helsinki, replied: "If someone does something horrendous, it is forgivable or even acceptable because they are drunk." No wonder Finland is the only European country I know which has a Minister with portfolio for Alcoholic Affairs.

The Finns, as this and other behavioural traits suggest, are essentially a simple people, in most cases no more than two generations away from their peasant forefathers. And the inner tensions caused by the 'fire-and-brimstone versus fun' paradox heighten the individual's appreciation of both - at the appropriate time. But these tensions also contribute to a relatively high suicide rate.

In addition to a rather melancholy style of singing, not unlike the Welsh, the Finns are accordion and tango fanatics, hosting two of the world's biggest festivals in these disciplines every year. They also have a pronounced fondness for cognac, despite a typically Nordic appreciation of white spirits, and are great consumers of onions, cabbage, potatoes, salmon and dill. They are also reputed to be Europe's biggest banana-eaters, coffee-drinkers and consumers of milk and butter.

If, after discounting the fact that they are great drinkers of milk, you still marvel at the high rate of heart trouble in Finland (though this problem has been vigorously tackled by the government), just consider how the average Finn spends his winter weekend: a slouch in the family sauna at 100°C, followed by a naked romp in the snow, followed by a warmup with lots of beer and sausages, then back into the sauna for a second round. The Finns are, indeed, heroic people with lots of 'guts' (what they call *sisu*).

Not surprisingly, since the Swedes occupied their country for four hundred years and acquired much of their best land in the process, the Finns have a rather ambivalent attitude towards their neighbours. It is not so much resentment at their riches (the Finns are too artless for that), it is envy at the apparently more cosmopolitan lifestyle and attitudes of Sweden.

There is still plenty of evidence of this historical connection in the Swedish-speaking communities along the west coast, and also in the Ålands, an archipelago of 6,000 islands speckled across the mouth of the Gulf of Bothnia. The 25,000 islanders, almost half of whom live in the capital of Mariehamn, enjoy a special self-governing status awarded them by the League of Nations in 1920. They use this strategic status - and location - to run a fleet of ferries (more accurately floating duty-free shops) between Sweden and Finland.

A fitting close to this chapter and to the section on the Nordics is provided by the proceedings of the Nordic Council meeting of March 1990, the scene of a bitter dispute over national claims to Santa Claus.

The Norwegians presented a carefully argued but sentimental case, matched by equally nostalgic pleas from the Icelanders and the Greenlanders, while the Swedes grumbled - and the Finns, being of another cast of mind, argued from the *de facto* reality of an established Santa Claus industry. Since then they have launched *Santa Claus Finland International* to promote their claim. This may in turn have contributed to a situation that prompted the Danish government, in late-1993, to grant a state subsidy to Santa's Greenland workshop.

But Norway, as always, intends to have the last word. News has reached the outside world that the Norwegian town of Dröbak is challenging the Finnish claim to the Father Christmas trade - on evidence, dating from the year 1602, that Santa was born under a tree there. Which only goes to prove that foreigners may sometimes be justified in calling Norwegians stubborn, obstinate, headstrong, pigheaded and so on.

Some people would also call them taciturn. Yet Peter Collett, who is a research psychologist at Oxford University, says the people of northern Norway have a reputation for being garrulous. Theodore Zeldin, another Oxford academic and a historian, asserts that the inhabitants of the Finnish province of Hame are the least talkative people on earth[44]. Which brings us full circle, Nordically speaking...

As Flora Lewis implies[2], consistency in diversity, even at the levels of Father Christmas and conversational styles, characterises the Nordic peoples. Whether it will be more permanent than any of the other national traits in this changing Europe of ours remains to be seen. With the progressive involvement of the nation states in something bigger than themselves, even these people - who have nurtured and sometimes regretted their individual, isolated cultures - are destined to come closer together, both to themselves and to the rest of the Continent.

Evidently not so the Norwegians, by their own choice the odd-ones-out. But the Norwegians will still have the afterlife to look forward to.

The Portuguese
The passive romanticists

"Travelogues tend to portray the Portuguese as easy-going, smiling, patient, good-natured, but imbued with an inner 'saudade', a feeling variously defined as a nostalgia or melancholy"
Insight Guide to Portugal

"The large majority of Portuguese are open-hearted, easy-going and tolerant. They possess an independence of spirit, a natural courtesy, a genuine hospitality and kindliness in which fortunate strangers are, for the most part, and as ever, warmly enfolded"
Marion Kaplan

"God gave the Portuguese a small country as cradle but all the world as their grave"
Padre Antonio Vieira

"Sixty Thousand Chickens Stolen During Lunar Eclipse"
Headline in Lisbon newspaper

"The present does not conflict with the past, but rather grows from it"
Mario Soares

"... these profoundly self-analytical people, absorbed by their own past, challenged by change, burdened with bureaucracy and defective services, pressed by low income, rising costs, high taxes"
Marion Kaplan

"Coimbra sings, Braga prays, Lisbon parades, and Oporto works"
Anonymous

"The Portuguese are not a very intelligent people"   Dr Salazar

Many people, me included, have set out relating our perception of the Portuguese to our understanding of the Spanish. It is a pernicious tendency, but difficult to avoid. Most of us get to know Spain first. We then fall into the trap of thinking that, because the two countries are neighbours sharing an idiosyncratic corner of Europe cut off physically by the Pyrenees - and sharing, on and off, a very tumultuous history - they must be close cousins. Cousins, yes, but not so close.

From talking to others and reading the guidebooks, you will quickly learn that the Portuguese are an Atlantic people by both location and temperament. By comparison the Spanish, without being by definition Mediterranean (take a look at the map), have a less atmospheric and more bracing view of the world overall.

The Portuguese personality reflects the mild, moist climate of the ocean littoral - a completely different world from the harsh, elemental environment of upland Spain. A business friend who was brought up in Portugal is even more emphatic, if geographically broadminded: "The Portuguese are like the climate of Madeira, never winter, never summer, always spring".

But it is difficult to explain the difference between the two peoples in terms of geography and climate alone. While Portugal has an exclusively Atlantic seaboard, the countries share a number of features - in particular a green and mountainous north, and an open and desert-like south extending eastwards from the plains of the Alentejo and Algarve in Portugal to the valleys of the Guadiana and Guadalquivir rivers and the mountains of Granada in Spain. At the extremes, the Iberian peninsula is markedly latitudinal in its physical makeup.

Yet there is one area where you really sense the change of country, and that is in the centre. Follow the expressway that links Salamanca in Spain with the Portuguese coast at Aveiro and you cross a geographical and cultural fault line. In a mere 20 kilometres the landscape changes from rolling upland country of vast bullbreeding estates to a rugged *maquis* startling in its wildness and infertility, with only the occasional small peasant farmstead to relieve the scene. The rest is hillocks, scrub and huge rounded rocks black with lichen, like the rumps of stranded whales. You are in the Ribacoa, a country for smugglers and highwaymen. Devious enough, it was also the preferred route of many of the invaders -

Romans, Moors and Spaniards (one would have thought they would have done better to stay further south).

Much of central and northern Portugal is just as wild. The expressway winds and ploughs its way from the Spanish frontier, through hill and scrub, to the fertile littoral stretching only a few kilometers back from the coast. One is left with the feeling that the country turns its back resolutely on the Iberian hinterland and faces equally resolutely towards the Atlantic.

History bears this out in the exploits of the great Portuguese explorers who, with the benign encouragement of Henry the Navigator, discovered much of the rest of the world for us Europeans. Today, there are some 200 million Portuguese-speaking people around the globe, outperforming even the Spanish who split the world with the Portuguese in 1494 under the Treaty of Tordesillas.

But it is the history of the peninsula that best explains the difference between the Portuguese and the Spanish. At the time of the Roman Empire there was little to distinguish the two races. And both peoples were later marked by the Vandal and Moorish invasions, both were engulfed genetically by the Celts and then by other arrivals from the northeast: the Visigoths, the Alans and, most importantly, the Suevi (the Swabians to you and me).

But as long ago as 1297, largely for reasons of dynasty rather than incompatibility, Portugal won its independence from Spain thanks to the efforts of its first king, Afonso Henriques. The fact that the Spanish temporarily reestablished dominion over the country for the 60 years from 1580 to 1640 helped reinforce the opposition. As Marion Kaplan says in her book[45]: "If the Portuguese, a relaxed, self-confident people, have a single national complex, it is over Spain, their only neighbour, five times as big, and inescapable. Rails and roads and the full panoply of modern communications and trade link the two nations, yet a barrier divides them that is invisible, intangible, perhaps even indestructible."

Hopefully without causing offence on either side, I would like to suggest that there are *some* similarities between the Portuguese and the Spanish. As people, they share two important qualities, style and humanity - although, again, there is a major distinction. Style is absolutely inbred in the Spanish, sombre as it may be. It is second nature to them and impinges as much on the observer as their sense of humanity (which occasionally escapes them). The

Portuguese also have style, but it is not an imperative. The humanity comes first. They are more intuitive about human relationships than the Spanish, who tend to have a conceptual approach.

As with all southern European peoples, there is lots of eye contact - although the Portuguese are more reticent about physical contact, whereas Spanish males will often lunge at one another for an enthusiastic *abrazo*. But where the Spanish are at times sententious, even withdrawn, the Portuguese are outgoing and eager to please. They are the pleasantest people to deal with - something said without a hint of condescension or disparagement. How dull, you think? That's the way they are. Be grateful.

The precept that language shapes attitudes and attitudes shape language certainly applies to the peoples of the Peninsula. Portuguese is a liquid language full of sibilants and soft sounds which contrast as dramatically with the staccato and rhythmic nature of Spanish as the climate and the geography. The nasal notes one associates with *fado* songs dominate. To the casual listener they could even be talking Russian.

But, curbing this pernicious habit of making comparisons with the Spanish, let us talk about the Portuguese *per se*. For once the guidebooks are right. What almost unfailingly impresses the foreigner about these people is their openness, their attentiveness, their courtesy, their charm and their hospitality: 'my house is your house' *('a minha casa é a sua casa')*. Where the Spanish invite you out, the Portuguese invite you in.

The astonishing thing is that they are almost all like that, from the *minifundia* of the north via the conurbations of Oporto and Lisbon to the *latifundia* of the south. They leave you with the impression that, more than most Europeans, they are at peace with themselves.

The homogeneity of character of the Portuguese is remarkable. Marion Kaplan puts her finger on it: "Through the centuries the singular essence of Portugal stayed pure. Eyes look at you that are the clear blue of the Celts and the dark brown of the Moors: from diverse origins the Portuguese became one intensely nationalistic people, with local rivalries but without linguistic, racial or religious minorities." *O povo*, the people, is not just a demagogic phrase used by both Portuguese dictators and revolutionaries. It is a staunch reality.

Flora Lewis speaks of the Portuguese as "stoic, impassive, unassuming. Pride is displayed by self-control, not by explosive behaviour, as in Spain" (here we go again!). Certainly the Portuguese are a stoic people, some would even say at times fatalistic, with a keen sense of the unattainable.

Some observers interpret this as a 'soft option', a symptom of spinelessness, but history proves them wrong, time and again. As for being "impassive", I'm not so sure: they are known to explode, but their emotional outbursts rarely lead to violence.

I would take issue with the Lisbon correspondent of the *New York Times*, however, when he says: "The Portuguese have the reputation of being a quiet, law-abiding, and introverted people who even in times of political turmoil go out of their way to avoid using violence." To me they are as noisy as anyone else except the Italians and just as extrovert - though I do agree that, on recent performance, they are fairly law-abiding. Unfortunately it seems that their complaisance is a blank cheque for rampant bureaucracy, with a less law-abiding element of corruption thrown in. Its mildest manifestation is a plea to bend the rules, the *jeitinho* approach. Also family and friends count for a lot in getting on in this essentially amiable society.

Marion Kaplan elaborates: "Portugal's passionate nature, it is frequently said, is expressed more in word than in deed. They are often thought to be people filleted of backbone, weakened by a crushing burden of unenlightened dictatorship [but please note that Salazar introduced bidets to all catering establishments], undesirable wars in Africa and unremitting poverty at home. The familiar image shows inertia, ineptitude, an innate reluctance to do that which can be left undone. Criticism flows in a steady stream, from foreigners, from the Portuguese themselves."

At this point one is reminded of the Greeks. The Portuguese share with the latter a distaste for thinking about the future. When disaster strikes, they make what they can of the situation and blame someone else, improvise (often very cleverly) and criticise. This extends to running down their own race in the presence of foreigners.

"Yet", Marion Kaplan adds, "the Portuguese, it is clear, have many rare and wonderful qualities. If they choose, they are capable of anything. The leap from impotent inaction to revolutionary fervour is an example, the sequence of events since the revolution ran its course another."

Still we are left, more often than not, with this sense of the unattainable. Never far below the surface of the Portuguese psyche, it is perpetuated in the Lisbon tradition of the *fado*, which induces catharsis in both singers and listeners. The Portuguese are an extremely sentimental folk, subject to a state of mind for which only they have the right word, *saudade* - a nostalgic longing for things that seem to be eternally out of reach.

Evidence of this abounds not only in their music, but in their attachment to their traditions and fellow-countryfolk when living abroad - maybe even in the urge to travel and explore that possessed the country five hundred years ago. Separation is part of this experience. Another is quite simply poverty - a historic fact of life for many Portuguese. All of these elements are there in the words and music of the *fado*.

The explorer spirit also survives in at least one contemporary pursuit, driving, where self-control or any sort of control seems to evaporate. Guidebooks speak of "the bravado of immortals", "complete indifference", even "naked aggression", yet the Portuguese are not aggressive, they simply have no automobile culture.

In fact Portugal had until recently, when Italy overtook it, the worst road accident rate of any country in the European Union. In 1989, the country recorded 1,163 motor vehicle deaths per million vehicles. Even Greece could only manage 764 per million, with Spain next at 635 and France at 439.

To quote the words of a Lisbon psychologist talking about his countryfolk: "They're normally very well-mannered and conservative, but all their repressed hostility and daring seems to come out behind the wheel." OK, hostility maybe, but not with pedestrians. In town, out of natural courtesy, the Portuguese driver gives way - something that distinguishes him or her from most other Europeans, and certainly the southern races. Yet a 1993 study by the Uniroyal Goodrich tyre company found that Portugal has the highest pedestrian fatality rate in the European Union.

Motoring in Portugal is indeed an instructive experience. My personal education was topped by an eager service station attendant who fuelled my 'lead-free' car with leaded petrol (evidence of my inability to cope with the language and Portuguese reluctance to respect European norms) and let me understand, in the friendliest way possible, that *I* was the idiot.

This led to a visit to the local automobile club, where the mechanics showed great acumen in siphoning the contents of the tank by mouth, with the aid of a liberal supply of peppermints. Pragmatic and amiable, they muddled their way through the problem with typical Portuguese goodwill.

While they are as instinctively a democratic folk as their Spanish neighbours (here we go again), a characteristic that reflects the historic influence of the Arab Moslem culture in both cases, the Portuguese are also prone to machoism. Again, the Arabs are partly to blame, but the Salazar regime also contributed to the issue by proclaiming, rather chimerically for a dictatorship, that everyone is equal before the law "except for women, the differences resulting from their nature and for the good of the family".

Even today the males in rural communities share with other races, the Greeks in particular, a tendency to stay in the family home until they marry. According to a Frenchman, Paul Descamps, permissive childrearing has a lot to do with the easygoing nature of the Portuguese character. Unfortunately this relaxed attitude does not extend to the marginals in society - homosexuals, Jews, Muslims and the emotionally unstable - who stumble onto Portuguese soil. A recent study suggests that the Portuguese are, in this respect, the most intolerant people in Europe: no doubt remote geography plus closeness to their roots explains this dichotomy.

Portugal is still essentially a matriarchal society, more so even than Italy and much more so than neighbouring Spain, where the old traditions are dying fast. Curiously, as Emmanuel Todd [46] also notes, without venturing an explanation for the deviation from the Portuguese norm, Southern Portugal has suicide and illegitimate birth rates "worthy of northern or eastern Europe".

As with all Mediterranean countries, there are still marked differences between the people of the north and those of the south. Historically, according to the *Insight Guide to Portugal* [47], "the south was still marked [at the time of the *Reconquista*] by refinement and urbanity; it was a culture with the tradition of tolerance [the Moors again]. In contrast, the northern culture had a rough arrogance, the attitude of invaders."

The northerners are indeed more work-oriented, they are more serious, less fun-loving and, appropriately, tighter with their money. The cosmopolitan Lisbon folk joke about the *continhas do Porto*, the 'little accounts of Oporto', with people keeping mental checks of who owes what to whom and everybody 'going Dutch'.

Conducting business in Portugal, while not necessarily very profitable, is certainly pleasant. I am astonished by the readiness with which even senior business people will give time to a visitor, even when called on without warning - something that is often unthinkable elsewhere. This relaxed manner extends to attitudes towards timekeeping and is buoyed up by the Portuguese spirit of independence and sense of self-esteem.

No chapter on Portugal can conclude without proper reference to the fact that this is the poorest country in the European Union, outperforming even Greece which has been described as a "poor country of rich people". This is affected by, and reflected in, the illiteracy rate which - at 16 per cent of the total population - is double that of Greece.

Household budgets are only one-quarter of what people in northern Europe are able to afford. Direct taxation thresholds are very low but, even so, 58 per cent of households pay no tax at all. And, on top of this, the Portuguese work the longest hours of anyone and, in terms of personal hygiene, are the cleanest people in Europe.

The fact that progress passed this country by is evident in the quaint juxtaposition of 1920s trams and fire engines with the massive invasion of modern cars. The belated but thoroughly deserved chance to catch up, sympathetically supported by the rest of the European Union, may erase some of the qualities the Portuguese show today. But I doubt it.

The Greeks

The intelligent improvisers

"Whatever it is, I fear the Greeks even when they bring gifts"
Virgil

"A sense of precariousness illuminates Greek life, its bursts of joy and storms of grief, its frivolity and angst"   Mary Blume

"The Greece of the classical heritage and of the romantic phil-hellene has gone, and anyhow has always been irrelevant to the Greek situation"   Philip Sherrard

"I have known uncertainty: a state unknown to the Greeks"
Jorge Luis Borges

"The modern Greek... when he begins to sing... breaks the crust of Greek logic; all at once the East, all darkness and mystery, rises up from deep within him"   Nikos Kazantzakis

"Among the Greeks every man is an actor"   Juvenal

"There is an overly powerful executive, a rigid, incompetent bureau-cracy and an anarchic and unruly population. The situation is impossible"   EC official, speaking about Greece in 1991

"Mythology is what never was, but always is"
Stephen of Byzantium

No European country has a more complex geography than Greece: islands, peninsulas, capes, gulfs, mountains and plains, all jumbled up. And the Greek, like many other Europeans, takes his personality from his country: he is complex, often contradictory. Few other Europeans can be so amiable and so infuriating, all at the same time. No wonder we all get confused and that Mary Blume speaks of "a sense of precariousness" where Borges speaks of "uncertainty: a state unknown to the Greeks".

Françoise Huart, the French writer[48], sums up the dilemma in the following words: "To portray a 'typical' Greek, you need to serve up a pot-pourri where every individual or collective trait is matched by its opposite: democracy and dictatorship, age-old heritage and urban horror, allegiance and rebellion, love and cruelty, suspicion and disinterest, candour and vengeance, self-satisfied egoism and an acute sense of duty, overflowing energy and apathy, honesty and venality, humility and exaggeration, hospitality and xenophobia, a gift for happiness and tragedy... How do they succeed in reconciling all these things?"

Appropriately it was the Greeks who invented the words 'anarchy' and 'chaos' - words that do them justice and give them a golden opportunity to demonstrate their powers of improvisation (a word which should have been Greek too, but isn't). Other classical Greek words like 'democracy' sometimes seem to have no relevance to the Greece of today.

Everybody's comprehension, including mine, is hampered by the fact that the Greeks have a different alphabet and a different religion from the rest of us Europeans. They tilt their heads back rather than from side to side when saying "no", like the Arabs. And they say *"né"* when they mean "yes". No wonder the rest of us get confused.

In European Union terms the Greeks are also geographically remote from the rest of us - separated by the minefield of the Balkans. But that is just the physical aspect. Psychologically, the Greeks are probably further removed from the epicentre of the European Union than anybody. A senior Foreign Ministry official in Athens commented wisely at the time of Greek accession to the EC that "it probably won't work because my fellow-countrymen won't open the mail!"

We have other problems in getting to terms with present-day Greeks. Fed on fantasies of blond, almost Nordic giants, with a cult of athleticism and a sense of civic responsibility that would put even a Swede to shame, we find ourselves confronted with a race of essentially dark and smallish people (there are exceptions!) with a Mr-Fix-It mentality, a talent for what the French call *combines* and a way of talking from the front of the mouth which reminds me of the Dutch.

One wonders what happened between 250 BC and today? A lot, of course, including Byzantium, the Ottoman Empire (nearly 400 years of it), and a bunch of Bavarians who turned up at the creation of the kingdom of Greece in 1832. That's enough to confuse anyone, the Greeks included.

Many Greeks dispute the fact that they were tall and blond. It seems there are some fairheaded people in the northwest confines of the country, also in the island of Crete. But tall? Even Philip II of Macedonia, the father of Alexander the Great, was only 1.58 metres when they laid him to rest. Maybe the mountainous terrain of much of Greece kept some of the people genetically intact (the semi-mythical Greek shepherd boy?) whereas, elsewhere, they mixed with others as the balance of power ebbed and flowed. Some observers, Greek included, say there is as much of the Levantine as there is of the European in the people today.

I have a theory that it's the early Celtic invaders who started this story of giants, before moving on westwards. After all the *keltoi*, as the Greeks called them, were "remarked upon for their height, their muscularity and their fair colouring". But I would not go so far as the German professor who made himself unpopular at the height of the Hellenist movement by categorising the present-day Greeks as Slav!

The mention of professors brings me to a scholarly analysis of the Hellenic psyche (another Greek word!) by Professor W H McNeil, an American who spent many years in this fascinating and often frustrating country. In his book *The Metamorphosis of Greece since World War II*[49], he explains much of the recent history and attitudes of the people in terms of a social diversity that reflects the country's geography.

Paraphrasing his conclusions, and adding a few thoughts of my own, Greek history and the Greek personality owe much to the traditional coexistence of three sociological groups: the mountain Greeks (the warriors), the plains Greeks (the farmers) and the coastal Greeks (the traders).

The coastal Greeks are the best known even today: Greek businessmen, Greek shipowners and Greek tradespeople are renowned for their commercial savvy and their ability to strike a lucrative bargain. This is the element in Greek society that least squares up with the traditional image of the noble, heroic Greek of the sagas. As McNeil says: "The middleman roles which gave the Greeks their most spectacular successes were intrinsically vulnerable. Traders and go-betweens, by the very nature of their activity, create distrust".

The plains Greeks were, and are, the farmers. Here, as McNeil explains succinctly, lies the real key to the Greek mentality. Geography and climate willed that Greek agriculture specialised in classical times and beyond in the cultivation of vines and olive trees, grain taking third place. Both wine and olive oil end up in bottles with a reasonable shelf-life, whereas the grain that the Greeks imported from neighbouring countries was weevil, rat and ergot-prone.

The result was that, while the Greeks were largely dependent on the product of a single crop of grapes and olives every year, they were not bargaining with their backs to the wall - thus enhancing their country's reputation for a market-wise mentality and negotiating skills.

It also meant that, when they weren't tending the vines (olives need relatively little attention) or gathering in the harvest, they had lots of time to sit in the village tavern, talk politics and recall past acts of heroism, legends and all.

As for the mountain Greeks - now decimated by the appeal of town life and mass emigration to other continents - they lived close to subsistence and, when even that was difficult, descended on the plains folk who naturally resented their attention. They were the ones who kept the Homeric tradition of heroism alive, partly by their existence, partly by their involvement as brilliant guerrilla fighters in the War of Independence and in WWII.

As McNeil says: "During the long centuries since classical times, [the Greek sagas and] other influential literary works re-affirmed and elaborated heroic ideals... it was commonplace to stud discussion in the village coffeeshop with quotations from and references to these poems, whose lines everyone had heard and often knew by heart."

So, reinforced with McNeil's analysis, we can find some clues to the dichotomy of the Greek temperament: the would-be hero engaged in a titanic struggle with the real-life pragmatist. This may help explain a number of traits in the modern-day Greek: his frequent cynicism, his talent for improvisation, his often disarming charm and his generosity.

Let's deal with the last first. Speaking of the tradition of heroism, McNeil says: "No Greek male could entirely forget what was daily betrayed. Suitably provoked, he often found himself strongly tempted to break away from the manners appropriate to ordinary routines by suddenly assuming a heroic pose. This could take many forms. Strangers were and still are most likely to see such impulses expressed in the form of reckless hospitality, offering food and drink on a lavish scale to persons who may never be able to return the favour, and offering it with no regard for how deeply the expense may cut into the host's available resources." Ah, yes!

Cynicism, even cunning, is the antithesis of this trait of generosity. A Greek business consultant confirmed my worst fears when he bewailed "the growing Machiavellianism" of his fellow-countrymen and described the prevailing mood as "never mind, who cares?" My fears had already been grounded in such minor but significant incidents as the taxi driver who deliberately misunderstood my instructions and drove me 50 kilometers too far and the service station attendant who filled the tank of my car when I had clearly indicated I wanted a half-tank.

As a western westerner, I am tempted to conclude that there may be an admixture of Oriental wiliness, maybe fatalism, in the average Greek - but that would be oversimplifying things. As ever, behaviour behind the wheel is revealing. Stand at the front of the line at a Greek traffic light and you can bet your bottom drachma that, within a half-second of the light turning green, someone will have hooted at you whether you are stationary or not. And yet I have seen a tailback of Greek motorists accept the dawdlings of a delivery truck in a single-file street with utmost patience and goodwill. A strange combination of Latin impetuousness and Oriental fatalism. Yet they are neither Latin nor Oriental!

Other epithets which crop up regularly when discussing the Greek character are, not surprisingly, 'philosophical' and 'romantic'. A resident Englishman pays the ultimate compliment by asserting that, on the 'romantic' side, the Greeks can "out-Byron Byron".

As for being philosophical the average Greek male can, in the Socratic tradition, start a conversation on a street corner and still be there, with at least two others involved, two hours later. As the debate warms up, voices rise to the level of a shouting match with practised theatricality.

The problem is that, as a much-travelled Belgian business acquaintance points out, they only listen to their own voices and don't hear what the other side is saying. Yet this doesn't inhibit them from being, at times, insufferably inquisitive: one foreign observer speaks knowingly of "their sublime curiosity, coupled with a truly wonderful skill at turning even the simplest situation into a world plot". This thirst for knowledge and sensation is a throwback to Greek village society, where everybody made it his or her business to know exactly what everybody else was up to.

This brings us on and back to improvisation. The Greeks have, as I hinted earlier, the Mr-Fix-It mentality par excellence, a scissors-and-paste approach to the art of living. One feels that they are always trying to catch up with the present. As one Greek puts it: "After 4,000 years, what else can you expect?"

Nothing in the country ever seems to be finished or complete - and not just the Parthenon. Buildings and even churches are abandoned when they are half up (there is no tax on unfinished buildings), streets are littered with debris, bridges are built over half-finished motorways with no ramps leading up to them (apparently this is done to please the local electorate - an unconnected bridge is better than no bridge at all when it comes to collecting votes).

Never, but never, look into a Greek backyard. It will be full of what any other European country would class as utter rubbish. It seems the Greeks hold on to just about everything because "it may come in useful one day". Four thousand years from now?

Civically, in short, the Greeks are a disaster (though they claim that the Cretans are even greater improvisers than themselves, particularly in *bouzouki* playing!). But personally, in matters of hygiene and the like, they are irreproachable.

An English friend of mine, who has spent many years in Greece, puts it like this: "Give a Greek a car and no one will damage or dent it faster... but no one will keep it going longer with bits of wire, string and ingenuity. They have a war syndrome". No wonder one-third of all cars on Greek roads were, until a recent government decision, more than ten years old.

A Greek informant, who has spent many years in Holland (socially the opposite pole), asserts that this adds up to a lack of standards, or the acceptance of low standards. "There are really no big problems, just lots and lots of small problems."

"We Greeks are impatient, unsystematic, we cut corners", he continues. "We are selfish, we think only of our personal gain. We have discovered that we can enjoy life in a society that suffers around us. So why bother about society? Greece is a poor country of rich people, whereas Holland is a rich country of poor people".

Pressed to explain this, he focuses on what he perceives as the root cause: "The problem is elementary education, the character-forming stage. We have poor teachers, because we pay them poorly and we shift them around all the time from one place to another. They are poorly motivated, they have no vision - and so they fail to communicate any lasting values to the children. Greek people are like badly programmed computers: they have the right hardware, the brainpower, but poor software, the value systems. You'll be lucky if you can get a Greek to give up his time voluntarily to a good cause." A sad comment on a state which gave birth to the concept of civism.

Lack of motivation, or cynicism, certainly does not imply lack of intelligence (the hardware bit). "Put a Greek in a dark room and he will find a way out, where a Dutchman or a German would take twice as long. He uses his natural ingenuity. Yet we tend to be too clever by half. We trip up on our own intelligence, we over-estimate our capabilities." Which may explain why foreigners charge the Greeks with ambiguity.

Another trait that surfaces from time to time is a gift for hysteria of a decidedly theatrical nature. Most evident at village funerals, it also has its uses in international relations, as for example the Macedonia Affair.

Of course, like other Europeans, the Greeks are caught up in a system which dictates to a large extent how they behave - to themselves and toward society. This system features two mechanisms in particular: political patronage and the parallel economy *(ricordi d'Italia?)*. The result is bureaucratic corruption and sloth on the one hand, adequate cause to cheat the authorities on the other. No wonder a recent feature in the normally well-informed French daily, *Libération*, rated the parallel economy at 30-50 per cent of GNP.

The problem goes back to the creation of the Greek state, when King Otto's Bavarian ministers tried and failed to grapple successfully with the time-honoured Greek way of doing things - namely clientage or what is known as *clientelismo* in Italy and *clientélisme* in France.

Professor McNeil's comments on an American attempt to get the country back on the rails in 1950 are particularly revealing. "Radical restructuring of the Greek economy", he says, "could not be carried through as long as the governmental administrative machine remained *democratic*, that is, *responsive to special pressures and traditional values* [my italics]. The centuries-old habit of seeking and finding favours through personal channels of patronage and friendship tore gaping holes in any kind of government-decreed general regulation designed to control economic processes." So that's what the Greeks mean by democracy!

And later: "To abide by the rules and let officialdom work its will unassisted seems to most Greeks a mark of stupidity or laziness. Things just do not get done that way, and everybody knows it." It seems to me that, in matters involving the settlement of conflicting interests, the average Greek will have a shrewd idea of the big guns lined up on both sides - implying a foregone conclusion and, in many cases, absolutely no action as a result.

My business consultant friend confirms the enormity of the issue. "The root problem is an oversized, dilatory and inefficient bureaucracy. Greek government officials do not consider themselves responsible for other people: by definition, the moment you are told you are responsible for other people, you are no longer a bureaucrat! Yet, on the other side, everybody knows somebody who can make a phonecall and cut the Gordian knot. If not, there are specialised professionals around to help you get even routine decisions from government departments. Moonlighting is the national pastime - both in the public and private sectors."

McNeil enlarges on the impact of this on business and the individual. "Extensively ramified patterns of patronage and clientage thus surround and supplement bureaucratically organised corporate structures. Conversely, income generated by short-term, personal contracts constitutes a significant part of many, perhaps most, urban family incomes. Needless to say, such arrangements very often escape the tax collector's net. This is one of the reasons for the energy Greeks put into searching out and making such deals. The bargaining involved gives scope for individual enterprise and cleverness." My English friend comments: "There are no real political parties here, just clans." And, as an afterthought, "the Greeks are not criminal by nature, they are just corrupt."

Politics tends to interfere with business as in other Mediterranean countries - only more so since party (or clan?) influence extends to subsidising industrial 'lame ducks', state patronage of banks, and manipulation of student organisations and trade unions. The last-named play the game meekly enough: both union officials and the people they represent are intent on protecting their jobs.

Having said all the above - and it's a mouthful! - I have to concede that, when the Greeks do things systematically and conscientiously, they do them extremely well. The evidence is there in many of the more successful businesses, in the better hotels, in the fruit farmers of the northern plains, in some of the fishing villages and in many retail businesses in the bigger towns (the Greeks don't have a reputation as traders for nothing).

Reports coming back from the business front are, of course, contradictory. On the one hand, the engineer of an American food products multinational with a production plant in Greece speaks warmly of the "flexibility and readiness of people to change shifts and workstations", albeit within union rules, and the administrative manager of a Dutch brewing subsidiary describes the workers as "adaptable and smart". On the other hand, a feature in *International Management* in May 1990 said "Greeks like to be independent and are reluctant to follow orders, making it difficult to achieve the teamwork necessary for large-scale ventures". They have difficulty in making decisions.

As owner-managers, the Greeks tend to be excessively autocratic and secretive: Greek SMEs are even reluctant to locate in industrial parks because they are afraid that, with things like perimeter fences and common services, the authorities will know too much about them.

As in Italy, the younger generation also seems to be playing it safe. A business consultant says their main motive is security, they have no sense of adventure. "If a state bank advertises for 40 people, they will get at least 2,000 to 5,000 applications. If it's a business firm, they'll be lucky with 100."

It is of course understandable that security is important to the Greeks. History records a diaspora - to Sicily, southern Italy and, later, to the Balkans and Anatolia (incidentally the Greek word for 'sunrise') that was only matched by the mass Greek repatriations from the latter and the Aegean Islands earlier this century. The reintegration of the Pontic Greeks left deep scars. And, like all Mediterranean peoples, the Greeks are excessively sensitive to criticism.

All of which, set against their illustrious classical past, leaves them with an image problem at the end of the 20th century. In trying to find a new *raison d'être*, they are casting a role for themselves as the honest brokers between the Balkans and the rest of Europe - something that tests other peoples' credulity from time to time. A Greek contributor to *International Management* magazine stated that "*the Greek reality* has become a catchphrase for problems without rational solutions".

Returning to the social mores of the country, it is a moot question to what extent Greek men are more or less macho than other European males. Greek society is certainly male-oriented. Whereas Ancient Greece, at least Athens, was reputed to have its fair share of homosexuality, the modern Greek seems to enjoy the company of his fellow-males on platonic grounds as much as anything else. Many of them, even in the bigger cities, frequent the same male coteries night after night - the women rarely get a look in. This tradition, the group of friends known as the *parea*, is fundamental to Greek life: it inspires a great sense of loyalty and respects the principle that, as the French say, *"un plaisir est un plaisir partagé"*. The only thing is that it's almost as if, socially at least, the other half didn't exist.

This may also help to explain the assertiveness I have noticed in the more emancipated Greek woman, a severity, sometimes a lack of elegance that is more masculine than feminine. One has the impression that this is less a response to the Greek version of the German triple-K syndrome (*Küche, Kirche, Kinder* = cooking, church, children) than the simple reality that the matter-of-fact behaviour of the men leaves them with little choice. Many Greek men have a pretty explicit attitude towards their womenfolk, and the opposite applies too. But the men do not seem to be so prone to bottom-pinching and infidelity as their Mediterranean neighbours. Unmarried sons in their 40s, still living at home and mothered mercilessly, are a familiar sight even today - the family objective being to marry off the daughters first.

Warmth, both familial and other, is ultimately what Greek society is all about. Flora Lewis puts things into perspective[2]: "Superstition, pride and sensitivity mark the Greek temperament, but charm is the highest value. *Charisma* is an old Greek word which never depreciated".

To come back to where we started from, these qualities reflect the physical environment - superb landscapes and seascapes, and a felicitous climate - a unique blend that leaves northerners spellbound. Geography has endowed Greece with the most unevenly distributed population of any European nation. The country boasts more than 4,000 villages with an average of 100 inhabitants each. Village life has given Greece the character that others admire. Sadly, these villages are now emptying and, with this trend, a distinctive way of life will dissipate.

And, in conclusion, a thought from our friendly business consultant, even if this makes both his opinion and my conclusions suspect: "Greece is a country of contradictions. You cannot find a typical Greek. I am *not* a typical Greek. I know there are people cleverer than me..."

The Hungarians
The articulate analysts

"Hedging is not a native Hungarian art form, however brilliant they may be at sitting on the fence"
Zsuzsanna Ardó, *How to be a European: Go Hungarian* [50]

"Look me in the eye when I'm speaking to you!"
Hungarian parent's admonition to Hungarian child

"An average day is worse than yesterday but better than tomorrow"
Hungarian dictum

"The leader of the Soviet Union convoked a Communist summit and put a thumbtack on each delegate's chair to test his responses. The Czech sat down and winced, but held his tongue. The Pole sat down and jumped up with a scream. The Hungarian, never trusting, looked first, discreetly brushed off the tack, sat down and then let out a yell"
Flora Lewis [2]

"Whoever has a Hungarian as a friend doesn't need enemies"
Austrian proverb

"Little Hungarians are taught mental gymnastics as well as getting physical training at school"
Georg Kövary [5]

"Hungarians talk with excessive verbal redundancy when they use a very concise language like English. It is bloody irritating for native English speakers!"
Hungarian sociologist

There's a 'paired' set of Finnish-Hungarian jokes - maybe I should just say Finno-Ugric - which tell how these two related peoples arrived at the eastern outskirts of Europe and found a stone tablet bearing a message.

In the Finnish version of the joke, the message read: "Turn right for a nice rich country". The Hungarians couldn't read, so they turned left.

In the Hungarian version of the joke, the message read: "Turn left for a nice sunny country". In this case it was the Finns who couldn't read...

You will have guessed from this that the Finns and Hungarians are vaguely related, even if they have little more in common than this joke. Even their languages are mutually impenetrable apart from sharing a special intonation and open vowels (something that, in a crowded room, tends to lead Finns towards Hungarians and *vice versa*).

A propos language, it is difficult to deny the fact that the Hungarians are articulate: with such a complex language they have no choice. They also, as you will have noticed if you've ever met a real live Hungarian, have strikingly analytical minds which, occasionally, they use for that purpose.

Philologists suggest this has something to do with the structure of the language, with all those noun endings or 'post-positions' as philologists call them. Political pundits think it may have more to do with the fact that, confronted with adversity throughout history, Hungarians have learned to use their wits.

Educationalists assert it is simply a consequence of the intensive and effective schooling system from the secondary level upwards - a system owing much historically to the Prussians. The young Hungarian is taught from an early age to think for him or herself.

Whatever the reasons, one or more of these things, there is plenty of evidence that Hungarians can think straight - tangentially, but straight - at least from time to time. Which does not mean, as Georg (György) Kövary [51] points out, that they necessarily think a straight line is the shortest distance between two points.

At least from time to time, I say, since some Hungarians, particularly the older generations, strike the casual observer as being mildly crazy. And 'professional Hungarians' - of which there are still a few, most of them elderly males wearing little 'Robin Hood' hats and short woollen coats, or sporting hussar-type moustaches in place of the little hats - are just plain crazy all the time.

Yet, whether logical or crazy, the Hungarians are often brilliant. Consider some of their race and the things they came up with. László Biró and the ballpoint pen. Dénes Gábor and the hologram. Ernö Rubik and The Cube. Bela Bartok and his strikingly (percussively) original and paradoxical music.

Two of 1994's Nobel Laureates were Hungarian-born: one of them, John Harsanyi, contributed significantly to a "pioneering analysis of equilibria in the theory of non-competitive games". And at least half the scientists engaged on the Manhattan Project were, for better or worse, Hungarians. One of them was Ede (Edward to you) Teller. Then there are the Polgár girls, all three trained by their father in the cerebral business of chess, and all three now famous internationally.

Cast by adversity into a foreign and often alien environment - as has happened to a lot of Hungarians in the course of the 20th century - many of them have survived and succeeded brilliantly. Heard of George (György) Soros? The pervasiveness of Hungarians in international life is such that it comes as a relief to the rest of us to learn that, of some 15 million identifiable Hungarians, at least four million live outside the country - primarily in Romania, Slovakia, Serbia and, for some reason, the US city of Cleveland.

This process has been helped on its way by Hungarian commitment to the concept of the extended family. You will find tight little knots of Hungarians everywhere. As George (György) Mikes, another expatriate genius, remarked: "London is a great English city, but it is also a small Hungarian village"[52].

With the demise of the communist regime, Hungarians are now even successful at home. One contemporary success story is that of Gabor Bojar of Graphisoft whose flourishing software company, testimony to his powers of lateral thinking, is now conquering world markets.

Lateral thinking? The Hungarian mind is more than just laterally competent. As an Irish business consultant who has worked in Hungary for many years puts it: "They have this ability, if they run up against a brick wall, to get past it - around, over or under it in one way or another."

In the words of Georg Kövary, the Hungarians are "as tough as Americans, as romantic as Slavs, as curious as the Japanese, as cunning as Arabs." Summing up all these characteristics they come closest, in his opinion, to the Italians or the French...

Cunning is an attribute readily acknowledged by Hungarians, who pride themselves on their shrewdness and practical approach to life. The native streak has been enhanced by historical adversity and, more recently, by the challenges imposed by a command economy and a state bureaucracy. The joke quoted by Flora Lewis at the head of this chapter makes the point. But even in a rural or a small-town environment, one had to use one's wits to get on (let alone, ahead) in life.

Some foreigners - particularly their Austrian neighbours but also the Americans - maintain that, even if you manage to get into a revolving door ahead of a Hungarian, he or she will be resourceful enough to get out first. Of course they, the Austrians, have the benefit of hindsight: they shared an empire with the Hungarians who, from those times, still call the Austrians *Labancs* - just as the Austrians still call the Germans *Piefkes*.

Despite such achievements, the Hungarians are still better known to the rest of the world for their folkdances, their wines and their *gulyas* - which happens to be a soup, *pörkölt* being the thing foreigners persist in calling 'goulash'. Those delicious Tokay wines, incidentally, were the work of the descendants of Walloon immigrants from Belgium (Tokay comes from the northeastern corner of the country and not, as some Hungarians would have` you believe, the shores of Lake Balaton).

As genetic outsiders casually related to the Estonians and the Finns, as well as to some of the people of the Urals and the Volga basin in the ex-USSR, Hungarians are entitled to be different. Indeed they are. They even used to have a social phenomenon, the Community Family (see Chapter 5), which set them apart from most of the rest.

Yet it would be wrong to think of the Hungarians as being a genetically exclusive nation - they wouldn't want that in any case, their culture is enough. A study conducted jointly in the early-1990s by a Budapest research institute and a German university identified 17 different racial groups in the Hungarian population, including more than one Magyar strain, Armenians, Ruthenians,

Croats, Swabians (who came down the Danube to repopulate areas laid waste by the Turks as they retreated) and, of course, gypsies.

The Hungarians are a delightful people, every bit as hardworking, intelligent, astute as any other race. They are also particularly responsive, subjective, empathetic, proud (in the words of a Scots businessman, "too proud to listen"), ultimately emotional and occasionally hysterical. Great individualists, they have a highly relation-oriented and high-context culture (see Chapter 7). They compete with the Mediterraneans in touching, intimacy and terms of endearment, though once-popular phrases like *angyalkám* ('my little angel'), *drágám* ('my dear one') and *édeském* ('my sweet little one') are now on the way out.

Sentimentality also expresses itself in a gloomy outlook on life. Opinion polls unfailingly chart one characteristic above all others - pessimism - even if Hungarians remain ever-hopeful. As one of their diplomats says: "Melancholy is not an alternative to euphoria but a natural corollary to it."

He cites an American friend who finds Hungarian "disinclination to see the whole picture, especially when the whole is brighter than the part," particularly upsetting. Failure to see the whole picture may also explain why, despite going through an educational system which makes them analytical and numerate, Hungarians have a propensity for living, quite happily, above their means.

None of this is particularly surprising when you consider what Hungarians have had to put up with. They suffer from the realisation that, more often than not, they have been on the wrong side throughout history. This inevitably leaves them with a residue of defensiveness and self-doubt. Ask too many questions and they think you don't trust them...

Speaking of his fellow-countrymen the writer, George Konrad, says: "It seems that people here, even when grown up, need a father to tell them what to do". This doesn't prevent them from telling their fellow-Hungarians what to do or in arguing intensely over minor issues - a tendency which Dr Lenke Simon, a Hungarian sociologist, believes highlights the pernicious effect of the country's history in fostering "lack of stability and value ambiguity: suffering equates with honour".

The obverse of this is envy and suspicion of the get-rich-quick, in a society which came to expect material betterment under 'communist consumerism' and now fails to see many of the improvements hoped for in the transition to a free market economy.

These problems may also help explain the phenomenon of the highest suicide rate of any European country, also the highest mortality from heart disease in Europe. Of course, these two factors could be linked - a case of Hungarians knowingly eating themselves, or romancing themselves, to death.

Moody introspection can however also explain an ability to adjust to hostile circumstances, a condition endemic in Hungarian history. This can manifest itself both in ingenuity and, by contrast, in a surprising degree of caution or even fatalism, a habit that was encouraged by decades of communism. Today, the free market has taken its place, but the frustrations are still there. If anything, they have increased: according to a Eurobarometer survey, whereas 51% of Hungarians had a positive image of the European Union in 1990, by 1994 the figure had dropped to 32%.

These frustrations were evident in the conversation I had with a young Hungarian economics student, who responded to my speculations on the future with typical Hungarian realism: "We have so many options, but we don't have any money." The maturity of mind of young Hungarians today is striking: they are learning from history. Obviously, in addition to keen minds, they have long memories. Three of them recently took part in a memory contest in France and ran off with the first three places.

In fact it is miraculous that the Hungarians have kept afloat in the sea of Slavitude that surrounds them, though they owe that as much to their hermetic language as anything else. But once they feel that things have gone too far for their taste, as in 1956, they are capable of acts of the most heroic defiance. Such defiance now even extends into more peaceful realms - as demonstrated by the readiness of Hungarian subsidiary and branch managers to 'do their own thing', despite instructions to the contrary.

Inevitably the streetwise quality of the Hungarians worries their old allies, the Austrians - particularly since the Hungarians, despite or perhaps because of their bizarre ethnic origins, are more committed Europeans than most, even if they're not as sure about the free market and the EU as they used to be. A senior Austrian diplomat, commenting on Hungary's application for membership of the

European Union, said with a sense of finality: "Once in, they'll take over". The revolving door complex...

Lenke Simon recalls a Hungarian joke, told at the expense of the sizeable gypsy community but which illustrates this side of the Hungarian character. A gypsy sold a horse to a villager. A few days later the villager ran into the gypsy at the horse fair and asked for his money back: "This horse is blind, he keeps on running into walls!", he complained. "Nonsense", said the gypsy, "he's not blind, he's brave!".

So we're back to walls, revolving doors, trapdoors, loopholes, etc, etc.

The Slavs

A cultural stew

"The Macedonian question has been the cause of every great European war for the last fifty years, and until that is settled there will be no more peace either in the Balkans or out of them. Macedonia is the most frightful mix-up of races ever imagined. Turks, Albanians, Serbs, Rumanians, Greeks and Bulgarians live there side by side without mingling - and have so lived since the days of St. Paul" John Reed, *The War in Eastern Europe*, 1916[53]

We've been beaten so many times and put in such difficult situations, we always think of survival first"
Stanislav Shushkevich, Belarus politician

"What's small, dark and knocking at the door? The future"
Romanian dictum

"How do you divide up the past?" Gane Todorovski, Macedonian poet

In the life of the Bulgarian reality is inextricably mixed with the symbolic and the abstract" Georgi Markov, *The Truth That Killed*

"A group of people united by a common error as to their origins and a common dislike of their neighbours"
Fred Singleton: a cynic's definition of a Balkan nation

"We want to be part of developed Europe, not part of the Balkans. Our mentality is closer to Mitteleuropa"
Miha Vrhunecs, Slovene foreign ministry official

The Slavs? We're in danger of getting out of our depth, since this definition is a dubious one - without even asking what the Estonians, Albanians, Bulgarians and Romanians are doing in this chapter. At least we managed to extricate the Hungarians.

The water gets deeper if we venture into the concept of 'east Europeans' and 'eastern Europe', definitions that have already been used in this book for the sake of convenience. The Czechs and Poles, as well as the Hungarians, reject such definitions, preferring 'central Europeans' - a preference they share with the Austrians - or at least 'east central Europeans'.

The Slavs (here we go) have been around for a long time, certainly since the fifth century BC in most cases. Yet being a rather mercurial folk by temperament, with a few exceptions like the Czechs, they managed to dissipate their influence on early European history to the point that, even today, many of us have difficulty in taking them seriously as Europeans. 'Balkanisation' is a polite way of saying that someone fouled something up.

Yet it wasn't the Slavs who fouled things up, it was the so-called Great Powers. And it was a clever Hungarian by the name of Lajos Kossuth who, in the late-1800s, proposed the creation of a 'Danube Confederation' to comprise Hungary, Austria, Bohemia and Moravia (parts of the Czech Republic as it is now known), Serbia and Romania. This would have represented a formidable cultural stew, but it might still have gone down better than the very mixed grill the Great Powers eventually dished up.

Any tendency by the rest of Europe to underestimate the Slavs does them less than justice. Much of the most creative artistic output of the last century has come from this part of the world. As relatively small communities, the Russians excepted, they have made their mark in art and literature. In music they have really excelled themselves - with distinctive geniuses like Stravinsky, Shostakovich, Prokofiev and Janacek. If their music is any guide, the Slavs offer us colour, surprise and, with notable exceptions, humanity.

They certainly have the potential to offer such qualities to the Europe of the 21st century if, in contrast to the past, the rest of us let them. For a start we need to get better acquainted. Recent politics have not given most of us a chance to get to know the Slavs properly.

The Russians, who got their name from the Swedish Vikings, are by their numbers and the sheer deadweight of their economy likely to need the most time and patience. For what we now call Russia still comprises 30 autonomous republics and five alphabets!

In his book *The New Russians*[54], Hedrick Smith describes the culture as "a people who historically have needed a belief system, an ideology to live by, whether Communism or Russian Orthodoxy. Many are uneasy with a political system in which the guiding principles of public life are concerned with means, not ends". Later he comments that "most Russians look to the state and the ruler to provide an ideology and a purpose as well as law and order". Shades of generations of czars, the brooding influence of the Orthodox Church ... and communism.

Peter Collett[5] expresses a similar opinion when he says: "In some respects the Russians are like Latins, because their relationships with their family and friends are extremely important to them, and they usually take precedence over the demands of time. The official values of the state, however, were just the opposite, because they were associated with efficient production, schedules and deadlines - in other words, issues which are of secondary importance to Russians."

So it is an irony of history that it should have been the Russians, rather than the Germans, who became the 'chosen race' for communism, despite their highly developed sense of community. Setting aside a marked tendency to oscillate between moods of ferocity and passivity, the latter predominating in the last 70 years, the Russians are individually as well attuned to anarchism, despite their Orthodox upbringing, as to any dirigist doctrine. This manifests itself in the sly ingenuity used by instinctively work-shy people to get round the system. Finding a substitute for the real thing - whether dodging work, building 'Potemkin villages' or just putting on a show *(pokazukha)* - seems to be an integral part of the Russian psyche.

I am talking about the Slavonic parts of Russia of course, including the 'Little Russian' and 'White Russian' versions thereof, as Ukraine and Belarus were known to 19th century romanticists. I have no brief here for the Turkic, Moslem, Georgian or Armenian peoples, either of today's Russia or of the other states of the ex-USSR (110 'nations', 112 recognised languages, five separate alphabets), all of which are beyond the confines of this book.

There are even some non-Slavic ethnic elements of Russia that, history turning reality upside down as it does, may well now qualify as 'European' even if they aren't. One Russian enclave houses 3.7 million Tatars, ethnically a mixed bunch now but decidedly Mongol in origin, while a smaller community lives in the Crimea along with Bulgars, Greeks and other minorities. Another enclave, currently called the autonomous republic of Udmurtia, is home to half-a-million Udmurts who speak a variation of Finno-Ugrian and apparently got left behind as what we now call the Hungarians and the Finns moved westwards. Yet another Finno-Ugrian group, the Ingrians, moved back into Russia some 50 years ago and now want to go back to Finland.

Some people will tell you that the only thing predictable about the Russians is their unpredictability. One of the striking features of the early stages of *perestroika* was that, in contrast to all the other freedom movements of eastern Europe, it seemed to evoke more response from the older folk than from the young (the Putsch changed all that). This was in stark contrast to the freedom movements of other eastern European countries, except those which were masterminded by an existing crypto-communist establishment, where in every case the young took the lead.

The obverse side of Russian unpredictability is their essential open-mindedness, good-heartedness and sense of hospitality: in this respect they are natural 'communists', in contrast to what I said earlier. They have a penchant for close physical contact and hyperbole. Unfortunately, this sense of hospitality does not always extend to non-Europeans: they tend to demonstrate a Pavlovian and extremely negative response to anyone with a brown skin, let alone a black one. Proud nationalism and xenophobia, as also evident in western Ukraine in particular, are close relatives. An almost permanent state of paranoia towards everything also plays its part.

In addition to the occasional outbursts of violence to prove their unpredictability, the last 70 years have provided ample evidence of the essential passivity of the Russian peoples - an echo of centuries of serf-like conditions under a series of tyrannical or, at best, blandly disinterested rulers. Suffering comes easy to the Russians: in the words of journalist Vitali Vitaliev (aren't their names harmonious?) "if a Russian husband stops beating his wife, she thinks he doesn't love her any more".

Recent history may also have contributed to the reputation of the inhabitants of Belorussia - ex-White Russia, now Belarus - as particularly passive. "Biddable Belorussia" was how *The Economist* put it. Belarussians have learned humility from their history, having been trodden on repetitively by their bigger neighbours, and have developed passivity in the face of misfortune as a way of life.

Similar things are said about Ukraine: in the words of a local pressman reported in *The Wall Street Journal Europe*, "the Ukrainian nation has a mentality that it is always better to be struggling and poor. Happy people are somehow not part of the Ukrainian sense of heroism". Curiously, Leopold von Sacher-Masoch was a Ukrainian.

But a long history of relatively silent suffering under both czarist and communist regimes cannot be dismissed as passivity and nothing else. The Russian people have shown a stoicism, better said a brand of courage, which no other European race, not even the Germans, has been able to match (and that's saying a lot when you consider our mutually bloody past). It is still difficult to get some people to realise that it was the Russians, with some help from the Americans and the British, who won WWII. In the process of living with communism and fighting off fascism, they sacrificed 21 million lives. There is a stoic heroism about this race which is too rarely recognised.

The people of the Baltic States have, in more recent times, shown the same sort of dogged determination as both the Russians and the Finns - with whom the Estonians, who share a related Finno-Ugrian language, blond angular looks and Lutheranism, have close affinities.

Where the Estonians look culturally to Finland, the Latvians share a cultural tradition including Lutheranism with Germany, and the Lithuanians are most closely linked through history and Roman Catholicism with Poland.

As a consequence of their reluctant association with the ex-USSR, all three Baltic states have had to live with very substantial ethnic minorities, Russian in particular: 20 per cent of the total population in Lithuania, where the principal minority group is Polish, 37 per cent in Estonia and 46 per cent in Latvia.

The Balts acknowledge that they are a sentimental folk with a passion for flowers. When asked to explain their differences, they are likely to say that Latvia produces the best politicians, Lithuania the best prophets and Estonia the best economists.

Certainly the Estonians are the most enterprising in business, on the strength of their short record, as well as being the dourest of the Balts. The Latvians are deeply attached to their folksong tradition of *dainas* and, despite nearly 50 years of communism, are fundamentally great individualists: eager to please, they are much addicted to understatement, but recoil at the kind of close physical contact dear to the Russians. And the Lithuanians, for their part, live up to a reputation as sentimentally religious people (they were, maybe significantly, the last nation in Europe to accept Christianity), with both historic and contemporary links to Catholic Poland. They are also known for their quick tempers, often at the expense of their Polish neighbours whom they regard as loud and arrogant.

Many Russian traits - including heroism (though of a more theatrical kind) but not passivity - are shared by the Poles. To these some of them, particularly the older generations, add exaggerated pretensions to nobility, real or assumed, and a great penchant for a swoony form of romanticism. No doubt Chopin has something to do with this, but the pastiche that results would do credit to Liberace. In its better moments the romantic streak can be interpreted as chivalry and, as Joseph Conrad put it, an "exaggerated respect for individual rights" - something that, tragically, did not extend to the Jewish community.

In conflict, and in other situations challenging their native ingenuity, the Poles are unsurpassed. As for normal hard work, in the opinion of the Germans and some others, this is something they are not so good at. Polish employers now benefiting from the relative work ethic of immigrant Russians, Lithuanians and Ukrainians are in agreement, even if they are by nature inclined to be xenophobic.

The consensus seems to be that the Poles enjoy being lazy, making up for this by using their wits. Hearing the stories about mobile Polish black markets all over eastern Europe, one is inclined to concur: shortly after the opening of the Berlin Wall, a Polish-registered Lada was apprehended crossing the Oder-Neiße line in an easterly direction with something like 70 kilograms of sausage-meat stitched into its lining.

My own Polish experience dates from the late-1970s when, standing at a Warsaw airport taxi rank, I was offered a ride, paying of course, in a public ambulance. Clearly the foibles of a command economy have brought out the potential of what is known worldwide as 'the Polish mafia'. As one of them put it succinctly: "one thing you learn under communism is how to be good at being corrupt". An independent observer of the ex-Comecon scene insists that this holds good for eastern Europe generally.

Certainly the wry humour of the Poles matches anything the Russians can produce. Russian joke: "Is it true that the Moskvitch car can be driven through a 90° bend at 120 kph? Yes, but only once." Polish joke: "What is 100 meters long and eats bread? A queue outside a Polish butcher's shop". Polish jokes draw liberally on events from everyday life.

The Poles have a humour born partly of desperation, some of them having fought off the armoured divisions of the Germans and the Russians on alternate days on horseback: the influence of Chopin made them feel gallant, if not particularly effective. They were certainly brave to the point of foolhardiness. The latter is a characteristic which survives in both behaviour and language.

Zaniness is evident in many aspects of Polish life, accentuated until recently by the trials and tribulations of coping with a centrally controlled economy and, currently, with something close to chaos. Even in worst-case scenario situations, the Poles manage to summon up a cheekily passive resistance. So, if a Pole tells you you are crazy, don't take it personally (you will probably think *he* or *she* is in any case).

Since we've broached the subject of humour - one of the great creative qualities common to most of the Slavs - let's deal next with the Czech Republic, a country that shares with Spain a reputation as a cradle of black humour, both verbal and graphic. Some of the best cartoons to be seen on western television come from this part of Europe. Their wit and originality, working with relatively modest means, is delightful.

And then there are the jokes, for example one doing the rounds in 1989: "Havel is offered three wishes by a good fairy. Each time he responds: 'I wish the Chinese would invade Czechoslavakia'. The good fairy asks why. 'That way', says Havel, 'they will have to march through Russia six times'."

The stereotype of the Czechs - solid, materialist, even depressive - suggests that their highly developed sense of humour belies, or finds its origins in, a tendency to introversion and submissiveness. The latter, a strikingly unSlav characteristic, may owe something to the fact that, until the demise of the Austro-Hungarian empire, they were socially subservient to a German-speaking elite and treated accordingly. Maybe it was this that prompted Winston Churchill, never a man to mince his words, to pronounce that 5 per cent of Czechs were scoundrels and 95 per cent cowards.

Flora Lewis expressed herself more elegantly[2]: "The Czechs are more stolid, cautious and practical than other Slavs, without the streak of wild passion, gaiety and cruelty". Maybe the submissiveness explains the fixed, sardonic smile that characterises so many well-rounded Czech chins, as well as a remarkable capacity for complaining about everything.

Note that Ms Lewis is speaking of the Czechs, not the Slovaks, who are a livelier, less inhibited lot. History may have something to do with this too since, in the Austro-Hungarian empire, Slovakia enjoyed relative autonomy as a province of Hungary and, indeed, still has a large Hungarian minority today.

In the opinion of the Czechs, the Slovaks are less inclined to hard work. This, compounded by the fear that the Czechs will dominate them economically, may contribute to the Slovaks' lingering fondness for state socialism. The tensions between the two peoples - heightened by the fact that, ironically, they have a characteristic in common, namely a marked distaste for compromise - make the progressive distancing of the communities inevitable. In the words of Jan Urban, a distinguished Czech commentator, "they only know how to win or to lose."

At the time of writing it is difficult to talk about a place that used to be called Yugoslavia, the 'country of the South Slavs'. Comprising Slovenia, Croatia, Serbia, Bosnia, Montenegro and Macedonia, it was a *potpourri* of cultures that almost defied analysis. Of all the Balkan countries, Yugoslavia was the most balkanised: it took shape in 1918 essentially as a barrier to the expansionist aims of the Italians and the Hungarian communists: from then on, no one could find a really good reason for its existence.

Even so statistically, if nothing else, this cobbled-together country had some homogeneity: 88 per cent of the population are South Slav, 75 per cent speak Serbo-Croat (or Croato-Serb, depending on who you are), and the vast majority are Christian of one rite or the other - a big difference, it seems.

It would take a separate book and a great deal of time to examine the temperaments of all these races, though the 'South Slavs' share characteristics with a disconcerting degree of overlap (disconcerting for both foreigners and fellow-South Slavs). Now with Slovenia out of the way, the pattern of its peoples becomes a bit clearer, but not much so.

Much of the 'Balkans problem' goes back to an arbitrary decision by the Emperor Diocletian, at the end of the 3rd century, to divide the country between the western and eastern Roman Empires (see Chapter 3). Yugoslavia inherited a Catholic/Orthodox fault line that, broadly, divided the Slovenes and Croats from the rest. The 11th-century schism between the two churches reinforced the *status quo* and, later, the Ottoman and Habsburg empires completed the balkanisation of the region.

So the Slovenes and the Croats use the Roman alphabet and belong to the Roman Catholic community, while the Serbs, Montegrins and Macedonians use the Cyrillic alphabet and worship according to the eastern Orthodox rite. Then there are the Muslim minorities of Bosnia and Montenegro totalling over 2.5 million people. In fact there are *two groups* of Muslims, those who are ethnic Albanian and speak a strange language descended from ancient Illyrian, and the remainder who are ethnically part-Slav, part-Turk. This Slav element is largely composed of descendents of 'Bulgar' heretics (see Chapter 3) who converted to Islam under the Ottomans.

Add the large Albanian communities in Kosovo and Macedonia, plus the important Hungarian minority in the Vojvodina autonomous province of Serbia, spice with 500 years of Ottoman rule, stir up vigorously - and you have, in ex-Yugoslavia, an excellent recipe for a Balkan stew.

Bosnia-Herzegovina, with a composition 17 per cent Croat, 31 per cent Serb and 44 per cent Muslim, was as complex a community as any in the Balkans. While life in Sarajevo had been reasonably harmonious up to the Serb onslaught, as Robert Kaplan points out in his book *Balkan Ghosts*[55], "the villages all around were full of savage hatreds, leavened by poverty and alcoholism". Yet, in the words of *The Economist*, the people of Bosnia-Herzegovina "muddled along together remarkably well". It would be more exact to say that, with striking exceptions, they existed side-by-side.

Bosnia's 'muddling along' certainly never applied elsewhere to the Serbs and Croats since, overlooking the hatred engendered between the two peoples in WWII, the mutual antagonism goes back a very long way. The best that can be said is that the younger generations of Serbs do not all share the enthusiasm of their elders for the Greater Serbia idea.

As the Croatian defence minister said at the beginning of the 1991 hostilities: "We have been waiting for this moment for eight centuries". Not as far back as Diocletian, but still a very long time. European history has a lot to answer for.

In western eyes - which includes the Slovenes and the Croats - the Serbs are folkloric with their rustic simplicity, their circumlocutions, and their tendency to Oriental mysticism and authoritarianism. For the Serbs, the people to the northwest are boringly systematic, bourgeois and sententious. They suspect the Croats, on the evidence of past and recent history, of being not just pan-Germanic but frankly fascist in inspiration.

The Montenegrins, who are both historically and ethnically close to Serbia, think of themselves as a warrior nation and tend to act accordingly. The Macedonians, in contrast, think of themselves as a race apart - a thesis it is difficult to argue with since there are as many theories on what constitutes a Macedonian as there are interested parties. This is hardly surprising since the two million people in this southernmost region of what was Yugoslavia are the ultimate racial hotchpotch.

Macedonia as a political entity only came into existence in 1945, when Tito declared the area a republic to suit his own ends, neatly administering one in the eye to both the Serbs and the Bulgarians. The Marshal's machiavellian manipulation of Yugoslav politics - playing off one community against another in order to scotch the Serbs' expansionist aspirations - has had more to do with the sad turn of recent events than anything else.

But the Macedonian issue also goes much further back into history - so far back, in fact, that it is positively daft. The Greeks evoke memories of Philip of Macedonia and his son Alexander the Great. The Bulgarians maintain that the people in this southernmost state are Bulgars, probably with some justification. And the Serbs, looking both to a far-distant past and to the future, claim they are Serbs.

But the Macedonians themselves, whoever they may be, have endorsed the independence claims of a governing party committed to a concept of a 'Greater Macedonia' which would ultimately include Salonika and Kosovo (consternation in Greek and Serb ranks). Even the Turks are getting worried about their ethnic minorities in northern Greece.

No wonder the name of the Balkans became synonymous with fragmentation and tribal politics. David Anderson, a former US ambassador to Yugoslavia, leaves you in no doubt: "The problem, I fear, is the Yugoslavs themselves. They are a perverse group of folks, near tribal in their behaviour, suspicious of each other (with usually sound reasons), friendly on the outside but very cynical within, ever ready for a war or battle, proud of their warrior history, and completely incapable of coming to grips with the modern world." Gulp.

That leaves us with the *Albanian* Albanians, the Bulgarians and the Romanians - none of whom, pace the title of this section, are strictly or certainly exclusively Slavs.

Their post-WWII brand of politics has ensured the Albanians the reputation of the least-known people in Europe. Their temperament, like their politics, is stubborn and fierce. Added to that they are exceptionally - and, for their neighbours, disturbingly - prolific. In fact nearly as many Albanians live in ex-Yugoslavia as in Albania itself. Maybe emigration is the answer after all.

As for the Bulgarians, in the 1989 thaw they took a leaf out of other peoples' books by using the environmental issue, in their *Eco-Glasnost* activist party, as a way to win popular support. This apparently inspired move may have reflected a wily and long-established art of making things look different from the way they really are. As Flora Lewis says: "The people tend to be big and muscular, solemn, suspicious, resigned to the blows of untender fate. They have learned to survive by accommodation, by mere doggedness, by self-effacement when that is prudent and by tricks when they may work well".

Robert Kaplan quotes the words of a Bulgarian journalist in his book *Balkan Ghosts*: "We are the most intelligent of peasants, and thus we know better than you how to survive". Their neighbours have been known to call the Bulgarians the Irish of eastern Europe: but local understanding of the Irish may not be sufficient to justify the analogy.

The Bulgarians are certainly industrious, having made a modest fortune by eastern European standards out of agricultural produce and forklift trucks (there seems to be a built-in logic there). They also seem to be more efficiency-oriented than their neighbours.

The Romanians surprised everybody in December 1989 by showing that they had the technical resources to listen to Radio Free Europe and the Voice of America. They also demonstrated that, far from being as submissive as legend has it, they were prepared to go out into the streets and fight.

Nicholas II, Russia's last czar, said: "Rumania: it's not a country, it's a profession". It seems that, as people who claim to be hot-blooded descendants of the Roman settlers (something not borne out by history, which suggests that the Vlachs turned up in the area a thousand years after the Romans withdrew), they have not entirely lost their taste for the occasional shootout. According to a source quoted in Robert Kaplan's book, there is no equivalent in the Romanian language to the word 'self-control'.

In the present state of affairs, understanding the Romanian mind is a superfreudian task. It takes a Romanian, Andrei Codrescu[56] to find the right analogy in the maze of tunnels built under Bucharest by the Securitate secret service: "The underground network was reputed to be a thousand miles long, multilayered, a complicated nervous system whose exact shape and direction no single person knew. Architects who had worked on portions of the system had been killed. When I told a poet friend that I could not think of anything similar in the modern world, he said: 'I can... the Romanian mind after forty-five years of dictatorship'." Ambiguity seems to be a permanent feature of the Romanian psyche.

Yet it has to be said that, when they really put their minds to a problem, the Romanians can be extraordinarily effective. They have even been called 'the Prussians of Eastern Europe' (in the old sense of the word of course - see Chapter 3!). They are untypically methodical, businesslike and reliable. Like the Spaniards, they need - and deserve - a thorough image overhaul.

A Case of Varying Values

"Long ago Pascal wrote: 'Vérité en deçà des Pyrénées, erreur au-delà' ('Truth on this side of the Pyrenees, error on the other'). This kind of ethnocentric perception prevails, whatever the nature of the mountains that separate one nation from others"
Professor Otto Klineberg

"Each society is a case of multiple personality, and it modulates without a qualm, without even being aware of what it is up to, from Jekyll to Hyde, from the scientist to the magician, from the hard-headed man of affairs to the village idiot"   Aldous Huxley

"When an American asks a European to carry out a simple request the German will say 'yes' and do it, the Frenchman will say 'yes' and not do it, an Italian will say 'no' but will do it and the Brit will say 'no' and bloody well mean it"
Anonymous American businessman

"In order to reach for the truth the Germans add, the French subtract and the English change the subject"   Sir Peter Ustinov

The national stereotypes indeed capture something of the temperament of a people. *Gründlichkeit* (thoroughness) in the Germans, *esprit* in the French, volatility in the Italians, a sense of honour in the Spaniards, independence of mind in the English...

Quite how these stereotypes emerged is hard to say: observation, folklore, poking fun at foreigners, an amalgam of influences that conspired over the centuries to reduce the irreduceable and define the indefinable.

Yet the 'raw material' of this process, the European nations and peoples, only took final shape and form in the last five centuries - and particularly in the last two, with the maturing of power politics and the nationalist sentiment. For much longer other influences, ones that take no account of modern frontiers, had been at work. They shaped common values that transcend the borders and other physical barriers that kept the peoples of Europe apart.

In his book *L'Invention de l'Europe*[46] Emmanuel Todd, a French demographer and Cambridge graduate, takes us back to our roots. Through a systematic analysis of population records (family size and structure, systems of inheritance, etc) between the years 1850 and 1970, supported by documentary evidence from much further back in European history, he identifies the essential forms of social structure.

His conclusions relate to agrarian communities or, in simpler terms, peasant families. This may seem a restrictive approach by today's standards but, historically, all of us find our origins on the land. As a people, our peasant years were our formative years.

The four families

Todd isolates four types of family structure: the absolute nuclear family *(famille nucléaire absolue)*, the egalitarian nuclear family *(famille nucléaire égalitaire)*, the 'stem' family *(famille de souche)* and the community family *(famille communautaire)*. The four categories reflect the varying realities of agrarian life and systems of inheritance.

The most easily recognisable of the four is the 'stem' family *(famille souche)*, the most hermetic and authoritarian of all these forms of social organisation. Traditionally it implied that only one son stays on the family property, ultimately inheriting the farm and the land: sometimes three generations will be cohabiting on the same property.

This family structure is historically present in four regions of Europe. The first is a *Germanic* region embracing Austria, German Switzerland, the South Tyrol area of Italy, the eastern fringes of the Netherlands and the southern part of mainland Denmark, as well as much of Germany itself. Second comes a *North/Scandinavian* grouping comprising the populated part of Sweden, the Swedish communities on the Finnish west coast, and north and west Norway. Third comes a Celtic region covering the western fringes of the United Kingdom from the north of Scotland to Cornwall, some areas of Ireland and the Breton peninsula of France.

All these regions, without respecting national frontiers, come close to ethnic reality. But the fourth grouping, dubbed *Occitan-North Iberian*, is a racial ragbag taking in the southernmost third of France, excluding the Mediterranean coast, and northern Spain from Catalonia through the Basque country and Asturias to Galicia (which, as an area with strong Celtic connections, I would have put in the preceding group).

Related to the 'stem' family is the community family *(famille communautaire)*, a relatively rare situation where two married sons and their offspring cohabit on the family farm, even when one or both parents are still alive. In the latter case the authoritarian nature of the relationship, with the 'patriarch' still in the home, is even more marked, but egalitarianism applies in the status of the sons. Evidence of such traditions can still occasionally be found in isolated areas of Western Europe including Finland, the Magyar-dominated province of Burgenland (the Finno-Ugrian connection) now part of Austria, central Italy, and the centre and Mediterranean coast of France (drawing on the tradition of male egalitarianism evident on both the southern and northern shores of this inland sea).

The absolute nuclear family *(famille nucléaire absolue)* implies what is today regarded as a conventional parent-children relationship, with the parents acting arbitrarily on the distribution of inheritance. This type of social formula is found in most of England, the east of Scotland, most of Denmark, southeast Norway (nb the Danish influence), the western and northern Netherlands, and the inland area lying behind the Breton peninsula of France. Curiously this grouping, the French and Dutch bits excepted, bears a close resemblance to the empire of King Knud (Canute to the British!). It basically reflects the presence of Germanic peoples originating from a clearly defined area: Anglo-Saxons, Jutes and Frisians.

Last, the egalitarian nuclear family *(famille nucléaire égalitaire)* features strict equality in the distribution of inheritance. This type of system is found in the north of France (excluding the areas bordering the Belgian and German frontiers), northwest Italy and coastal Provence, southern Italy including Sicily and Sardinia, and central and southeast Spain and central Portugal. Absent from the UK and much of Germany, with the exception of Baden-Württemberg, Hesse and Rhineland-Palatinate thanks to Napoleon, it reflects the historical influence of Rome on the laws of succession.

What do these findings tell us? In the first place, they confirm the traditional hermeticism of family life (the 'stem' family) in Germany, Sweden and Finland. They reflect the principle of parental authority as applied in southern France, northern Spain and Portugal and the eastern provinces of the Netherlands. They also confirm the relatively liberal, egalitarian nature of family life in northern France and central Spain (the *meseta*).

Emmanuel Todd also comments on the Belgian practice of young couples living at home with one of the parent families for the first years of their married life. And, perhaps more significantly, he notes the egalitarian nature of family life along the Mediterranean seaboard extending, at the western limit, right across southern Spain to the Algarve region of Portugal - a reflection of the traditions left over from the Moorish occupation of these regions. In fact, his demographic map of the Iberian peninsula looks uncannily like the division between the Moslem and Christian worlds at the height of the Arab occupation!

Also for those, like myself, who tend to sentimentalise about the demise of large families, it is instructive to see that the nuclear family had already arrived in the UK back in the 17th century. There were very few English families extending so to speak vertically over three generations - or horizontally to include uncles and aunts - even in those days.

The collectivist concept of family and society is the exception in Europe, where Christianity put the emphasis firmly on the individual. Some people assert, though, that communism took hold in Eastern Europe precisely because the Orthodox Church encouraged the cult of passivity in its congregations. As an ethnic Hungarian exile from Serbian Vojvodina, who now runs the 'Marxim' (note the spelling!) bar in Budapest, puts it: "The Orthodox always provide an icon: a person, a father, a pancreator of the world. These nations never got the chance to think autonomously, freely; they were permanently oppressed by sultans and dictators." And tsars and marxists, of course.

In recent times the principles of the nuclear family and lower birthrates have taken hold across Europe generally, with the notable exception of Ireland. Western European families now average 1.6 children, compared with 2.6 in 1962.

Even the poorer countries of the Mediterranean, which used to respect the malthusian principle that poverty breeds population, have joined the movement. It is now Europe's 'Deep South' that returns the lowest birthrates in the world: 1.27 children per mother in Italy, under 1.3 in Spain, and under 1.5 in Portugal and Greece (the standard for survival is 2.1). Eastern Europe is not far behind, with birthrates still falling in Hungary, Poland and the Czech Republic (a process that started some years ago) and now plummeting in Romania, Ukraine and parts of Russia.

The populations of France and Germany are also aging drastically fast, with the birthrate dropping in the *neue Länder* of Germany by nearly 50 per cent from 1989 to mid-1991. Since 1960 the overall fertility rate in the European Union has dropped from 2.6 children to 1.6 per mother. If things go on the way they are, we shall wipe ourselves out and there will be no reason for books like this.

European single parenthood, by contrast, is on the increase. A report published by Britain's Family Policy Studies Centre in 1992 showed that almost one in five UK families is headed by a single parent, compared with one in seven in Denmark, one in eight in Germany and France, and one in 20 in Spain, Italy and Greece.

A concomitant of falling birthrates is the aging of the population, with less young people to help support the elderly. The role that used be played by the family has now, particularly in northern Europe, been assumed by society. With national debt levels rising in many countries and some social security regimes close to bankruptcy, the future doesn't look too rosy!

Yet there are signs of a turnround in the European north. The fertility rates of Britain, Germany, Belgium and the Nordic countries

- including even Sweden, which seemed to be dying on its feet a few years ago - started turning gently upwards from the mid-1980s.

Much of this smacks of 'corrective action', a cybernetic process of social alignment as the cultures of Europe settle down within a narrowing band of economic and social parameters. To quote *The Economist*, "despite obvious differences of language and culture, the once-varied societies of Western Europe have grown remarkably alike. And where they still do differ in family and work patterns, they tend to be moving in the same direction. Europeans are becoming safer to generalise about not just for statisticians but for Europe's politicians and businessmen." Be thankful for small mercies.

Uncertainty Avoidance and all that...

An influential figure in the study of cultural influences on human behaviour is Professor Geert Hofstede, a Dutch social psychologist. His *magnum opus* on cultural differences [57] is based on 117,000 questionnaires he and his staff analysed when he was working in the human resources department of IBM. The study, conducted among all levels of company employees in the late-1960s and early-70s, covered 40 countries both in Europe and outside. It was subsequently extended and updated by further studies undertaken in the late-70s and early-80s.

Hofstede categorised national cultures in terms of four 'dimensions': (1) *Individualism* versus *Collectivism*, (2) *Large Power Distance* versus *Small Power Distance*, (3) *Strong Uncertainty Avoidance* versus *Weak Uncertainty Avoidance* and (4) *Masculinity* versus *Femininity*. The main conclusions of his study are featured in the box opposite.

Since defining these dimensions - which are applicable in varying degrees to all European cultures, Professor Hofstede has identified another pair that particularly set off Europeans against the cultures of other continents: *short-term orientation* versus *long-term orientation*. Witness the difference in the attitudes to time between the Europeans (or Americans) on the one hand and the Japanese (or Arabs) on the other.

For me the most revealing of Hofstede's original four dimensions are (2) power distance and particularly (3) uncertainty avoidance. The latter is the least easily comprehensible on first acquaintance but, over time, it becomes highly illuminating - throwing light

Hofstede's Dimensions

(1) *Individualism* can be correlated to a large extent with national wealth. Understandably the northern European countries lie at the 'individualistic' end of the scale with, perhaps surprisingly, Austria and, not so surprisingly at the time, Spain trailing behind and Portugal even further to the back of the pack.

(2) *Power Distance*, which means the extent to which a society accepts the fact that power in organisations is unevenly distributed, is small in the northern European countries of Scandinavia, the UK and Germany (also again rather surprisingly Austria) and relatively large in France, Belgium, Italy, Spain, Portugal and Greece. Fortunately the extreme attitude quoted in the section on the Belgians (Chapter 4), namely "the boss is on holiday and no decisions are taken in his absence", is hardly true any longer of Belgian, German, French or other Continental industries, although there are still some examples around.

(3) *Uncertainty Avoidance*, the extent to which a society feels threatened by unsure and ambiguous situations and consequently searches for statutory structures, is weakest in Denmark, Sweden, the UK and Ireland, and particularly strong in Germany, Austria, Switzerland and Finland, as well as in the Large Power Distance countries of the Mediterranean. As Hofstede points out, it is no coincidence that the Germans have a law in their constitution to cope with the eventuality that none of the other laws work.

(4) *Masculinity* versus *Femininity*, which represents opposing poles in social attitudes (showing off, 'performing', achieving, 'big is beautiful' versus putting personal relationships, respect for quality of life etc, before money) rates the German-speaking countries as relatively 'masculine' and the Netherlands and Scandinavia as 'feminine'. The record in the case of the Mediterranean countries is mixed: Italy and Greece turn out to be very 'masculine' while Spain, contrary to the macho folklore, proves to be 'feminine'.

into corners of national cultures that would otherwise go unnoticed.

Uncertainty avoidance has little to do with risk avoidance, although the two are obviously related. It is perhaps best illustrated by the fact that, as Hofstede points out, the Germans have a law in their constitution to cope with the eventuality that none of the other laws work (the *Notstandsgesetz*), while the British do not even have a written constitution.

In fact, strong uncertainty avoidance is clearly a mindset, or form of mental programming, which is reinforced by the existence of a structured statutory environment.

The reverse of the medal, of course, is that weak uncertainty avoidance cultures are allergic to such constraints. André Laurent, a French researcher and consultant, notes that the Swedes and Dutch are far less comfortable with precisely defined roles than are the Germans, French, Belgians and Swiss. That goes for the British too!

The ultimate explanation of these striking differences is historical and worth putting into a nutshell: the origins of strong uncertainty avoidance - and by implication high power distance - lie in the intensive codification of the laws of the Roman Empire, extended to Germany beyond the *limes* through the efforts of Charlemagne and his successors in the centuries that followed. Essentially this explains why the Nordic peoples and the people of the British Isles (some of whom were late arrivals in the Roman Empire, but kept well clear of Charlemagne and Napoleon), register such weak uncertainty avoidance compared with the rest.

Three other pieces of research seem to go some way towards confirming Hofstede's findings. The first is the work of Edward Hall described in the next chapter. The second is a study by Richard Lynn[58] into anxiety levels which places European cultures in three categories:

High Anxiety: Austria, Germany, Belgium, France, Italy

Medium Anxiety: Denmark, Finland, Norway, Switzerland

Low Anxiety: The Netherlands, Britain, Ireland, Sweden.

The third, a very recent piece of research by Dr David Weeks of Edinburgh Royal Hospital, examines European eccentricity[59]. "I estimate there is one eccentric for every 10,000 people in Britain", says

Dr Weeks, summing up his findings. "The figure for Europe as a whole is only half that, and Germany has the fewest eccentrics of all." Of course, his definition of what does or does not constitute an eccentric is a cultural value judgment in its own right.

By contrast another piece of research, an analysis undertaken by the Boeing Corporation, suggests surprisingly that countries with *Low Individualism* and *Strong Power Distance* indices record air traffic accident rates 2.6 times greater than countries at the other ends of these scales. But, more surprisingly, *Uncertainty Avoidance* offers no correlation with accident rates.

Security versus risk

The Germans were the big savers of Europe, but this image has been dulled recently by the spending spree of the Ossies and increased taxes for the Wessies.

When saved, much of this money goes into the local Raiffeisen-kasse bank. The German saver's natural instinct is to keep his money in a safe and unspeculative environment close to home. Even closer to home are some of Europe's rural communities, particularly the French, who still retain the peasant habit of keeping their savings stitched into the mattress or, at least, hidden in a box in the chimney.

If he or she goes further afield, then the German's preference, like that of the Belgians and the Luxembourgers, is for government bonds or fixed interest securities rather than shares. Bonds are also a favourite with the Italians, who manage to save nearly a quarter of their incomes, but high interest rates on cash deposits often divert these funds to the banks. It is the French and the British who go for equity share investments with, in the case of the British, a substantial proportion of their savings finding their way there through pension and life insurance funds. Swedes are starting to follow suit.

According to OECD figures, the Europeans now most addicted to saving, even if they don't have that much to save, are the Greeks. Britain and the Netherlands come at the bottom of the league. Thrift has in any case ceased to be a marked characteristic of Europe's economies.

Insurance figures, as a percentage of income, rise more or less in keeping with Europe's lines of latitude from Greece to Germany.

Britain, a poor saver, does well on the insurance scale, but this is more a reflection of poor state and company pension schemes than on any foresightedness.

Readiness to take risks is another aspect of security. In the inflamed imagination of northerners, the peoples of the Mediterranean live exciting, even dangerous, lives - images of *mafiosi*, passionate love affairs, etc. But the reality is often the opposite.

Perhaps because they have the automatic luxury of lives more or less cocooned in state security systems, Nordics, Britons, Germans and others have acquired a moderate sense of risk. By contrast, it is the Mediterranean folk, from Spain to Greece, who are seduced - even at an early age - by the sirens of security.

The fact that historically these were essentially peasant societies, hiding their modest savings in the mattress, doesn't really explain the present-day attitudes of the South. All of Europe started life as a pastoral, then agrarian (hence essentially peasant) society, and even Sweden was such until the 19th century.

France has one of the strongest peasant traditions in Europe: a good nine-tenths of the country's population in the early Middle Ages were peasants. By virtue of the remoteness of so many areas of this large and mountainous country, mediaeval people had to be self-supporting - something that, in the opinion of the historian Geneviève d'Haucourt[60], bred a spirit of parsimony and of saving for its own sake that is still evident in rural areas there today.

The roots of this distaste for risk in the European South are more recent. As the experience of the older generations has shown, life is a constant battle against unpredictable and mainly uneven odds: World Wars, civil wars, slumps, inflation and the like. So, in an environment of governmental featherbedding, administrative and professional cheating, handouts and bribes (including, in Italy, pensions for phoney invalids), if one can gain title to a lifelong income and pension, why think twice?

This only goes to show how time - and, paradoxically, improved living standards when all the basic needs are met - changes people, even the Spanish. A 1991 study by the Santa Maria Foundation found that only 30 per cent of Spaniards seek jobs with responsibilities. For them work is mainly a source of income, not satisfaction, and they prefer security to responsibility and any chance to prove themselves. Sociologist Francisco Andrés Orizo comments that

Spaniards "seem to have fewer experiences, fewer interests than other Europeans. They are... more stuck to routine."

I would have liked to think that the younger Spanish generations, with the benefit of a secondary education, would be more inclined to look for opportunities than their elders. The latter, after all, were coming out of a period of history that taught them to keep their mouths shut and enjoy the good life, such as it was. As a nation, the Spaniards certainly have 'de-politicised', which is a good thing. But, as a Spanish sociologist, Amando de Miguel, comments: "If you look at our youth, we're becoming a nation of narcissists, concerned mainly with the cult of the body, of comfort, of consumption, of money. They read less and spend more." One might think this would make them more ambitious, more ready to take risks, but it seems not.

Hedging one's bets is also evident in other aspects of the way Europeans run their lives, private and professional. British entrepreneurs look aghast at the readiness with which their Continental counterparts consult an astrologer before making a major business decision. Both graphology and, increasingly, astrology are accepted as legitimate candidate screening techniques in both the German and French cultures.

As Europeans' need for security may also be reflected in (dare I suggest it?) their religiousness, let me just add that, as a group, the Latins are more fervent churchgoers than the Germanics, even if their zeal is diminishing rapidly. The Dutch, with their respect for the pillars of society (zuilen), still do a fairly good job, both Calvinists and Catholics. But the top scorers at churchgoing are the Irish, year-round, and the Greeks at Easter.

Incidentally, if you remember the great debate in 1633 between Galileo and the Catholic Church about whether the earth went round the sun or vice versa, you might be forgiven for assuming that the Catholic countries of Europe would still be at deviance with Galileo. On the contrary. According to a Eurobarometer survey, whereas only 5 per cent of Italians still believe that the sun goes round the earth (and 6 per cent of Greeks and 7 per cent of Spaniards), no less than 18 per cent of the Dutch (Calvinists and Catholics) now adhere to this 20th-century version of the heresy and 16 per cent of the British.

Different nationalities show varying degrees of accommodation to original ideas. The most striking contrast is between the

Germans on the one hand and the French and, to a lesser extent, the British on the other. John Ardagh makes the comment that "... the French enjoy novelty and exhibitionism, and they like to be startled by ideas they do not necessarily share: the German public, much less secure, more anxious and conformist, does not."

The next-to-last haven

Nothing can be more significant than the choice of retirement, voluntary or imposed.

If it's voluntary, then northern Europeans tend to end up in dream residences, the English in cosy little cottages with names like 'Magpies' or 'Whispers', the terminal 's' being one of the more modish manifestations of English fashion in the last 30 years (calling your retirement home something like 'Mon Abri', 'Sai Wen' or 'Dunroamin' has gone out of fashion).

Such solutions are facilitated by the fact that the English insist on owning their homes in any case: "an Englishman's home is his castle". In other countries - Ireland, Greece and Spain in particular - home ownership rates reflect the predominance of agrarian or peasant communities. By contrast, more than half the Germans and Dutch live in rented property, private or public, and the Swiss live in apartments.

If, as is increasingly the case, retirement is imposed prematurely, then the reality is often different. The English - particularly those relieved of jobs in the marketing, advertising and PR fields - take over the management of pubs, most often in the West Country: this is the best they can do to emulate the sentimental tradition of the country squire.

In similar circumstances the French (those not born and brought up in Paris), being a far less sentimental race, go genuinely native and return to their roots, probably somewhere in wildest Brittany or the Massif Central. This tendency is also present in the Italians and, to a lesser extent, the Spanish.

The Germans, being well set up whether they retire or are fired, have no need to rationalise their discomfort by pretending to be country-lovers, even though they are. A lot of them seem to end up in spas.

The European way of death

Most Europeans die naturally, the principle of death by violence having suffered a serious if not final setback after World War II (though it appears to live on in Luxembourg, which has the highest homicide rate in the European Union).

Some Europeans die by their own hand, though the stories about sensationally high suicide rates in crazy little countries often turn out to be rubbish (unlike the homicide rates). Those figures that are available suggest that countries in Central Europe - notably Hungary (with the highest recorded rate of nearly 40 suicides per 100,000), the Czech Republic and Austria - have a particular proclivity for this kind of thing. In Western Europe, the Finns come top of the league with just under 30 per 100,000, followed by the Swiss and Belgians with 23.

Portugal (with the lowest suicide rate at 8 per 100,000, subject to a glitch referred to in Chapter 4), Spain and Greece come at the bottom of the list. Whether it is religion or the sunny climate that keeps them out of trouble is uncertain. Shortage of daylight certainly rates as a factor in seasonal affective disorder (SAD) in the Nordic countries, with over 5 per cent of Swedes slipping into fully fledged winter depressions from November to February.

When it comes to the ceremonial accorded the loved one, Europeans behave individualistically and sometimes atavistically. There are at least a dozen different European 'ways of death', ranging from the Irish wake, which is if anything a celebratory event, to the morbid pomp and circumstance of a Flemish funeral (it is no coincidence that Flanders was occupied by the Spanish at one of the peaks of the latters' death-wish culture).

In between comes the English way of death, which is typically low-key. In the words of the American writer Mary Blume: "If English funerals came to lack the voluptuous grief, and statuary, of Catholic countries, they did contribute to the nation's pastoral beauty with their churchyards and simple graven headstones."

These days growing irreligiousness encourages Europeans to take death less seriously than they used to - they frequently pop off totally unprepared. One exception is the Irish, a religious people of whom 85 per cent claim to be regular churchgoers (with the Italians next in line at only 45 per cent). Perhaps because 'the faith' is so closely linked with their own peculiarly Celtic form of mysticism, the Irish manage to handle the whole business with a fair degree of levity.

Anyone who has participated at an Irish wake will remember the experience fondly: Paddy whiskey for the men, Cork gin-and-orange for the ladies and a great deal of lyrical reminiscing which, being conducted in the past tense, can be expected to include passing reference to the defunct.

However some pockets of genuine morbidity still remain, Spain being the most single-minded. Sure enough, they have a long established tradition to go on: Don Juan and the Man of Stone, the Inquisition, Philip II, the Foreign Legion *("Viva la muerte!")*, etc. Something survives, if only the habit of pensioners in Alava province of accepting free bus trips to funerals paid for by the relatives of the departed.

Their peninsular cohabitants, the Portuguese, while slightly less inclined to be morbid (*saudade* encourages one to hang on to life rather than hanker after death), still put on a good show today. Portuguese peasant custom dictates, as Marion Kaplan[45] points out, "two years' mourning for a father, at least a year for any other relative. A widow traditionally wears black for the rest of her life and, in rural communities at least, is considered sexually provocative if she does not." To justify the two years' mourning, the coffin of the dearly departed is opened at the graveside so that the bereaved can check that the right person is in it.

A traditional Italian funeral, in the words of Luigi Barzini[15], comprises "prancing black horses, their harness decorated with black plumes and silver ornaments, a glass-enclosed hearse surmounted by a flight of golden wooden angels, more black feathers and sundry symbols of eternal life, followed by weeping relatives and friends". The Italians always have a sense of occasion.

In most such cases, of course, the principal players are not the dearly departed but the nearest and dearest left behind, the "relatives and friends". The most astute performers are the southern Italians and the Greeks. Some newly widowed Greek ladies, particularly those descended from the Pontic immigrant communities, still observe the rite of 40 days' mourning, a very noisy and strenuous affair for all concerned. Clearly the Greeks enter into the spirit of things: in one case, the blood relatives of the dearly departed, who all happened to be Italian, caused great indignation because they managed to control their emotions with dignity. The Greek ladies present concluded that the Italians were a cold-blooded lot!

In one Greek case known to me, the poor widow put so much effort into the ritual that she had to be hospitalised halfway through from sheer exhaustion. This, in extreme cases, could provide a striking example of the domino effect.

Life after death for some Europeans does not necessarily end with the funeral or even interment. In the frozen north, for the obviously practical reason that the ground is like concrete for six months of the year, the Swedes and others sometimes consign their defunct temporarily to deep-freeze bunkers.

The alternative, cremation, is also widely practised up north. Britain records a cremation rate of 70 per cent (up from three persons in 1885), compared with only 10 per cent for France. The Germans are catching up fast, egged on by less government largesse on death allowances, although they still prefer to be interred in coffins of teak and other exotic timbers. Burial at sea goes down well with the wealthy in Bremen and Hamburg. But cryogenics has not yet become a fad in the Old World, not even in the permafrost-bound north.

Tough terrain also poses problems for the Greeks, limiting the land surface available for gravedigging. Their solution is to bury their dead for three years, then dig up the remains and put the choice pieces in a little box. That way there's space for the next generation. Similar considerations apply, with less urgency, elsewhere: in Belgium you get five years' grace, in Germany and Switzerland a maximum of 25.

Even Britain is thinking that some degree of regulation will be necessary, since many cemeteries in this high-land-cost country are expected to reach saturation point by the turn of the century. Respect for tradition will be maintained, however, since incumbents will still be left undisturbed for 75 years, when they will be reburied deeper down and new tenants installed on top.

Space also poses a problem for the people of Hallstatt in Austria (which, significantly, gave its name to the *Hallstatt* culture when an important Celtic cemetery was found there). After a maximum of ten years in the steep and rocky town cemetery and at the discretion of relatives, skulls are painted with floral garlands and with the late owners' names, and then displayed on racks in the communal charnel-house. Neapolitans used to consign the bones of their dead to the Fontanella tufa caverns on the edge of the Old City. In Norway, a particularly democratic country, all gravestones have to be exactly the same height.

When it comes to land for construction as opposed to burial, the Greeks - in the same spirit as the Maltese, the Spanish, the Portuguese and the 16th century Dutch - really excel themselves: they build exceptionally large churches with beautiful blue roofs, and often bankrupt themselves in the process. What price the afterlife?

Values and cultures

While general values such as a regard for human rights and respect for the environment are increasingly common to all European nations, specific values lie at the root of many of our cultural differentials.

One of the points on which we Europeans tend to differ is the freedom - nay, status - we accord the media. An investigation into press law and practice, published in March 1993 by the 'ARTICLE 19' International Centre Against Censorship[61], shows wide variations in the way the supposedly mature and developed nations of Europe approach this sensitive issue.

The most enlightened country, without doubt, is Sweden which adopted its first Freedom of the Press Act as early as - wait for it - 1766! The Netherlands also emerges with a relatively clean bill of health. Importantly, Austria, France and Germany offer legal protection on the key issue of the confidentiality of sources. Even Spain, precisely because it emerged only recently from the Franco era of dictatorship, offers strong protection for the media. The UK on the other hand, because it has no written constitution, provides no fundamental guarantees for freedom of speech.

Attitudes to film censorship also vary widely. The most permissive countries are, surprisingly, Italy, Portugal and Spain (which does, however, operate an age classification system) and, unsurprisingly, the Netherlands. Britain lies at the other extreme, thanks to the British Board of Film Classification, while Ireland, Germany and France (in descending order, so to speak) lie in between. Some funny things happen as a result. The French film 'Betty Blue' was presented as suitable for consumption by 12 year-olds on French TV, but rated 'Adults Only' in the UK. 'The Lover', based on the Marguerite Duras novel, was rated 'Adults Only' in the UK and Ireland, found fit for seven year-olds in Denmark and suitable for all in the Netherlands.

Yet often the most evident impact of value judgments is in the trivia of life rather than the grand designs. A Dutchman of my acquaintance who spent a couple of years working as a tourist guide found that the English complained about his accent and the French complained about the food (the Americans simply compared everything with home).

Geert Hofstede notes a series of peculiarities: "British people will form a neat queue whenever they have to wait; not so the French. Dutch people will as a rule greet strangers when they enter a small closed space like a railway compartment, doctor's waiting room, or lift; not so the Belgians. Austrians will wait at a red pedestrian traffic light even when there is no traffic; not so the Dutch. The Swiss tend to become very angry when somebody - say, a foreigner - makes a mistake in traffic; not so the Swedes."

Yes, but... if the Dutch bother to greet strangers in a railway compartment, they are equally capable of passing the next two hours without as much as exchanging a word with them. The Belgians are at their politest in elevators. And, if the Austrians respect pedestrian lights, it may have something to do with the fact that the penalty for infringement is severe.

But leaving aside the folkloric trappings of our cultures, there are some fundamental and very clearly defined lifestyles which distinguish many countries from their neighbours.

The most easily recognisable, folklore or not, are the ones that reflect a long established agrarian or peasant tradition. These I might class as the 'cocoon cultures', cosily bound up in a way of life that has survived the centuries. Examples are Flemish Belgium and German Switzerland, which happen to share a Germanic value system.

At the other end of the scale are liberal and open cultures which impress by the graciousness of their lifestyles. In this class I include Italy, particularly of course Tuscany and adjacent provinces, Sweden, Poland (with reservations) and, I dare say, England. Not much in common here!

In between come other cultures, some of them varied but distinctive, such as France and Spain, others rather dull and stereotyped with Germany as the prime example.

Some cultures, despite the inexorable march of material progress and its levelling-down effects, still have an essence that assails the senses. It is compounded of many things - sights, sounds, smells - and is difficult to analyse. For me, 'essential' cultures are definitely to be found (but not necessarily everywhere) in France, Spain, Italy, Greece, Austria, Sweden and Poland. But that's simply the way things get through to me as a northerner and an Anglo-Saxon.

The absence of such an essence in no way implies that a culture is characterless. Germany has a very clear culture - what a British consultant, Paul Thorne, calls "a culture of containment and precision". Here philosophical traditions are also evident. The most obvious contrast is what *The Economist* calls "the comic struggle between wholesome Anglo-Saxon common sense and the slurred, obfuscatory, garlic-and-*sauerkraut*-flavoured verbiage of 'continental' thought."

National cultures reveal themselves in matters of taste - not just gastronomically but in design taste too. Nothing could be more distinctive than the 'artless aestheticism', to quote a phrase, of modern Italian furniture or the finesse of Danish interior design.

Cultural conflicts even surfaced in the styling and layout of the high-speed trains planned for the Eurotunnel link. *The International Herald Tribune* reports how "the British favored a stylized replica of the classic Orient Express; the Belgians wanted the interior divided into traditional six-person compartments; the French wanted open airline-style seating. After months of discord, a gentleman's agreement was reached. The British would design the exterior, the Belgians would do the toilets and the baggage compartments and the French would handle the rest". As usual, the British and the Belgians compromised and, of course, the French won.

Subtle variations in national value systems are likely to have a surreptitiously divisive effect for a long time to come. The national responses to a public opinion poll on human rights published by the European Commission in November 1989 are illustrative. With the exception of Britain and France, all countries put the *right of association* and *asylum* bottom of the list. The British gave that distinction to the *right to information* of all things (the French did the same with *personal safety*). Of course, values take root in many ways: maybe the fact that Britain doesn't have a written constitution explains disinterest in what others consider a fundamental right.

One wonders, in passing, whether the absence of a written constitution might not have a permeating effect on British attitudes generally. Speaking of the UK delegation's performance at the Maastricht Summit, Flora Lewis made the comment, in an article in the *International Herald Tribune*, that "... this is a typically Anglo-Saxon approach, by experiment, not at all in the continental manner of perfecting a grand design and then trying to apply it." It also reflects the tradition of English common law.

The consequences of this devotion to pragmatism are sadly evident in the realities of life in Britain today. The English are still suspicious of the value of a vocational education - one of the things that has made Germany great - and have not yet got the message, despite the example of the French, that investment in one's infrastructure is a precondition of economic success.

A Eurobarometer study conducted for the European Commission in 1990 (ref 34.2) also showed some striking variances in value systems. A pan-Union sample - nearly 4,000 young people aged 15-24 - broadly agreed that the causes they most closely identified with were *world peace*, *protection of the environment* and *human rights*. But the Greeks also cited *freedom of the individual* (52%), the French (48%) and not surprisingly the Portuguese (64%) gave priority to the *fight against poverty* and, interestingly, Italian young people (52%) put emphasis on the *fight against racism*. It was also encouraging to see *defence of one's country or one's religion* continuing to lose ground.

The study also found often poor and widely varying levels of awareness of the European Union itself. Asked to identify the Member States, the Luxembourgers and the Germans did best, with 10% and 9% giving the right answers. The Greeks, the Portuguese, the Italians and, not surprisingly, the British came last, with 2% each.

The younger Western generations, in the opinion of French sociologist Bernard Cathelat who masterminded the *Euro-Styles* study described in Chapter 7, now seem most concerned with personal issues. He sees evidence of newly emerging standards, both 'technical' (for example, consumerism and quality-consciousness) and moral (respect for professional hierarchies, social conventions, cults, religions and of course the environment). He also detects a growing elitism among the young: maybe the yuppies are here to stay?

Variances in value systems surface clearly in international affairs and in business. At the level of politics, it is remarkable how different government responses to the approach of the Gulf conflict laid bare national temperaments. The British joined in pragmatically and enthusiastically, the French were too clever by half (egged on by their perpetual search for *la gloire* and the desire to be different) and tripped up in the process, the Belgians tried to muddle through and upset themselves, and the Germans displayed their usual hermeticity and upset just about everyone else.

As *The Economist* said, commenting on this dismal set of events: "Foreign policy is the outward expression of a country's internal instincts, habits and history."

But, generally, pan-European value systems provide a reasonably level playing ground where everyone knows the rules, even if they do not abide by them. They also help bring out the best in everyone: the method of the Germans, the wit of the French, the empiricism of the British, the opportunism of the Italians, and so on.

Not long ago I received a cameo of value judgments from an eminent committee of international university professors. Their manner of response highlighted the differences in their cultures. They were asked to provide arguments in defence of a scientific publication threatened with termination by its American management.

The Spaniard's response was statesmanlike, the Frenchman was challenging and cheeky, the German's reply was seriously argued and substantive, the English professor was pompous, and the Dutchman didn't think it necessary to reply. Each of them, even the Dutchman, said something about his value system and the culture he comes from...

Talking about the differences between the European cultures often produces the response, "OK, do the Europeans have anything in common?". Here are some of the things which, I believe, are shared by, and in some cases are exclusive to, the European cultures (feudalism missed much of the northern Nordic countries, maybe to their advantage!).

The megalith-builders. The Celts, Greeks, Romans and Vikings.

Christianity, individualism, missionaries, monastic orders, saints, naming practices, charters.

An open Europe with a common history up to +1200 AD (see Chapter 3).

Feudalism, burgess rights, contractual relationships.

The Age of Enlightenment. Scientific inquiry.
Il Rinascimento.

Music, architecture (especially Gothic), art, philosophy, etc.

The *Kaffeehauskultur* (street cafés): 19th century Continental.

The oaktree: the 'Green Man', the Sarakatsani people of northern Greece, 'touching wood'.

The sheepdog: 13th century Iceland, 15th century British Isles.

The garden gnome: 6th century Cappadocia, then Central Europe (see box, page 368).

Santa Claus/Sankt Nikolaus/Sint Niklaas/Saint Nicolas/etc, and Knecht Ruprecht/Zwarte Peter/La Befana/Barteln/*katchikali*, etc.

Conscience, freedom of speech, tolerance and other things we are occasionally in danger of losing.

The European Anatomy

"English patients, according to persons who have lived abroad, tend to know little about their bodies. 'French people know their blood pressure,' said Dr. Inch. 'Not one English person in fifty knows their blood pressure'"   Lynn Payer, *Medicine and Culture*

"Despite the scientific advances made in this century, attitudes to health and its achievement are still heavily influenced by myth and superstition. And the cultural barriers are likely to persist way beyond the end of this century"   Dr Michael O'Donnell

"Everybody usually sits silent for the first hour or so. Then the light begins to work. We get more and more cheerful, and there's usually almost a party atmosphere by the time we're finished"   Birgitta Larsson, Swedish SAD sufferer

"There is still an Emma Bovary in all women, even if they dress in miniskirts and look like executives"   Bernard-Henri Lévy

"Under communism making love was better"   Zek & Misha Halu

"On the continent they have sex. The English have hot-water bottles"   George Mikes

National cultures help shape individual and community attitudes toward the human anatomy.

A Swiss anthropologist, Felix Moos, asserts that the Germans' historical inclination towards romanticism (I would prefer the word 'mysticism', but he's right) makes them view their bodies in a spiritual rather than a functional way.

British medical expert Dr Michael O'Donnell observes that German doctors diagnose circulatory and other heart-related problems "on grounds that would not mean heart disease elsewhere". Germans consume six times more heart drugs than the Dutch and the British, despite the fact that the death rate from heart disease is the same for all three countries.

The French also claim a lower incidence of heart disease, despite some very Gallic dietary habits. Curiously it is lowest in Gascony, of all places, where the natives eat vast quantities of *foie gras*, goose and duck fat. However French statistics have recently been shaken by the realisation that many doctors have been recording fatalities like cardiac arrest in the hold-all category of *mort subite* ('sudden death!), a category unknown to much of the rest of the European medical profession. *Vive la France!*

Belgians, particularly those of the older generations, go bonkers about blood pressure. Most British people complain about constipation where the French invoke a *crise de foie* (most British people probably think a *crise de foie* is a crisis of conscience in any case). It is an almost folkloric fact that the British talk about their intestines while the French talk about their livers (the British aren't very sure where their livers are).

Historically, the issue of constipation has dominated the British health psyche: the country's foreign policy at the end of the 18th century was dictated by the need to keep Far Eastern trade routes open to ensure the safe and regular arrival of Chinese rhubarb. Just to be safe, self-respecting Britons purged themselves with sea water on the principle that, to quote a medical guide of the time, "a pint is commonly sufficient in grown persons to give them three or four sharp stools." Sounds painful.

An American, Lynn Payer in her book *Medicine and Culture*[62], reports on an extensive survey of European medical idiosyncrasies. She records the abnormally high incidence of manic depressives diagnosed by British doctors, almost five times higher than the same diagnoses in France. Also where French doctors go for *spasmophilia* (stress-induced tetany), German ones talk about *dystonia* (muscle tone). And the rate of appendix removals in Germany is three times that of any other country in Europe.

Drug prescriptions can also tell you something about a country, although the exact cause - incidence of illnesses, hypochondria or structure of the national health system - is difficult to determine. Levels of medication are far higher in Germany and France than in the UK, though patterns of pathology are similar ("the French are all hypochondriacs", says a pharmaceutical industry pundit). The Italians and Portuguese do pretty well too: the latter seem to be fascinated by illness and, for a generally poorly educated people, are extremely literate on matters medical.

Figures suggest that, with deviations, medication levels increase the further south you go, Greece being a spectacular exception (classical stoicism?). Germany and, seasonally, Italy - also France and Spain - attach a lot of importance to preventative medicine: vitamins, tonics, etc. Germany is also keen on homeopathic medicines, which are virtually unknown in Spain and Greece.

These and many other health attitudes go back to the days of pre-scientific medicine and to the historic relationships and expectations developed between a society and its GPs. But the fundamental cultural differences go even deeper: as in other fields of human endeavour, the French are cartesian in their approach to health matters, the English empirical, the Germans both methodical and mystic.

Hardly surprisingly, national medical infrastructures (themselves a reflection of cultural influences), differ by country and reinforce attitudes to health, and not just in terms of the amount of drugs prescribed or the treatment provided. A 1987 study showed that Spain had the highest ratio of doctors to total population in Western Europe and, not surprisingly for anyone who's ever had toothache in Spain, the second-to-lowest ratio of dentists, neighbouring Portugal being the lowest.

Despite the high ratio of Spanish doctors, it has to be said that the Latin countries have a poorer record on public health than the Germanics and others. Investment in public hygiene programmes, measures to prevent general epidemics, etc, generally come much later in the south than in the north.

Teeth are also a good way of distinguishing one group of Europeans from another. If the subject's mouth is full of gold, there's a good chance he or she is from somewhere between Austria and Russia (unless the development took place in WWII, in which case the mouth may be full of stainless steel). If the person has lost a lot of his or her teeth, then there's a fair chance you're looking at a non-pensioned Belgian (Belgian pensioners used to get their teeth removed at the state's expense on condition that they had them all pulled out, bad and good, at the same time).

Deborah Thomas, an American dental hygienist working in Switzerland comments that we Europeans have rampant gum disease and smoke too much. Her front-line observations have convinced her that the Germans and Swiss specialise in periodontal problems, the French rinse their mouths with wine, the British have good teeth but lots of plaque, all Eastern Europeans use toothbrushes for something else, South Slavs and Turks have lots of gold teeth right up front, and the Italians just look after their front teeth for appearance' sake.

If no teeth are evident at all, you're probably looking at a Belgian pensioner or an inhabitant of Galicia in northwest Spain where, until not all that long ago, it was the village barber who pulled them out. The only other thing I can tell you about Spanish dentists, what there is of them, is that they love crossword puzzles.

Hygiene, private and public

Which brings us on to hygiene. Personal hygiene being a particularly intimate matter by definition, the cultural divisions are likely to last quite a while yet.

What we all had in common in the later Middle Ages was a mistrust of water and washing which, at the time, was thought by both the English and French (and, for all one knows, the Germans) to be a potential percutaneous conductor of viruses. The English simply stopped washing and left it at that. The French stopped washing... and developed the perfume industry.

Even so, the French still appreciated body odour enough to prompt Napoleon, perhaps apocryphally, to send a message ahead to Josephine on his way back from Egypt: *"ne te laves pas, j'arrive!"* ["don't wash, I'm coming!"].

Coming closer to the present day, a study undertaken in 1984 showed that the Danes recorded the highest per capita consumption of soap, detergents and cleaning products at 29.5 kg per annum, followed by the Germans (26.5 kg), the Belgians/Luxembourgers (26.1kg) and the Spanish (24.6 kg). Surprisingly, the Norwegians came low down the list (19.1 kg), with the Austrians (18.2 kg), the Portuguese (17.8 kg), the Greeks (16.6 kg) and the Finnish (12.6 kg!) bringing up the rear.

The Finns are more respectful of the Nordic tradition when consuming tissues and household paper, ringing up the respectable figure of 12.11 kilograms per person, ahead of Germany (11.50) and Switzerland (11.44). They are, however, outstripped by the Norwegians (13.12) and Danes (13.62), with the Swedes well ahead of the pack at 19.06 kg per person per annum.

But such things tell us very little about absolute standards of cleanliness. When it comes to personal hygiene, nobody is more scrupulous than the Portuguese, even if they use far less soap than most other Europeans. Even the French, their appreciation of body odour notwithstanding, have caught up with the rest. Whereas, as late as 1951, the Larousse medical guide was still saying that "a bath or shower may be taken weekly", by 1995 the average French person was taken over five baths or showers a week.

Unlike many Continentals, the British still prefer the bath (61%) to the shower (39%) regarding the latter, like the bidet, as slightly suspect. "The British are quite satisfied with their lot", concludes a psychologist quoted in the Graham Bathroom Report, a study undertaken in 1991 by a supplier of bathroom fittings in the UK. "The British preference for bathing shows that as a nation we do not mind wallowing in our own strengths and weaknesses, while those who shower are continually trying to improve themselves through further exertions." One in the eye for the Continentals.

National attitudes towards the practice of shaving under the armpits have also been a source of cultural conflict, leading to such silly jokes as: "Q: how do you tell a French airplane? A: it's got hair under its wings". This issue, which does less than justice to upper-class Parisiennes, causes endless titillation among the English.

There are, of course, some subtler and more lasting nuances in personal hygiene: the precise configuration of toilets and tap mechanisms, the use of bidets, the quality and format of toilet paper (French paper tends to be shiny and come in individual sheets, while the perforations in toilet rolls come more frequently in Greece than elsewhere). But, as the French say, *"vive la différence!"*.

Bidets are a great European institution and the inspiration for a subculture of jokes, all of them in dubious taste. Nobody disputes that they were invented by the French. What not so many people know is that they are a statutory feature of all restaurant washrooms in Portugal, being about the only surviving evidence of the Salazar regime.

On another subject Jean-Claude Kaufmann, a Frenchman who has made a study of his compatriots' laundry habits, says: "Taken separately, each undergarment washed, every lone sock seems minor, but all society is there, forming the individual who thinks he or she is controlling them. Laundry conceals within its folds the perfect investigatory tool: it is everywhere, all the time." So, obviously, a comparative multinational study into personal hygiene habits is called for to explain the real differences between us Europeans...

Research data on bathroom habits is also thin. The only extensive study I know of is the Graham Bathroom Report from the UK. This showed that 68% of the British daydream in the bath, over 50% (not mutually exclusive with the 68%) read in the bath, 30% sing, 14% chat on the phone (a sign of the times), 10% play with *their own* toys, and 4% have sex. One respondent uses his time to organise "duck races".

Times were when British northerners used the bathtub, when they had one, for storing coal. It will be interesting to see what answers we get when the same questions are put to the French. Spanish gypsies, incidentally, used to be renowned for flogging off the bathroom fittings. Incidentally, according to a recent study, there are more TV sets than bathtubs in the European Union.

The subject of hygiene also demands, these days, a reference to European drinking and smoking habits. Education and prosperity is inhibiting both. The French provincial working man no longer starts his day with a *petit coup de rouge*. Cynics will say he drinks beer instead, and there's some truth in that. Yet the consumption of alcoholic beverages is on the downward slope Europewide: less wine in the southern countries, less beer in the north, less spirits in traditionally hard-drinking countries like Germany and the Netherlands.

Thanks to a virulent anti-tobacco lobby in Europe, the same goes for smoking.

Environmentally the most conscientious of the Europeans are without question the Dutch, the Nordics and the Germans (the five new *Länder* excepted, thanks to the marxist concept which conveniently dismissed any value inherent in natural resources). The Dutch have good reason to be exercised about such things, having the sea at or over their doorsteps on one side and the Rhine delivering toxic waste and vast loads of salt from the Swiss, the French and, to a lesser extent, the Germans on the other. The Belgians also worry the Dutch despite, or perhaps because of, the fact that politically they turned distinctly Green (and simultaneously racist) in November 1991.

Overall, the Belgians and the British share the pollution laurels in northern Europe, the latter having a particular fondness for dumping unwanted matter in holes in the ground. These countries also vie for first place in discharging untreated sewage into the sea. The less said about the Mediterranean countries the better, since *mare nostrum* has been converted in recent times into little more than a cesspit.

Sex and the Swedish Woman

European reproduction may have its ups and downs, but sex goes on... and on. It suits the stereotype relished by many European male machos that our source should be Malena Ivarsson, a Swedish female sexologist.

Malena enlightens on the sexual strengths and weaknesses of at least some of us Europeans. To start with my own race, it seems we are feeble on foreplay and short on experimentation. "The Englishman", she says without beating about the bush, "is a catastrophe as a lover". This seems to be borne out by a survey conducted by the British *Good Housekeeping* magazine in early-1994, in which a majority of the 1,010 respondents said the prospect of a delicious meal in a restaurant was "more tempting than making love". The survey added insult to injury to the British male by identifying a preference for Italian cuisine, followed by Chinese and French. Ah, but if the lovers were Italian, Chinese or French...?

But let's move on hastily to the Germans. Malena describes them, not surprisingly, as 'well organised' and 'perfectionist', but lacking in passion and creativity.

Equally surprising for most of us other Europeans, Malena Ivarsson gives Swedish men as poor a rating as the English and the Germans. And curiously, while the Swedish male's attitude to sex is simple and straightforward, his foreplay tends to be more intellectual than physical. The 'outing' of sex has apparently subdued the male libido, making younger Swedes less sure of themselves and encouraging them to unburden such complexes on their companions. Most Swedish women see their relationships in terms of comradeship, with the odd moments of excitement thrown in.

Next comes the Dutchman. Despite his often calvinist upbringing, he has no taboos and has learned a lot about female sexuality. The evidence is there: 78 per cent of Dutch women say they have "a very happy sexlife".

Superior ratings on sexual competence are accorded to the Portuguese and the Greeks. While the Greek is seen as 'sensitive' to the needs of his companion, the average Portuguese is an 'old-fashioned' lover, jealously regarding his woman as his property.

So we move irresistibly upwards, to the Frenchman. He, says Malena, grooms his 'irresistable lover image' but often fails to live up to it, paying the bill but offering little more in terms of female satisfaction. He also, she adds appropriately, is a terrible *voyeur*. But, says Frenchwoman Françoise Giroud, ex-minister and author, "love has a special place in our society and literature, and relations here between men and women are, while imperfect, the best in the world."

Which brings us to the Top Two of this European hitlist, the Spanish and the Italians, *ex aequo*. Spanish men's attitudes towards sex vary by region - a reflection of things said in Chapters 2 and 4 - and particularly between the north and the south. Spaniards are dashing and attentive lovers - yet 30 per cent of all Spanish women say they have no sex life at all.

As for the Italian male, well, he is even more dashing and attentive. But much of the 'dashing' is between his wife, his mistress, his children and, most importantly, his mother. His relationships are noted neither for their discretion nor for their longevity. No woman

Sex and socialism

One of Malena Iversson's more emphatic findings offers an interesting comment on the relationship between social organisation and sex. To quote her words, "the East Germans, both men and women, jump into bed more readily than the West Germans" - 26 per cent of them, it seems, on the first date. Malena attributes this to the greater professional and sexual equality practised under communism, when 90 per cent of women of working age had a job.

Her findings receive confirmation from other sources, including a Czech couple, Zek and Misha Halu, who have sampled the joys of sex in a socialist society. "Under communism making love was better", they said to a reporter from *The European* newspaper. "With no competition or career pressure, time was on your side."

The Halus have now turned their attention, and not a moment too soon, to the rest of us in the West. They find, among other things, that "the Germans are eager to know more about sex and are quite pragmatic about it". By comparison the British tend to be shy. "Once they open up, they want to go ahead. It's a reserved approach but there's a genuine interest behind it."

The Swiss, they add, are no more physically emancipated than the British. But (here we go again!) it seems that the Netherlands and the Nordic countries - the most emancipated societies of western Europe - are, like the old communist world, the places where sex is best.

Russia, it seems, is not part of this, if we are to believe the findings of an early-1995 poll conducted among 1,700 of its female readers by the Russian edition of *Cosmopolitan* magazine: 57 % of them said they didn't make love often enough.

Yet 55 % of them admitted being unfaithful to their partners – "a fact which surprised us only because we expected it to be higher", commented the magazine's editor, who added that such infidelities are "a reaction to the sexual strictures of past years", a reference one assumes to the moral code of communism.

Which only goes to show that the socialist world had its cultural differences too...

has exclusive rights to his attentions, though *mamma* generally comes off best.

This empirical evidence suggest that none of us Europeans really excel ourselves in such matters. Such serious research as has been undertaken so far - with the Dutch, Scots and rather surprisingly the Norwegians as pioneers - doesn't add that much, apart from examining the more mechanical aspects of the subject. But two major studies into sexual lifestyles, one on the British, the other on the French, were published at the end of 1992.

Apart from finding that the percentage of people refusing to answer questions on such matters was, at 35%, the same for the two countries (so much for the British idea that the French are totally engrossed with matters of sexuality!), these studies showed up incompatibilities in the responses of the sexes. In the words of the French researchers, these differences are "presumed to stem from both female understatement and male overstatement as well as from a greater diversity of male responses", whatever that may imply.

The British research, on its side, disproved Madame Cresson's assertion that 25 per cent of UK males are homosexual, while the French study led the influential German newspaper *Die Welt* to report incorrectly that "52% of French women between the ages of 35 and 49 admit having two partners at the same time [another way of saying they have a lover]; for men the figure is 33%". This was clearly a case of German wishful thinking, since the percentages related simply to those respondents already admitting to a 'multipartner relationship' (even French women, it seems, have difficulty in handling more than one lover at a time).

One thing to be said in favour of both French and Italian males is that they don't discriminate on age. In stark contrast to Anglo-Saxon attitudes in particular, any representative of the other sex is fair game if even just modestly mobile. But where the French think it a matter of honour and gallantry to flirt with an older woman, Italian males seem to be driven by the urge to get anything female on two legs into bed as fast as possible, more as a matter of self-respect.

No reference is made in any of this research to the inhabitants of the Kingdom of Belgium, so let me share the insight offered by an operator on a Belgian sex-line service. To quote her words to a local newpaper reporter, "I try to be flamboyant and imaginative with French callers because they don't accept mediocrity. Francophones, let us not forget, have an enormous store of culture on this subject: De Sade, *Les Liaisons Dangereuses*, etc. The Dutch are more simple, more direct, more natural." And the Belgians? "They have a fantasy, for example, of making love in a church, because religion is a big taboo here."

But let us leave the last word on the subject to a Flemish woman university professor. "People have completely the wrong idea about Swedish girls", she says. "They think that, because the Swedes have a reputation for permissiveness, they are promiscuous. Not so. Even the Spanish with their Catholic upbringing could show them a thing or two these days."

"From what I know", she adds, "it's the British girls who most easily cross the line." So much for the sexual stereotypes...

Women's wrongs and rights

This brings me to a subject which is difficult to approach in the same spirit of scientific pragmatism. For a start, I am too much of a realist to attempt a meaningful distinction between the *machismo* levels of European males. In any case European women, regardless of nationality, find we're all the same.

I am inclined to believe that this trait is most highly developed in societies with a tradition of strong male confraternities, generally of an energetic nature, as for example the fishermen of the Basque country or the mining communities of Wales and elsewhere.

But today, as such pursuits go out of fashion, it is perhaps more instructive to look at what goes on in the family car. I note that the British show a distinct readiness to let the women do the driving, which must mean something.

The only thing I can really assert with confidence is that, if you see a car driven by a man with no one in the front passenger seat and a woman or women at the back, then the odds are it is a Maghrebian or Turkish family, not a European one (unless it's a Swiss peasant *ménage*).

On the other hand, if you see a car driven by an extravagant male with a fierce-looking female in the front passenger seat and two old people at the back, then it's a Flemish family (not necessarily peasant) on an excursion. The fierce-looking female is there because she's the driver's wife or whatever and, as such, is entitled to glare at other drivers who look like taking liberties with the family property: all Belgians have bricks in their bellies, but it is the family car that's closest to their hearts. In fact, the Belgians are not all that macho.

The best that can be said on the subject is that some nationalities are better at helping in the house than others, but that's about it. A Eurobarometer survey in 1987 did indeed suggest that European couples are moving gradually towards an egalitarian relationship where both have a career and share the domestic chores.

While there may be some wishful thinking in the responses (though they have largely been corroborated since by the conclusions of a Henley Centre study published in late-1992), it seems that the most enthusiastic male communities in the matter of dishwashing and the like are the British, the Dutch, the Danish and - surprisingly for many of their fellow-Europeans - the Spanish.

According to a study by the Institute of the Woman in Madrid (which woman?), the Spanish male averages the fairly respectable rate of 2 1/2 hours a day looking after the home and kids. Even so, the Spanish government launched a TV campaign in 1994 to persuade men to be less macho and do more housework. But the least enthusiastic males must surely be in Austria, where a proposal has been drafted to make a husband's participation in the housework legally enforceable.

This trend indicates that more and more European women have careers of their own. Indeed they do, but the career ladder is not as long as it should be: it stops short, in most cases, a couple of rungs from the top. In this respect, when you look carefully, you find that no one country is better than another. There are exceptions, of course, but they tend to be either in certain narrow sectors of industry or in family-owned firms. Germany, where the family-owned firm predominates, is typical of Europe generally: "In banking, business and industry, it is reckoned that only 2 per cent of all top positions are held by women," says John Ardagh[4].

At the time of writing, sexual harassment at work is the big issue. The Spanish were the European pioneers in legislating against such things. The matter is being taken half-seriously by the British (English law does not recognise the concept of sexual harassment) and solemnly addressed by the Germans and the European

Commission, the latter on behalf of everyone. The French have since followed the example of the Spanish - but Gallic cartesianism was clouded in the process by the divagations of a female prime minister who, on the one hand, praised British males for their attitude towards women in society and, on the other, condemned them for their homosexuality.

The only firm conclusion I can draw on this vexed issue is that the most macho countries are located at opposite ends of the European Union. At the northwestern end, Ireland and Scotland, where many golf clubs still bar entry to the weaker sex (maybe handicaps should never have been invented?): most Irish males also prefer to drink on their own, as do the Scots if they admit it. And at the southeastern end, Greece, where male matter-of-factness produces two types of female: the assertive type and the over-feminine type.

What is happening in between is hard to guess, although there are still male social enclaves like the Greek *parea* to be found, the German *Stammtisch* for example. Maybe George Mikes[34] had a point when he said: "We are all male chauvinist pigs, except for women who are female chauvinist pigs". But, then, he was thinking of the Swiss.

Or was he? A survey carried out in 1994 by the Gestalt psychotherapy centre in Florence found that over 35 per cent of men questioned said they had been subjected to sexual harassment at work by their female superiors. A similar survey by the Italian Association for Demographic Education (AIED) came out with a similar figure - but added, not a moment too soon, that only two per cent of the men found the experience not to their liking. So the Latin Lover lives on...

The Demands
of Daily Life

"It is useful to know something about other nations' habits in order to judge our own in a healthier fashion, and not to imagine everything which differs from ours should be dismissed as ridiculous or illogical, as is frequently done by those who haven't seen anything"
Descartes

The British spent the most on toilet paper - nearly four times as much as the most frugal users, the Dutch" The Economist, 23/10/93

Northern Europeans want large refrigerators because they shop only once a week, in supermarkets; southern Europeans prefer small ones because they pick through open-air markets almost every day" William Echikson, Fortune

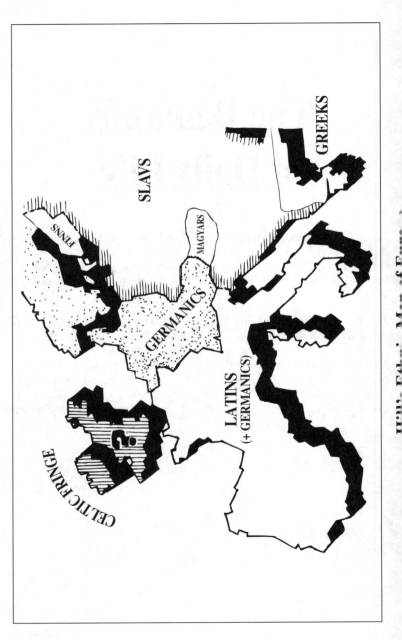

H°lly Eákai: Map of Europe 1

320

First, a caveat for any reader looking for comparative statistics on the daily living habits of the peoples of Europe: this is *not* the book.

Statistics abound - as books, as reports, as plain statistics - and there's no difficulty in finding them. The problem is what to do with them when you've got them. For one, they are often not very meaningful and, secondly, they'll be superseded sooner or later by another set. As I said at the beginning of this book, the fact that "30% of Europeans under the age of 30 snore and 50% of over-60s", as reported in a responsible newspaper on god knows what authority, leaves me unmoved.

It is even questionable whether inter-country comparative statistics, which is what we are really concerned with here, can really help. A lot of official data, when you look at it closely, turns out to be comparing apples with pears. As Franco Ferrarotti, the Italian sociologist, says of matters in his country: "Statistics have little to do with reality here". But I will quote a few where I think they tell us something.

In their place and in the spirit of the book so far, I offer what could be laughingly called Hill's Ethnic Map of Europe (see opposite). It makes the subject more manageable, and may even help to explain what follows, by summarily dividing the continental western Europeans into two main groups, the *Germanics* and the *Latins*.

Like all the other generalisations in this book, it is a gross over-simplification, but it contains a germ of truth. Of course it overlooks the Basques, also the Finno-Ugrian peoples and a few others. Significantly the dividing line between the two groups tends to follow the frontiers of the first Roman Empire.

How people cope

Taking this graphic interpretation of the Germanic/Latin fault line as our guide, let us explore the manner in which the different nations conduct their lives - an extension of the value systems talked about in the previous chapter.

Dr Edward T Hall and Mildred Reed Hall[63], an American anthropologist couple, have probably learned more about us Europeans than we have ourselves. They analysed national characteristics in terms of two different parameters, one relating to social organisation (*High Context* versus *Low Context*), the other to attitudes towards time (*Polychronic* versus *Monochronic*).

If we use Hill's Ethnic Map of Europe as our guide, unbeknown to them of course, we can see that the Halls basically identified the Latins as 'high context' and the Germanics as 'low context'. This means that the Latins - including of course the French in case there's any doubt - are, to use the Halls' words, a "people who have extensive information networks among family, friends, colleagues and clients and are involved in close relationships... As a result, they do not require much contexting (in-depth, background information) because they keep themselves informed about everything."

The 'low context' Germanics, on the other hand, are by no means so strong in terms of informal networks and need more information to feel comfortable in a situation and arrive at a rational decision. Their approach to life generally is highly segmented and compartmentalised (the Halls use the phrase *screen-dependent*), and this complicates things further. The Latins, by comparison, are interactive in their personal and professional behaviour patterns.

The second parameter examined by the Halls is peoples' attitude towards, and their *use* of, time. They describe those cultures that tend to do more than one thing at a time as 'polychronic' and those that do one thing after another as 'monochronic'. The correlation between 'high context' and 'polychronic' and between 'low context' and 'monochronic' is striking.

The polychronic Latins are culturally adept at doing a number of things at the same time and in any order that pleases them at that moment. The monochronic Germanics prefer to do one thing at a time and in a predetermined order. This makes the Germanics *schedule-dependent* and the Latins *schedule-independent* (a polite way of saying that they're always late!). We are not sure where all this puts the English, which explains the query on the Ethnic Map.

Eating and sleeping

Out of respect for European gastronomic traditions, food comes first as the aspect of consumption most worthy of consideration. Here, attitudes to time play an important part.

Enough has been written about English as opposed to Continental breakfasts, and all the variations in between. Suffice it to say that, taking lunch as an example, national approaches vary widely. Whatever they actually end up eating, the British working class sits down to lunch (they call it dinner) at 12 o'clock, like the Germans generally, while the rest of the British, supposedly the leisured lot, eat at 1. The Norwegians leave for lunch at 11 and the Spanish at 3. Italian public officials, of whom there are a lot, only officially work from 8 to 2, and the Greeks are trying to stop the habit of shutting down year-round from 2 to 5.

The bastion of national gastronomic traditions is naturally the home. Even this is being infiltrated as the younger generations start up on their own. The motive for change comes in two forms: *time pressures* leading to the increasing use of convenience foods, particularly deep-frozen meals, and changing *fashions* in gastronomy, with the young favouring fast foods and almost everybody acquiring a taste for ethnic cuisines.

Another growing influence is health concern - even in a gastronomically inclined community like the French who, since the 1960s, have sharply reduced their intake of potatoes and cheap wine in favour of cheese and yoghurt. In fact, the French now eat five times more frozen meals than they did in 1979, and drink two-thirds less wine than they drank in 1965.

The growing inroads of ethnic dishes like *pasta, pizza, pitta* and *moussaka* are paralleled by a curious snobbishness about imported products that would be regarded as very ordinary in their own countries: Belgian 'Tuc' biscuits and 'Stella' beer in Britain for example and, *vice versa*, British 'Peek Frean' biscuits and 'Crosse & Blackwell' sauce in Belgium. 'Barilla', a medium-range *pasta* in Italy, is sold as a luxury product elsewhere.

Eating-out habits vary enormously from country to country though, here again, time pressures are encouraging a trend upwards: even the French, according to the *Institut National des Statistiques*, now dine out about three times a week and spend almost 20% of their food budget in restaurants and canteens.

Europe is under permanent threat from McDonalds and its local look-alikes. Greek youngsters are particularly fond of fast food, an attitude now increasingly and alarmingly shared by their French peers. The Germans and the Dutch are equally enthusiastic but, then, they don't have so much to lose. Ethnic restaurants are also gaining ground all round: some of the best eating out Spanish-style is to be found not in Spain, but in Berlin, Hamburg and

Zürich. And it was a rude experience for me to end up in a small town in the backwoods of Sweden and find nothing but Italian, Greek and Chinese food.

Back home, the British are turning to the microwave oven while the Italians still spurn it. Even so "only 60 per cent of British families have got round to buying a toaster, self-weeding lawns and intelligent lavatories" says a *Euromonitor* report, which attributes this fact to "a love of self-reliance". Maybe this also explains the northern Europeans' preference for single beds (see below).

Kitchens, to use a phrase coined by John Quelch, assistant professor of business administration at Harvard University, seem to be the most 'culture-bound' of the rooms in the common European house, not surprisingly in view of the widely ranging traditions embodied in European cuisine. Follow, in descending order of importance, the bath/bedroom, the living room, the garden and the garage.

Plenty of formal research has been done into the habits of the European nations. One pioneering study into caravan design (a provocative subject since, to other motorists, the whole of Europe seems to migrate in caravans in the summer season) found that "the Dutch regard a toilet compartment as a waste of space; the French-speaking Swiss want end kitchens while the German-speaking Swiss favour central kitchens; some countries want all single beds, some double, and Germany and Holland outsize doubles" (presumably to get warm after going to the toilet outside).

This research was confined to the countries of northern and central Europe. More recently a Frenchman, Gérard Mermet, has drawn on a three-year pan-European study for his book *Euroscopie*[29]. Among other things he finds that double beds are more popular with southern Europeans, who have no particular need to keep warm at night, than with northern Europeans who often prefer single beds - 80 per cent of the Germans compared with only 5 per cent of the French (who said the French weren't Latins?). The argument that this is because the Mezzogiorno peasant gets better value out of a double bed by putting the whole family under the same set of sheets does not explain the phenomenon.

Other bed-related quirks include the use by the French of sausage-shaped bolsters in the place of pillows and the fondness for duvets and soft pillows in the *deutschsprechende Raum* as well as the far north (the Norwegian *dyne,* etc). Italian insistence on hard pillows has been known to create chaos in German hotels. The French *sous-proletariat* is also accused of changing its bed-sheets only once a month - a revelation that quite understandably put our Spanish concierge into a state of shock, the Spanish being one of the cleaner nations of Europe.

Durables and consumables

The market researchers can also point to European differences in the purchase of investment goods like domestic appliances, where the choice tends to be more careful.

British housewives, for a start, tend to spurn the dishwasher: only 12 per cent of UK households own one, possibly reflecting the helpfulness of British husbands at the sink (see Chapter 5). They also covet front-loading washing machines while the French prefer top-loaders. The Germans, being environmentally minded (less soap and water needed), want a larger choice of settings than their neighbours. And northern European countries go for higher spin speeds than the Mediterraneans (almost, but not quite, synonymous with 'Latins'), because their clothes don't dry as easily.

Northern Europeans need larger refrigerators than Mediterraneans, obviously not because of the climate but because they shop less regularly than southerners, who regard a walk to the open-air market as part of the daily routine. Northerners also prefer to have the freezer at the bottom of the refrigerator, southerners on top.

Meanwhile the Swiss of all persuasions - German, French and Italian - still cohabit with kitchen appliances 5 cm narrower than anywhere else. This is not so much an expression of the spatial frugality of Swiss housewives as a reflection of the lengths to which Swiss manufacturers will go to block foreign imports.

The Germans cook with electricity, the Italians with gas, the British with both. Italians put great emphasis on the visual aspect of domestic appliances, the others less.

Deviations are also evident, though with increasing signs of convergence, in consumables too. The most obvious variations are in the culinary area, but a glance at market shares will also show wide discrepancies in things like perfumes and toiletries. International toothpaste marketers, say the people at the JWT Europe advertising agency, sell a lower-quality product to the

Dutch for half the price, while Spanish women shave their armpits more than women in France or Germany.

Pan-European marketeers can afford to overlook many of these idiosyncracies, while treading warily through sensitive areas like the kitchen, bedroom and bathroom of the common European House. Some specialists have isolated pan-European behaviour patterns in specific aspects of everyday life, particularly in fast-moving and fashion-conscious areas like ready-to-wear, branded toiletries and cosmetics. High-flyers include *Benetton* in the fashion field and *Dior* and *L'Oréal* in cosmetics.

Some observers are even encouraged to talk about *Eurobrands*, examples being up-market *Dior* perfumes (and down-market *Nivea* skin creams) which recorded awareness ratings in 1991 of respectively 84% (and 95%) in Germany, 92% (also 92%) in France, 81% (and 84%) in Great Britain, 66% (and 88%) in Italy and 97% (and 92%) in Spain. Few people would argue that *Nestlé* and *Knorr* qualify as Eurobrands in the food sector. But how and when a product becomes a Eurobrand is an issue that will exercise marketeers for a long time to come. The subject, like the sex of angels, creates more heat than light.

Eurobrands and Euroconsumers

The international marketing confraternity seems to be rallying to the view that the future lies in specific consumer segments or niches across the whole of Europe. This may sound like wishful thinking when you consider, for example, that the Greeks spend twice as much on jewellery as the Swiss and 20 times as much as the Portuguese...

The development of Eurobrands presupposes the existence of *Euroconsumers*. French sociologist Bernard Cathelat has developed what he calls, with appropriate French *esprit*, 'social meteorology', a form of behavioural analysis using a three-dimensional frame which goes beyond demographic and economic conditions of life to examine behaviour and habits, opinions and attitudes, motivations and emotional responses.

Working from a Herculean research study undertaken with 20,000 citizens from 15 countries and 78 regions of Western Europe[64], Cathelat concludes that Europeans tend to fall into one of six groupings classified as: *Withdrawn*, a category that includes the

A Question of Taste

For a number of years now Hennes & Mauritz, the Swedish ready-to-wear manufacturer, has been promoting its lingerie and swimwear lines through seasonal advertising campaigns in all European markets. The chosen media are poster sites, particularly at bus and tramway shelters.

Throughout, the company has used attractive and appealing models, suggesting real-life femininity rather than the stylised chic of the fashion houses, and has combined this with outstanding creative photography to achieve high noting rates.

Every year, H&M meets the challenge of re-arousing interest in a highly competitive market by being a bit more daring than the rest: "our campaigns are done with a twinkle in the eye". The parent company prepares a choice of photographs of each subject, with treatment ranging from conservative to provocative.

Inevitably this causes controversy from time to time, though reactions tend to reflect the cultural predispositions of the countries concerned.

Here are some of H&M's experiences:

Netherlands: recurring complaints from feminist movements.

Belgium: judicious choice of photographs has precluded any negative reactions and prompted requests for copies of posters.

Britain: moralising by intellectual elite, approval by public.

Germany/Switzerland: same as Britain, with amusement at elitist reactions among the general public.

Norway: condemnation by the Lutheran church (moral) and by the motoring associations (practical!).

Sweden: theft of posters by members of the general public who, in the process, damaged shelters and distracted the police from their normal duties.

H&M accepts controversy as inevitable in pluralistic societies, and special interest groups such as the church and the feminist movement are only doing their job. But, as for the ordinary man or woman in the street, "they like our advertising. They write to tell us so and, in the final analysis, our sales show that it works".

older age groups, *Dreamers, Ambitious, Contestors, Militants* and *Notables*, which includes the socially motivated and the professionals. Altogether Cathelat and his colleagues have identified 16 sociological groups, generically dubbed Euro-Styles and individually labelled *Euro-Rockies, Euro-Romantics, Euro-Pioneers, Euro-Gentry*, etc.

Cathelat maintains that various niches in the European consumer market can be tackled by a process of horizontal segmentation, even if individual components do not correspond exactly in socio-demographic or socio-economic terms. Euro-Styles can also be used to identify regional 'micro-civilisations' and simplify the consumer marketing process. One thing, in Cathelat's view, is absolutely certain: "Manifestly national frontiers are not the right breakdown if you want to take account of the diversity of sociological types". So much for the nation state.

A simpler and more recent approach to European consumer segmentation is provided by the 'Young Adult Europe' study undertaken by Yankelovich Partners Inc. (see also Chapter 11). This identified five distinct population groups among young people, age 16-34, in eight European countries. Yankelovich dubs these groups *Islanders, Armchair Magistrates, Quixotians, Groovers & Shakers* and *Highest Bidders*.

Of the eight countries studied, Spain comes out with significantly the highest share of *Islanders* - a relatively down-market, ethnocentric (as opposed to cosmopolitan) and conservative segment, generally living-in with family connections.

The Germans star as the *Quixotians* - often full-time students (Germany boasts the oldest undergraduates of any country), tolerant and intellectually inclined, with a sizeable dash of idealism.

Italy heads the *Groovers & Shakers* - creative and cosmopolitan, tuned into trends, socially alert, yet tolerant of others.

Sweden, followed by the Benelux countries, heads the list of *Armchair Magistrates* - judgmental, conservatively minded people (yes, the Swedes and the Dutch can be like this, contrary to the popular image!), typically male with above-average income levels.

Finally, the French and the British come close to sharing the honours as *Highest Bidders* - people who, as the Yankelovich study explains, are "bold, brash and out to impress". But, unlike the *Groovers & Shakers*, who just happen to be in the lead, the *Highest*

Bidders are still striving to be part of the lead group and, as predominantly young males, need feedback and approval. But they are big spenders (marketing people please note).

The trivia of life

Some of the most formidable obstacles on the path to a United Europe are what I like to call the 'trivia of life'. Many of them, like the English Channel, divide the British from the rest - *pace* the Chunnel.

Some of these obstacles are of a purely practical nature. Others, the 'totems' of European life, are artificially imposed.

Most of them have something to do with the geometry or dimensions of civilised existence. Here are the ten most recalcitrant:

1. *Knives and forks:* Why do Continentals insist on confusing the British by putting their knives and forks face-down on the plate somewhere between 09.15 and 07.25 when they've finished eating? The British, those who know, put them face-up at 06.30.

Until not long ago the French bourgeoisie put the forks and spoons face-down when laying the table. Some of them still do.

2. *Condiments:* The British put their salt in what some Continentals think are pepperpots (single hole) and *vice versa* (multiple holes). This confusion can have serious practical consequences.

3. *Hands versus tables:* Why do the Germans, the Dutch and the Belgians insist that people, particularly their own children, put their hands on the table during meals whereas the British, those who know, expect quite the opposite?

Hands, tables notwithstanding, are a divisive factor on their own. The French give a Gallic shrug of the shoulders and spread their hands wide, an apparently generous but deliberately vague form of expression. The English put their hands in varying degrees over their mouths - because they're not sure what will come out. The Germans stand stiffly to attention and keep their hands to their sides. The Spanish use their hands to pat the back of whomever is nearest (they used to clap them authoritatively to command the attention of waiters, but that's now frowned upon in the new democratic Spain). The Italians put their hands everywhere.

4. *Kissing:* A very complicated matter, though normally limited to kissing the opposite sex, women excepted.

In Belgium, the Walloons kiss three times (left, right, left, as seen from the viewpoint of the party doing the kissing) and noisely - even man-to-man, though normally once only and less noisely. The Flemish Belgians kiss sparingly, generally once and man-to-man rarely.

In France, outside Paris and Lyons where two kisses suffice, the amount of kissing depends on regional loyalties. In Normandy they kiss four times (left, right, left, right), in the Ardèche three times (starting untypically with the right cheek), further south also four times (left, right, left, right), but in Provence, surprisingly, also only twice (left, right, and that's your lot).

The Germans kiss once (right), occasionally twice (right, left), never man-to-man. The British also kiss just once (generally right), but at every possible opportunity. This comes as a surprise to older British generations, among whom I count myself. Yet, in the words of a 17th century Englishman, "to salute strangers with a kiss is considered but civility (in England) but with foreign nations immodesty". In those days the English, male and female, even kissed on the lips (some still do), which neatly - messily? - removed the cheek priority problem.

Even the tolerant Erasmus found English kissing overdone: "Wherever you go, you are received on all hands with kisses; when you take your leave you are dismissed with kisses... wherever a meeting takes place there is kissing in abundance."

Today the Germans, the Italians and the Spanish of the older generations don't normally kiss at all, ladies' hands excepted. Peter Collett[5] remarks that the Irish and the Welsh are also rather cautious in this regard. That leaves lots of room for handshaking, essentially a Continental habit.

5. *Handshaking:* Although much less complicated (only one-armed people shake with the left hand), it can also cause embarrassment - particularly with the English who, if they're upper class and/or female, don't shake hands at all except on first introduction and, if they're working class, simply grunt.

6. *Forms of address (letters, etc):* Horribly complicated, whether oral or written. Consult your local librarian, language school or business advisor.

7. *Titles:* Honorary titles are still important in Britain, France and Germany. In Britain, manifested through the Queen's Honours List, they buttress a redundant social system.

In Italy you can get one whether you want or deserve one or not: although it is illegal to do so, they are even bought (particularly by the young, it seems). In Austria as well as in the democratic Netherlands, the system has been officially abandoned, which means that titles are valued even more highly than before. Meanwhile Belgium has the highest incidence of *titres de noblesse* of any country in Europe.

As for professional titles, the Austrians take the highest honours *("Ich habe die Ehre, Herr Professor Doktor Doktor")* followed by the Swedes *("God dag, Ingeniör Svensson")*, the Italians and the Germans. Titles of this kind leave the British totally unmoved...

8. *Book titles:* English (and American) books feature their titles on the spine top-downwards, the Continentals bottom-upwards. The English (and Americans) argue that it is logical to have a spine which can be read when a book is lying 'cover up', as it should do, on a tabletop.

The Continentals argue that, accepting that the normal place for a book is in a bookcase, it is easier for a right-handed person to tilt his or head leftwards, ie at a bottom-upwards title, without getting a crick in the neck. And since most Continentals are right-handed...

The Commission of the European Union should address this most vexatious issue for once and for all. Currently, if you happen to have a large and multilingual library, you're likely to end up with a stiff neck in any case.

9. *Driving:* It seems that, inspired by the precedent of Ancient Rome, Napoleon decided that his subjects should drive on the right because, most of them being understandably right-handed, there was less likelihood of their whips entwining if they did so. The British, being implacably hostile to Napoleon, decided to stay on the left.

10. *The fourth dimension:* See 'Polychronic' and 'Monochronic', above. And do the British, the Irish, the Portuguese and the Greeks have to be out of step timewise with the rest? But here, for once, the Greeks have a good case.

The Europeans at Play

"We won the second half"
>> Norwegian daily reporting a 2-1 defeat by Sweden at football

"We beat England 1-1"
>> Norwegian daily reporting on an international draw

"Vier Österreicher unter den ersten drei!" ["Four Austrians in the first three"]   Austrian daily reporting on an athletics event

"... the Belgian management and staff will be kept in order to make sure that you receive the same personal welcome."
>> Announcement of Brussels hotel takeover

"On dude ranches in Saskatchewan and Alberta, citified Germans put on crisp new western gear to ride the range"   *The Economist*

The Europeans at work have come under the microscope in another book of mine, *EuroManagers & Martians*. But what about the Europeans at play?

Though the new market economies of Eastern Europe have a lot of catching up to do, the continent is rapidly becoming a leisure society. Europe is playing its part in realising the OECD's prediction that tourism will be the largest single sector in the world economy by the year 2000.

It is the Germans who, contrary to foreigners' folklore about their work ethic, are actually showing the way. In 1993, according to the *Institut der deutschen Wirtschaft*, industrial employees in the western half of Germany spent less time per year working than any other European nation - an average of 1,524 hours (Britons, at 1,847 hours, worked the most). This didn't prevent the Germans from outproducing everyone else...

The overriding reality is that, regardless of nationality, we Europeans are rapidly becoming a race of couch potatoes (another type of potato introduced from the New World), much of this effort being devoted to TV coverage of football games and cycle races. Germany and Denmark head the pack with at least one TV set per three people, which is the same thing as saying a set in every family home. There can be no question that, in the domain of sport at least, television is the most potent influence in breaking down the cultural barriers that remain.

It is also a potent catalyst of sporting chauvinism, particularly when one of the smaller nations has something to shout about - not only in front of the TV set, but also in the stands (with the English still claiming the title of Euro-Rowdies *par excellence*) and in the papers. The Norwegian and Austrian newspaper headlines at the start of this section are evidence enough...

But some brave and active souls are still searching out idiosyncratic leisure pursuits that reflect their environment, physical or cultural. In broad and very racial terms, the Germans go on long hikes, the Swedes go boating, the Dutch go camping, the British go to the beach when the weather's not beastly, the northern Italians and Austrians go to the lakes, the Swiss and Norwegians go climbing, the Italians go for long lunches in the countryside, and the Spanish just go out (14 per cent of their household spending, alcoholic drinks not included, being devoted to restaurant, café and hotel bills). Come the winter most of them, with the exception of the Mediterraneans, go skiing.

In looking at leisure pursuits, it is not inappropriate to remember that, until recently, many parts of Europe - particularly the more mountainous or inaccessible bits - were peasant communities. Because they were poor, too busy or had too much sense, most peasants were not keen sports enthusiasts, unless it was playing cards over a bottle of *schnaps* or rolling in the hay with the girl from over the hill.

The result today is that those regions with a strong peasant background have few sporting traditions other than the aforementioned - to which one can now add watching football and cycle racing, either on the box or in the flesh. However, there are some exceptions to this rule, a number of regions which have an ethnic sport very much of their own.

Close to the Arctic Circle, the people of northern Sweden indulge in an extra-rowdy form of ice hockey known as *bandy* and the Finns have a Nordic version of baseball called *pesäpallo*.

Not to be outdone the northern Frisians - who live on the North Sea coast close to the Danish frontier - practise a vigorous winter sport called *Boßeln*, a form of weight-putting where a heavy round object is thrown as far as possible and allowed to roll even further over frost-hardened fields. Both this and *bandy* are accompanied by the enthusiastic consumption of local versions of white liquor by spectators and, in the case of *Boßeln*, by participants as well.

The good people of the Orkney Isles, north of Scotland, have a ball game called *bá* (sounds like something from 'Star Trek'). This, which is rumoured to have been played originally with a human head, is indulged in once a year, not in the island's fields but in the streets of Kirkwall, the capital.

Their neighbours the Scots engage in tossing the *caber* (also calculated to remove human heads) and a local form of wrestling - an activity they share with the people of Cumbria further south, as well as with the Swiss and with the Bavarians, who practise a form of arm-wrestling.

The people of southern Ireland favour *hurling*, a venerable and dangerous form of hockey which features a hide-covered cork ball travelling at high speed some three metres above the ground. That it is both venerable and dangerous is borne out by the comments of a spectator in 1699, who pointed out that sometimes, if a player misses the ball, "he knocks one of his opponents down, of which no resentment is shown."

The Frisians of the northern Netherlands have a thing called *fierlejeppen* which involves vaulting with a long pole over a canal. More gregarious Dutch people go in for *korfbal*, a slow version of basketball. This might have been thought more appropriate to the German Swiss but the latter, being a contrary lot, practise a potentially murderous game called *Hornisse*, whipping discs in the air and arresting them in flight with the aid of miniature billboards.

Further south, the Basques have a particularly lethal sport called variously *pelota vasca, frontón, baloncesta* and *jai alai*. This is a betting sport like horseracing and the dogs, with bookmakers in attendance.

Shooting projectiles is a particularly Basque pastime: they have been doing this kind of thing for centuries in the Pyrenees, throwing discs into the air over mountain passes to fool southwards-bound pigeons into thinking they are in the presence of hawks - persuading them to fly lower and straight into the nets of Basque accomplices. Other less energetic Spaniards amuse themselves throwing horseshoes into the mouths of cast-iron frogs.

The further south you go, the less sport you find - evidently the folk are content with card-playing and rolling in the hay, plus the occasional Saints Days. But in Europe's southernmost manifestation, the Canary Isles, a local version of wrestling pops up again. Not unlike rolling in the hay...

Some of the more recent European sports have a working-class rather than a peasant origin, though the concept of 'working class' is strictly dated, there probably being more peasants than workers in contemporary Europe. The French claim a sport called *pétanque* which, despite its aura of antiquity, is a game that, in its present form, was only developed at the end of the last century. They also share pigeon-fancying (what a lovely expression!) with the Belgians and others.

Greyhound racing is essentially a British working-class pursuit: some other nationalities have emulated it but their 'greyhounds', as I have found out to my financial advantage, are more like whippets in various stages of genetic decomposition.

The Belgians, for their part, can claim *balle pelote* or *kaatsen*, a mainly airborne ball game played by opposing teams, which may have a long pedigree though nobody seems sure. They also have a residual sport which involves getting your pet cock to crow more times within a given period than anyone else's: since it involves no physical exercise other than drinking beer and placing bets, it's surprising that it's dying out. In fact the pet cock is in the process of being supplanted by the songbird, a genteel variation of the same thing.

Some sports are culturally and socially ambivalent. The prime example is rugby, which in its 'League' form (as played in the north of England) is working-class and in its 'Union' form (as played in Wales and the south of England) decidedly pukka.

A sport of more recent origin is dwarf-throwing, which involves heaving small people across a bar (the drinking variety). Imported, not surprisingly, from Australia in the 1980s, it enjoyed a short-lived popularity in France before being outlawed by the ministry of the interior (nb *not* the ministry for small-to-medium enterprise). An older sport, goat-tossing, has also been banned in northwestern Spain.

There are of course better known games which are fairly ethnic without being closely linked to peasant or working-class cultures. The most famous are the striking of leather-covered balls with willow bats of the English and other non-Europeans, known as cricket, and the organised slaughter of bovines by the Spanish (and, in a more elegant way but with equally fatal results, by the Portuguese), known as bullfighting.

Golf is one sport which it is difficult to classify. It certainly has ethnic origins - Scots or Dutch depending on whom you talk to, though I think the Scots have the better case - but it is now, like tennis, in the process of pan-European gentrification. Shortly after reunification the east German *Land* of Mecklenburg-Vorpommern, previously a so-called people's democracy, had received more than 80 applications for the construction of golf courses.

This raises the question of whither European leisure? One thing seems certain: with the prospective release of large areas of land onto the European market, thanks to the progressive inroads of the Common Agricultural Policy (will all those peasants become workers?), there will be lots of room for space-hungry leisure sites like golf courses and theme parks.

The Europeans on holiday

Vacation habits are changing fast. The packaged holiday boom, which got off the ground in the second half of the Sixties, opened up vistas for ordinary people whose perspective had been limited to their national frontiers. A glut of beer-drinking northerners in short pants and 'kiss-me-quick' hats destroyed large swathes of the Mediterranean littoral. The only major exception to this trend was the French, who more often than not preferred quite sensibly to stay in their own large and varied country.

The Spanish also tend to stay at home, not because they cannot afford to travel (according to Visa International they spend more per head on holidays than anyone else), but because they are so attached to their roots and their relatives. They leave the Mediterranean coast to the foreigners. However a young but growing community of ski-mad Spaniards migrates seasonally to the French Alps, untypically demonstrating as great a talent for drunkenness and rowdiness as its British and Swedish counterparts.

The other nations on the Mediterranean littoral also tend to be stay-at-homes. The poorer folk don't have the money to go abroad, and neither they nor the better-to-do have any particular incentive or inclination to do so, unless it's to head for the fleshpots of the French Riviera. One thing they all do is keep away from the beaches the northerners frequent, unless they are making money off them.

Even more on holiday than at home, the Dutch demonstrate their native genius for saving money - a subject that exercises their Mediterranean hosts as much as the fortunes of the local football team. Figures complied by the Austrian National Tourist Board, for example, show that in 1994 even the Czechs outspent the Dutch on subsistence, at ECU40 and ECU37 per day respectively.

The Germans are the European tourists *par excellence*. Like the Dutch, they are great caravaners, the difference being that their caravans are generally motorised and tend to be bigger (see Chapter 7, toilets and double beds). They also have the most money: according to the World Travel & Tourism Council (WTTC), they alone accounted for more than 35 per cent of all European expenditure on international travel in 1995. The second biggest spenders, the British, could only manage 13 per cent of the total, despite their anxiety to invade other peoples' beaches where the sun could be expected to shine, Spain for the hoi polloi, France for the rest.

As for the French, they came third in the international travel and tourism stakes, slightly ahead of the Italians, but they still spend one-third of their holiday time visiting family and friends, by definition mainly in France. They also claim the highest ratio of holiday homes: 12 per cent of all French families have a *deuxième résidence*, outperforming the Danes with 10 per cent and even the Belgians. Maybe this is one way of avoiding the worst of the traffic snarl-ups, since one thing their dirigiste government has not succeeded in doing is stopping the French taking to the roads all at the same time.

There are still some hardy souls who remain loyal to the risky pursuit of trans-European hitchhiking - risky because, these days, the bourgeois motorist mind equates hitchhiking with promiscuity of some kind or another. Katie Wood, editor of *The Hitchhiker's Guide to Europe*, insists that the characteristics of each country are reflected in their attitudes to hitchhikers. "The French are their usual mean old selves and don't give rides. The Scandinavians are great, as are the British, especially the Scots and the Welsh".

Winterwise, however, the Europeans stay in Europe. From its early days as a 19th-century diversion for a few pioneering and inevitably eccentric English gentlefolk (they brought it to Switzerland), skiing metamorphosed into a popular upper-class diversion after WWII and, more recently, into a sport for the masses. Having systematically spoiled the Mediterranean's beaches, the Europeans are now taking collective responsibility for the destruction of the Alps.

Another thing English gentlefolk did, egged on by Queen Victoria, was popularise the seaside holiday at home long before it became popular abroad. English 'bathing resorts', places like Brighton and Bournemouth, have since moved down-market in varying degrees, but the concept still flourishes in northern continental Europe. Germany has the island of Sylt, the Netherlands has Noordwijk, Belgium has Knokke, and France has Deauville and other places on the Atlantic coast. These places have a lot of things in common: society life, snobbishness and the desire to see and be seen.

Incidentally, the Irish spent more of their household budget on recreation than anyone else in 1993, according to Eurostat. Presumably most of this went on Guinness, gin-and-orange and whiskey.

The downside of it all

Once addicts of colonialism, we Europeans have now developed a taste for international tourism. Again, the Germans have been the trend-setters, heading for exotic or romantic destinations which take them away from home as far as they can get - often in search of, among other things, *Kultur*. In the words of Karin Minke, a German escapee, "this is pure escapism". Other nationalities are now starting to follow this trend to far-away places with strange-sounding names.

But the herd instinct is, once again, all too apparent. Canadians, for example, look aghast at the German invasion of their western provinces, first as tourists but then, increasingly, as 'settlers'. A report in *The Economist* in early-1995 comments that "rich Germans are buying up lakefront property, ranches, wilderness resorts (they now own most of these) and local businesses. With them come Bavarian-style cafés, bakeries and sausage shops." Yuck!

Whether we're in Europe or outside, we Europeans often make a pretty dubious impression. The Germans do a particularly thorough job of it, upsetting both the natives and fellow-Europeans who are staying in the same resorts. On the other hand, they please the natives but offend their fellow-Europeans by having more money than the rest.

They apparently have more of some other things too, if the complaint of Austrian parliamentarian Horst Wendling is anything to go by: "Everywhere naked male chests with sloshing fat stomachs, female rear-ends hanging out of short shorts" (and there speaks a right-wing fellow-member of the German-speaking community). Evidently even this is not enough to put off the French: Club Med is planning a series of villages exclusively for German tourists. A policy of containment?

The Germans set the example for most other Europeans by behaving contrary to type when outside their own country. Loud and vulgar in the more popular resorts of the Mediterranean, they indulge what territorial impulses they have left by claiming poolside places with their bathing towels and fiercely defending their rights to the best tables in beach restaurants. They are particularly pushy in skilift queues in the Alps.

Where the Germans tend to the exotic(?) in their choice of leisure activities, the Dutch prefer 'the home away from home' approach.

Consider this cameo from the *Wall Street Journal Europe*: "It's a glorious summer afternoon here at the Petit Paradis campground [in the Belgian Ardennes]. Fred Buitenhuis [an invented name, I hope], a Dutch insurance man stripped down to his lime-green swimming trunks, is perched on a plastic chair outside his caravan. He looks up from the sports section of his Dutch newspaper. His Dutch neighbors' laundry is strung from tree to tree around a murky pond. Gas canisters rust in the brush. Cars, many bearing Dutch license plates, buzz along the highway 20 meters away. "We came here to see the nature," Mr. Buitenhuis explains." Good reporting but, again, yuck!

Evidently the northern Europeans like baring themselves. They certainly make an impression when enjoying themselves abroad. The Mediterraneans, by comparison, are positively discreet. They see the British get extrovert and boisterous, the French get moody and assertive, the Germans get noisy and arrogant, the Dutch get devious and the Swedish get drunk - and they take their money. As a general rule the smaller countries are less Jekyll-and-Hydish when abroad than the bigger ones.

Unfortunately, popular tourism has turned large, mainly coastal and alpine, areas of Europe into international ghettoes: one visit to Spain's Costa Blanca or Italy's Val d'Aosta should convince you. A compact form of the same phenomenon, football-fan(atic)ism, has laid waste some of our inner cities.

The grass is greener...

Short-term stays are transmogrifying into long-term settlement as Germans invest in property around the lakes of southern Switzerland, northern Italy and the western provinces of Austria, as well as in coastal Spain, Ireland and Denmark. Action by the Danes in fact ensured that the European Union treaty negotiated at Maastricht included a protocol banning the purchase of summer houses by EU citizens, a concern that now also exercises Austrians, Finns and Swedes since their accession to the Union.

In fact, such initiatives come late in the day for some countries. The French - and not just the radical right - are distressed at the number of British, Dutch and German nationals buying holiday or even permanent homes in their vast country. Jean-Yves Le Gallou, a leader of the National Front party, tactfully evoked regional rather than racist issues when he said: "Come the day when 80 per cent of the population of Dordogne will be English, then it will not quite be Dordogne even if the English there are very amiable." *Verrie Frensch*. And look what the English have been doing to Normandy!

George Mikes comments that the Swiss, not particularly known for turning down a quick Deutschemark, dislike the idea that the Germans, having lost the Cameroons, should set about colonising southern Switzerland instead. Meanwhile the Dutch buy holiday cottages in the Ardèche, and the British buy up Portugal's Algarve. The French, sensibly, put their money into property at home, which is almost as good as keeping it in the mattress.

A Gallup poll conducted in February 1993 suggested that 49 per cent of Britons would leave their country given the chance. No doubt many of them would gravitate, if only for reasons of language, to the ex-Colonies, Australia in particular.

But not entirely. Other parts of Europe also have their attractions, France in particular. An EC-wide survey conducted in December 1992 by the Sofres research institute, on behalf of the French daily newspaper *Le Parisien*, showed that 6 million Britons would choose France in preference to other European Union countries.

It seems that the Dutch - of whom over 53 per cent declared themselves ready to leave their mother-country - are even more footloose Francewards. But the reason here, according to *Le Parisien*, is not so much despair at the way their country is being run as sheer suffocation resulting from population density, traffic jams and bureaucracy.

These conclusions prompted *Le Parisien* to banner-headline its cover page with the unashamedly chauvinistic headline *"L'Europe aime la France"*. It then justified its crowing by using a strangely Gallic English equivalent of *cocorico* which, for some Freudian reason, is "cock-a-*little-do*". English cocks, for some equally Freudian reason (because they don't take themselves too seriously?) say "cock-a-*doodle*-do"...

The same article concluded that France came top of the EC pops because it is *"à la fois riche et latine"*. I'm not even sure about the 'rich' bit, but 'Latin'?

All this living in one another's laps should at least help us Europeans get to know one another better. Yes, but not necessarily for the better. The INRA study described in Chapter 2 shows that not everyone trusts everyone else.

Eurobarometer also conducts periodical studies into the attitudes of the European Union's member nations towards one another, in terms of an 'index of confidence'. This suggests that the most trusting are the Danish and the least trusting are the Italians. In terms of *earning* trust, the most favoured are the the Germans, the Dutch and the Danes (one good turn deserves another). The ones earning the least trust are the Greeks, even when they bring gifts.

Here parle man europees

"A language is not just a dictionary of words, sounds and syntax. It is a different way of interpreting reality, refined by the generations that developed that language"
Federico Fellini

"Language disguises thought... The tacit conventions on which the understanding of everyday language depends are enormously complicated"
Ludwig Wittgenstein

"The man that has two languages is worth two men" [L'homme qui possède deux idiomes vaut deux hommes"]
Charles V

"Whenever the literary German dives into a sentence, that is the last you are going to see of him till he emerges on the other side of the Atlantic with his verb in his mouth."
Mark Twain

"If thought corrupts language, language can also corrupt thought"
George Orwell

"Translation is treason" ["Traduttore = traditore"] Italian dictum

"It is quite an illusion to imagine that one adjusts to reality essentially without the use of languages and that language is merely an incidental means of solving specific problems of communication or reflection. The fact of the matter is that the 'real world' is to a large extent built up on the language habit of the group"
Edward Sapir

"'When I use a word,' Humpty Dumpty said in rather a scornful tone, 'it means just what I choose it to mean - neither more nor less'"
Lewis Carroll

anguage shapes attitudes and attitudes shape language.
Witness the French fondness for abstraction, which is ideally served by the tools of communication available to them. In contrast, Castilian Spanish admirably conveys the elemental nature of an environment that has done so much to shape the country's culture.

It may even be that language projects itself daily onto the lifestyles of its speakers. The Luxembourgers suspect that the less definitive nature of their vocabulary leads to misunderstandings with their German and French neighbours, and may even influence their own behaviour. And the fact that a small country like Hungary can produce so many people of genius may owe something to the logical structure of the grammar, which encourages clarity of thought.

In his book *Language, Thought and Reality*, Benjamin Lee Whorf says[65]: "We dissect nature along lines laid down by our native languages... We cut nature up, organize it into concepts, and ascribe significances as we do, largely because we are parties to an agreement to organize it in this way - an agreement that holds throughout our speech community and is codified in the patterns of our language."

As long as a language continues to be used as a vehicle for a distinctive culture, it will nuance human behaviour. From my own experience, I know that switching from one language to another can have a slight but subtle effect on the way one thinks and reacts. So it should. In the words of an American translator interviewed by the *International Herald Tribune* in Prague, "Czech is a terrible, insidiously difficult language. To make heads or tails of it vis-à-vis English requires understanding the differences in how Czechs and Anglos think." The same goes, in varying degrees, for the others.

The physical structure of a language indeed affects the way people communicate, and not just in the sense that German can suggest excitement simply because the verb comes at the end of the sentence. Language is a matter of vocabulary as well as structure and the resources of expression available in different languages also vary strikingly.

Most of us use one or other of the Indo-European family of languages where, if you look closely enough, the similarities are as striking as the differences. But there are remarkable variations in the nature and extent of individual vocabularies.

English draws on something like 500,000 words excluding technical vocabularies (600,000-800,000 in the opinion of the German *Duden* organisation), of which the average English person in fact uses no more than one per cent. Duden gives estimates of 300,000-500,000 words for German, of which the average German (being slightly more committed or articulate?) uses some three per cent, and only 100,000 words for French.

The other Latin languages are equally impoverished, though Spanish and Portuguese assimilated an Arab vocabulary as well as the one they acquired from the Romans. This impoverishment may be both a cause and effect of the southern Europeans relying more heavily on oral communication than their northern neighbours, who are much more inclined to commit themselves to writing.

Standing apart from all this, of course, are the Finno-Ugric languages - primarily Finnish and Hungarian - which have a logic and a structure ('agglutinative' is the word) entirely of their own. They distinguish themselves by, on the one hand, great compactness of expression and, on the other, by a simply monstrous vocabulary. It is reckoned that the Hungarian has access to a vocabulary of well over one million words, of which he or she may use up to 250,000!

There are also striking variations in the compactness of the Indo-European languages (what French translators call the *coefficient de foisonnement*). Of course it is impossible to set norms; the outcome of any translation, in terms of both quality and length, depends on at least three factors: (1) the subject, (2) the originator, and (3) the translator. But in the case of the average non-technical text, and taking English (the most compact language) as a base, it can generally be said that, with the exception of some of the Nordic tongues, the foreign-language versions will be anything up to 25 per cent longer.

In his book *Word Play*[66], Peter Farb cites the number of *syllables* needed for the different language versions of the Gospel according to St Mark. Taking English with 29,000 syllables as his base, he arrives at 32,500 (+13%) for the Germanic languages, 36,500 (+26%) for French and the Slavic languages, and 40,200 (+39%) for the Romance languages.

Different languages also lend themselves in different ways to deformation to suit social purposes. Professor Ringel[35] says of the Austrians' use of German: "... we have accustomed ourselves to a language which consists of phrases and formulas, and represents perpetuation of the 'ceremonial of the Spanish court' in rhetoric... We have learned to speak without being obliged to express our feelings...".

At the other end of the scale - in the realms of verbal clarity - lie certain forms of intimate expression which are appropriate to some languages but not to others. The fact that, in earnest discussion, male Spaniards and Germans are prepared to address one another as *hombre* and *Mensch* respectively, whereas other Europeans do not, says something. These are expressions of mutual esteem, the language of love being something else again.

There are also some overused phrases which offer cameo insights into national temperaments. Without knowing it, the English upper classes use the word 'actually' to avoid appearing too direct: it prevents what follows from sounding confrontational. The Germans do much the same thing with the introductory phrase *'Im Grunde genommen'* but, in their case, the intention is to let the interlocutor understand that they have thought about it carefully, therefore there should be no grounds for offence.

All languages, of course, have their OK words which, I suspect, also tell us something about the people that use them, even if I'm not sure what. The ones that stick in my mind are:

English:	nice!
German:	toll!
French:	dingue!
Dutch:	gek!
Spanish:	vale!
Italian:	ciao!
Greek	rè!
Swedish:	skol!
Irish English:	now!

Significantly, with one exception, they are monosyllabic.

Although a lot of Europeans grunt like this - and use an infinitesimal fraction of the vocabulary available to them - there is enormous richness and variety in the European family of languages. My favourite is Spanish, but French and Italian come very close. Even German, far from resembling dogs barking, can sound beautiful with the right voice. And there's even a European language which doesn't use words: the whistling vocabulary of La Gomera in the Canary Isles.

A Babel of Voices

Stereotyped attitudes to the way a particular culture 'gives voice' to its language are often wide of the mark. Many Germans use sounds which, far from being guttural, as most Anglo-Saxons fondly believe, are wonderfully melodious. It is only comic-opera Italians who enounce their beautiful language in such a sing-song way. Real-life Italian can be surprisingly flat.

But there are indeed very distinctive *physical* differences in the way languages are spoken. The French, as an American puts it, put their tongues way back in the gargle position and their lips pouted way out, as if they're sucking grits through a hose. The Scots, some of them at any rate, use a soft 's' which comes out as an 'sh', as in 'S(h)ean Connery'. The Greeks speak from the front of the mouth and the Dutch even more so, so that their teeth and the top of the palate seem to get in the way. A lot of supposedly sing-song Italians sound decidedly gravelly. And there are Germans who talk from the chest or with a decidedly Maghrebian catch of the throat.

Elsewhere I have said that Spaniards speak as if they have pebbles in their mouths, but the sound is often more like running a finger over the teeth of a metal or plastic comb.

In many cases, the way people speak reflects their temperament and, by deduction, something of the elemental nature of their physical surroundings. I suspect it is true of the Dutch, exposed as they have been for many centuries to wind and water. Certainly the abrasiveness of Spanish speech echoes a harsh, arid yet very beautiful environment, just as the melodiousness of Italian reflects the pastoral nature of much of the country, particularly Tuscany and Umbria.

For reasons that so far escape me, the women of the race demonstrate even stronger idiosyncrasies, some of them unrelated to the way the language is spoken by males (see Chapter 10). English women may have well modulated voices but, for the sake of stress (or because of it?), tend to go over the top and end up in the squeaky zone. Spanish women sound impressively emphatic (modulatedly so if they are well groomed, penetratingly so if they are not), Greek women sound matter-of-fact. German women often have very low-pitched and melodious voices while, for me, far too many Belgian women (particularly the French speakers) have strangely fluting voices which sometimes make them sound, and even behave, like ventriloquists' dummies. As for French women, well, the size and variety of the country makes it impossible to say anything sensible at all.

Body Language and Bubbles of Space

An extension of the Halls' theories referred to in Chapter 7 is that we all, mostly without knowing it, work within a self-defined territory.

"In 'Low Context' northern European cultures," they say, "each person has around him an invisible *'bubble of space'* which expands and contracts depending on his relationship to others, his emotional state, his cultural background and the activity he is performing".

In the words of WH Auden:

Some thirty inches from my nose
The frontier of my Person goes,
And all the untilled air between
Is private *Pagus* or demesne
Stranger, unless with bedroom eyes
I beckon you to fraternize,
Beware of rudely crossing it:
I have no gun, but I can spit.

The Germans, who are particularly 'screen-dependent', reinforce the bubble by resorting, in some cases, to double doors in offices - and also by an almost aggressive protectiveness when defending their rights to tables and chairs in public restaurants. The Dutch, too, still tend to keep their office doors closed, much more so than their neighbours to the north and west.

The 'bubble of space' phenomenon is also evident in the behaviour of Germanics in two other situations. The first is the lift, or elevator, where most people look up, down or directly ahead - unless there's a pair of eyes there. The second is the queue, surprisingly a French invention which was taken over in the last century by the British, possibly encouraged by exaggerated ideas about the importance of time - something that Latins, if not necessarily the

French, treat much more casually. But I would not go so far as to suggest, as some people have done, that 'bubble of space' criteria prompt Germanic peoples to queue where Latins do not. Norwegians, whose impatience can often get the better of them, hate to stand in line and wait...

Generally the 'High Context' Latins, as well as many of the Slavs, like close contact and are much more sensorially involved with each other than the relatively contact-shy people of northern Europe (which does not prevent the average, autocratic Latin manager from keeping his office door firmly closed!). Hungary is also very much a tactile culture.

This proclivity is also shared by the Greeks, in the view of an American professor, W H McNeil[49] (see Greece, Chapter 4), who observes that "small Greek children maintain close physical intimacy - touching each other, holding hands, sitting or standing near one another - whereas American children", he adds, "establish a distinctly greater social distance".

Not just Americans, according to an Australian specialist[67] who also finds that the average European manages with a relatively small space: even Danes are happy with an 'intimate zone' of 20-30 centimeters compared with an Antipodean standard of *46* centimeters (sic).

Norwegians, by comparison, can be very jealous of their bubbles of space - to an extent that even astonished an American visitor. "One of the first things I noticed when I moved to Norway was that Norwegians need a lot of personal space", he remarked to an interviewer[6]. "Once I went into someone's office for an informal chat and sat down on the edge of his desk, some two meters from him. As I did that, I thought he would try to crawl out the window behind him! I had the distinct impression that I was on his territory. Also, I have found that if one reaches out to touch another during conversation, there will almost immediately be a recoil from the listener."

Maybe that's why Norwegians, whenever they get the chance, prefer life in the Great and Underpopulated Outdoors.

Cultural differences are also evident in body language responses to person-to-person situations. Body language, which is closely related to the 'bubbles of space' phenomenon, is every bit as important as language itself. In fact some experts maintain that over 85% of the impact of a spoken message is non-verbal, much of the balance coming from intonation and physical expression rather than the words themselves.

Body language is part of the national stereotype: the Gallic shrug of the French, the stiffness of the Germans (heel-clicking is now out of fashion), the shuffling hands palms upwards of the Italians, and so on. But it goes a lot further than that.

Consider a particularly complex example of ethnic body language (Gerald Brenan speaking[22], my italics): "One of the rituals to which the foreigner in Spain must adapt himself is the friendly stroll. Watch two men of the middle classes taking one. They *walk ten paces* and then, as the conversation warms up, *stop* and *confront one another*. Spaniards cannot converse, as the English do, with averted looks. They like to *meet one another's eyes* and *watch the effect* of what they are saying in one another's expressions."

I can attest to the fact that the Spanish really *do* conduct perambulatory conversations like this, some Italians too. The Spanish approach is measured, almost hieratic. The Italian approach is animated. The Germans, by comparison, turn towards one another in an uncoordinated manner as they walk, bumping into others on their way. The English prefer to advance steadfastly, hands in pockets, heads down, sneaking the occasional sidelong glance. The French maintain their progress, but turn from time to time to look at one another as they go. The Italians are often too excited, too busy gesticulating and eyeballing one another, to move forward at all.

Eye contact is a related phenomenon - something that is not easy for the shier type of Briton or Swede, whereas a Spaniard is capable of transfixing you with his stare *(la mirada fuerte)*. The Hungarian is, too, as Zsuzsanna Ardó points out[50]: "Ongoing eye contact, gazing openly and honestly into the other's eye, is considered imperative, especially for the more manipulative discourses and transactions." Which, of course, is exactly the kind of situation in which the Brits and the Swedes, contrary to type, look you in the eye...

No wonder the British are grateful for the eye-level advertising in the trains of the London Underground. It gives them something to look at absorbedly, rather than having to look at one another. And put British, French, German, Spanish and Italian people all together in the same lift and see how they respond individually!

352

Where the British, even the English, do make eye-contact is in responding to advances made by others in serious conversation. We - I say 'we' advisedly - find it difficult not to make supportive gestures when somebody else, British or foreign, is trying to make a point in earnest debate. We are involved to the point that we feel encouragement is deserved. It's only afterwards that we realise we have given moral support to a viewpoint that we don't really subscribe to. And then we back off. And, quite rightly, we're charged with hypocrisy.

There are also variations in acceptable degrees of intimacy in social activities, including sharing the facilities of a urinal. As a male I have noticed that it is possible to conduct an animated conversation in such circumstances with an Englishman, a Frenchman and occasionally a French-speaking Belgian, but rarely with anyone else.

How people use their hands can be particularly revealing. Maybe that's why the Dutch book on etiquette, *Hoe hoort het eigenlijk*, includes the following admonition (English version taken from William Shetter's book)[33]: "making violent gestures is still considered vulgar and talking with the hands is still impolite. Well-bred people gesture as little as possible, and if they do, it is done gracefully and harmoniously..."

"Greeting someone with a big hug is also something that isn't done", this stern Dutch authority continues. "In public we should use nothing more than words to communicate with. Words which normally are not amplified by gestures. We don't use gestures of revulsion, horror, satisfaction, or surprise. That is the way things should be done, and that is in keeping with our national temperament, because we don't wear our hearts on our sleeves." Yet the Dutch have invented a sign language of their own: for them, tapping the forehead with a raised (as opposed to lateral) index finger means they think the other person is clever, not stupid.

Sign languages are even more open to misinterpretation in the European south. The cheerful thumbs-up sign of a British tourist means something very different to a Sicilian female or even a Greek male. And a tug of the earlobe, which tells a Portuguese he's about to get something he'll appreciate (generally food), is also a nice way of telling a Spaniard he's a sponger, a Maltese he's sneaky, an Italian he's gay and a Greek he's going too far. And never put a raised hand, palm forward, anywhere near the face of a Greek: it will remind him of an old custom, *moutza*, which I won't bother to go into here.

Another rude gesture, of course, is the extension of the first and second finger, palm inwards, of the British (nothing to do with the Victory 'V'). A wonderful even if apocryphal story tells that this goes back to the Hundred Years' War. English longbowmen captured by the French in battle had the misfortune to have these two fingers cut off so that they could no longer practise their trade. On the next occasion, when lined up to do battle, the British extended their first and second fingers to signal to their enemies that they were able-bodied and that the French had better watch out.

There are, inevitably, infinite variations on such themes. Peter Millar, who writes for *The European*, quotes the following examples: "A right hand limp from the wrist and waved furiously while pouting is an instantly recognisable sign of a bad day or sympathy with someone else's, but only if you happen to be French. Similarly, a flick against the chin with index finger and thumb, followed by one or two fingers held horizontally across the arm is a perfectly clear signal that you are set on a bender but need a companion or two to split the cost of a vodka bottle; at least, it is perfectly clear in Moscow."

In his book *Euroscopie* Gérard Mermet [29] cites probably the most extreme example of geographic differentials in body language. The 'frontier' in this case is an Italian river, the Volturno, which flows east-west just north of Naples. The people living on the north bank of the river indicate disagreement by moving their heads from side to side, just as most of us Europeans do. But the people on the south bank move their heads *backwards* and make clucking noises with the tongue, a gesture also common to Greece, Bulgaria and part of Turkey. The difference is explained by the fact that, in classical times, the southern Italian seaboard up to the Volturno river was colonised by the Greeks.

Further light on this appropriately byzantine matter is cast by Peter Collett in his fascinating book *Foreign Bodies* [5]. Apart from the fact that, in his opinion, the 'frontier' runs more precisely between the Garigliano river on the Italian west coast and the Gargano peninsula on the Adriatic, he insists that the Bulgarians have their own exclusive way of indicating *agreement*: "To signal 'yes' the head is wobbled from shoulder to shoulder". He labels the Bulgarian yes/no combination the 'Roll-Toss' code, compared with the Greek/Turkish 'Dip-Toss' code and the 'Nod-Shake' code that most of the rest of us are accustomed to. He further points out that the richness of the Neapolitan gestural vocabulary also owes much to the ancient Greeks.

Another Italian trait, particularly noticeable among younger males of the Stallone type, is the military manner in which the chin is held in, almost like a stallion (no connection) at dressage. This of course helps the proud owner use his flashing dark eyes from under the brows to great effect and lends emphasis to his admirable chest.

This proud deportment is not untypical of Latin children of both sexes. It is astonishing to see the erect, mature bearing of little Italian and Spanish girls, not even in their teens, as they fuss and mother the smaller fry in their care. The kids from further north look positively childish by comparison.

Colours, Characters, Commercials

Not surprisingly, culture and climate have an influence on colour preferences - and not necessarily in the way one would expect.

Colours communicate cultures. The differences are most evident in illuminated signs. Where the Finns tend to use deep rich reds and blues, the Swedes use blues and whites, showing particular restraint and elegance. Dutch colour preferences can be surprisingly garish. The Italians are keen on bright primaries, the Germans on dark rich colours and, increasingly, acid drop greens, mauves and yellows. Paris is pure white light.

When I discussed such preferences with a Spanish architect he pointed out that, next to planning control, national colours might play a part. But the Irish, being a contrary kind of folk, don't like green because they associate it with bad luck!

Differing aesthetic judgments pop up in many aspects of life. A marine architect specialising in luxury cruise-liner interiors complains of the difficulty of reconciling German preference for dark colours with Italian insistence on white marble and British fondness for oak, brass and knick-knacks.

Cultural predispositions are also evident in preferences for typestyles, with the letters of some German typewriters still show-

Eight different ways of advertising the same thing

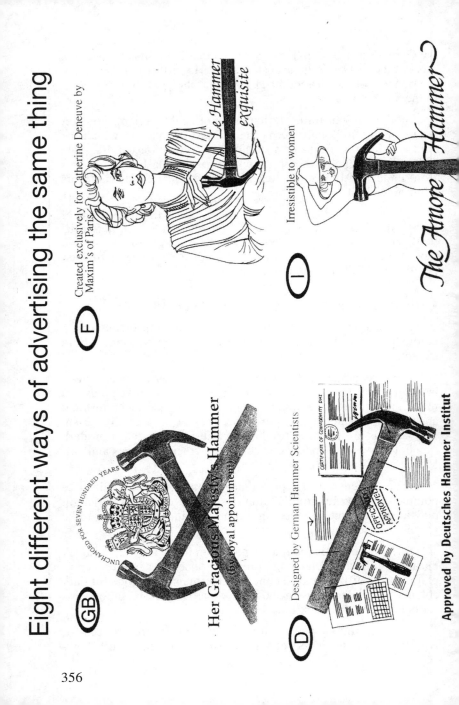

F Created exclusively for Catherine Deneuve by Maxim's of Paris

Le Hammer
exquisite

Irresistible to women

The Amore Hammer

GB UNCHANGED FOR SEVEN HUNDRED YEARS

Her Gracious Majesty's Hammer
(by royal appointment)

D Designed by German Hammer Scientists

CERTIFICATE OF CONFORMITY DHI

OFFICIALLY APPROVED

Approved by Deutsches Hammer Institut

356

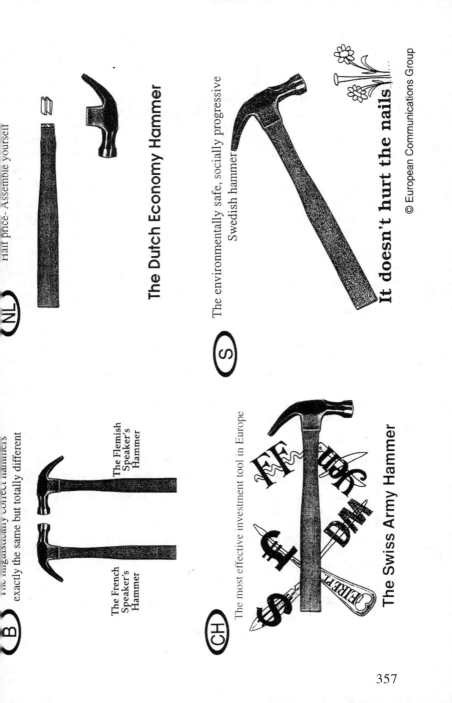

(NL) Half price- Assemble yourself

The Dutch Economy Hammer

(S) The environmentally safe, socially progressive Swedish hammer

It doesn't hurt the nails......

© European Communications Group

(B) The linguistically correct hammers exactly the same but totally different

The French Speaker's Hammer

The Flemish Speaker's Hammer

(CH) The most effective investment tool in Europe

The Swiss Army Hammer

357

ing a decidedly vertical cast. In printing, the Germanic peoples generally prefer typographical characters from the Helvetica family, while the British show a predilection for *Times* and Bodoni. The Swedes in particular go crazy over Baskerville and its relatives, and the Spanish used to adore **DAVIDA**. And the French, once again demonstrating the uneven taste that surfaces in various facets of their culture, are particularly fond of a display typeface the name of which escapes me, but which looks as if it were drawn with a worn-out paintbrush.

Equally, in the fetish-ridden field of symbols and logos, the Germans favour symmetric designs and the French asymmetric ones. Italian preferences go to the economical and classical, while British tastes tend towards the atmospheric and emotive.

On a related subject, the Germans have a monopoly in promotional flags which, instead of being 'landscape' format, are 'portrait', i.e. the main axis is parallel to the flagpole. I haven't had time to find out why this is, though I suspect the concept has its origins in mediaeval tradition.

Much of all of this is fashion. But there is still plenty of evidence, *pace* the advocates of global marketing, that an advertising appeal that has an *ah-hah* effect in one country may have a *ho-hum* effect in the country next door. Sometimes the intellectual content just doesn't travel, sometimes the message doesn't mesh with national mores. An example is Benetton's poster advertising, which met with disapproval in Britain, but went down a treat in France and Italy. Another is the H&M campaign (see page 327). It is also an open question whether the countries of Eastern Europe will appreciate the blatant appeals of the consumer society: there are signs already in the *neue Länder* of Germany that some people do not.

Some advertising approaches, humour and wordplay in particular, are inevitably condemned not to travel - yet it is surprising how many self-claimed international agencies still fall into the trap. Two languages lend themselves to the game of wordplay or puns, English and Dutch. Is this the language working on the national psyche or the national psyche working on the language? Both of course.

But all is not lost for global pundits. A study undertaken by Ipsos, the French research company, on behalf of the British CDP advertising agency, showed that some degree of unanimity can exist even among Europeans of different sociological types. A

358

cross-section of European consumers was shown 88 award-winning TV commercials from France, Germany, Italy, the Netherlands, Spain and the UK and asked to vote on their preferences. Everyone except the Germans - curiously enough in view of their normal affinity with things Spanish - opted for the Spanish commercial (the Germans went for a commercial for Levi's jeans which, admittedly, all the others put a close second). The Spanish commercial featured a dog leaving the house with its bowl and bone because its young master preferred to watch television. It seems all Europeans now like animals.

Incidentally but unsurprisingly, France's contributions were found to be so idiosyncratic that, to quote *EuroBusiness* magazine, "some of its most popular campaigns were detested elsewhere. On the other hand, the Dutch adored commercials from Britain and Germany, but disliked most advertisements of Latin origin."

Common Factors
and Divisions

"The first condition of understanding a foreign country is to smell it"   TS Eliot

"The fate of nations depends on the way they eat"   Brillat-Savarin

"The empire of the climate is the first, the most powerful, of all empires"   Montesquieu

"To travel you simply need to exist... It is only within us that landscapes become landscapes... The traveller is the journey"   Fernando Pessoa

"One of the small marvels of my first trip to Europe was the discovery that the world could be so full of variety, that there were so many different ways of doing essentially identical things, like eating and drinking and buying cinema tickets. It fascinated me that Europeans could at once be so alike - that they could be so universally bookish and cerebral, and drive small cars, and live in little houses in ancient towns, and love soccer, and be relatively unmaterialistic and law-abiding, and have chilly hotel rooms and cosy and inviting places to eat and drink - and yet be so endlessly, unpredictably different from each other as well. I loved the idea that you could never be sure of anything in Europe"
        Bill Bryson, *Neither Here Nor There*

Despite rearguard actions by Little Englanders and Non-Compliant Nordics, the Great Homogeniser is slowly and silently working his will on the countries and cultures of Europe.

With the help of the Single European Market, the political establishments of the member states and the support of many of the mass media, we can look forward to the maturation of a standardised European individual.

But that may be a couple of centuries off yet, even if we Europeans realise more and more that - if we delve back a bit and, more importantly, cast off our prejudices - we have a lot of *common factors* in our past (see box, page 303).

Unfortunately the *divisions* are still very evident. There are some substantive issues which will have a marked impact on the way individual racial or linguistic groups behave for a long time to come.

We Europeans share the fact that we are creatures of habit. The problem is that our habits are different and deep-seated. Try getting the French to take their holidays any other month than August, for example, or moving their lunch hour from one o'clock!

Different conceptions of time and space, discussed in the preceding chapter, have a lot to do with this. But other factors are equally important. Here they are, in alphabetical order and not in order of importance:

Bread: The Germans and British rarely eat bread with their main meals, the rest eat their main meals with bread. To the tourist the bread *par excellence* is the type the bereted and bicycling Frenchman of legend carries under his arm, the *baguette* and the *bâtard*. But they're a shade of their old self these days.

Some Europeans, particularly the Nordics, put sugar in their bread. Others put a lot of salt, some a lot of milk. The Danes, the Germans, the Dutch and the Portuguese also use rye. And bread comes in a giddymaking variety of shapes and sizes ranging from the loaves and rolls of northern Europe to the *ciabatte* and *grissini* of the Italians and the *colouri* of the Greeks.

Jan Morris believes the best bread comes from the Iberian peninsula: "One of the glories of Spain is her bread, which the Romans remarked upon a thousand years ago, and which is said to be so good because the corn is left to the last possible moment to ripen upon the stalk. It is the best bread I know, and its coarse, strong, springy substance epitomizes all that is admirable about Spanish simplicity."

Yes, but Greek bread and Portuguese bread are even better.

Coffee: No European seems to agree on what constitutes good coffee. The Germans roast it differently from the Belgians, who roast it differently from the French, who roast it differently from the Italians, not to mention the Greeks. My view is that Spanish coffee (done *espresso*, the Italian way) is best, but then they get their beans from South America. Presumably the Portuguese do as well, because their coffee is every bit as good. What the Dutch will make of this, I can't imagine, though it seems they're the ones who cure the beans that go into all these coffees in any case.

Mr McClumpha (cross my heart!) of Nestlé maintains, as reported in the *International Herald Tribune*, that "the Germans like their Nescafé roasted on the light side, the Italians on the heavy side, and the French like their breakfast coffee to have a bit of chicory in it." So there you are.

Northern Europe drinks the most coffee, southern Europe the least (despite the Italian habit of dropping in for a *ristretto* every five minutes). Top drinkers are the Finns (like other Nordics they tend to boil it), backrunners are the Portuguese.

Curtains: Some Europeans keep them open, others closed. The Swiss leave their curtains open so that they can show they have nothing to hide. The Dutch keep them open so that, despite their natural modesty, they can make the point that they have something to boast about, even if it is difficult to see inside because of the forest of potted plants on the windowsill. The Belgians keep their curtains closed - and often pull down the shutters as well - as a natural reaction to a history swarming with unwanted foreigners. A few keep them open but, as I have learned from rude experience, a fine cut-crystal chandelier seen from outside is no guarantee that there is any other furniture within.

Driving traditions: Automobiles encourage atavism in Europeans as much as in other nationalities. The British will continue to drive on the left as long as they can get away with it. The Belgians will still insist on their priority from the right, probably even after the law has changed. The Swedes drive with their headlights on, day or night (not that you can always tell the difference).

As for how people drive... the Latins, and here I include the French, will go on treating motorways like Formula 1 tracks with nervy, athletic demonstrations of their driving skills. Among the Latins, the Italians will continue to cross red lights at night and the Portuguese will persist in driving like suicidal idiots while showing the utmost respect for pedestrians in towns. Further north, the Swiss will continue to be aggressive, the Swedes will persist in charging when they see a pedestrian, the Luxemburgers will retain their single-car accident record, and the Germans will go on behaving like supercharged lemmings until their luck runs out.

There's also a difference in the generations. Young Europeans, regardless of nationality, drive upright and leaning slightly over the wheel, with their chins down. Old Europeans drive slumped down, with their chins up so that they can just see over the dashboard. This proves both that the Europeans are getting taller, also that the younger generation wants to make a better impression. They also drive better, although young female Europeans in VW Golfs can be dangerous.

Young Italians of both sexes can be dangerous too. The new Italian highway code, according to a report in the *International Herald Tribune*, "puts safety above romance by banning kissing, ear-nibbling, embracing and other amorous effusions at the steering wheel." It doesn't specify what they may or may not do when they're both in the back seat.

The 1994 Pan-European Motorist Report, published by Europcar Interrent International, plumbed the depths of driver attitudes and found among other things that, contrary to popular legend, European men are less critical of their women counterparts than the women are of the men. Female accolades, which seem well-founded, go to Irish and German men for aggressivity, to Danish men for impatience, Italian men for dangerous driving and French male drivers for rudeness.

The report found that Germany and Denmark came top in the use of unleaded petrol (80% and 73% of respondents respectively) and France, Spain and Italy lowest (34%, 27% and 18%), results that will not surprise those familiar with general environmental attitudes in these countries. Do-it-yourself maintenance skills are most highly developed in the UK, least developed in Greece and Spain. The

German and Spanish motorway systems were judged the worst in Europe, Germany essentially on traffic volumes and Spain on bad driving (the Spanish or the holidaymakers?). The UK also got special mention for its inevitable roadworks.

Nearly three-quarters of all respondents, out of a sample of over 11,000, felt that drivers should be banned from using car telephones when on the move, which only goes to show how sensible most Europeans are. And, in the words of the Europcar report, "the Swiss, more than any others, seem to experience car crime when on holiday in another country". Is this Swiss chauvinism or the belief that a car with a Swiss numberplate must inevitably contain more valuables than any other?

Speaking of numberplates, the only Europeans daft enough to spend money buying personalised numberplates for their gratification are the British and the Austrians. Others have the possibility, but are much too sensible...

Education: European education, like the media, is a great leveller, although one sometimes wonders whether up or down. The 'upside' is the consistency of the younger generation's attitudes towards broad issues such as democracy and the environment: the teaching profession is obviously saying much the same thing around Europe, both East and West, to great effect. The 'downside' is that educational standards are eroding and the end-product is increasingly illiterate. But this may not matter much since the jobs are not there in any case.

In terms of educational approach, some fundamental differences in teaching styles are apparent. Nordic education, which is generally participative, contrasts starkly with Belgian education which tends to be autocratic and French education which is still surprisingly militaristic. An American sociologist who has spent a lot of time studying European educational standards tells me that British secondary schools increasingly 'spoonfeed' their students, while German education is moving from a dogmatic style to a discussive one. Meanwhile an Italian educationalist assures me that teaching there, like everything else in Italian life, is opportunistic: students flatter teachers in order to get good marks and then laugh behind their backs.

A fundamental inconsistency that will hopefully be remedied in time is the intensity of instruction. 81 per cent of Germans are still in full-time education at the age of 18, as against 70 per cent of the French and only 36 per cent of the British. Even this last figure contains a 'hidden difference', since the Scottish educational system is more demanding than the English one. And the resources and infrastructures of the individual educational systems are likely to vary substantially for a long time to come.

Where there is so obviously a need for more levelling is in the teaching of 'European history', a subject alien to many teaching traditions and educational establishments. The British continue to ape Good King Knud (Canute to them) on this issue: when the matter of a national curriculum came up in the early-90s, the Ministry of Education blue-pencilled various references to Europe in the draft and replaced these with sections on British constitutional law...

First names: Don't think you can go to the births registrar, *maison communale* or whatever and give your offspring any name you want. Countries under the Napoleonic influence have traditionally insisted you stick to an approved list: France has now shrugged off the habit, but some other countries still have to follow suit.

In Germany parents are forbidden to choose names that are either ambiguous gender-wise or "endanger the wellbeing of the child". Not surprising when they have been known to propose names like *Bierstübl* ("watering hole"), *Störenfried* ("disturber of the peace") and *Whoopy*.

In Greece, just to be different, no name is given at all until the child is baptised. And, in Hungary, the first name is the second name and the second name the first!

Flowers: As a male guest, you can offer red roses to your host's wife if she's Italian, but emphatically not if she's German or French. Give a German hostess carnations or white lilies and she'll think you're trying to bury her - the same thing with chrysanthemums if, rather than German, she's French or Belgian (but not, incidentally, if she's an Australian mum). And please, if she's French, no carnations (they're bad luck), no hydrangeas (perish the thought) and absolutely no yellow flowers of any kind (yellow implies her husband has a mistress...). Whoever dreamed up the phrase 'the language of flowers' must have been dreaming.

Cultural inclinations also interfere with the way flowers are grown and displayed. A Frenchman, Dr Maurice Mercadier, observes that "the English garden is rich in a great variety of flowers chosen with taste and arranged with nonchalant elegance, whereas the French garden consists of a limited number of types of flowers, strictly selected and arranged in careful geometric patterns. The one is a harmony of colours, the other a harmony of lines. The first belongs above all to the world of the concrete, the other essentially to the world of the abstract". And the Italian garden...?

Food generally: Would need a book on its own - and a greater gourmet than your's truly. To save space and avoid an excursion into gastronomic dialectics, it might be better to sum things up by saying that the Italian-language instructions on a well-known *pasta* pack recommend five minutes' cooking time and the German instructions say ten.

Unfortunately, it's not as simple as that - least of all for those of our American friends who have a straightforward approach to the business of eating. We Europeans, quite a lot of us, don't stop at steak. We go on to the other parts of the animal, starting with the liver and kidneys and progressing via the lungs, the sweetbreads, the stomach lining ('tripe'), the brains and so on. Some of us even make sure that everything ends up in the form of a sausage, of which there is an endless variety. I even know of two nationalities that sometimes end up eating even the wretched animal's testicles if it has any: the Spanish (bull's balls) and the Icelanders (sheep's).

Culture clashes in the gastronomic area generally involve the British and the French, the former favouring a sterile approach to things like sausages and cheese where the latter love stuffing them with protein, microbes and the like. Behind the protagonists lies the usual European North/South divide (see below).

The use of salt in food, and not just bread, is also a great source of division. Some European countries like their butter salty, some not. The Belgians add salt to just about everything.

Milk can also be a source of division, some countries favouring plain, others pasteurised. The inhabitants of the British Isles are the only ones to persist in having milk delivered in glass bottles to their doorsteps. This system, idle tongues claim, gives bored suburban housewives the chance to jump back into bed, this time with the milkman. But it now seems, on evidence from Stoke-on-Trent, that milkmen are being enlisted by the local police to watch out for early-morning signs of break-ins and burglaries on the 'beat'.

The European Garden Gnome

Long before Walt Disney popularised Snow White and the Seven Dwarfs, we Europeans had been working hard on the 'garden gnome' concept. Once again we had the idea, only to have the Americans cash in on it (although, according to the Germans, the Poles are now getting more than their fair share of the action from counterfeit gnomes).

The story, it seems, starts in the copper mines of 6th century Cappadocia, a province of the Greek Empire in Anatolia (the Greek word for 'East', ie what is today Turkey). For some reason, mining became associated with vertically challenged people (remember the diamond mines in 'Snow White'?) and the idea caught on of immortalising them in 'life-size' sculptures.

These dwarfs or gnomes are then reputed to have found their way, over the centuries, to central Europe where they popped up in the salt mines of Poland. It was a short step from there to the gardens of Germany.

The biggest assembly of 20th century garden gnomes witnessed, with horror, by this writer is the proud property of a hotelkeeper in Freiburg, in the heart of the Black Forest.

Due to overcrowding in the garden, a detachment of them has found its way into the breakfast room.

Germany also has a garden gnome museum and shop, located at Rot am See in Baden-Württemberg. Proprietor Günter Griebel reports, in an interview with *The European* newspaper, that his best-selling lines now include 'Flasher Gnome', 'Stabbed Gnome' and 'Sexy Susie'. He also complains about the vast quantities of counterfeit gnomes that have been flooding the German market from Poland.

Though particularly favoured by Germans (though not all of them), the garden gnome has migrated to other European countries where it finds itself facing local competition from such things as miniature atomia (Belgium), Eiffel Towers (France), beer crates (Britain) and rubbish (Greece).

Germans who do not appreciate garden gnomes include a Hamburg couple who took the people next door to court for installing specimens of the species on their front lawn. This, said the plaintiffs, lowered the tone of the neighbourhood (for other examples of what Germans perceive as anti-social behaviour, see page 100).

The garden gnome originally found favour in Germany because people had had enough of garden cherubs. Chief perpetrator of the garden gnome cult, before Walt Disney, was Günter Griebel's great-grandfather (how's that for a mouthful!). Sensing that cherubs had had their day, he started replicating figures of old men in miner's outfits which progressively mutated into garden gnomes.

So there must be something in the 'mines in Cappadocia' story after all.

There are rumours, though, that the days of the milkbottle on the doorstep are numbered.

Different countries literally go bulimic over different types of food. Thanks to General de Gaulle, most people know that France boasts 246 types of cheese - or did at the time he said this in 1951 (they probably have more now). Germany has more than 200 types of bread and Italy has just as many types of *pasta*. And Portugal, not to be outdone, reputedly has 365 ways of cooking dried cod.

Curiously, the denizens of the frozen north are the greatest amateurs of icecream, summer and winter, with the Swedes outright winners in the European icecream stakes and the Spanish coming a poor last.

Despite these and other deviations, European eating habits can be expected to harmonise increasingly at the top (gourmet food) and bottom (fast food) ends of the scale. As the Norwegian manager of a fast food company said recently: "You will never get the French to eat like the Dutch but there is a convergence." He should know.

Our guess and hope is that the ethnic foods native to, and increasingly migrating from, the countries of southern and eastern Europe will both survive this process and continue to curry favour (oops!) with all nationalities.

And, if it's true that you are what you eat, then maybe this convergence of eating habits will foster greater European togetherness.

Geography: Independently of the North/South issue (see below), there are obvious geographical divergences which, global warming notwithstanding, will continue to set countries, and even regions, apart.

The vexed 'Irish question' is easier to understand when you know that there is a marked geographical and climatic change between Ulster and what used to be called, quaintly, 'the Free State'. The same is true of Spain: the people of the meseta are a very different lot from the people who live on the littoral. The Greeks are at least three different people: the mountain Greeks, the plains Greeks and the coastal Greeks (if not nearly 10 million different people, since every Greek is a law unto him or herself). Even the differences between the Flemish and the Walloons in Belgium cannot be explained by culture alone.

The availability and choice of building materials between one country and another also vary dramatically. Latitudes leave their mark in terms of the quality of the light which, in turn, influences colour preferences as they apply to the decoration of buildings - even the use of colours in illuminated signs, which tend to be pastel in the north, primary in the south. Colours also have a subliminal significance: black suggests prestige to the British and the sophisticated Spanish, mourning to other Mediterraneans.

Gullibilities: Every nationality has its weak spot. In France, according to James Randi, ex-magician, conjurer and escape-artist, 10 per cent of companies insist on a handwriting test before hiring anyone and another 40 per cent make some use of the practice. Some of the French even think it is possible to find a missing person by waving a pendulum over a map.

A recently enacted French law reveals the true extent of these bizarre practices, which included the use of astrologers, numerologists, clairvoyants and, last but by no means least, morphopsychologists (who judge your potential from your facial features.). One French company even interprets the car licence plates of prospective employees in favour of those those with 'magic numbers'.

Graphology and psychometric tests are also popular with many Belgian and German managers. There are German captains of industry who refuse to make strategic decisions until they have consulted their astrologers. Some Germans are devout believers in water divining - though not necessarily in a business context.

The English, James Randi suggests, have a fondness for communicating with the other world via a medium. While we're on the subject, he also points out that the Americans tend to believe in anything that is scientific and the Japanese believe in anything that is American.

Health and hygiene: Individual attitudes to health vary enormously, state health systems less so. Yet it is extraordinary how patient attitudes can shape the practices, if not the structure, of a country's medical profession (see Chapter 6).

Heights: Something else we can blame on the poor old nation state, with everyone doing their own thing when measuring heights above sea level. The trouble is that no one can agree on where sea level is.

The consequence is that the intrepid traveller drops a sudden 2.31 metres when crossing the line from Belgium into Germany. You can either blame it on the Germans, who curiously enough work from a benchmark established in Amsterdam, or on the Belgians who have a benchmark of their own. Travel on eastwards and you drop another 16 cm as the Saint Petersburg benchmark takes over or 27 cm if you happen to wander into Austria. Denmark lies 11 cm below the Amsterdam benchmark, Switzerland 8 cm. It must all mean something terribly significant, but I can't think what.

Holidays: The Germans look like outstripping us all in terms of the number of days they take off. Being the wealthiest of the Europeans, they can afford to do so, also because they are intelligent enough to stagger their holidays state-by-state, thus avoiding bringing the German economy to a halt.

Inevitably, in order to be different, the French (pardon, the Parisians) go away on August 1 or thereabouts and return on August 31 or thereabouts. They not only bring the economy to a halt, they clog the motorways. Of course, being French, they complain bitterly about this ridiculous state of affairs but do nothing about it. The rest of Europe tries to avoid travelling through France on those dates.

Other nationalities have their habits too. The British grill themselves pink on the Costa del Sol. The Dutch clog up the highways with their caravans. And, as the *Wall Street Journal Europe* adds, for the sake of its American readers, "the Americans are handing Italian lire or Greek drachmas to French waiters". *Vive la monnaie unique!*

Humour: Now there's a real cause of culture clash, as you will have discovered when trying to tell your favourite joke to a bunch of foreigners. As Theodore Zeldin points out in his book *The French*: "The reason why the humour of foreign countries is seen as odd is that one of the characteristics of humour is that it breaks the rules of reason, creating surprises by bringing together ideas that do not normally go together; and these juxtapositions seem more bizarre in foreign contexts". Amen.

Labels: Some status-conscious Continentals leave the labels on their Lalique glassware so that visitors are in no doubt: others don't. Most Belgians leave the bands on their cigars whereas no self-respecting Brit would dare be compromised in this way. Other, younger Continentals are now wearing the labels of their Saville Row suits on their sleeves. *Autre pays, autre mœurs.*

Since we're on the subject of clothes, let me add a couple of points. First, there is a strange wilfulness in measurement systems: what passes for a 'size 42' blouse in Germany or the Netherlands is a 'size 44' in France or Belgium and a 'size 46' in Italy. It goes without saying that it is a 'size 16' in Britain.

Second, the influence of climate in deciding what one wears is diminishing. National styles, however, are still idiosyncratic. Dutch and German males tend to wear their trousers short (I am *not* talking about Lederhosen), Italian males wear them tight.

Overall, dress fashions are changing fast. Witness the fervour with which Spanish women now go hatless to church. But why is it that women in the European south, from Portugal to Greece, still seem to be so set on polka dots? At least it makes a change from peasant black.

Language: Likely to be the most lasting difference yet. Not because everybody won't eventually use English as a *lingua franca*, but because, thank god, most of us will continue to start off life in our traditional mother-tongue.

To sense the cultural differences inherent in language, consider the instructions on the typical European food or drink package. The German, Dutch and Flemish instructions say the equivalent of "at least 'conservable' till end (month and year)": very authoritative technically. The French, Italian and Spanish instructions say "to be consumed preferably before end..." which is more of a value judgment or a philosophical statement than a technical definition. And the English instructions, epigrammatic and unbothered, simply say "best before end..."

Every language has its strengths and weaknesses as a communications tool. The French like to think French is lucid, but many foreigners would disagree. By comparison German is opaque but well suited to the more abstract streams of thought. Jan Morris describes Spanish as "one of the most subtly precise" of the European tongues. English could be precise but, because of the sheer enormity of the vocabulary, can be used with effect to conceal meaning.

There are linguistic fads, even snobberies, as well. The Dutch and Germans love affecting French, as do some British folk. The

French love importing Anglo-Saxon words into their vocabulary, despite anguished cries of the *Académie Française*. Some of the importations into both French and Belgian French are of very dubious origin - words like *standing* (status), *footing* (jogging), *talkie-walkie* (guess what), *aquaplanning* (designing marinas?), etc, etc.

But the biggest damage to the English language is probably done by the Belgian misuse of the possessive apostrophe: you really wonder what's going on when you see advertisements for the Brussel's English Nursery School (sic).

Legal systems: It should be self-evident that any society takes shape within a set of self-protecting customs or laws, whether they are common law or codified. Yet one of the outstanding issues facing the European Union is the harmonisation of its legal systems. The British and Irish have common law, the French have the Napoleonic Code (which they have generously shared with some of their neighbours), the Italians, Spaniards and Portuguese rely on Roman law, and the Germans, Austrians and Nordics have hybrid systems of their own. As long as these different systems subsist, gulfs will exist between member states too.

Gulfs in both judgments and speed of delivery. The average wait between issuing a writ and obtaining a court judgment varies from six months in Germany to 42 months in Italy, say London solicitors Davies Arnold Cooper.

Meanwhile, in Luxembourg, the jury system poses problems. "We're a small country where everybody knows one another", comments a local attorney. "It's impossible to have an impartial jury in Luxembourg."

Music: You have Anglo-Saxon pop (the dominant trend in Europe). You also have the lyrical French tradition where the emphasis is on the words as much as the music, the raucous Italian vocal approach, the heavy German technique with synthesised music and groups in harmony and, god help us, the German/Dutch/Flemish schmalzy ballad singers. They're apples and pears, but they all have a public - and they all come across better than the European anthem, the 'Ode to Joy', which sounds like barking dogs.

At the more serious end of the spectrum, while the Europeans generally make good music, different nationalities approach the issue in different ways.

The German approach is as disciplined and emphatic - think of von Karajan and the Berlin Philharmonic! - as it is in anything else. Ronald Pisarkiewicz, an American tuba player who deserted a German orchestra for the more congenial environment of the Vienna Philharmonic, said with great finality apropos Mahler, "I don't think he could have written the Third Symphony for a German orchestra". Elaborating, an American colleague William McElheney said, "the Vienna ideal corresponds to how I was trained at home: a warm, round, full, brass sound, almost fat, not playing accents overly hard". Sounds right for Vienna.

According to the Japanese conductor Seiji Ozawa, who should be about as objective as anyone, both orchestras and conductors reflect a country's character: "The English are very disciplined, clean, professional... When the Italians get hot, at La Scala, their Puccini is incomparable... In France, before they play, they talk about what they ate for lunch. When they're 'on', they're fantastic."

Daniel Barenboim echoes this last comment: "The French sensitivity to colour and their imagination is much greater than that of their colleagues in other countries. But they lack discipline." Where have we heard that before?

In similar vein, an eminent British choirmaster describes French singers' voices as "dark and grainy" and trains his altos to sing French works appropriately, rather than in the traditionally light English manner. Maybe the dark and grainy bit comes from what they ate for lunch.

Rather than share the Reverend Sydney Smith's view of heaven as eating *foie gras* to the sound of trumpets, I prefer the idea of eating *ratatouille* to the sound of French horns. That's dark and grainy.

North/South (agri-cultural): This comes close to superstition, but there is some evidence that every Western European country - Andorra, Luxembourg, Lichtenstein and Monaco excepted of course - has a North/South divide. In France, the Loire marks the point at which climate, cultures (including the agricultural variety) and eating and drinking habits tend to change. In Germany you have the Main, in Spain the central plateau, and so on.

Climatic change sometimes coincides with frontiers of both the ethnic and nation-state kind. There must be a subtle historical link between the two, perhaps determined by things like natural barriers, crop preferences, and so on. But this does not explain why different weather systems seem to apply at Belgium's frontiers with Germany and northern France - and even less why, at the time of writing this book, meteorologists are recording different rainfall rates on opposite sides of the linguistic border between Flanders and Wallonia.

On the agricultural fringe, maybe inspired by the 'back to nature' movement of Jean-Jacques Rousseau, the town-dwellers of northern Europe have compensated for the dreariness of backstreet existence by creating daytime mini-settlements on the urban outskirts. Variously known as *Schrebergarten* (Germany), *volkstuinen* (the Netherlands) or just plain *allotments* (Britain), they are something a southern European wouldn't be seen dead in - although you will probably find plenty of maghrebians and gipsies living round-the-clock in similar or worse conditions not far away.

North/South (socio-political): This is a divide that, at first sight, seems more rooted in folklore than in reality. Yet, in the early Middle Ages, what became France was emphatically divided between the people of the *langue d'oc*, the *hoc*-speakers, and those of the *langue d'oil*, the *hoc ille* or *oui*-speakers.

The folklore - or the reality? - lives on. George Mikes speaking: "Why do people always look down upon those who live to the immediate south of them? Germans look down upon the Swiss Germans; Swiss Germans look down upon Swiss Italians; Swiss Italians look down upon North Italians; North Italians upon South Italians; South Italians upon Sicilians; Sicilians upon Maltese; Maltese [and here we leave the confines of Europe] upon Arabs; Arabs upon black Africans. Luckily there are no Eskimos at the South Pole, because who could they look down on? They would be psychological cripples." I suppose the buck stops with the South Africans, where the whites look down on the blacks, and the blacks on the whites. Checkmate.

But there is a separate European 'intra-national' issue, which is in no way prejudice but a self-evident fact: many, if not most, European countries are traditionally powered from the North, but governed from the South.

Let's look at the evidence, especially striking the further south you go. In Greece, the industrial power is in Thessaloniki (North) but the bureaucrats are in Athens (South). Likewise Italy (Milan/ Rome), Spain (Oviedo-Barcelona/Madrid) and Portugal (Oporto/ Lisbon).

Some people would add Belgium (Antwerp/Brussels), the Netherlands (Amsterdam/Den Haag) and the United Kingdom (Scotland-the North/London). With greenfield industries replacing smokestack ones, the balance is shifting, but only slowly. The only major exception to the rule is France, a country that is still centralised enough not to count.

Oil/fat: Europe is divided between those that cook with olive oil (the Mediterranean nations) and those who prefer other vegetable oils, margarine or animal fats. The Danes, the Belgians and the Dutch are hot on margarine while the Irish, as well as the French north of the Loire, are still butter-oriented. The Germans, depending on income level, are torn between margarine and butter.

Old age: The Italians and Spanish respect old age for practical reasons (grandparents are the guardians of the children), the British make fun of it (look at the TV programmes), the Germans sentimentalise about it (look at the TV programmes) and the French pretend it doesn't exist.

Despite or maybe because of this diversity of viewpoints, the European Commission made 1993 the 'European Year of Older People and of Solidarity between Generations'. Not a moment too soon considering the birthrate.

Parliamentary styles: The British line up face-to-face and throw light-hearted insults at one another ('Her Majesty's Government' versus 'Her Majesty's Opposition', with the Speaker acting as umpire). It's a game, a good-humoured confrontation.

Continentals sit in a hemisphere, are earnest and polite, an act of consensus. The Italians fight.

Plumbing: The subject of lasting inter-European ribaldry, most of it inspired by the French who, as latterday high-technology plumbers, deserve better. Even so, they still specialise at the European level in ceramic holes-in-the-ground, often accompanied by a high-pressure flushing system called *La Trombe* that is guaranteed to carry you down the hole with everything else. I even found a public lavatory in France where the act of pulling the chain in one cubicle activated the system next door... on the occupant's head. But, though French plumbing is still decidedly idiosyncratic, these things are rare today.

What is not so rare is the two-tier pedestal, in Germany and the Netherlands, which enables the party concerned to look at things passed. A strange arrangement which puzzles anyone who doesn't happen to be German or Dutch. The Germans also used to have a bath outlet system, particularly popular in spa resorts, which resembled a Russian samovar but was much more difficult to use.

The British are essentially conservative on the plumbing front. Their heyday was the Nineteenth Century when, with surprisingly un-Victorian humour, they put cast-iron cisterns onto the European market with names like 'The Thunderer', 'The Deluge' and, as a particularly nasty dig at the French, 'The Waterloo'. 'The Crapper' was a different case, as it just happened that the boss was called Thomas Crapper.

Predictability: Something else than punctuality (see next paragraph). The French are unpredictable because they have a natural taste for confrontation, heightened by the need to show off. They love a good argument because it gives them a chance to show they are intellectually superior to the rest.

The English are unpredictable because they prefer to *avoid* confrontation. They *know* they are intellectually superior to the rest and, out of lip service to their reputation for fair play, prefer not to make things too obvious. Hence the charge of hypocrisy.

The Germans are unpredictable because they need to work things out for themselves. They withdraw into their all-German mental bunker, deliberate cautiously and methodically - but nobody else has the slightest idea what they are really thinking.

The Italians are unpredictable because they prefer to wait and see which way the wind is going to blow.

The Spanish are unpredictable because their self-esteem forbids them to be read like an open book.

So we do share a *common factor* here: unpredictability rather than predictability. But it comes in various flavours.

Punctuality: Back to the Fourth Dimension... Socially, Europeans tend to be more or less punctual with the exception of the British who prefer to turn up 15-30 minutes late, as they see it out of consideration for their hosts. More of this in other chapters.

Smells: TS Eliot travelled, if the quotation at the head of this chapter is anything to go by. Smell is the most evocative and associative of the senses and every country offers, sadly to a diminishing extent, its own olefactory 'label'. The ones that made the most powerful impression on me were the smoky smell of the typical Austrian *Gaststube* in the late-1940s, the aromatic disinfectants of the public washrooms of post-WWII Switzerland and, of course, that genial amalgam of garlic, Gauloises and warm human bodies in the Paris Metro.

Apart from their strictly evocative powers (what turns on an Italian when he goes abroad?), our senses of smell as Europeans of different nationalities may be on a convergent course. According to research undertaken by the University of California in 1990, the universally preferred aroma is banana. But national Number Ones range from aniseed for the French - and, rather surprisingly, the British and the Finns - to 'woodland fragrances' for the Germans and lemons for the Norwegians and Swedes. Antiseptic countries like antiseptic smells.

According to other research reported by Gérard Mermet in his book *Euroscopie* [29], the British also go for patchouli, the Germans prefer pine, the French and Italians like lavender, and the Spanish fall for fern of all things.

But, to return to the subject of association, Europe's only olefactory label shortly will be the hamburger-and-onion aroma wafting over the main squares of our cities. The Great Homogeniser moves on...

Telephones: Harmonisation just can't move fast enough in this field. At the time of writing, countries still have different charge rates, different access codes, even different dialling tones. When calling out from Sweden, you get a dialling tone not before but *after* the country code. And it's not all that long ago that what goes for an engaged tone anywhere else was used as a dialling tone in Norway.

At least the European Union is attempting to harmonise long-distance charges and has at last decided we should have the same international access code.

Voting systems: Like national constitutions, a current source of diversity. The Germans have a dual voting system - one vote for individual constituency MPs, another for the party of choice. The French have a two-round system for the presidency. The British are supposed to vote for a candidate at constituency level, but vote more for a national party: they also squabble about the merits of proportional representation. Everyone can vote for candidates for the European Parliament, but most don't. Time for a clean-up.

Water: A major and lasting source of division. The French drink it, the Irish live in it, the Dutch canalise it, the Germans brew beer with it, the Spanish and Italians irrigate with it, and the British and the Belgians pollute it. But more and more Europeans, including the British, now drink it out of bottles.

Wine/beer: There are many Europeans who cheerfully drink both, me included, but the choice of beverage can still be a source of division, as in Germany where the Rhinelanders prefer to be *thought* of as winedrinkers and the Bavarians as beerdrinkers.

Despite such regional differences, one can still depict Europe in beer/wine terms, with the beer-drinking countries to the north and the wine-drinkers to the south. But packaged tours, prosperity and the Single European Market are slowly changing all that. France, geographically a borderline case, still boasts the highest consumption of wine: nearly 75 litres per inhabitant in 1988 (a significant shortfall on the 1950 figure of 135 litres!).

The North/South divide is still occasionally evident in attitudes to getting drunk. Generally, the further north you go, the greater the chance of seeing someone inebriated in public. The British lager louts do a good job, the Swedes (even educated women, as I have witnessed) let themselves go from time to time, and the Finns simply get paralytic.

Women's voices: Surprising as it is for many people, German women probably come tops for the melodiousnesss of their voices, low-pitched and well modulated. The same applies in lesser degree to the Spanish and the Italians, who can be low-pitched too but positively raucous. The English tend, by comparison, to have high-pitched, even squeaky, voices (what a Danish journalist described as "voices that can cut cheese") and the French wobble around in between.

All of these are deeprooted *divisions* which may be with us as Brits, French, Germans, etc, for a long time to come. In fact most of us - as Brits, French, Germans, etc - hope they will survive because they are, individually, the things that make Europe so distinctive, so varied and so interesting.

At a signing session for the original edition of this book, I was charged with sexism by a young American woman for singling out the issue of female voices. Why, she asked, did I make these remarks about women only and not men? Because, I said, I had only noticed these differences on the distaff side. Also men's voices, though not all, tend to operate only in the lower register. Pressed for a reason for these differences, I ventured the possibility that, in some classes and communities, it is the women who are most exposed to social expectations of behaviour (expected by their menfolk of course) that result in these traits.

❦

So much for the *divisions*. Back to the *common factors,* the most important of which, after due thought, I have assembled in the box on page 303.

Today, though, the single most unifying factor must be the realisation that, despite what the nation states have tried to tell us, we Europeans have ultimately the same roots and much the same history, particularly in the first half of the present era, ie the years AD1 - AD1000 (when, it seems, some of us thought the world was going to end in any case).

Also most of us, if not all, claim to be increasingly convinced supporters of the great 'isms' of the second half of the Twentieth Century: consumerism and environmentalism in particular, even a degree of elitism.

We have all, *pace* the peoples of Eastern Europe, started to discover the value of a free enterprise society and to learn to live with its vices.

We all share of course the not-invented-here (NIH) complex and, in varying degrees, all contribute to the growth of the parallel economy by trying to avoid taxes (nb in Germany, tall people benefit from tax concessions).

We all have an ambivalent attitude toward our immigrant communities and as males we all tend to be macho, consciously or subconsciously, toward our womenfolk.

We all tend to drive too fast, the Germans fastest of all.

Also we all drive around with stickers in our back windows saying either 'baby on board' (*bébé à bord*, etc) or 'I ❤ whatever'.

We all know the lure of the lucky number. The Spanish are in the lead on *lotto* and the Portuguese outperform everyone on *bingo*. Miriad variations of these games of chance offer hope to all of Europe's milling masses.

We all worship at the altar of Association Football.

We all receive the same news and interpretation of world events thanks, currently, to the wire services and, shortly, to satellite TV as well.

Finally, we all display varying degrees of the *club* mentality - a word that has cropped up again and again in this book. After all, every European nation state was and still is, when all is said and done, a club. Yet, in our European way, each of us has a different idea of what constitutes a club.

For the British, particularly the English, a club is a device for drawing a firm line between classes (the Old Boys Club, the working man's club, etc), thus simplifying the business of living. For the *dirigiste* French, a club is a cosy conspiracy between the public and the private sectors, for the greater glory of *La France*. For the Swiss, the only club is the Swiss army.

For the Italians, a club is *La Famiglia*, something that enjoys a wide range of interpretations. For the Spanish, a club is *la familia*, something that means more or less literally the family, nuclear or extended. For the Germans a club is quite simply all Germans, *'wir sind ja unter uns'*. The German concept is the ultimate, all other interpretations (Dutch, Belgian, Danish, etc) lie somewhere in between.

At the core of all these clubs are the 'old boy' networks. These can be as virulent in the apparently democratic Netherlands ('The Mertens 200') and Finland ('The Sauna Society') as in Germany (the bankers), in France *(Les Grandes Ecoles)* and in Britain (the Old Boys Club).

So behind our apparent differences lurk a lot of similarities, some of them not very flattering. A dubious scenario, maybe, but it shows that we *do* have things in common. Within the Global Village, there is another smaller and increasingly homogeneous village called Europe.

A cynic's view of European organisation charts

BRITISH

FRENCH

SPANISH

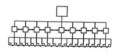

IRISH

PORTUGUESE

BELGIAN

SCANDINAVIAN

LUXEMBOURGER

GREEK

ITALIAN

SLAV

GERMAN

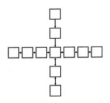

SWISS

DUTCH

AUSTRIAN

VATICAN

Where do we go from here?

"The triumph of culture is to overpower nationality"
Ralph Waldo Emerson

"In spite of all the differences between its various provinces, Europe is a whole shaped by a common past" Czeslaw Milosz

"Across the West, from Canada to Slovenia, the problem of what makes a nation is poking up its head. And the answer is plural everywhere. It lies in the curl of the rivers and mountain-ranges; in rituals of worship; in language and dialect; in shared beliefs about what kind of people "we" are; and in old, repeated biases in classrooms" The Economist

"If ever there is another war in Europe, it will come out of some damned silly thing in the Balkans" Bismarck, 1897

"Never forecast, especially about the future" Sam Goldwyn

"'Would you tell me, please, which way I ought to go from here?' 'That depends a good deal on where you want to get to,' said the Cat" Lewis Carroll

"Anyone who doesn't know where he's coming from and doesn't know where he's going to, doesn't know where he is"
Otto von Habsburg

"The plurality of cultures is irreducible" Sir Isaiah Berlin

"'We are absolutely at one," Mr Major said. "The Community needs to move together as 12"
The International Herald Tribune, October 1 1992

Mr Major was right. We absolutely have to be at one, even if we are 15 at the latest count - and are likely to be a lot more as the years go by.

The only future for Europe is Europe - bringing together this patchwork quilt of cultures and creating unity out of diversity. A tough enough challenge in its own right.

Yet we have come a long way since I started on the original version of this book, at the time that the barriers were coming down between east and west Europe. Now, as I write these lines, we have Maastricht behind us and, not content with that, are planning the 1996 European IGC (Inter-Governmental Conference). Both of these past events - the demise of the eastern empire and the Maastricht summit - posed the same question: "What kind of Europe do we want?"

The answers we got were strangely different. The opening up of eastern Europe in 1989, heady with a strange mixture of nationalism and environmentalism, was the spontaneous response of people emerging from a 40-years timewarp.

The Maastricht summit, muffled and muddled with macro-political compromises, was the weary response of nations plagued with their past histories and desperately looking for a future.

One was a grassroots phenomenon, the other the work of an inner cabal of nation state representatives. The first was the life and soul of democracy, the second a case of macropolitical haggling. *L'Europe des peuples* versus *l'Europe des gros chats*.

In the two years separating these two events - the collapse of the Berlin Wall and the Maastricht summit - the euphoria generated by developments in eastern Europe had completely evaporated. We are back to earth with a bang.

But the question remains: what kind of Europe do we want? And what kind of Europe can we reasonably expect?

Perhaps the best way to approach the issue is by accepting a basic fact. Not the fact that, as Chapter 3 tried to demonstrate, we are all more closely linked than the history books and the politicians would have us believe. That would be turning too many totems upside down.

I mean the fact that, until we produce 'Global Man' (an awesome thought), we will be dealing with human beings who need a more or less localised sense of identity to feel safe - the kind of identity, subtle and evolutionary, I have tried to pin down in the preceding pages.

How this sense of identity evolves depends on many factors, macro, micro and media. In an eastern Europe still emerging from nearly a half-century of superimposed ideologies and suppressed self-awareness, the disintoxication process has produced the nastier forms of nationalism and urgings of 'ethnic purity'. In western Europe, spurred on by the anti-war movements of the 60s and relative prosperity, it has led to an emotive pan-Europeanism and, as a countercurrent, regionalism with at least a taint of xenophobia.

As the Americans say, where you stand depends on where you sit. Or, put another way, which way you vote depends very much on where you happen to live. But that introduces another issue, the question of who got their first. I was stunned to hear a representative of the *Volgadeutsch* say on television: *Das Land gehört uns* ("the land belongs to us"). The Volga Germans may indeed feel justified in claiming that they have earned rights to such property, precisely because they have put more into the soil than their Russian counterparts, but they certainly weren't the first. Who was in fact first? I doubt if anybody knows.

Nationalism in its purest form is practised by the political right wing. In the face of unemployment and rising immigration rates, it is a useful outlet for an increasingly disgruntled electorate, particularly people in working class areas. But even such defensive, if not offensive, sentiment contains the germ of racism.

In some cases this starts with complaints about the other party's lifestyle or cooking smells. In other cases - for example anti-Semitism generally, but also Russian fear of the *Volgadeutsch,* Romanian dislike for the Germans of the Siebenburgen, and British resentment of the Indian immigrant community - it finds its origins in the suspicion that the others are smarter, better organised or work harder.

Nationalist and regionalist sentiments, frequently magnified by the media, cloak people's real intentions. This is just as true of the right-wing movements of western Europe. Even the Lega Nord has its racist side, though it purports to be pro-separatism and anti-Rome. Political Rome, not religious Rome, I hasten to add.

Regionalism and separatism in western Europe go hand-in-hand with conservation movements - conservation of nature, conservation of lifestyle, conservation of dying languages. Much of this thinking, when it is not naive, is wishful. It overlooks the fact that its promoters benefit from a living standard which they could never have achieved on their own. It also overlooks the fact that there are a lot of other people who, asked to prioritise lifestyle and living standards, would prefer to have decent living standards in the first place.

One other ingredient is present in some countries, particularly eastern Europe. Religion, where it hasn't gone out of fashion, can polarise nationalist instincts: the most striking examples of this are the Catholic church in Poland and Lithuania, and the Orthodox church in Greece and Russia.

Where the established church is in danger of losing its authority, other sects like the Church of Scientology and Transcendental Meditation are poised to fill the spiritual void left by communism - a creed that not only offered some intellectual appeal for a while but, through the Cold War, provided the other side with a mobilising force.

If pan-Europeanism on the one hand and regionalism on the other have been the main currents of western European opinion since 1945, another trend has emerged with time - a trend that may have helped encouraged eastern European calls for self-determination. This is the reemergence and legitimisation of national sentiment as a non-political phenomenon.

Max Jacobson, a retired Finnish ambassador, summed up this process in 1986 when he said: "We now know that the view of the world prevailing at the end of the Second World War was profoundly mistaken. Instead of an irresistible trend toward greater political unity, we have witnessed a continued fragmentation of political authority. The membership of the United Nations has tripled in forty years. Stalin's great empire has broken up into several warring factions."

"In the West, no one speaks of a United States of Europe. Nationalism has ceased to be a dirty word: no longer an aggressive or expansionist doctrine, it has become the last defence of peoples against the anonymous forces of integration that threaten their identity. Contrary to beliefs widely held at the end of the Second World War, ideologies have failed to maintain an enduring hold over peoples' loyalties: national interest has proved to be a stronger force than ideological commitment."

The speaker was inadvisedly dismissive of a 'United Nations of Europe' and treated ideology too lightly. Environmentalism is a very powerful ideology. But, for the rest, events have largely proved him right.

Of course the Finnish perspective is a special one, as is the Austrian. Both countries, which have only recently resolved their international alignments, are still resolving their national identities. Professor Ringel[35], talking of the mistrust many adults feel towards the attitudes and aspirations of Austrian youth, quotes the words of Friedrich Torberg: "In one respect at least these young people are better than their elders: when you say Austria, they know what you mean and when they identify themselves with this Austria, they know why". But self-awareness is one thing, insistence on self-determination another.

Nationalism is Suspect

It is my belief however that, at the end of the second millenium, nationalism in all its forms is suspect. It implies an arbitrary definition which, inevitably, favours some and disfavours others. And the ones caught in the middle - children of mixed parentage, Serbo-Croat for example (to give fresh meaning to this phrase) - can't win either way.

Ex-Yugoslavia is a particularly striking example of the arbitrary manner in which European frontiers have been drawn up. When Woodrow Wilson, Clémenceau and Lloyd George got together in a post-WWI conference room to clean up the Balkans mess ('Balkans', it seems, is the Turkish word for mountains), a kind soul gave them a map to help them with their deliberations. Unfortunately Lloyd George misread the map: he thought the green bits were the Christian enclaves and the brown bits were the Muslims, whereas the green bits were the valleys and the brown bits the mountains...

The cavalier treatment of European cultures is as bad as it ever was. Moreover, nationalist zeal that ignores the rights of minorities is a contradiction in itself. And the current rise of what political observers call ethnic populism - in erstwhile Yugoslavia, the ex-USSR and elsewhere - is a step backwards in time.

In its worst excesses it produces a government that lays claim to Kosovo province on the grounds that a historic battle (a Serbian defeat as it happens) took place there six hundred years ago. Or another that resorts to a 14th-century map to extend the territorial claims of Georgia to the detriment of its neighbours.

A letter published in *The Economist* at the time of the eastern European revolution gave expression to something that many have thought but few have said: "Nationalism is an emotive doctrine that commands vast support among any ethnic group that it purports to represent... If we are honest it must be admitted that a tyranny of a majority can be as bad as the tyranny of one man".

Of course, that assumes that there is a minority. The impulse to redraw the map of eastern Europe along ethnic lines is particularly sinister. The Baltic States want to exclude ethnic Russians, while the Serbs have been furthering their concept of a 'Greater Serbia' by a brutal process of occupation and eviction.

Appeals to the right to self-determination should always be suspect. The writer of a letter to the *International Herald Tribune,* appropriately an ex-citizen of Yugoslavia, went so far as to declare that "we have had enough of the sacrosanct principle of self-determination of peoples". How many crimes have been committed in its name?

Separatist sentiments at the regional level are not much better than the nationalism of the nation state. When the people of South Tyrol claimed a 4,000 year-old corpse recovered from an Alpine glacier as 'one of their own' - thereby trumping competitive claims from the Austrian and Italian governments - the only winners were the gods who must have laughed their heads off.

Anti-semitism is a close relative of separatism. It is disturbing to see it manifest itself in the current eastern European context of a new generation's demands for democracy and respect of the environment. After all, the Jewish community is part of the environment even if, in the case of Poland for example, there are very few Jews left. The Polish problem may be partly explained by the historical role of the Jewish community in the Polish economy but, even so, the strength of feeling is perplexing.

A long time ago, in the reign of Queen Victoria, Lord Acton expressed an opinion that is just as valid today: "A state which is incompetent to satisfy different races condemns itself; a state which labours to neutralise, to absorb or to expel them is destitute of the chief basis of self-government." Antonis Tritsis, the mayor of Athens, put it more bluntly when he said "the Europe of the States doesn't work any more".

A Europe of the Regions?

So where should Europe's policymakers be looking for inspiration? Eminent men such as Victor Hugo, Richard Cobden and Richard Coudenhove-Kalergi, an Austrian count whose name betrays his pan-European origins, all championed the concept of European union long before the Treaty of Rome.

Specifically, are there any existing European political models which could serve as a guide? As a sop to aspirations to self-determination, Spain hastily established 17 autonomous regions - but it was little more than a sop. Belgium, for the wrong reasons, created a federalist state while Switzerland boasts a cantonal structure that has withstood the test of time. But my vote would go to the German system.

Perhaps the architects of the New Europe should go back to the drawing board after all. The idea of a Europe of the Regions has been bandied about for a long time. In 1941 an Austrian, Leopold Kohr, published an essay entitled "Disunion Now: A Plea for a Society Based Upon Small Autonomous Units". He argued that Switzerland had thrived, not because of a national sense of identity but because of the smallness of its administrative units, the cantons.

Mike Zwerin, one of the most cosmopolitan of journalists, published a book in 1976 under the title of "A case for the Balkanisation of practically everyone". And a number of other eminent people have taken up the idea of a Europe of the Regions since WWII. These include Richard Mayne, Professor Northcote Parkinson of 'Parkinson's Law' fame, and A H Heineken of the Dutch brewing dynasty.

In proposing a redivision of the European landmass into units of no more than 10 million inhabitants, dubbed 'the United States of Europe', Heineken sees this as a way of both reviving the traditional cultures and extricating ourselves from the present political mess: "We have begun to realize that a state of thirty to fifty million people is hopelessly incompetent, with a deadening effect on provincial culture and a drearily standardizing effect on social life.

Heineken's
'United States of Europe'

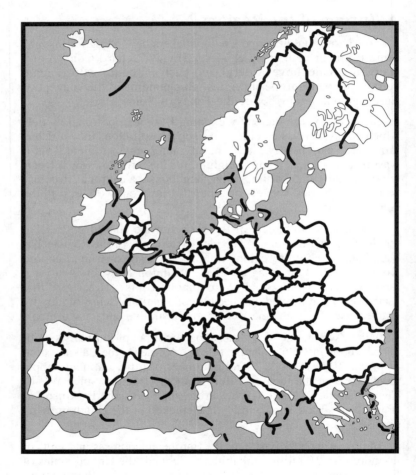

For all purposes of internal administration we want a government which is accessible and economical, administering an area which is culturally unified and reasonably small."

The redivision proposed by Heineken and his associates (see map opposite) respects administrative boundaries currently effective within the existing nation states. It could, they concede, be improved on. "Obviously the plan is far from ideal and does not offer solutions to every problem, but it can be adopted and adjusted according to actuality. Let us in this context not forget that our present nations are also artificial and, in many cases, quite recent inventions. Government and cultural elites may have made us think otherwise, but let us remember that their line of thinking is embedded in (accepted) chauvinistic nationalism." Amen to that!

If the Europe of the Regions concept seemed to make sense years ago, in the heyday of western European separatism, it certainly has merit today. Separatist movements in western Europe are motivated as much by administrative inefficiencies as by tribal instincts. Italy's Lega Nord, which argues for a Europe based on loosely federated regions, is largely a reaction to the politics of patronage - a sentiment shared in countries as far apart as the ex-USSR and Spain, one of whose movements Alan Whicker of BBC fame immortalised as the 'Catalonian separationists'...

The Lega Nord is certainly more effective than some of the longer-standing separatist causes, hangovers from the late-60s, which degenerated into vague and sentimental hankerings after a long-lost past. They implied a conceptual, essentially artificial, attempt to go back to one's roots. Yet the fabric of traditions is unravelling fast (to have known the Europe of the 1950s is enough to persuade one of this) and you cannot reconstitute it artificially.

Folklore is indeed a poor and only partially representative substitute and the intellectuals' approach to recreating a lifestyle that has been lost is even worse. Not much good is done, either, by wishing to revive languages that are virtually dead and which serve no other purpose than to make a political point.

This Europe of the Regions should not just be an outlet for separatism in its various guises. In his book *The French*[1] Theodore Zeldin comments that French regionalists "do a very delicate balancing act between seeking economic revitalization and developing their own brand of chauvinism". In that respect, they are like most other regionalists.

The two objectives of separatism and economic viability are not entirely compatible, even if they are not mutually exclusive. It is questionable how far, regionally, you can have your cake and eat it. Below a size that is difficult to define, depending on natural resources and other factors, independence may not make economic or administrative sense.

Even the relatively wealthy and, in some cases, heavily subsidised German *Länder* are under pressure to accept a redefinition of their borders in order to create larger and more viable units. In the words of the German constitution, federal territory should be reorganised "to create *Länder* which by their size and capacity are able to fulfil the functions incumbent upon them". Where does this kind of thinking leave places like Wales, Corsica and FYROM?

The potential for such putative states largely depends on the rate at which the Old Continent develops an open trading system. Denmark and even little Luxembourg have managed to do very well, thank you, in the Single Market. And Switzerland, a country of independent cantons, has done pretty well too. But separatists, like environmentalists, should be aware that realisation of their ideals brings its responsibilities as well as its opportunities.

EU member state governments are well enough aware of the power of the separatist argument - at least as a vote-getting device - and are attempting to dodge and defuse the issue in a number of ways. At the Union level, they have even paid lip service to the cause by creating an advisory body called a Committee of Regions. But the nation states are not going to give way that easily.

As an admirer of the 'Open Europe' of the early Middle Ages, I have a lot of sympathy with the regional approach. But, even with a Europe of Fifteen, it needs the kind of massaging, in terms of administrative size and organisation, that many regions might find inacceptable. There is no commonality in the way the existing counties, *départements, Länder*, etc are defined and run. With the prospect of further enlargement of an already large European Union, the establishment of a coherent and cohesive administrative structure at regional level may well be an unattainable ideal.

Moreover, there is no point in breaking Europe down into its real constituent parts - many of them rich, many poor - unless the acceptance of a common future and a commitment to solidarity are part of the process. Separatism cloaking an abandonment of moral and financial responsibility for our fellow-Europeans is

"Europe's major advantage is that almost all its people are well educated. Europe is the only region in which one country, Germany, is a world leader in production and trade, and another, the republics of the former Soviet Union, have in the aggregate been a leader in high science and the world's largest producer of natural resources. Add the design flair of Italy and France to a world-class London capital market efficiently directing funds to Europe's most productive areas, and something unmatcheable could be created.

Those who guard the entrances to the world's largest economy have always written the rules of world trade. The 21st century will be no different. The Europeans will write the rules for world trade.

But Europe will first have to overcome two problems. The economies of Western Europe have to really integrate, and that integration has to be quickly extended to Central and Eastern Europe. And the ex-communist economies of the region have to become successful market economies. Neither is an easy task. Both will require European citizens to make sacrifices today to create an economic juggernaut tomorrow: Western Europe must provide the large amounts of economic aid needed to get capitalism started in Central and Eastern Europe; both West and East must put aside ancient border and ethnic rivalries.

Europeans know that they must and will change. Western Europe is already making the changes necessary to create the world's largest integrated market, and Central and Eastern Europe are already moving from communism to capitalism.

For these reasons, future historians are likely to record that the 21st century belongs to the House of Europe."

Lester C Thurow, Dean of the Sloan School of Management, Massachusetts Institute of Technology, in *The Washington Post,* April 1992.

unacceptable. In the words of Magnus Wijkman, a director of the EFTA secretariat: "Community enrichment through diversity; protection of diversity through community. Popular respect for minority rights and their constitutional protection are two pillars of European society... To be European is to belong to a community of foreigners."

The present system at least has the advantage that it subjects the member states of the Union to peer pressure, as was evident in Maastricht. Would this work in a commonwealth of literally hundreds of regions? And is there any evidence that the nation states would accept such an act of disenfranchisement?

The monolithic concept of the European Union, as it is conceived at present, seems untenable in the face of further enlargement. The most imminent solution, to get things moving again, is a 'multi-speed' Europe.

Another is the creation of satellite groupings with common institutions. For example the Nordic nations, who are talking of a Baltic economic area reminiscent of the Hanseatic League and are already planning a Council of the Baltic Sea States that will bring together Denmark, Estonia, Finland, Germany, Latvia, Lithuania, Norway, Poland, Russia and Sweden. Or the countries of central Europe who hanker after the old *Mitteleuropa* ideal. Or maybe even an association between Turkey (which certainly deserves inclusion in a Greater Europe, if only in recognition of the contribution made by its immigrant workers) and its Turkic neighbours in the ex-USSR.

Whatever formula wins the day, the regions are sure to feature more prominently on the future map of Europe. One group of regions that certainly stand to gain are the Regio's, those unfortunate areas located along the frontiers of the old nation states. No one can deny the legitimate claims of communities that just happened to come close to a dotted line drawn, often arbitrarily, on a map. Traditionally, these frontier areas have suffered from underdevelopment, low land and property prices, and disruption through defence measures. They may be the best nature reserves in Europe - as evidenced by a recent book, *De Groene Grens/Die Grüne Grenze*, which describes the no-man's-land between the Netherlands and Germany - but the development and integration of their infrastructures cries out for attention.

The Diktat of the Dotted Line

Maybe we will learn something from the turn of events in eastern Europe, including a lesson that many European observers have overlooked, namely that you can't turn your back on the past. It needs an American, Robert Littell, to make the point: "We should shed a tear in recognition of the millions of our best and our brightest who - through the Bolshevik Revolution, through the 1920s and '30s in the Soviet Union when it was still possible to believe in a brave new world, through the Spanish Civil War, through the resistance to Hitler - sacrificed their lives for an idea..."

"We should worry that the demise of communism has created a vacuum in the realm of ideas by which men live. Call it what you will: communism or Soviet-style socialism, by its mere existence had a profound impact on the capitalist world over the years... Now that the alternative is being buried in a mass and unmarked grave, what will keep the capitalists of the world honest?"

The Third Way, the Nordic approach to the concept of a society caring enough to dig deep into its collective pocket, is now challenged by economic reality. Also recent events suggest that the desire for better material standards is stronger than any ideology, however socially sensible this may be. But isn't it possible that some cultures conceal within them a 'ceiling' of prosperity, beyond which considerations of quality of life will outweigh living standards? Taxation may hasten the process.

There are signs of this in some of the more genteely gentrified areas of England, particularly the southeast. It may also be there in some of the remoter (and certainly less genteel, but more genuine) areas of France and Spain, also on the Celtic Fringe. Maybe, despite their loss of interest in the Third Way, the Swedes sense it too.

As the breeding ground of capitalism, the European nation state brought great glory to many parts of the continent, enriching culturally through a process of patronage and influence, and accelerating the material improvement of its peoples. Yet in the process it generated sentiments that, by any judgment, will sooner or later lose their validity. One of these is the concept of sovereignty (ie "it's none of your bloody business"), which will hopefully be dropped from the agenda in a new world order. Maybe something that draws on the inspiration of the Nordic Third Way will, some day, take its place.

Another American, god bless 'em, this time Stuart Miller in his book *Painted in Blood* [23] - explaining the differences between Americans and Europeans (yes, he speaks in terms of a European culture!) - says the following: "For us, nurture is everything and nature nothing, and in our giving opportunities to masses of people of many races to become successful Americans in similar ways, we have gone a long way toward proving that race is vastly less important than many people used to think. We would go further and say that it is inconsequential. And perhaps that is so, for all practical purposes of social functioning. But Europeans are utterly at odds with such a view".

Race *per se* is no longer a real issue for Europeans either - except for those who invoke it spuriously, like the Serbs and the Greeks. We have now reached the point where we rationalise such matters in terms of frontiers - fondly imagining that these frontiers define a reality which, more often than not, they do not! Ultimately, we have to question the value of such frontiers, other than as a means of bringing continents down to a manageable size administratively.

Europe has suffered enough from the 'diktat of the dotted line'. Samuel Butler spoke of grammatical definitions as "the enclosing of the wilderness of an idea within a wall of words". Geographical definitions - frontiers and borders - are in the same class. European frontiers show little respect for the historical reality of race and culture. The best thing we can do is grow out of them.

In the words of Xabier Arzallus, the leader of as distinctive and determined a lobby as the Basque Nationalist Party (and no one in Europe could be more distinctive genetically or more determined politically than the Basques): "Why should we found a new state in the new Europe? The states will whither away".

Let me quote the advice offered by a Bosnian mother to her daughter, as expressed in a letter to the *International Herald Tribune* in 1992 (a genuinely cross-cultural message since the mother's name was Vanita Singh Mukerji and she was living at the time in Tashkent, Uzbekistan): "I will teach her honestly and teach her that a person is a person, regardless of where he was born or where he lives. For me, the world was always without borders. That is why this creation of a tribal community on the threshold of the 21st century is incomprehensible to me."

Let's look ahead

That was a mother speaking. But what do the younger generations think? Since writing the first version of this book, I have had a lot of enthusiastic reactions from people of my own generation, often with memories of WWII and related events engraved in their minds. But the most solid endorsement has come from people who are just now embarking on life, in particular those who have had the good fortune to graduate through college or university.

I have also had the great opportunity since then to talk to more than 5,000 secondary school students, university graduates and young professional people in Belgium, the Netherlands, France, the UK, Sweden, Finland, Austria and Hungary. Much of what they have told me throws an intriguing light on the aspirations of young Europeans, with many opinions shared by many nationalities. What I have heard is largely reflected in the findings of the MTV Europe/Yankelovich Young Adult Europe MONITOR™ study (see following pages).

Despite all the patent mistakes made by their elders and despite the difficult times we are living through, I think young people still identify with the European ideal - even though, as the study shows, they respond in different ways to the formalised concept of a 'United Europe'. To some extent they espouse the enthusiasms and inhibitions of their elders, but they also project dissatisfaction with their national political heritage on the European institutions.

Many young people feel more European because the American Dream no longer satisfies them. They relate to Europe through fashion, pop music and films rather than through high-minded initiatives from the Commission of the European Union. The German news magazine *Focus* even dubbed this new generation with the title of 'yeppy', meaning 'young, European and proud of it'...

Speaking for these and other generations, if I may presume to do so - and if we can grow out of our personal cultural 'fixes' - there is every reason to think that the good things about Europe, its languages, its traditions, its gastronomies and its landscapes will survive and prosper to the benefit of everyone.

So let us preserve and cherish the essence of Europe, a heady blend that transcends frontiers and never ceases to surprise and

The View of the Young

If anyone has the right to determine the future of Europe it is Europe's young people. What they think has been the subject of a lot of speculation, including the often contradictory findings of research studies sponsored by pan-European marketing and advertising groups.

In Autumn 1994 an international market research organisation, Yankelovich Partners Inc, undertook a substantive and detailed study into the attitudes and priorities of over 3,000 young Europeans in the 16-24 and 25-34 age groups (the MTV Europe/Yankelovich Young Adult Europe MONITOR ™).

Individual interviews, of up to one hour in length, were conducted with 500 respondents in each of seven European countries - the United Kingdom, Germany, France, Italy, Spain, Belgium and The Netherlands - plus a further 250 interviews in Sweden. Responses were analysed by nationality, age group (16-24 and 25-34) and gender. Many of the findings of the Yankelovich study match the comments I have been receiving from contacts with young audiences.

The single most disturbing conclusion, with very few contacts dissenting, has been the lack of confidence in, or credibility of, the political classes of most European countries. Even more serious is the total disinterest in party political issues generally.

On this point, the findings of the Yankelovich study are clear. Of the total of 3,278 respondents only 645, or 20%, claimed to be "interested in politics". The highest percentages were in the Netherlands and Sweden (28% and 24% respectively), the lowest the UK (13%) and Belgium (7%). Not surprisingly, the females of all nationalities expressed less interest than the males.

Religion, evidently, does not provide an alternative to politics for European youth. Only 14% of the total sample described themselves as "religious", the highest percentages being Italy and the Netherlands (20% each), the lowest the UK,

Germany (both 10%) and, again not surprisingly, Sweden (4%). Females, in this case, were markedly more enthusiastic than males, but there is little difference between the age groups.

To a separate question, "How important would you say religion is in your life?", 81% of Swedes, 73% of Germans and 71% of the British said "not very important" with Italy, at 41%, at the other end of the scale.

The environment continues to attract attention from young people, the most concerned still being the Germans (69% "very concerned") and the Spanish (65%), and the least concerned the British and the French (38% and 37% respectively). Yet there appears to be a nuancing of environmentalist concerns in the younger (16-24) age group: only 35% felt "very concerned" compared with 41% of the older age group. This difference applies, in varying degrees, in all the countries sampled.

Asked whether or not they agreed with the statement that "you used to be able to believe what people in authority told you, but that's not as true as it was", 84% of British respondents concurred, together with 83% of the Dutch and 80% of the Belgians. The Germans, at 66%, were the ones who agreed least.

But, even if they have less respect for authority than they used to, British youth is still relatively law-abiding. Asked about the notion of "rebelling against authority", only 32% of them found this acceptable, compared with 85% of the Germans, and 72% each of the Swedes and the Dutch. It seems that the socially docile British are as wary of revolutionary impulses as ever they were...

Yet, individually, the British are ready to fight it out with the best. Asked whether they agreed with the statement "I'm one of the leaders in my group of friends", 51% of the British answered in the affirmative. The next were the Dutch and the Italians (42% each) and the least sure were the non-competitive Spanish, with 27%.

Cultural differences showed up again in responses to some of the major issues of the day. On sexual harassment, 53% of the Spanish, 49% of the British and 48% of the Italians expressed themselves "very concerned", compared with 'lows' of 20% for France and 19% for Sweden. The figure for France may owe something to French women's appreciation of attention from males, while the Swedish response may reflect the orderly nature of Swedish society as well as the level of emancipation. Both countries showed the same, and by far the smallest, gender differential of all the eight nations sampled: only 22% of women declared themselves "very concerned" and 17% of men.

On discrimination against women, two Latin countries showed markedly divergent views: 49% of Spaniards declared themselves "very concerned", but only 21% of Italians. This gives the lie to the idea that Spain is a 'macho' country.

Another myth, 'the promiscuous Swede', is also challenged by the Yankelovich findings. When questioned whether they thought affairs outside of marriage were acceptable in today's society, 84% of Swedes - the highest percentage of all eight countries - said 'no'. 75% of Dutch respondents, also considered a permissive society by many foreigners, equally found extramarital affairs "not acceptable". The most permissive on this issue in fact turned out to be the French and the Germans (52% and 48% "not acceptable").

Asked to rate their degree of personal happiness, Dutch young people came out well on top, with 62% of them rating themselves "very happy". Following them came the Swedes (45%) and the Belgians (41%). The least happy were the Italians (only 11% "very happy"), the Spanish (17%) and the Germans (19%). With the exception of the British, the Germans and the Swedes, the younger 16-24 age group were markedly happier than their elders. There were also significant gender differences in the case of two countries: Italy, where the men were much happier than women the (34% against 19%), and Sweden where the women were much happier than the men (68% against 45%).

402

French youngsters in the 16-24 age group are the most pessimistic of European youth. Asked whether they thought their generation would be better off than their parents' generation, only 18% answered "yes". The most optimistic of this age group were the Italians and the Spanish (65% each).

Asked whether they were in favour of a United Europe, youthful attitudes tended to mirror those of the population at large: 90% of Italians pronounced themselves in favour, compared with 76% of Spaniards, 69% of Germans, 62% each of the French and Dutch, 59% of the Belgians, and only 43% of the British and 41% of the Swedes. Asked if they thought people in different countries were becoming more alike, 52% of the sample agreed, the most emphatic being the Italians (67% agreeing) and the least certain the Germans (38%).

So Europeans still agree to differ!

delight. The magic of a hot August afternoon at Foz do Porto with the foghorns booming as the sea mist rolls up the gorge of the Douro. The incongruously autumnal colours of a Swedish spring in the Stockholm archipelago, with the gulls crying at midnight. The symphony of light, laden with wild flowers, of northern Greece. The vibrance of a village street in Ireland's County Clare busy with old men and jackdaws. The blue-green sky of a Spanish dawn in Valencia, with the wind rising gently off the Mediterranean. The impeccably English sight of Lincoln cathedral rising out of a gold and silver-flecked haze. The balmy mist-laden, gold-flecked air of a late summer's day in the woodlands of Franconia. And the brilliance and gaiety of the Italian lakes as you sweep down from the Alps.

Whatever the future holds for us Europeans, it deserves to be a happy one. But the way we interpret a happy ending depends on our culture. For, here again, we beg to differ: our fairy tales end in different ways.

If we're English, we say: "and lived happily ever after." If we're French, we say: "and lived happily ever after and had lots of children." If we're Spanish, we say: "and lived happily ever after and ate partridges." If we're German, we say: "and if they have not yet died they are still living." And if we're Greek, we say: "and they lived happily - and we lived better!'."

Which only goes to show that the English are pragmatic and sentimental, the French are still intellectually expansionist, the Spanish are down-to-earth, the Germans are as mystical as ever, and the Greeks know better than anyone else...

BIBLIOGRAPHY

1   Zeldin, Theodore. *The French*. London: Collins Harvill, 1988.

2   Lewis, Flora. *Europe - A Tapestry of Nations*. New York: Simon & Schuster, 1987.

3   Marsh, David. *The Germans*. London: Century Hutchinson, 1989.

4   Ardagh, John. *Germany and the Germans*. London: Penguin, 1988.

5   Collett, Peter. *Foreign Bodies*. London, Simon & Schuster, 1993.

6   Habert, Kjell and Lillebø, Arild. *Made in Norway - Norwegians as others see them*. Oslo: ALICOM Publishing, 1992.

7   Borrow, George. *The Bible in Spain*. London: Century Hutchinson, 1985.

8   de Madariaga, Salvador. *Spain*. London: Jonathan Cape, 1942.

9   Barzini, Luigi. *The Europeans*. London: Penguin, 1983.

10 St George, Andrew. *The Descent of Manners*. London: Chatto & Windus, 1993.

11 Critchfield, Richard. *Among the British: An Outsider's View*. London: Hamish Hamilton, 1990.

12 Platt, Polly. *French or Foe?*. London: Culture Crossings, 1994.

13 Harris, Philip R, Moran Robert T. *Managing Cultural Differences*. Houston: Gulf Publishing, 1979.

14 Granick, David. *The European Executive*. New York: Doubleday, 1962.

15 Barzini, Luigi. *The Italians*. New York: Atheneum, 1964.

16 Frischer, Dominique. *La France Vue d'en Face*. Paris: Robert Laffont, 1990.

17 Fernau, Joachim. *Deutschland, Deutschland über alles...* Munich: Goldmann Verlag, 1972.

18 Ebert, Wolfgang. *Das Porzellan war so nervös*. Munich: Bastei-Lübbe, 1975.

19 Marsh, David. *The Germans*. London: Century Hutchinson, 1989.

20 Morris, Jan. *Spain.* London: Penguin, 1982.

21 Pritchett, VS. *The Spanish Temper.* London: Chatto & Windus, 1954.

22 Brenan, Gerald. *The Face of Spain.* London: Penguin, 1965.

23 Borkenau, Franz. *The Spanish Cockpit.* London: Pluto, 1986.

24 Miller, Stuart. *Painted in Blood.* New York: Atheneum, 1987.

25 Christophory, Jul. *Luxembourgeois, qui êtes-vous?.* Luxembourg: Guy Binsfeld, 1984.

26 Kartheiser, Josiane. *Ent-Grenzung.* Echternach: Editions Phi, 1982.

27 Christophory, Jul. *A Short History of Literature in Luxembourgish.* Luxembourg: Bibliothèque Nationale, 1994.

28 Trausch, Gilbert. *Histoire du Luxembourg.* Paris: Hatier, 1992.

29 Mermet, Gérard. *Euroscopie.* Paris: Larousse, 1991.

30 Huizinga, Johan. *Dutch Civilisation in the 17th Century.* London/New York: Macmillan, 1968.

31 Schama, Simon. *The Embarrassment of Riches.* London: William Collins, 1987.

32 Hofstede, Geert. *Cultures and Organizations: Software of the Mind.* London: McGraw-Hill, 1991.

33 Shetter, William Z. *The Netherlands in Perspective.* Leiden: Martinus Nijhoff, 1987.

34 Mikes, George. *Switzerland for Beginners.* London: André Deutsch, 1975.

35 Ringel, Erwin. *Die österreichische Seele.* Vienna: Hermann Böhlaus, 1986.

36 Evans, E Estyn. *The Personality of Ireland.* Dublin: Lilliput, 1992.

37 Chadwick, Nora. *The Celts.* London: Penguin, 1971.

38 Muecke, Donald. *The Compass of Irony.* London: Jonathan Cape, 1980.

39 Himmelstrup, Per. *Discover Denmark.* Copenhagen: The Danish Cultural Institute/systime, 1992.

40 Phillips-Martinsson, Jean. *Swedes as Others see Them.* Lund: Studentlitteratur, 1991.

41 Anderson, Bengt. *Swedishness.* Stockholm: Positive Sweden, 1995.

42 Laine-Sveiby, Kati. *Företag I Kulturmöten*. Akademitryck: Edsbruk, 1991.

43 Hill, Richard and Haworth, David. *The Newcomers*. Brussels, Europublic, 1995.

44 Zeldin, Theodore. *An Intimate History of Humanity*. London: Sinclair-Stevenson, 1994.

45 Kaplan, Marion. *The Portuguese*. London: Viking, 1991.

46 Todd, Emmanuel. *L'Invention de l'Europe*. Paris: Editions du Seuil, 1990.

47 Hill, Alison Friesinger. *Insight Guide to Portugal*. London: Harrap, 1989.

48 Huart, Françoise. *La Vie en Grèce*. Paris: Solar, 1991.

49 McNeil W H. *The Metamorphosis of Greece since World War II*. Chicago: University of Chicago, 1978.

50 Ardó, Zsuzsanna. *How to be European: Go Hungarian*. Budapest: Biograf, 1994.

51 Kövary, Georg. *Ein Ungar Kommt Selten Allein*. Graz: Verlag Styria, 1994.

52 Mikes, George. *How to be a Brit*. London: Penguin, 1984.

53 Reed, John. *The War in Eastern Europe*. New York: Boni & Liveright, 1919.

54 Smith, Hedrick. *The New Russians*. London: Hutchison, 1990.

55 Kaplan, Robert. *Balkan Ghosts*. New York: St Martin's Press, 1993.

56 Codrescu, Andrei. *A Hole in the Flag*. New York: William Morrow, 1991.

57 Hofstede, Geert. *Culture's Consequences*. London: Sage, 1980.

58 Lynn, Richard. *Personality and National Character*. London: Pergamon Press/Elsevier, 1971.

59 Weeks, David Joseph and James, Jamie. *Eccentrics*. London: Weidenfeld & Nicholson, 1995.

60 d'Haucourt, Geneviève. *La Vie au Moyen Age*. Paris: Presses Universitaires de France, 1987.

61 *Press Law and Practice*. London, ARTICLE 19, 1993.

62 Payer, Lynn. *Medicine and Culture*. New York: Henry Holt, 1988.

63 Hall, Edward T and Mildred R. *Understanding Cultural Differences*. Yarmouth (Maine): Intercultural Press, 1990.

64 Cathelat, Bernard. *Life Styles for Europe*. Paris: CCA, 1990.

65 Whorf, Benjamin Lee. *Language, Thought, and Reality*. New York: The Technology Press and John Wiley & Sons, 1956.

66 Farb, Peter. *Word Play*. New York: Bantam, 1984.

67 Pease, Allen. *Body Language*. London: Sheldon Press, 1984.

INDEX

Have You Heard This One?

An Anthology of European Jokes

Compiled by Richard Hill
136 pages
format 195 × 130 mm (7 3/4 × 5")
ISBN 90-74440-08-8

€ 9,75

Here are some of the better jokes we Europeans tell about one another. There are a lot of bad ones – far too many – but you will find none of them here.

Good European jokes are neither stupid nor abusive. They tell one something instructive about the way people from different cultures perceive one another. And some of these jokes shed light on the cultures of both the 'sender' and the 'receiver'.

Humour is the subtlest expression of culture, which explains why English people have difficulty in understanding German jokes. Even the psychology of humour is coloured by the attitudes of the different cultures. Yet there is common ground in European humour: some of these jokes turn up in various guises in various places.

As that eminent European Johann Wolfgang von Goethe said, rather severely: "There is nothing in which people more betray their character than in what they laugh at". Taken in the right spirit, humour is an excellent starting point for cross-cultural comprehension.

Sharks and Custard
The Things That Make Europeans Laugh

Author: Richard Hill
190 pages
format 195 x 130 mm (7 3/4 x 5")
ISBN 90-74440-14-2

€ 14,95

With his new book **Sharks and Custard: The Things That Make Europeans Laugh** Richard Hill sets out to do two things: first, throw light on the different styles of humour of the English, the French, the Germans etc, and, secondly, offer a careful selection of what he thinks are the best jokes by and about the countries concerned.

For Hill, **Sharks and Custard** is a logical progression from the spadework he did on European cultures in his earlier bestsellers, WeEuropeans and EuroManagers and Martians. Humour is an important component of international business life that needs to be handled with tact and understanding. At best it can defuse the difficult moments of a major negotiation, at worst it can ruin a relationship!

Styles of humour can be very revealing for, as Johann Wolfgang von Goethe said in one of his lighter moments, "there is nothing in which people more betray their character than in what they laugh at". If the title of the book needs explanation, that is deliberate. Behind it lies a classic English joke - "Q. What is yellow and dangerous? A. Shark-infested custard." - a joke that makes foreigners feel culturally challenged. Custard is a traditional English sweet which should rightfully be as famous as pudding, but isn't...

"Sharks and Custard is like a pleasant evening with friends, planned but not overly organized, not too long and not too short, serendipitous, a place to share feelings and opinions and nonsense. Scholarly discourse drops in, but doesn't stay long. We go away a bit more connected as human beings."
Dr. George Simons, Intercultural Consultant and Trainer, France

".... a perceptive analysis of German humor and, especially, of one of its essential components, self-deprecating Jewish humor - a fundamental element in the humor of all central European countries."
Polly Platt, author of the best-selling "French or Foe?" and "Savoir-Flair!"

"The book is hilarious!" **Alan Tillier, Journalist, France**

"This is a great book because it is not just a list of jokes but jokes in a social and cultural context." **Andrzej Szoszkiewicz, Editor, "BM Magazine", Poland**

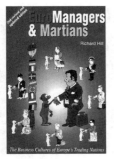

EuroManagers & Martians
The Business Cultures of Europe's Trading Nations

Author: Richard Hill
272 pages
format 195 × 130 mm (7 3/4 × 5")
ISBN 90-74440-02-9

€ 17,25

Looking at them simply as people, when we see them in the streets of Paris or when we visit them *chez eux*, our fellow-Europeans come across as a pretty odd lot – a far cry from the Single Market, harmonisation and all those dreary things.

But how do they behave in business? Put a German, a Frenchman, a Spaniard, an Italian, a Swede and, of course, a Brit together around a negotiating table and what happens? Either nothing at all – they just don't know how to deal with one another – or a lot! It's then that you realise that, despite all the constraints of working within a business environment, life *à l'européenne* is still full of surprises.

The simple fact, of course, is that it would need a superhuman to leave his cultural baggage behind him simply because he puts on his coat to go to the office. This book examines the business cultures of Europe's main trading nations and offers useful insights into differences in attitudes to time, hierarchy, protocol, negotiating styles, acceptance of management disciplines and multicultural teamwork.

With so much cultural diversity even in business, the author wonders how on earth we are going to develop the Euromanager we keep hearing about, the person who is going to save us from the Japanese, the Asian Tigers and others. Will this Euro-superman-ager ever exist?

"As an Australian in Europe trying to study and work, this book provided me with some fantastic tips on what and what not to do when!! The mix of anecdotes and factual content means that it is very readable and the relaxed style and humour are very refreshing!! For any non-European it is a definite must, whether you are going over to work or to study and irrespective of what country you are going to! The appropriate theoretical basis and use of Hofstede's cultural dimensions give Richard Hill credibility and allow readers of any education level to understand the points being made. A thoroughly enjoyable and informative read!"

Sydney, Australia

GREAT BRITAIN
LITTLE ENGLAND
Who's fooling whom?

Author: Richard Hill
152 pages
format 195 × 130 mm (7 3/4 × 5")
ISBN 90-74440-04-5

€ 12,95

Britons have recently been bombarded and bludgeoned with books examining the reasons for their country's dramatic decline.

But, while offering heavily documented analyses of culprit 'constituencies' - labour, management, educators, civil servants, government itself - these books have stopped short of examining the mindsets, motivations and mannerisms common to the actors in the drama.

In this book, Richard Hill sets out to fill the gap. Starting with himself, he tries to get under the skin of the British - more specifically, the English - and understand where they go right and why they go wrong.

This is an entertaining and thought-provoking book by a Briton who has had the advantage of living outside his island culture, yet consorting closely with it, for the last 30 years.

"I found it fascinating reading. If I weren't British (sorry, English), I would have enjoyed it."

Stanley Crossick,
The European Policy Centre

"Wonderful stuff. Witty and accurate without being cynical."
John Mole, author of 'Mind Your Manners'

"I am thoroughly enjoying reading it... it cheers up a Scottish Nationalist of a London evening!"

Margaret Ewing, MP

'The NewComers'
The Austrians, Finns and Swedes

Authors: Richard Hill,
David Haworth
176 pages
format 195 x 130 mm (7 3/4 x 5")
ISBN 90-74440-06-1

€ 14,95

Many years after Austria's, Finland's and Sweden's accession to the European Union, ignorance about these countries is as great as ever.

Maybe not where they are, or what they represent economically, but who they are, how they do business, what things are important to them and what are not.

Now Richard Hill and David Haworth, a public affairs consultant specialising in the Nordic countries, have collaborated to write **"The NewComers"**.

This book sets out 'to take the lid off' the Austrians, Finns and Swedes, and explain them to their fellow-Europeans and others. The Norwegians were also supposed to be included but, sadly, things didn't work out that way.

"The NewComers" presents a family portrait of each of the three countries - their virtues, their quirks, tastes, habits and sensitivities, together with relevant background on history and politics.

"I would like to congratulate you on this publication, which is not only a delightful read, but gives at the same time a very comprehensive insight into these countries, their people and mentalities."
Austrian Embassy Official

"Delightful! You seem to have got the essence of this extremely complex society."
British businesswoman in Vienna

US & THEM

Author: Richard Hill
175 pages
format 195 × 130 mm (7 3/4 × 5")
ISBN 90-74440-10-X

€ 14,95

In his book **Us & Them** Richard Hill examines European separatism in its various forms: the regionalist movement, attitudes to minorities, the bonding instinct and, most significantly, the silent separatism that is now distancing the younger generations of Europeans from the world of politics.

Since his first book, **WeEuropeans**, came onto the market ten years ago, Hill has had the opportunity to address audiences of students, undergraduates and graduates totalling over 10,000 young people of every European nationality.

In discussing European issues with them, he discovered that these young people have largely disengaged from conventional politics. They regard politicians with, at best, disinterest and, at worst, distaste or disrespect. This attitude is prevalent across all western European countries, with the possible exception of the Netherlands and Ireland.

Hill concludes: "The world has changed massively in the last fifty years, but western Europe still lives with the threat of social dislocation. Then, the problem was the divides that separated countries and cultures. Us was the mother-country, Them was the rest. Now, the dislocation is within countries and cultures, the growing gulf between Europe's young people and the society they were born into. Today Us is Europe's youth and Them is the rest of us".

Hill's conclusions are supported by the findings of national and international opinion studies, reviewed in detail in the book.

"This is an astonishing book, not only because of the superbly lucid and vigorous writing, but also because the thoughts are equally rigorous and right in both form and substance. I have recommended it to my students."

Adelino Torres, Professor, Universidade Técnica de Lisboa

'WeEuropeans', 'Us & Them', 'EuroManagers & Martians' and other Europublic books have been selected as course material by the following institutions:

BELGIUM	Antwerp University (UFSIA), English Dept.
	Erasmus Hogeschool, Brussels
	European University, Brussels/Antwerp
	Gent University, Department of Sociology
	Hoge Technische Instituut, Brugge
	ICHEC Business School, Brussels
	Institut für Erwachsenenbildung, Eupen/St Vith
	ISC Saint-Louis Business School, Brussels
	KUL Leuven
	KVH Interpreters School, Antwerp
	Solvay Business School (ULB), MEB Programme
	United Business Institutes, Brussels
	Université de Mons, Sciences Economiques
BRITAIN	Institute of Management (IM)
	The Centre for International Briefing
	The Open University
DENMARK	Copenhagen Business High School
FINLAND	Helsinki Institute
	Jyväskylä University, European Studies
	Vaasa University, European Studies
FRANCE	Groupe EM, Lyon
	INSEAD, Fontainebleau
GERMANY	Hochschule der Künste, Berlin
	Mercator Universität, Duisburg
NETHERLANDS	HEAO business course
	Netherlands Institute for MBA Studies, Utrecht
	Nijenrode University, Breukelen
SWEDEN	Swedish Institute of Management (IFL)
	University of Lund
USA	Antioch University, Ohio
	Chicago University, Graduate School of Business
	Massachusetts University (Plymouth)
	Michigan State University
	New York University, Stern School of Business
	Temple University School of Business and Management, Philadelphia
	UCI Graduate School of Management, Irvine (CA)
	University of Pennsylvania
	and the training arms of various international corporations.

'WeEuropeans', 'Us & Them', 'EuroManagers & Martians' and other Europublic books have been selected as course material by the following institutions:

BELGIUM	Antwerp University (UFSIA), English Dept. Erasmus Hogeschool, Brussels European University, Brussels/Antwerp Gent University, Department of Sociology Hoge Technische Instituut, Brugge ICHEC Business School, Brussels Institut für Erwachsenenbildung, Eupen/St Vith ISC Saint-Louis Business School, Brussels KUL Leuven KVH Interpreters School, Antwerp Solvay Business School (ULB), MEB Programme United Business Institutes, Brussels Université de Mons, Sciences Economiques
BRITAIN	Institute of Management (IM) The Centre for International Briefing The Open University
DENMARK	Copenhagen Business High School
FINLAND	Helsinki Institute Jyväskylä University, European Studies Vaasa University, European Studies
FRANCE	Groupe ESC, Lyon INSEAD, Fontainebleau
GERMANY	Hochschule der Künste, Berlin Mercator Universität, Duisburg
NETHERLANDS	HEAO business course Netherlands Institute for MBA Studies, Utrecht Nijenrode University, Breukelen
SWEDEN	Swedish Institute of Management (IFL) University of Lund
USA	Antioch University, Ohio Chicago University, Graduate School of Business Massachusetts University (Plymouth) Michigan State University New York University, Stern School of Business Temple University School of Business and Management, Philadelphia UCI Graduate School of Management, Irvine (CA) University of Pennsylvania *and the training arms of various international corporations.*